to my parents

CONTENTS

INTRODUCTION

IDEA, FORM, OBJECT

This book consists of a planned sequence of furniture designs. A design is included on condition that it has its place in the overall narrative and formal structure of the book. As such, the book aims to present a coherent body of work. And it is precisely in a book, in the form of drawings, that relations between objects within a project, as well as relations between projects, can be read.

The designs collected in this book make use of mathematical ideas, theoretical constructs, derived and invented rules in order to generate form.

The aesthetic ideal is the achievement of perceptual complexity by means of conceptual simplicity, using the least number of rules to generate the greatest number and variety of forms. The creation of complexity from simplicity is necessarily a debasement of, but it also aspires to, the condition of Creation *ex nihilo* in which everything comes from nothing.

In using mathematics in design, geometry, which is the study of the properties of space, is always already related to, and can be represented by, spatial form. Numerical relations too, in so far as numbers measure extension and indicate position, can also be represented by spatial form.

There are also designs in which their formal structures are derived from musical forms such as the Passacaglia, the Fugue and the Sonata, so that while the musical form organises pieces of music in time, the derived musical form, reduced from its cultural and historical references, can be used to structure objects in space.

In some projects it is the imagined form in search of its mathematical origin ('Undulating tables with triangles and arcs', 'Screens with obstacles', 'Stars and constellations', 'All-interval clock'…), while in other projects it is the mathematical idea in search of its formal expression ('Music box', 'Three mathematical screens', 'Invention on a number', 'Even number, two primes'…).

Objects across some projects look very different even though they share common generative material ('Stars and constellations' and 'All-interval clock', 'Non-square mirrors' and 'Non-square towers'…), while objects across other projects appear somewhat similar even though their generative material is unrelated ('Screens with obstacles' and 'Truncated screens', 'Derangement' and (Ana(gram)matical) shelves'…)

There are some projects in which each object in the project is generated by the same rule ('Four measures, six boxes', 'Quasi una passacaglia'…), while there are other projects in which each object in the project, even though the objects are related, is nonetheless generated by different rules ('Quasi una fuga'…).

There are some projects in which the rule generates a set of objects in the project synchronically ('Four measures, six boxes', 'Quasi una passacaglia'…), on the other hand there are other projects in which the rule applied recursively generates a sequence of objects in the project diachronically ('(Ana(gram)matical) shelves'…).

A 'closed' project is that in which a finite and specific number of objects are generated ('Four measures, six boxes', '(Ana(gram)matical) shelves', 'Odd number, prime, power of two'…), while an 'open' project refers to a potentially infinite number of objects within which a finite and specific number of objects are realised ('Undulating tables with triangles and arcs', 'Even number, two primes'…), and also to a potentially unlimited extent of a form within which a limited form is realised ('Distribution of primes', 'Primes as sum and difference of squares'…).

In some projects the generative material is merely the means to make form ('Undulating tables with triangles and arcs', 'Screens with obstacles', 'Derangement'…), while in other projects the generative material has its intrinsic worth beyond its particular application ('Music box', 'All-interval screens', 'Picking out types of number'…).

An object, in its formal complexity, is perceived to be enigmatic, perplexing, puzzling, amazing —like a maze.

The form of the object is not immediately readable. But through attentive looking, it is revealed to be a coordination of parts, which gives rise to the supplementary act of analysis and sets in motion the process of decipherment.

While from a mathematical theorem to its proof requires a chain of reasoning, from the mathematical material to the formal object cannot just be a linear unfolding process, so that while a mathematical proof is always the unique result of its theorem, the formal object is never the only possible translation of its mathematical material.

This is to say, in contradistinction to the mathematical proof which is always already embodied in its theorem, the formal object is not given by its mathematical material. This means that the lack of ultimate correspondence between the formal object and its mathematical material opens up a gap which is to be filled in by subjective intervention in making form from mathematics.

Subjective intervention in this sense refers to aesthetic choices, which necessarily place the formal object in a cultural-historical context.

In the effort to reproduce the objectivity of the mathematical material for the formal object, there is to be the minimum of subjective intervention and aesthetic choices, there is to be the rhetoric of reasoning and justification, so that the formal object is able to show itself, to a certain extent, to be as such and not otherwise, so that the formal solution must appear, as far as possible, to be the only one and no other.

To be sure, subjective intervention and aesthetic choices can never be wholly avoided.

In the translation from mathematics to object, properties such as scale or orientation can never be determined by mathematics. A form generated by mathematics does not yet have a specific scale of orientation, and it is the form being put to use, being realised as object, which suggests that particular scale and orientation.

Putting an appropriate form at an appropriate scale and orientation into the context of use reverses the process in Duchamp's Ready-Mades in which functional objects are lifted out of the context of use to be appraised purely and simply as form.

Therefore, a raised horizontal surface at a certain size can be used as a table, a vertical plane at a certain height can serve as a screen, and so on.

A form is invented for which a function is found. Ideally, forms are invented without the teleology of function, but in cases where forms can be convincingly adapted for use, or where use has been marginalised but not subverted, function is an effect, not a cause, of formal invention. This reverses the modernist dictum "form follows function" to "function follows form".

Function follows form in the sense that form has priority over function, so that the traditional attribute of efficiency of arrangement has been marginalised. Objects are not shaped or sized to optimise usefulness.

In cases where anthropometric and ergonomic requirements cannot be accommodated within the generated form, objects which defer to the human body such as chairs and sofas will have no place in this collection of furniture.

Function follows form in the sense that form exceeds function, so that the traditional attribute of economy of means has been marginalised. Objects are not designed to facilitate construction or minimise material, even though the amount of material used demanded by form has exceeded the functional requirements of stability and rigidity.

Forms are realised in spite of themselves.

Architecture has a long and distinguished history of unrealised designs such as utopian and visionary schemes of various sorts, as well as deliberately unrealisable projects, such as the polemic works by Eisenman and Libeskind, in which the drawings, and the text, are accorded a privileged status.

The following conceptual/formal designs, while not unrealisable, privilege drawings over the realised objects.

With the existence of drawings the conceptual and formal work of a design is complete and objectified.

Drawings point forwards to the realisation of the design. To realise a design is to be an act of interpretation in which the method of construction is worked out and materials are chosen. The specification of the realised object is not given in this book of formal presentation.

Drawings point backwards to the analysis of the design. To analyse a design is to be an act of clarification in which the design process and the generative ideas are described and explained by texts and diagrams.

Conceptual/formal works are indeed transparent to analysis. Sol LeWitt remarked that, as a conceptual artist, in making art, he had to go from A to B to C to D. This, then, suggests the possibility of the reverse tracing of the creative process from D to C to B to A.

There is, therefore, analysis in the sense of the reverse tracing of the creative process from the finished design to its origin, or what amounts to the same thing, a step by step reconstruction of the development of the work from its beginning to the end product, while all the time looking for connections between ideas, in order to show the work why it is as such.

And there is also analysis which makes the potentially infinite demand of showing the work not only why it is as such but also why it cannot be otherwise.

Why it is as such but not otherwise: this is just what our surrounding world cannot show itself to be. This lack then gives rise to the project of the making of an ideal delimited conceptual/formal world which is as such but cannot be otherwise, within which nothing is superfluous, nothing can be different and everything is necessary, and which aims to present, within its own limits, the best of all possible worlds.

Analysis which intends to show the conceptual/formal work why it is as such but not otherwise must be able to describe and explain, in every stage of the creative process, not only every decision taken but also every alternative not chosen, so that the decisions taken are shown up to be, in some cases the most convincing, in other cases not.

In these other cases, analysis provides that critical tool which points the conceptual/formal work towards the fulfilment of its potential.

Measured against the exacting demands of analysis, the texts and diagrams included do not constitute analysis, but are just supplementary conceptual summaries in this book of formal presentation.

This document of plans, elevations, axonometrics and introductory texts, which enables the designs to be realised as well as analysed, is therefore analogous to the music score, the playscript, the screenplay, the architectural partis and so on.

The following furniture designs are arranged into types of projects—tables, boxes, screens, cabinets…—and into groups of projects where projects within the same group are conceptually or formally related.

TABLES

G1. FORMS CONSTRUCTED BY GEOMETRY

Curves are usually associated with immediate gestural expression, directly formed by hand without the medium of drawing instruments.

In these projects, the fluid contours of the tabletops are, in fact, rigorously constructed by geometry, where curves are formulated as arcs.

In this way, the objects appeal to the intellect without sensual pleasure being renounced.

P1. Undulating tables with triangles and arcs

Every step of the design process is built upon an original grid of equilateral triangles. The plan of each of the three legs in shape and size is a typical unit triangle and each leg occupies a certain displacement from the apex of the grid.

An arc is constructed from the centre of each leg and the arcs are joined tangentially by further arcs in order that the tabletop will be a continuous curve.

By repositioning the legs, different forms of the tabletop will be generated.

Therefore, it is by establishing geometric rules for generating arcs that a series of different but related objects can be analysed.

This is an 'open' project in the sense that the generative rules can, theoretically, produce a potentially infinite number of instances of forms.

Two tables, A and B, are represented

Table B – Displacement of the three legs by 2, 4, 6 units from the three apexes of the triangular grid

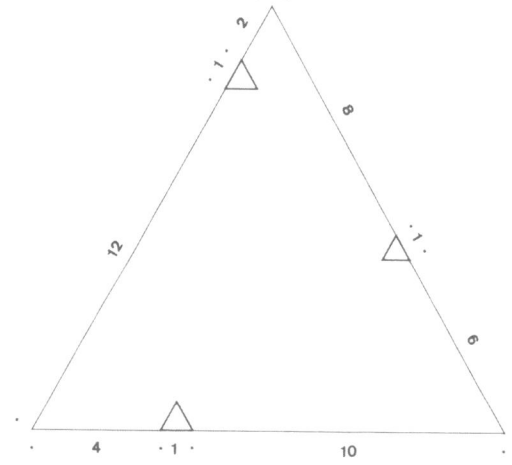

Table B – Construction of the arcs to form the tabletop

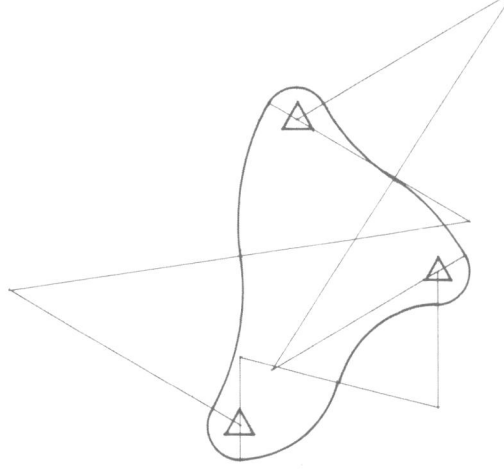

Table A – Displacement of the three legs by 1, 2, 3 units from the three apexes of the triangular grid

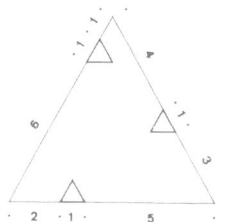

Table A – Construction of the arcs to form the tabletop

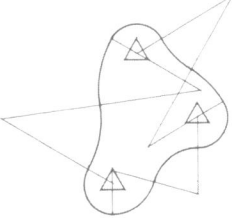

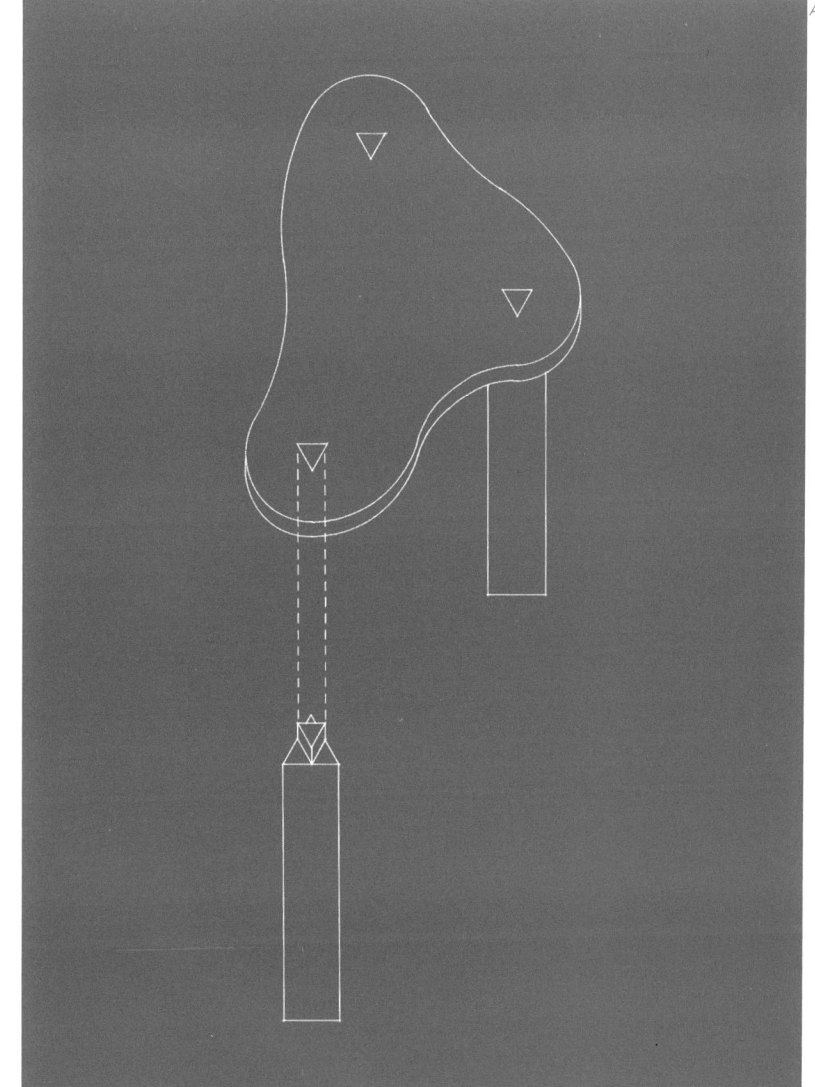

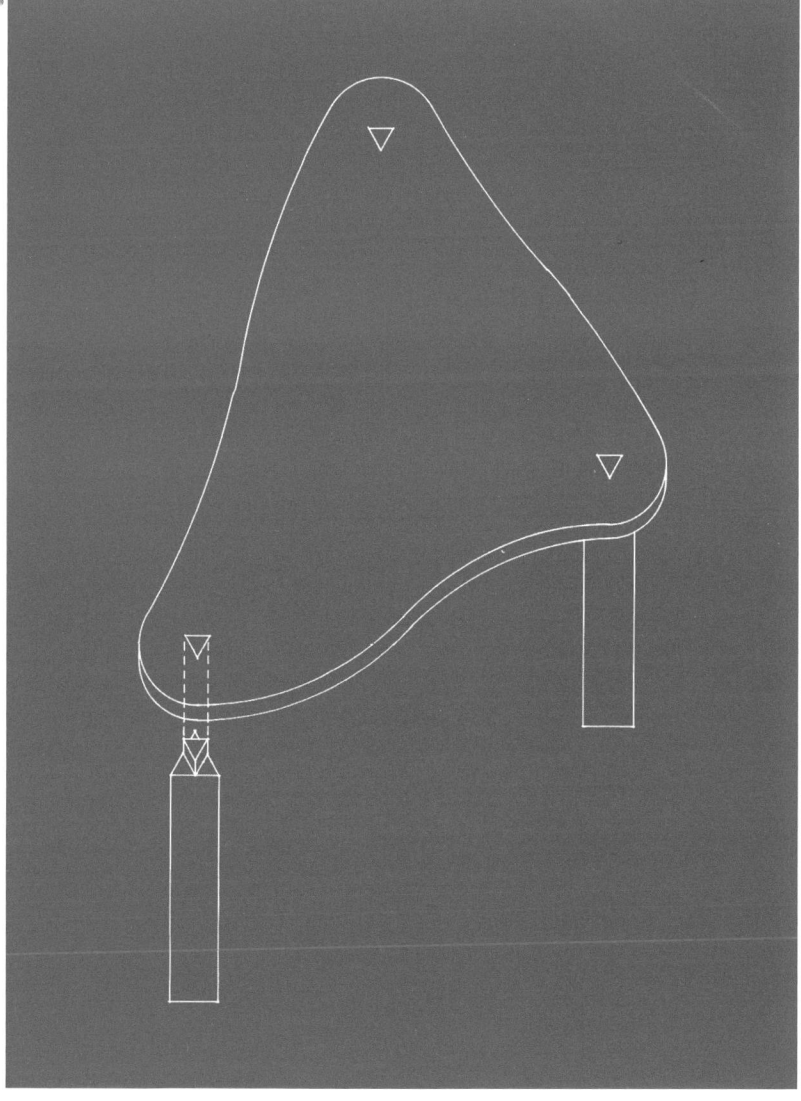

Symmetry is a formal device which reaffirms the form by means of repetition.

And yet a symmetrical form is conceptually superfluous to its reflected double.

Every repetition engenders superfluity.

In this table, the symmetrical initial form is transformed into the asymmetrical final form by rotating slightly one arc relative to the other arc in order to remove the conceptual superfluity of symmetry.

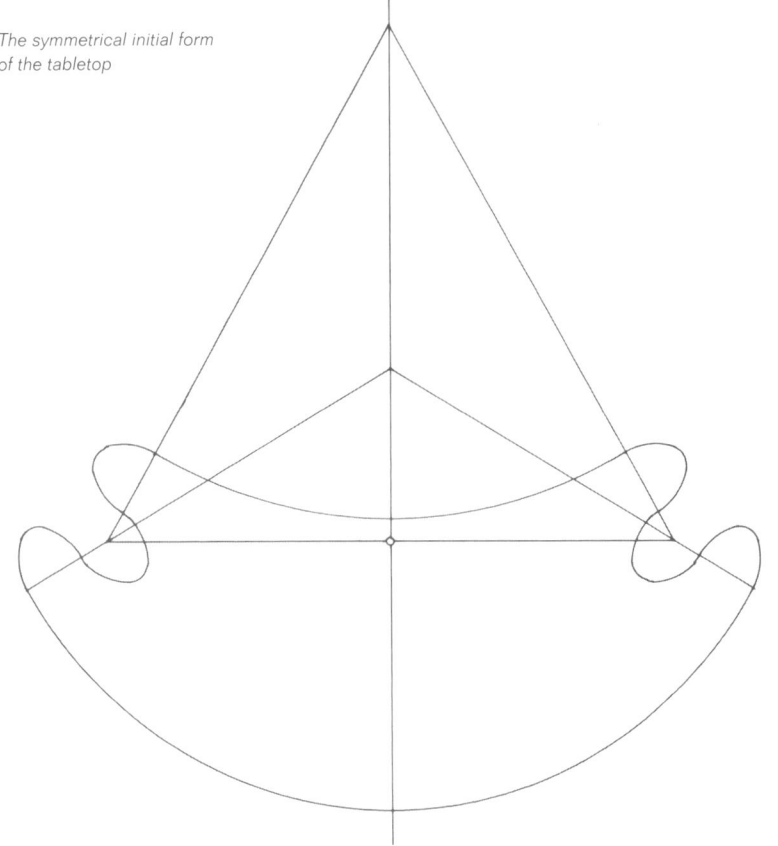

The symmetrical initial form of the tabletop

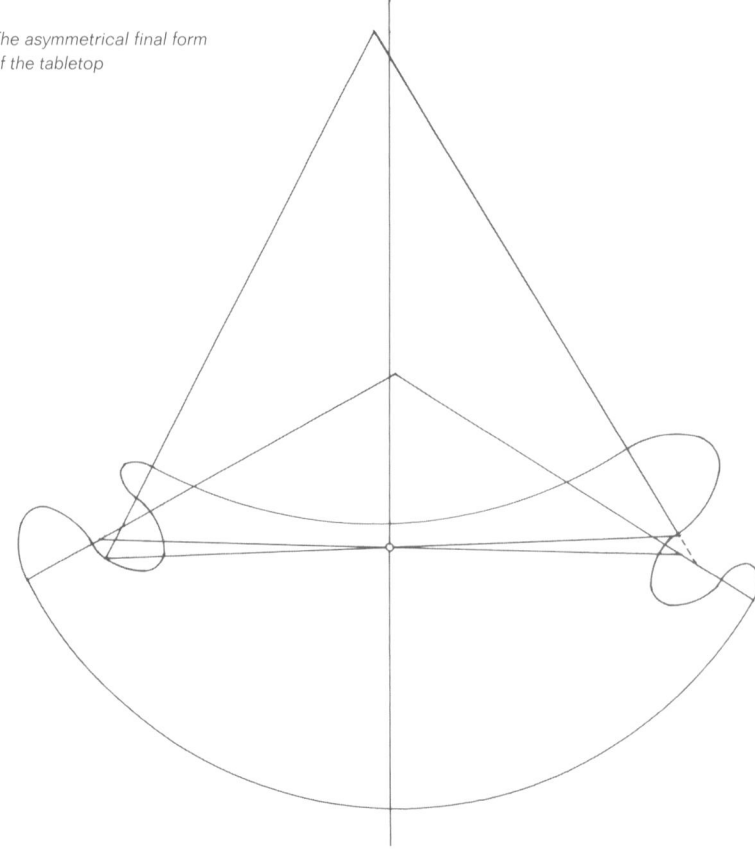

The asymmetrical final form of the tabletop

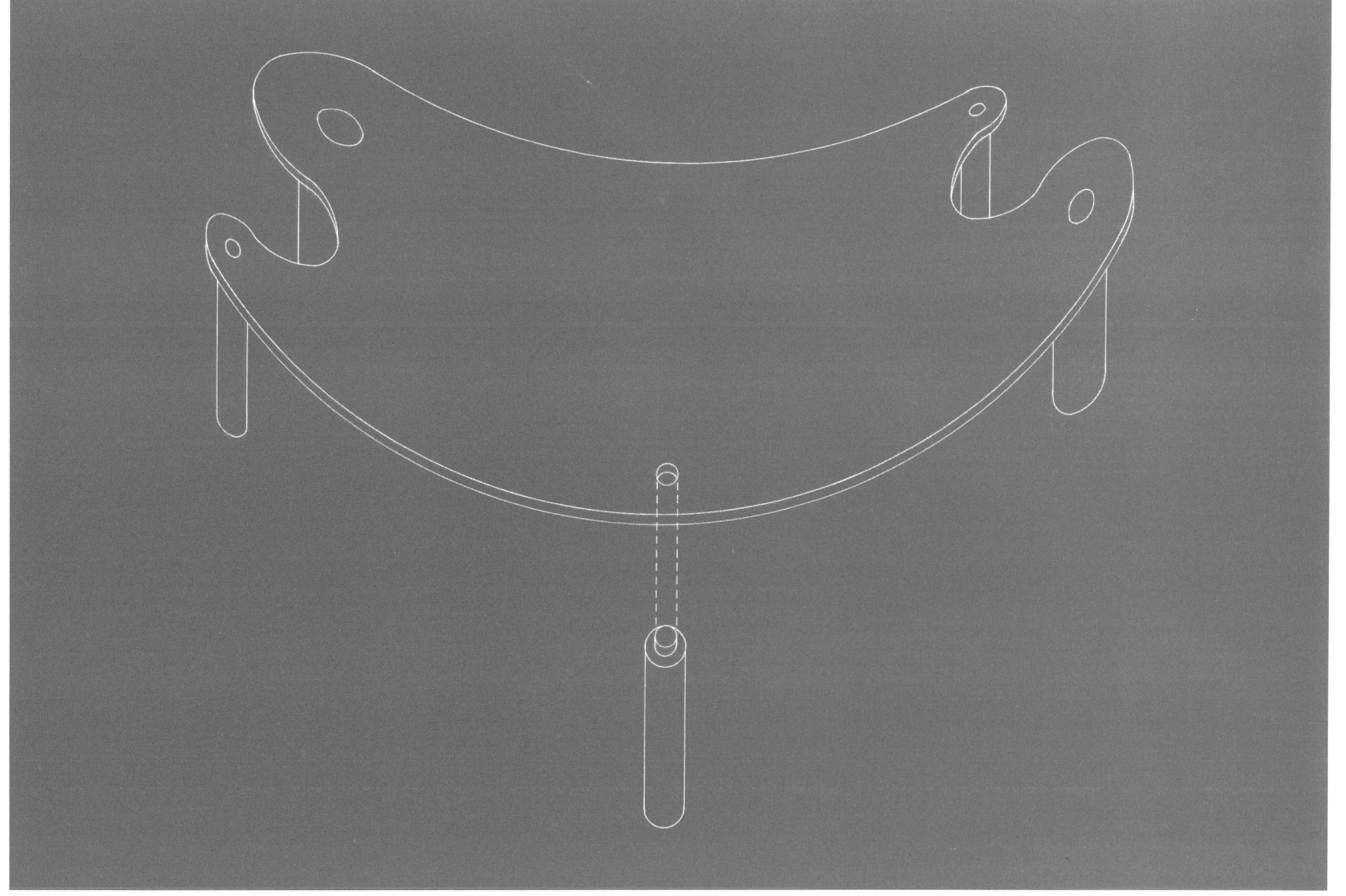

G2. FORMS ORGANISED BY DRAWINGS

Drawings are usually a means of representing forms.

In these projects, not only do the drawings represent form but also the form of each table is, in fact, developed from a composite drawing of its plan and its four unfolded elevations.

Furthermore, the formal relations between the diagonal and horizontal bars in 'Tables with diagonal crosses' and the geometrical relations between the sloping bars in 'Tables with sloping bars' are revealed in these composite drawings.

Thus the composite drawing can be used as an analytical device.

P3. Tables with diagonal crosses

On each tabletop a diagonal cross is inscribed, each arm of which extends diagonally down an elevation and then continues horizontally across to the adjacent elevation of the table.

The two tables are related by the plan of each table given by the longer side of the smaller table measuring the same as the shorter side of the larger table, and also by the difference between the length and width of both tables being the same.

The height of each table is given by the composite drawing of the plan and the four unfolded elevations of one table occupying the same area as the composite drawing of the plan and the four unfolded elevations of the other table, and also by the height of the smaller table exceeding its longer side by the same amount as the shorter side of the larger table exceeding its height. Thus, the method of generating form is derived from certain technique of representing form.

The ostensible purpose of the diagonal and horizontal bars on the elevations of each table is structural strengthening, but these bars are in fact a formal rather than a functional device.

This project consists of two tables, A and B.

Table A – Composite drawing of the plan and the four unfolded elevations

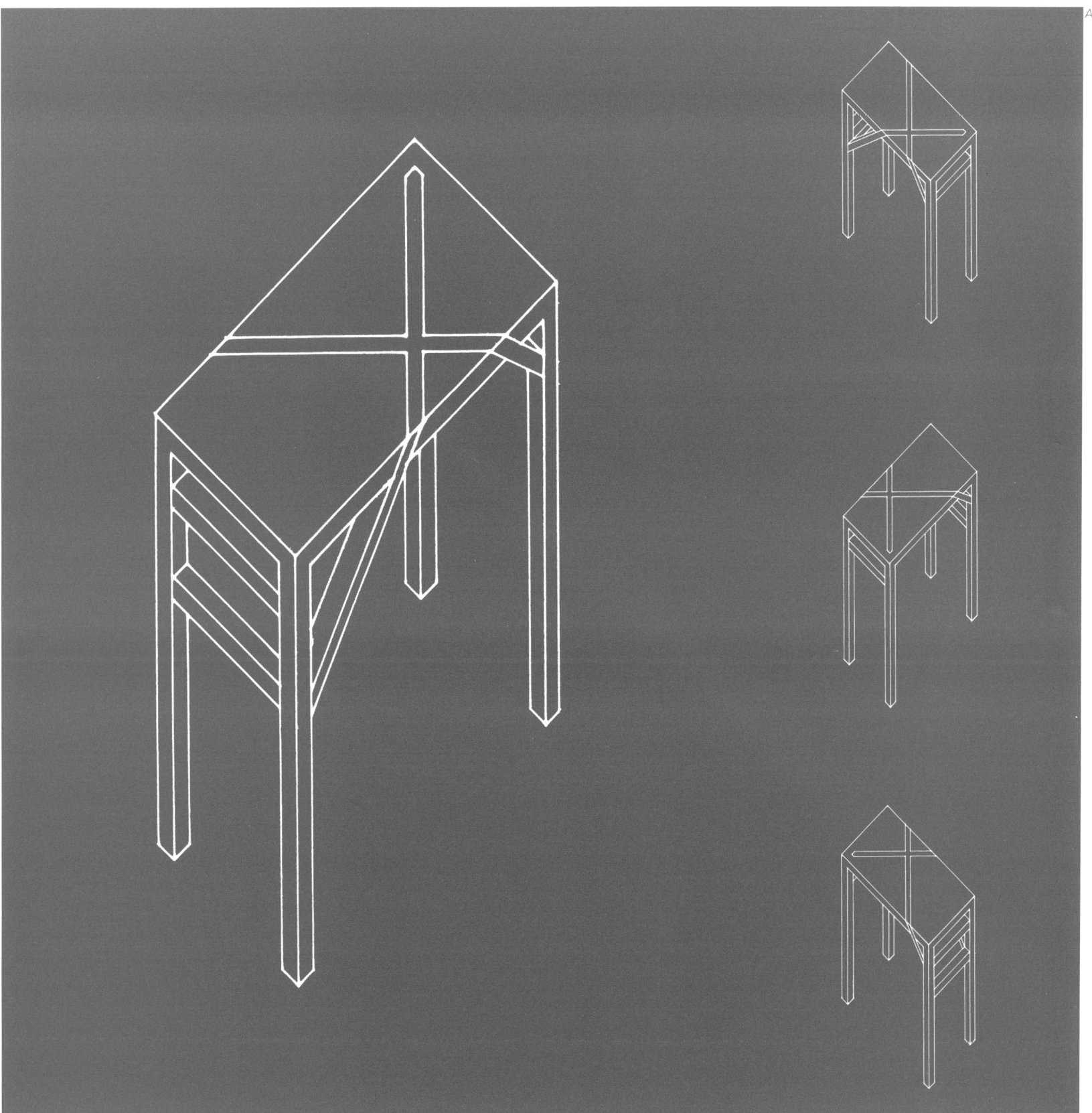

Table B – Composite drawing of the plan and the four unfolded elevations

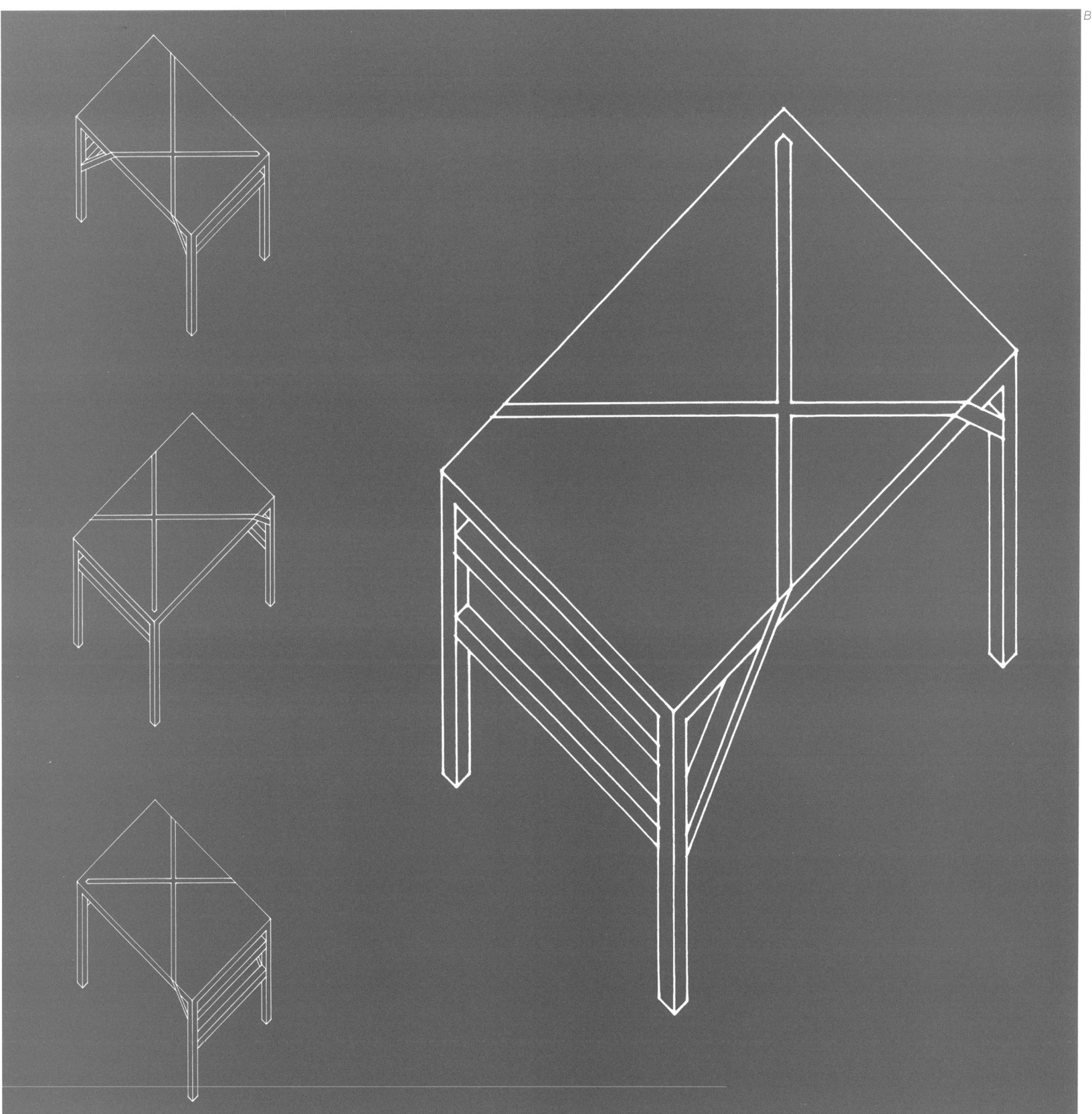

P4. Tables with sloping bars

On each table sloping bars are attached to the elevations. Viewing the object itself, the geometrical relations between the bars are not shown. The geometrical relations between the bars are revealed in, and are indeed generated by, the composite drawing of the plan and the four unfolded elevations of the table.

Like 'Tables with diagonal crosses', the method of generating form is derived from certain technique of representing form.

The strengthening function of the sloping bars on the elevations of each table is merely a means to enable formal elaborations on the object.

This project consists of two tables, X and Y.

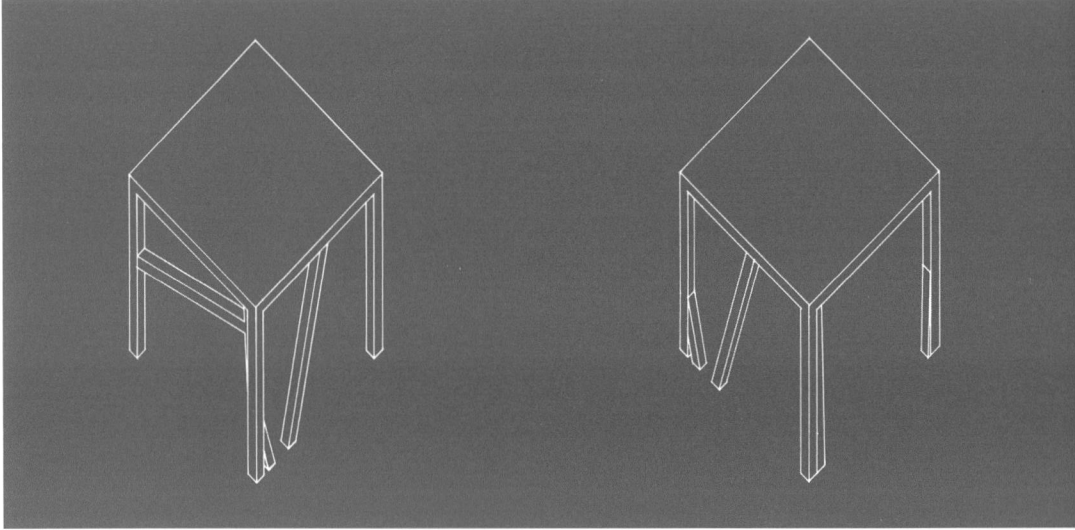

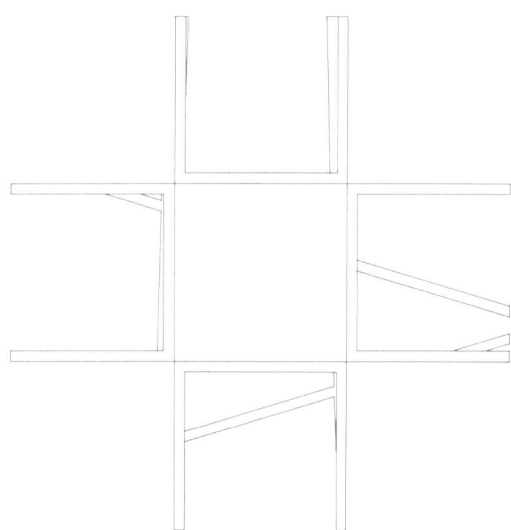

Table X – Composite
drawing of the plan and the
four unfolded elevations

Table Y – Composite
drawing of the plan and the
four unfolded elevations

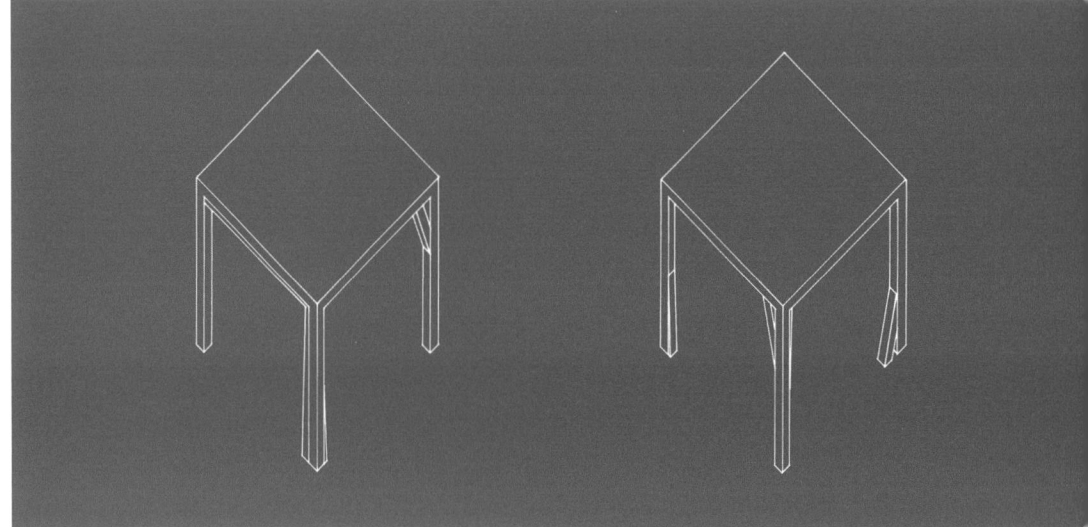

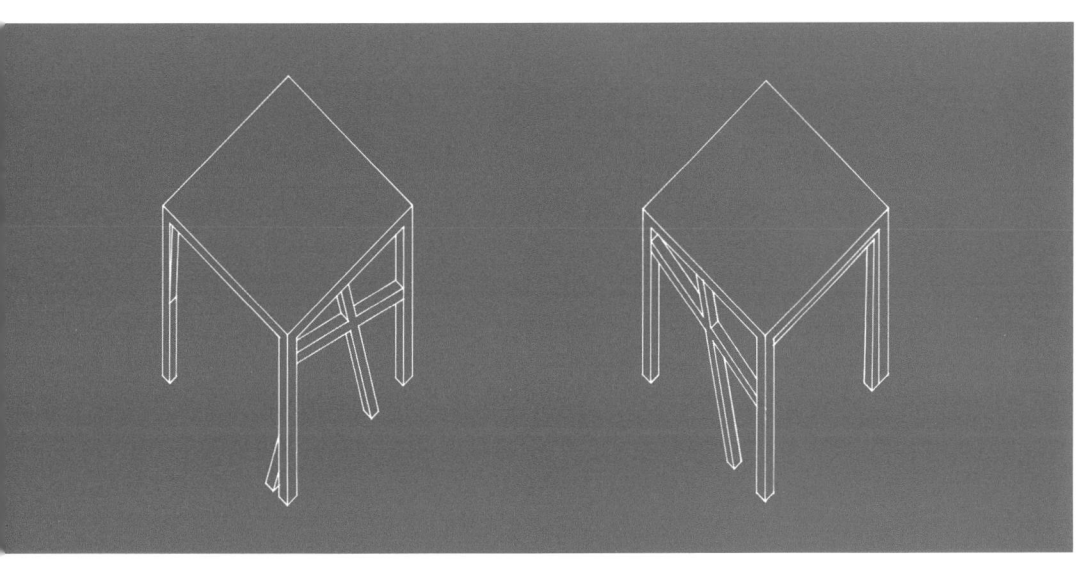

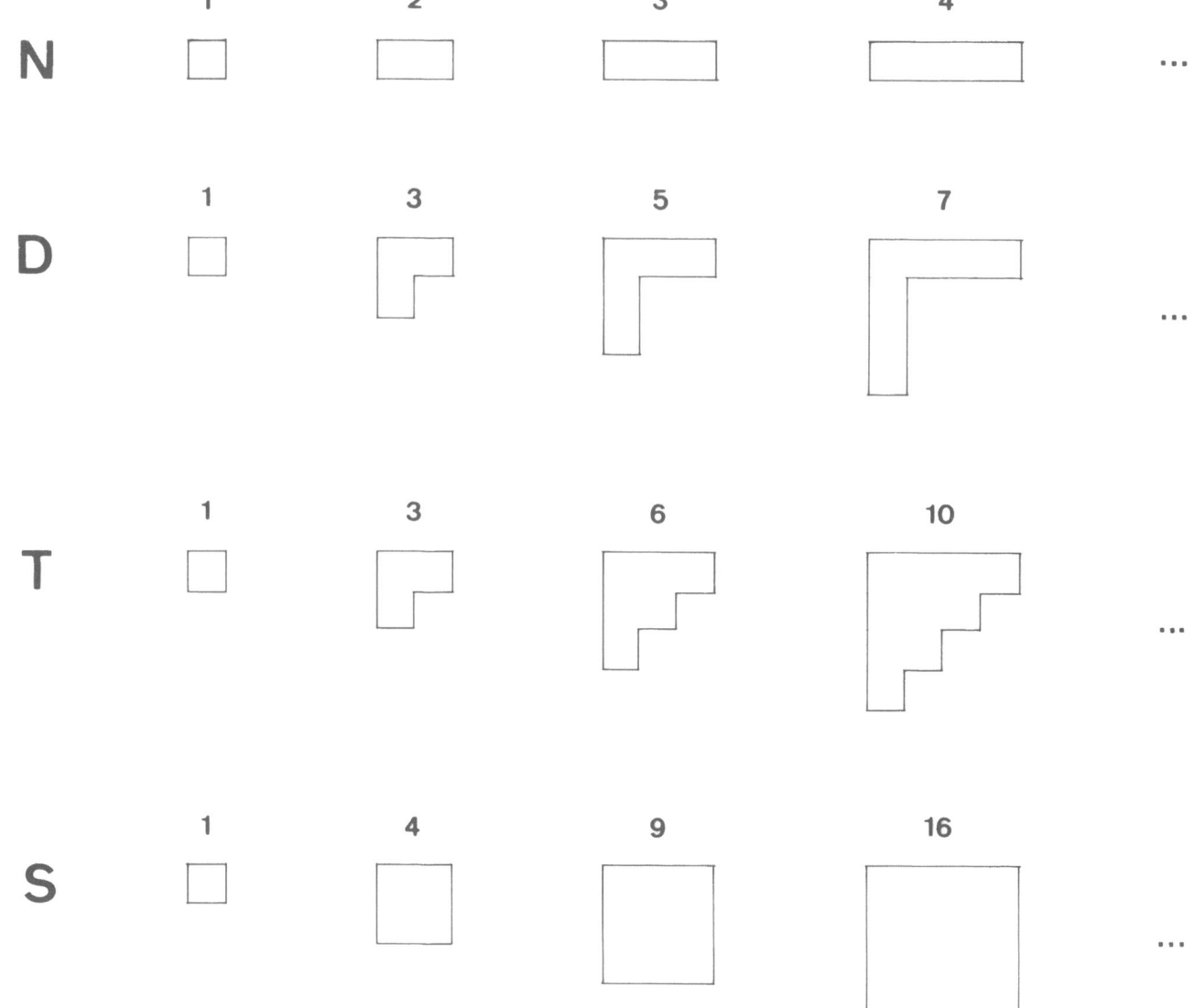

G3. NATURAL, ODD, TRIANGULAR AND SQUARE NUMBERS

Numbers can be represented by their shape. Certain types of numbers—triangular, square, pyramidal, cubic…—are even named after their shape.

In these two simple projects, the shape of numbers are combined to make the form of two tables. The group of projects 'Shaping numbers', consisting of cabinets, are elaborations on the subject.

G3.1 The shape of the first terms of natural (N), odd (D), triangular (T) and square (S) numbers

P5. Table with four types of number

Like 'Tables with diagonal crosses' and 'Tables with sloping bars', 'Table with four types of number' takes the function of structural strengthening as the starting point in order to make form.

Where the table is read within a certain cultural context, it is seen to relate to traditional Chinese furniture.

So the strengthening structure on the elevations fulfils its practical function while it also conveys its stylistic meanings.

But this strengthening structure in fact originates from abstract ideas. It has the shape of a natural, an odd, a triangular and a square number joined up from end to end.

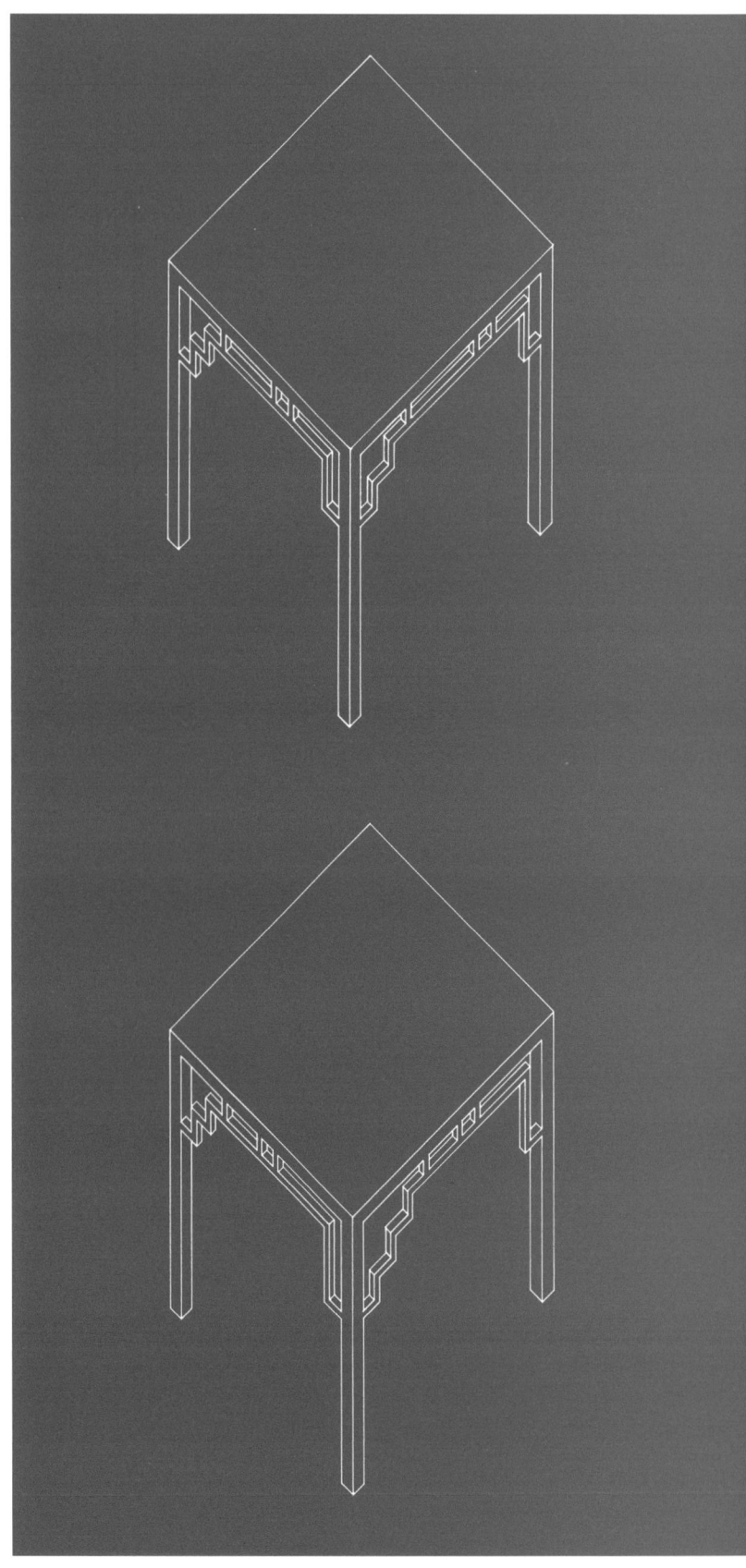

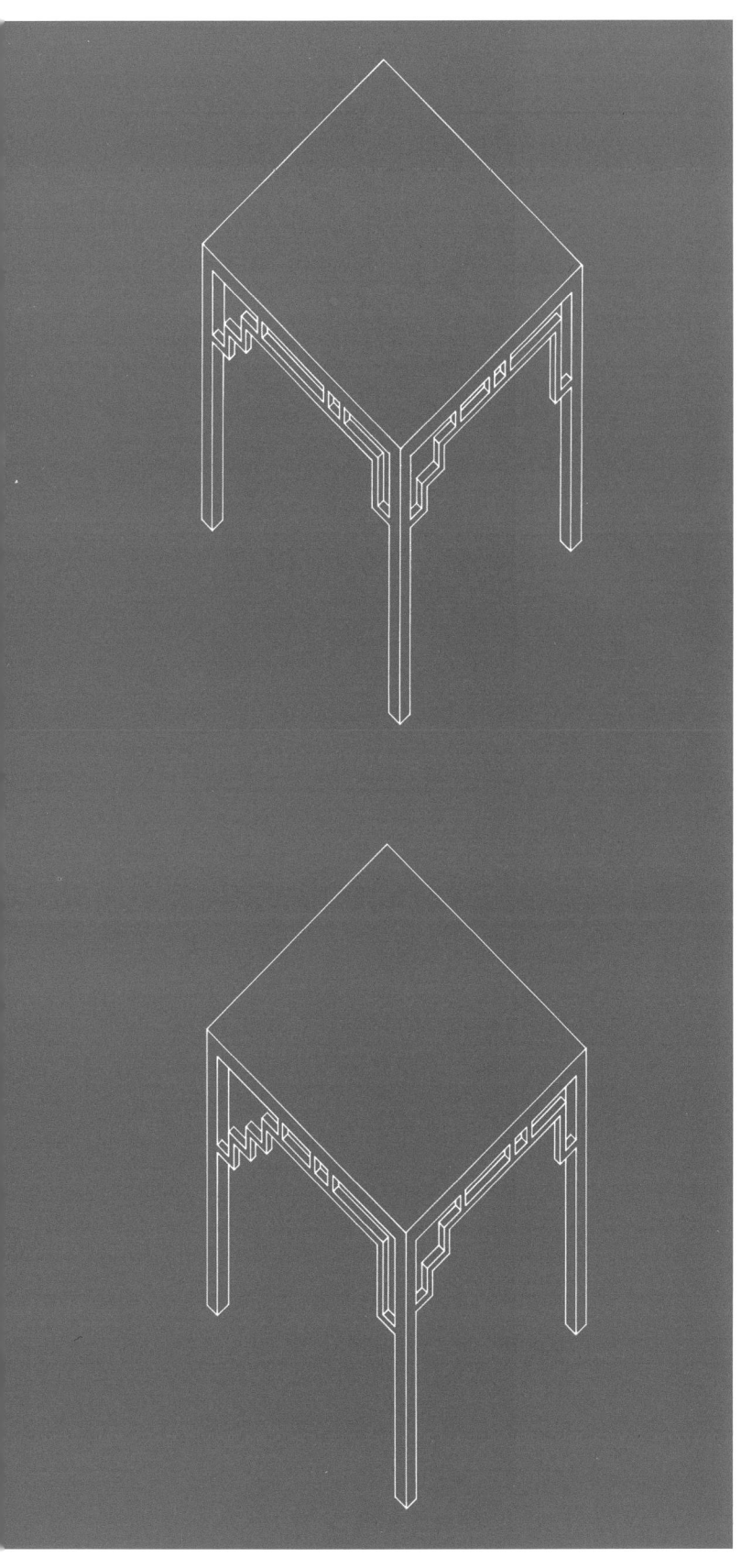

On the surfaces of the table, the upper structure of solid planes using the shape of a natural, an odd, a triangular and a square number is interlocked with the lower structure of open frame also using the shape of the same natural, odd, triangular and square numbers.

In order for the object to function as a table, the tabletop is to be a raised horizontal solid plane, which is to be a square surface representing the chosen square number.

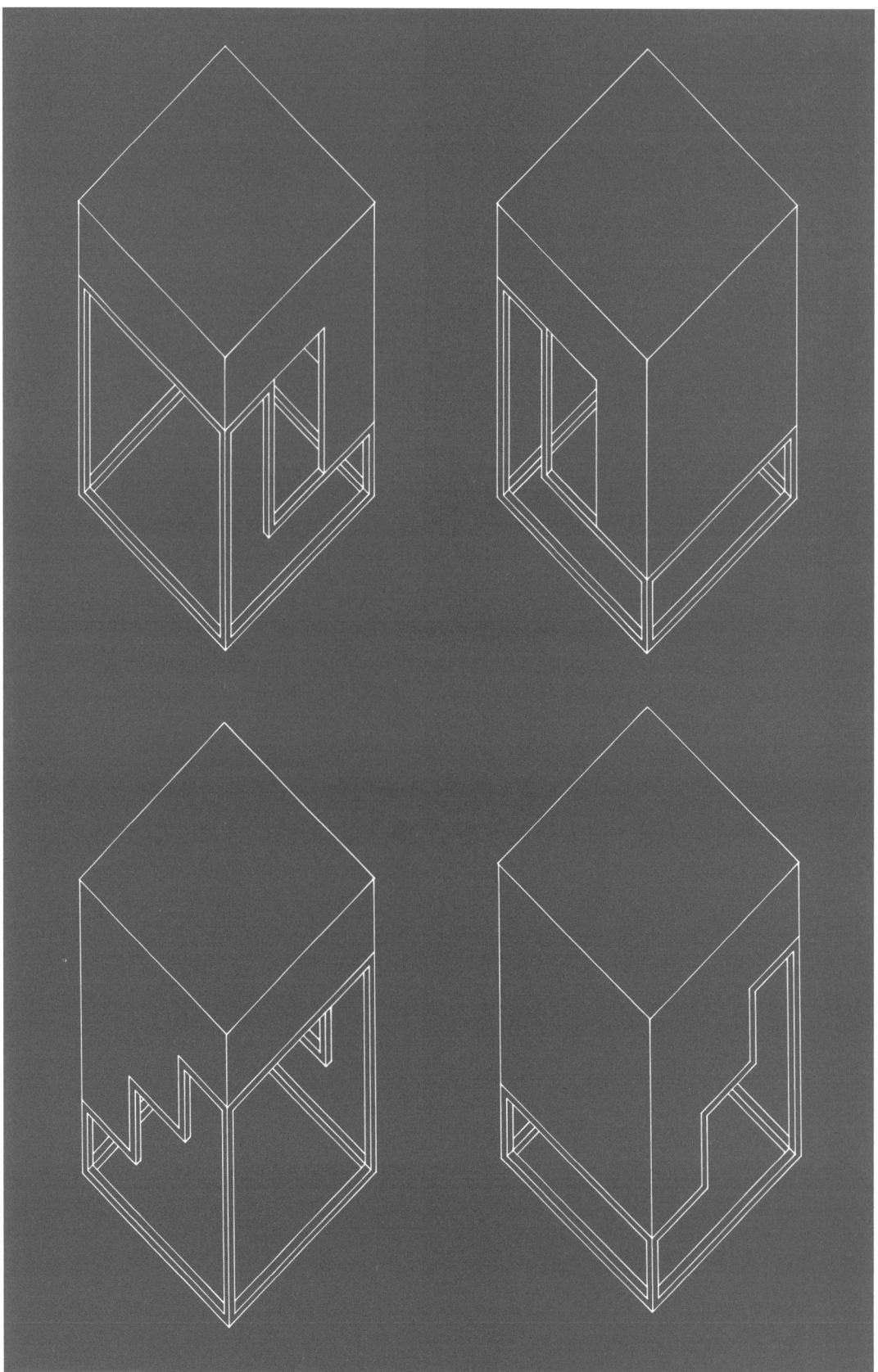

G-4. TRIANGLES, TRISECTION OF ANGLES

The polygonal tabletops are each formed by combining triangles while the quadrilateral tabletops can be analysed into triangles.

It is known that by trisecting the angles of any triangle the lines of trisection intersect to form an equilateral triangle. This equilateral triangle will then be the plan of a leg for the object.

From this, each combining triangle of a polygonal tabletop and each analysed triangle of a quadrilateral tabletop will now have a leg in place.

P7. Polygonal tables with triangles

Three right-angled triangles are conjoined to give a polygonal tabletop from a minimum of three sides to a maximum of six sides.

By trisecting the angles of each of the three triangles, the lines of trisection intersect to form an equilateral triangle, and this equilateral triangle will then be the plan of a leg supporting the tabletop.

Four tabletops from three to six sides are used for four tables A, B, C, D

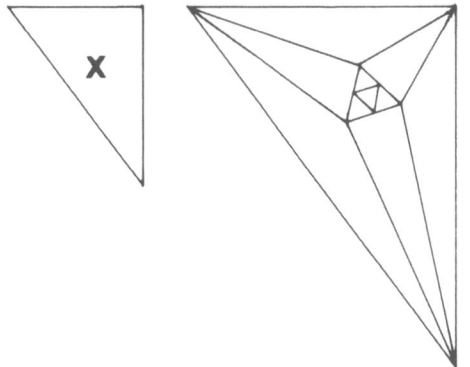

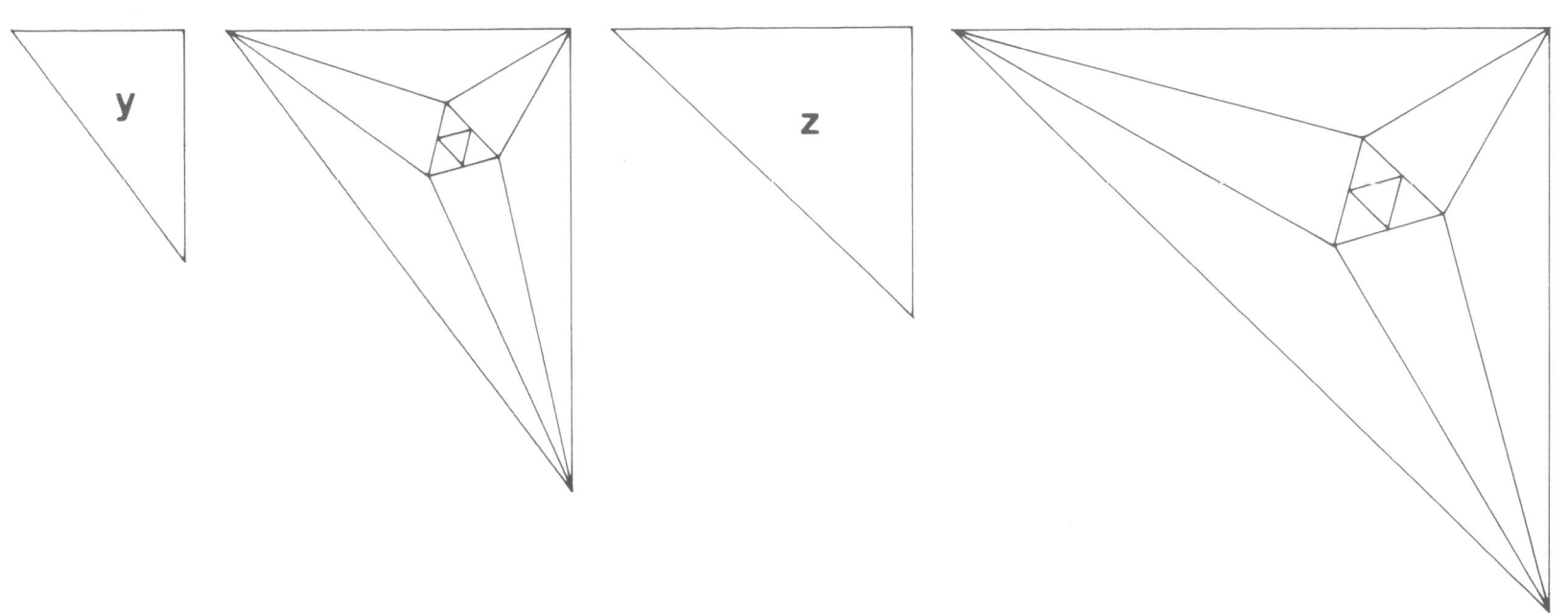

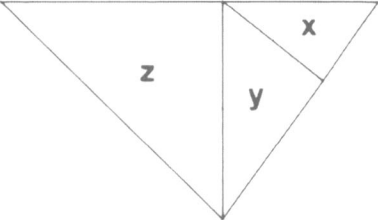

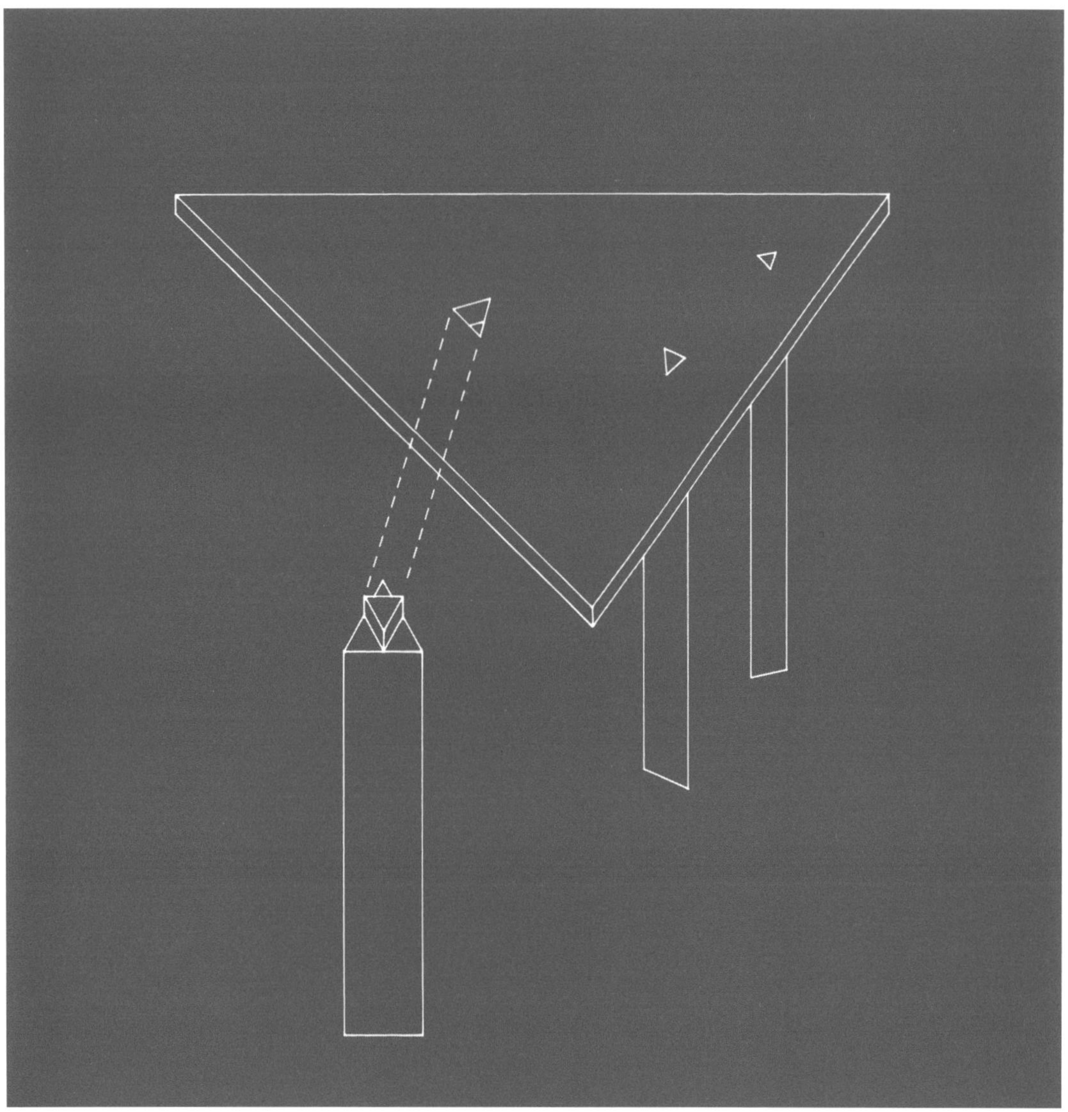

*Table B – Cojoining triangles x,
y, z to give a four sided figure*

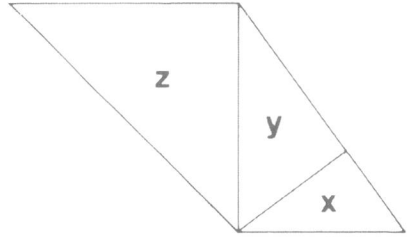

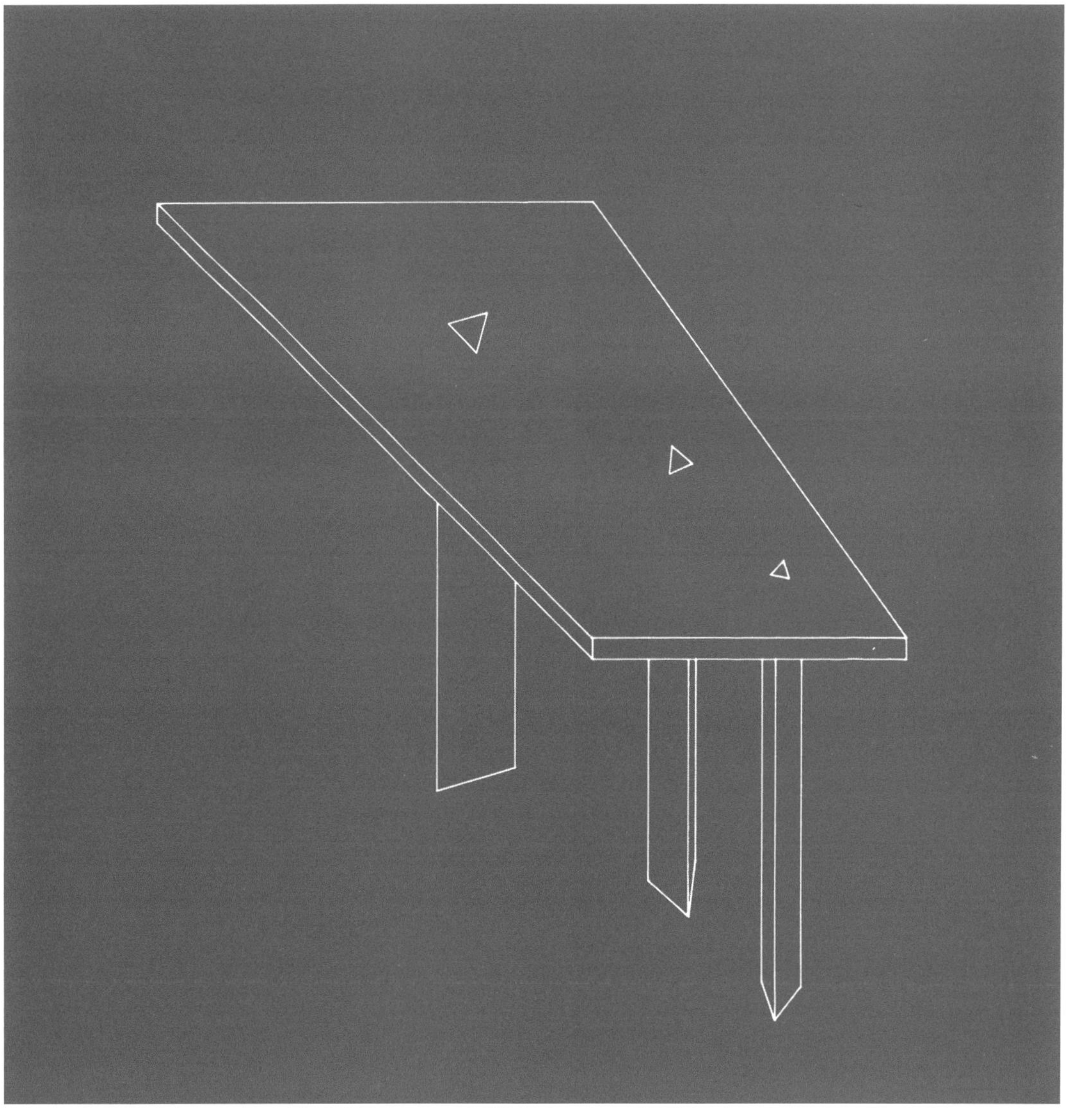

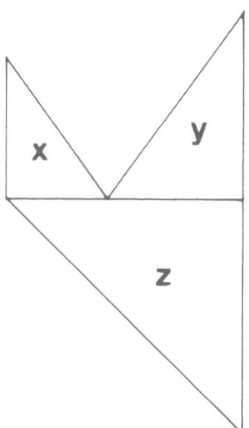

Table C – Cojoining triangles x,
y, z to give a five sided figure

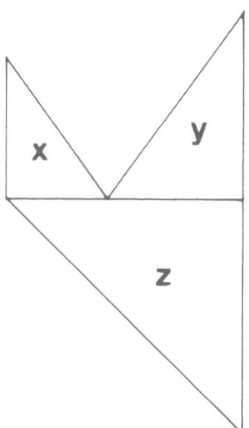

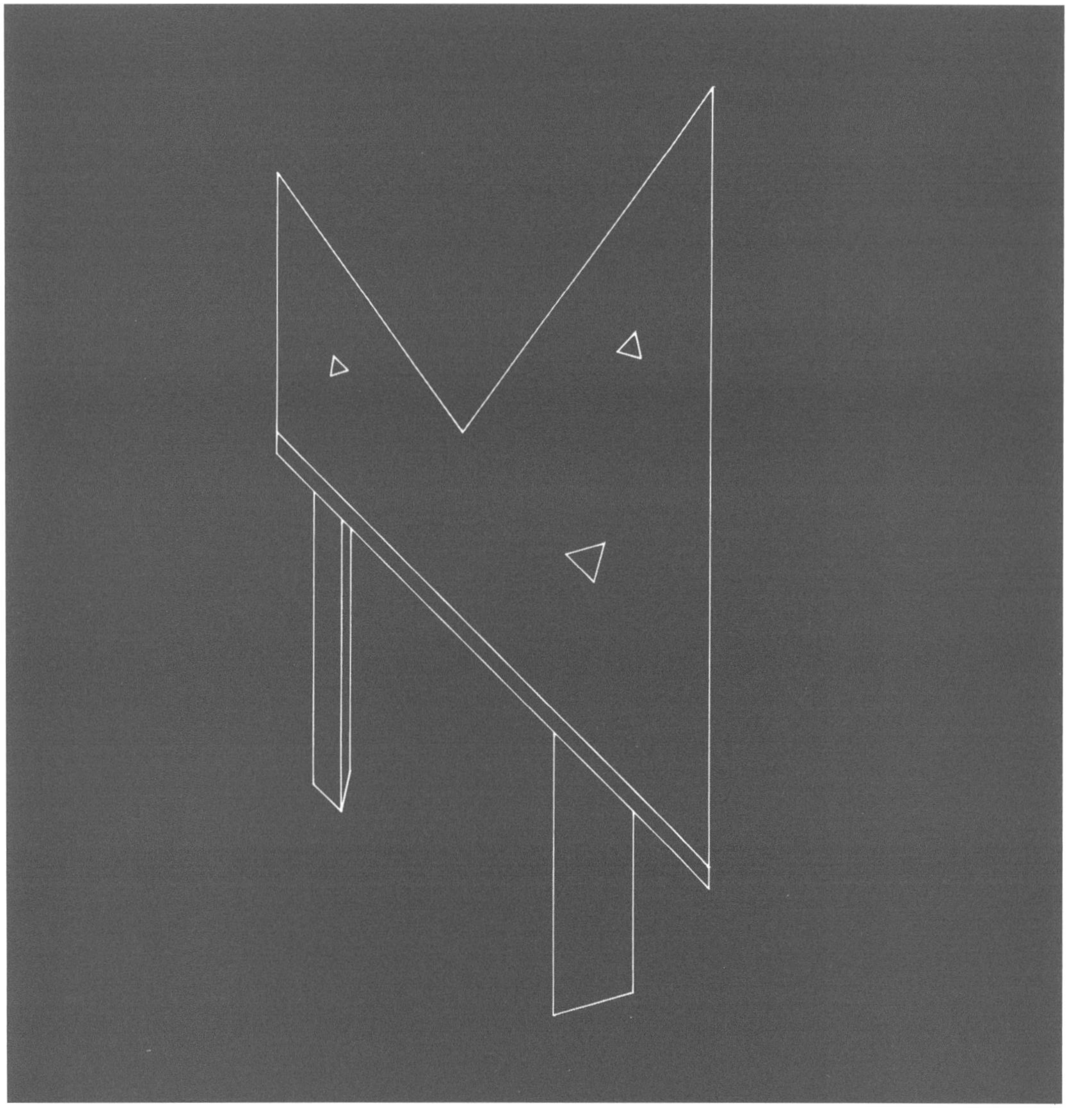

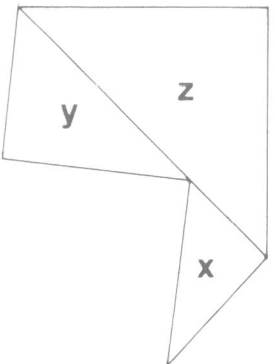

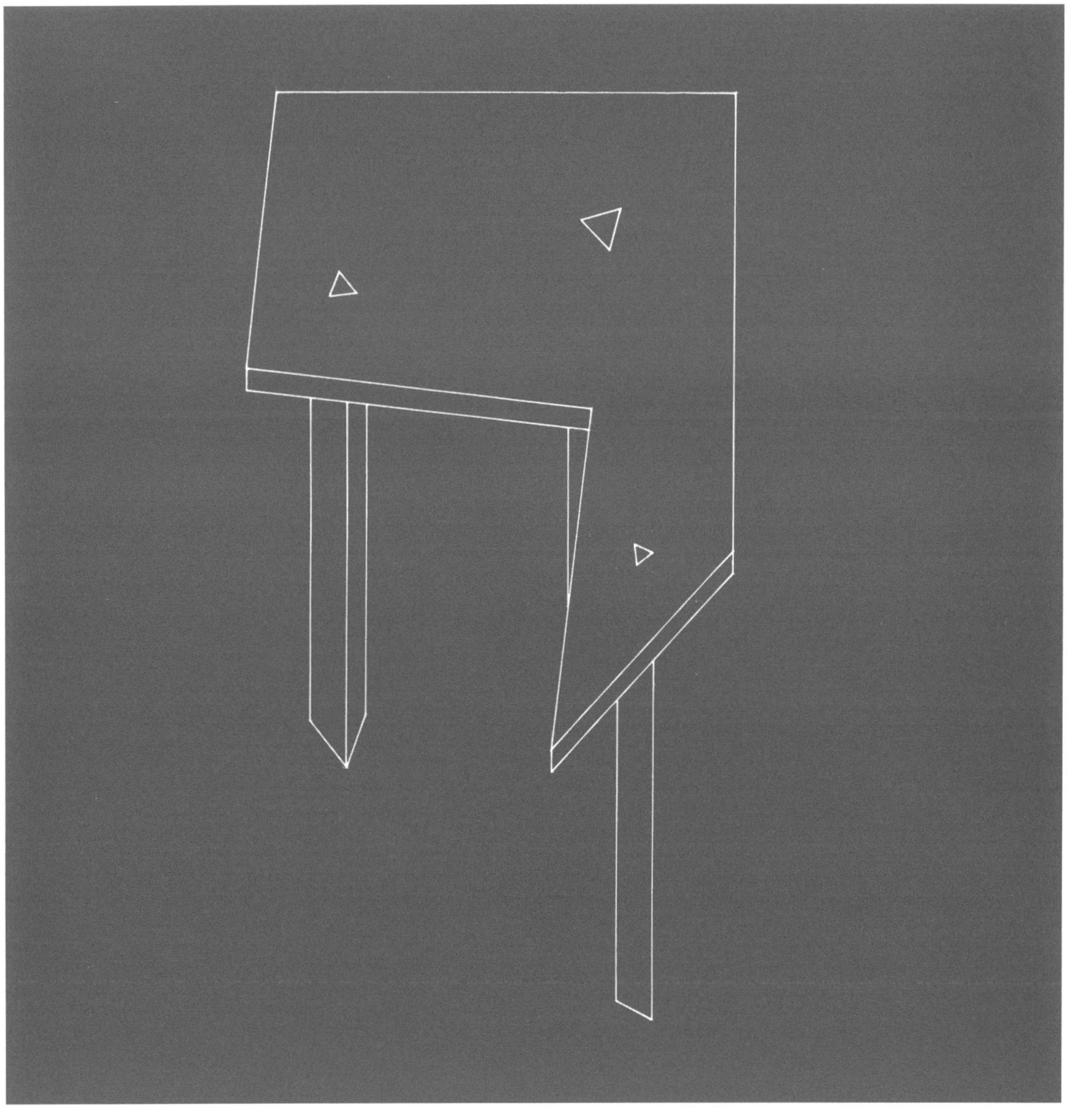

P8. Quadrilateral tables with triangles

A cyclic quadrilateral is constructed to give the form of the tabletop.

Join up one pair of opposite corners of the quadrilateral one way to form two triangles, and join up the other pair of opposite corners of the quadrilateral the other way to form two more triangles.

By trisecting the angles of each of the four triangles, the lines of trisection intersect to form an equilateral triangle, and this equilateral triangle will then be the plan of a leg supporting the tabletop.

Three different quadrilateral tabletops are used for three tables X, Y, Z.

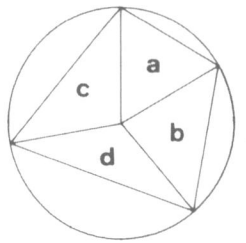

Table Y – Its cyclic quadrilateral is given by cojoining triangles a, b, d, c in this order

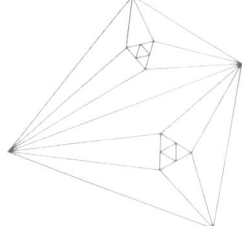

Table Y – Forming four equilateral triangles from the two ways the quadrilateral is divided into two triangles

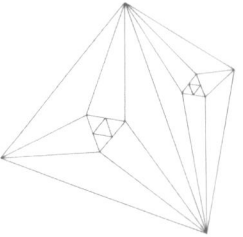

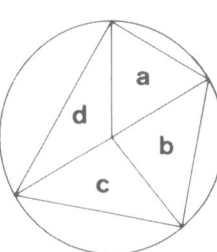

Table X – Its cyclic quadrilateral is given by cojoining triangles a, b, c, d in this order

Table X – Forming four equilateral triangles from the two ways the quadrilateral is divided into two triangles

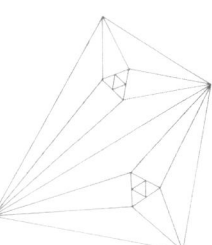

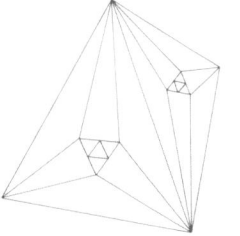

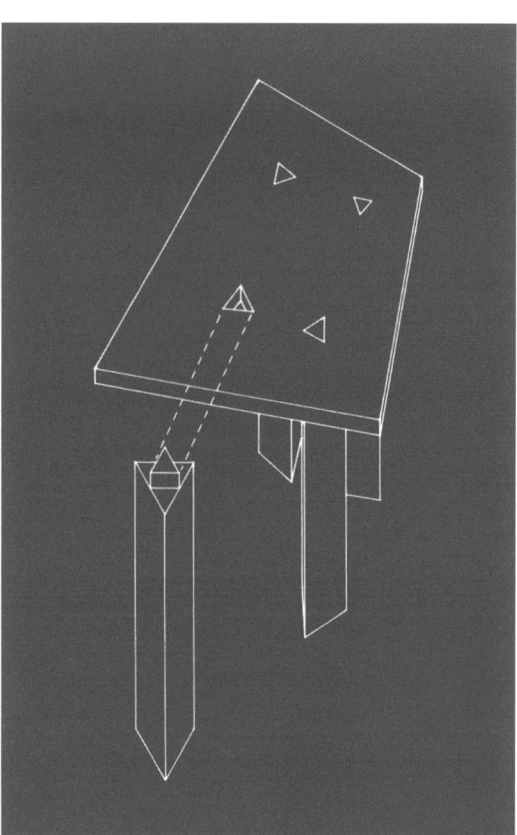

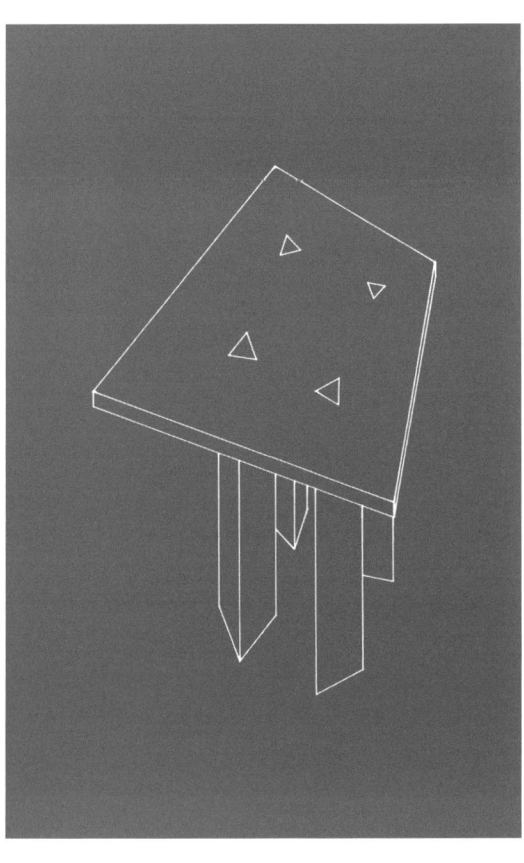

Table Z – Its cyclic quadrilateral is given by cojoining triangles a, c, b, d in this order

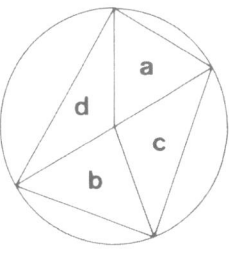

Table Z – Forming four equilateral triangles from the two ways the quadrilateral is divided into two triangles

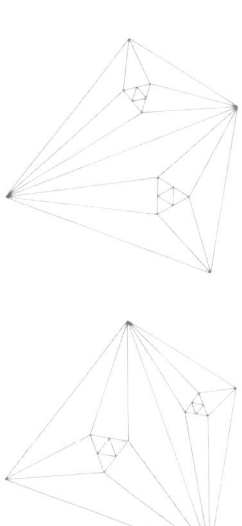

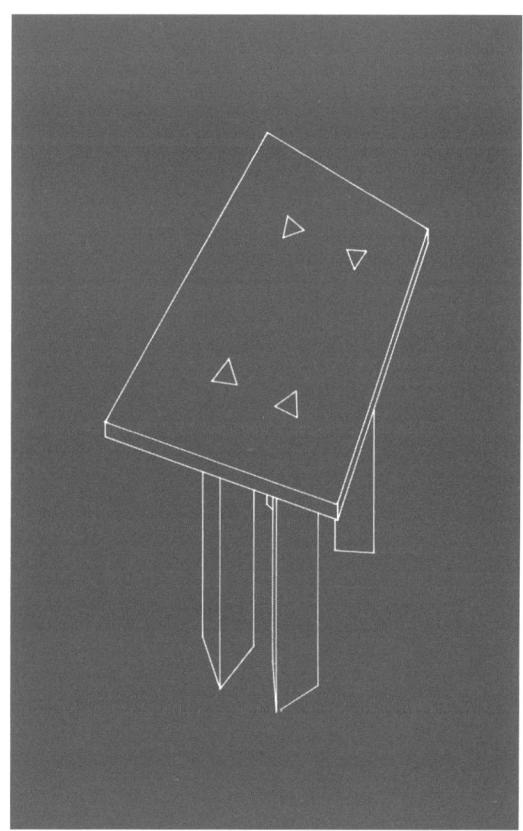

BOXES

G5. MUSICAL CONSONANCE

In music there are consonant as well as dissonant intervals. Since Pythagoras musical consonance have been defined by means of numerical ratios such that the simpler the ratio the greater the consonance. The following mathematical structure uses three numbers to give six numerical ratios as the six consonant intervals:

The three smallest integers where the largest integer is less than twice the smallest integer are 3, 4, 5.

The six ratios formed by using these three numbers are 3/4, 3/5, 4/5, 5/4, 5/3, 4/3.

Let these six ratios be expressed within the octave, that is between 1 and 2, by doubling those three ratios the values of which are less than 1, then the six ratios become 3/2, 6/5, 8/5, 5/4, 5/3, 4/3.

The six ratios are separated into the two sets, with set A consisting of the three smaller ratios 6/5, 5/4, 4/3, and set B consisting of the three larger ratios 3/2, 8/5, 5/3, then

(a) the three multiplications of two ratios in set A will give the three ratios in set B:
6/5 x 5/4 = 3/2
6/5 x 4/3 = 8/5
5/4 x 4/3 = 5/3.

(b) the three multiplications of two ratios in set B, to be expressed within the octave by halving the product of each multiplication, will give the three ratios in set A:
1/2 (3/2 x 8/5) = 6/5
1/2 (3/2 x 5/3) = 5/4
1/2 (8/5 x 5/3) = 4/3.

(c) every ratio in one set will have its inversion in the other set, where two ratios (intervals) being inversions of each other are defined by the product of their multiplication being two (octave);
6/5 x 5/3 = 2
5/4 x 8/5 = 2
4/3 x 3/2 = 2.

The six consonant intervals are spatially represented as follows:

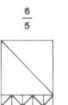 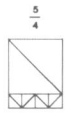 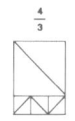  

P9. Music box

The six surfaces of the object represent the six consonant intervals in music—minor third, major third, perfect fourth, perfect fifth, minor sixth, major sixth—using the six related ratios in mathematics – 6/5, 5/4, 4/3, 3/2, 8/5, 5/3 – which define musical consonance.

The six consonant ratios are arranged on the six surfaces of the object such that reading three adjacent surfaces on the x, y, z planes will show that mathematical relation in which two consonant ratios multiplied give the third consonant ratio.

The top panel of the object opens to a storage space.

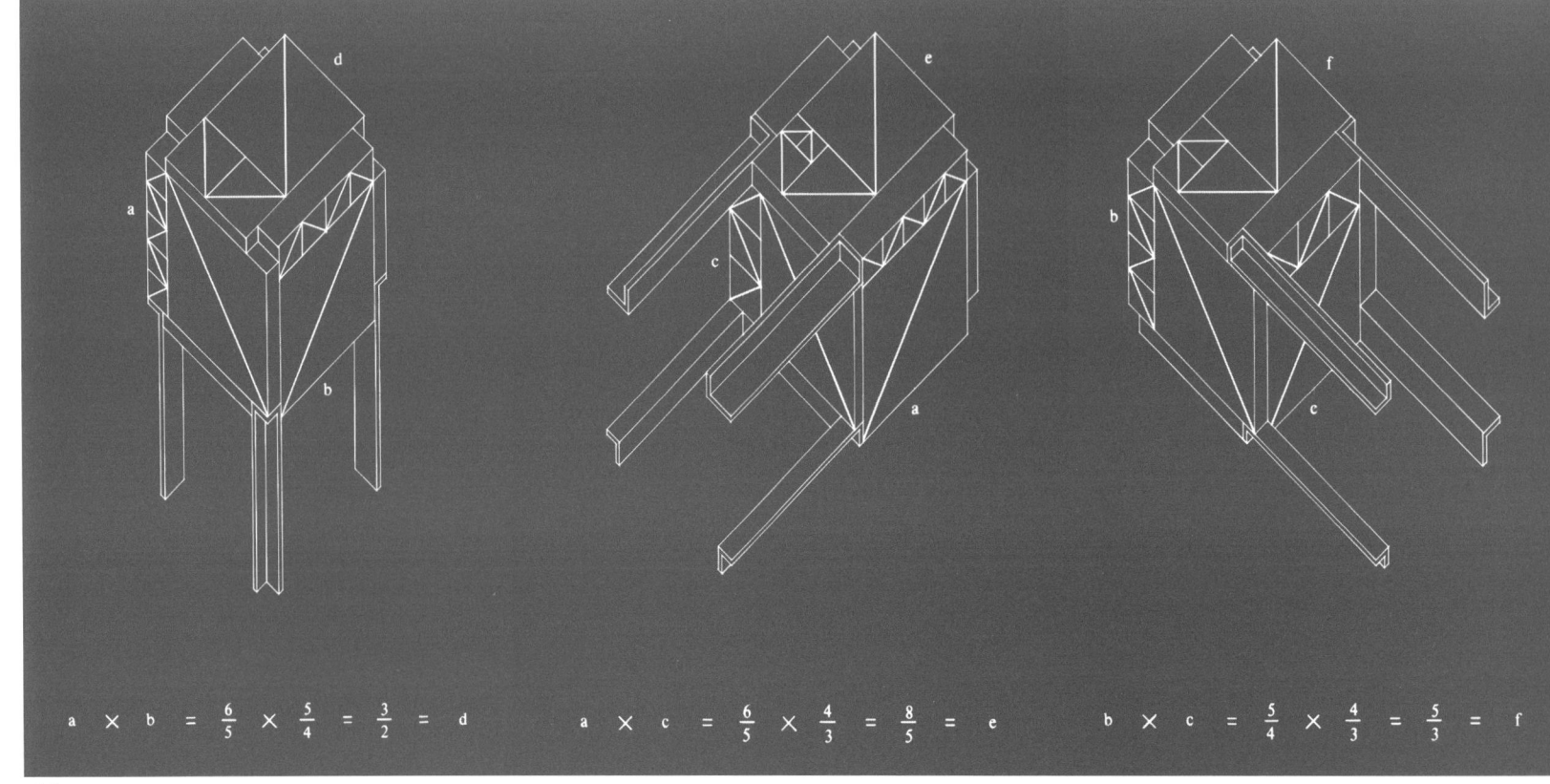

$$a \times b = \frac{6}{5} \times \frac{5}{4} = \frac{3}{2} = d \qquad a \times c = \frac{6}{5} \times \frac{4}{3} = \frac{8}{5} = e \qquad b \times c = \frac{5}{4} \times \frac{4}{3} = \frac{5}{3} = f$$

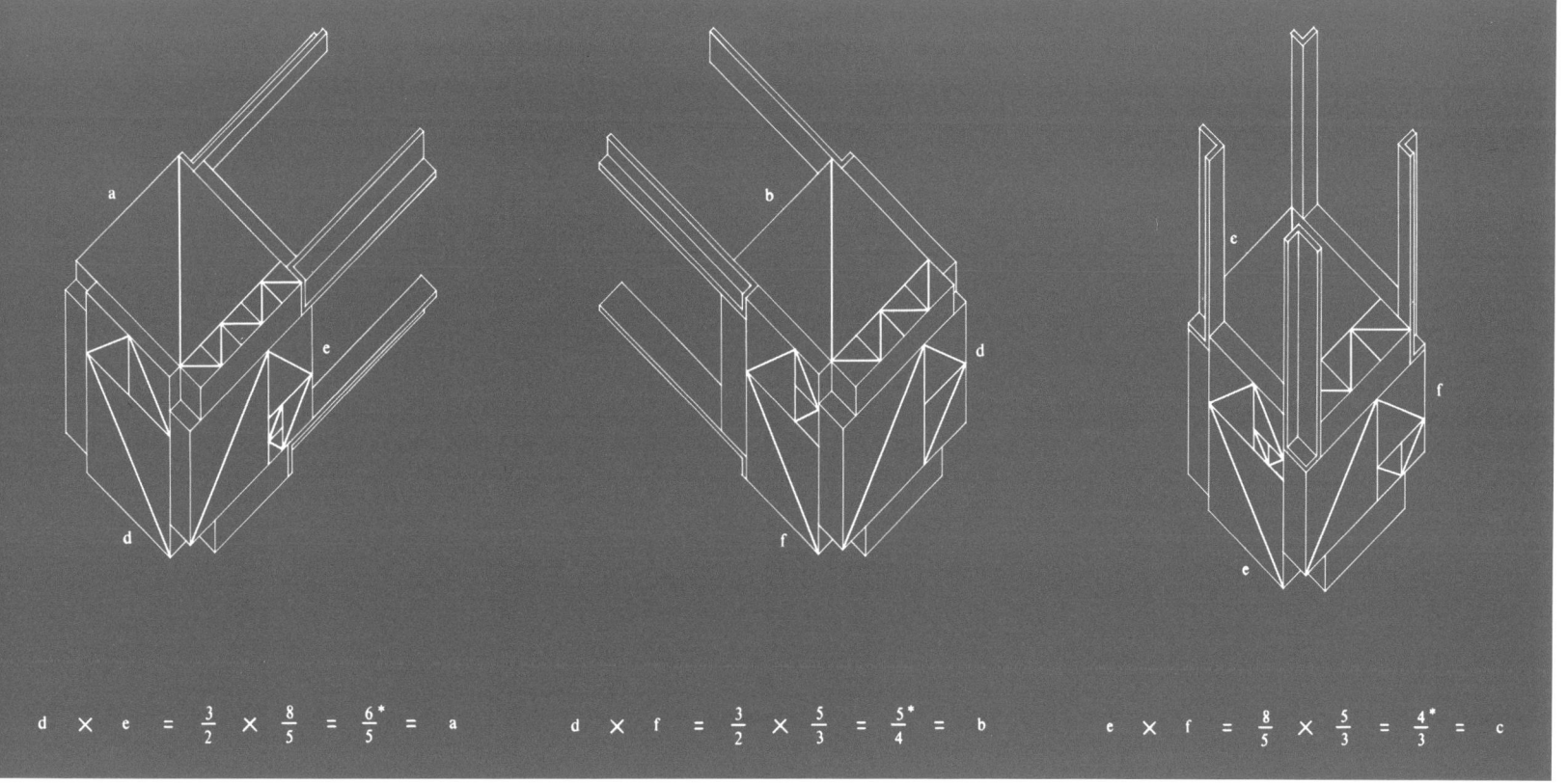

$$d \times e = \frac{3}{2} \times \frac{8}{5} = \frac{6}{5}{}^{*} = a \qquad d \times f = \frac{3}{2} \times \frac{5}{3} = \frac{5}{4}{}^{*} = b \qquad e \times f = \frac{8}{5} \times \frac{5}{3} = \frac{4}{3}{}^{*} = c$$

P10. Diatonic box

There are all-interval note-rows in each of which not only
each of the twelve notes within the octave is used
exactly once in sequence but also each of the eleven
intervals within the octave appears exactly once between
adjacent notes.

Analogously, are there also all-consonant diatonic-rows
in each of which not only each of the seven notes of
the diatonic scale within the octave is used exactly
once in sequence but also each of the six consonant
intervals within the octave appears exactly once between
adjacent notes?

There are in fact six all-consonant diatonic-rows, excluding
retrograde and pitch transpositions. This discovery is
celebrated in a hexagonal box on the six vertical surfaces
of which the six all-consonant diatonic-rows are represented.

Let A, B, C, D, E, F, G refer to the seven diatonic notes
and let a, b, c, d, e, f refer to the six consonant intervals
where, expressed as numerical ratios, a = 6/5, b =
5/4, c = 4/3, d = 3/2, e = 8/5, f = 5/3, then the six
all-consonant diatonic rows, excluding retrograde and
pitch transpositions, are shown as follows:

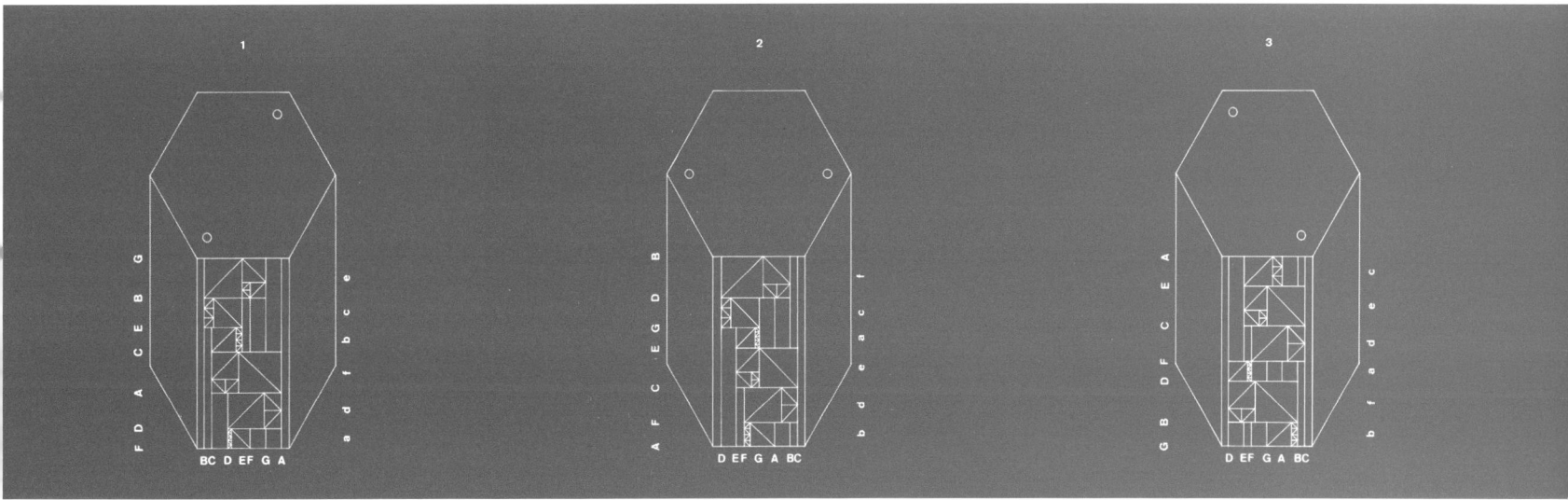

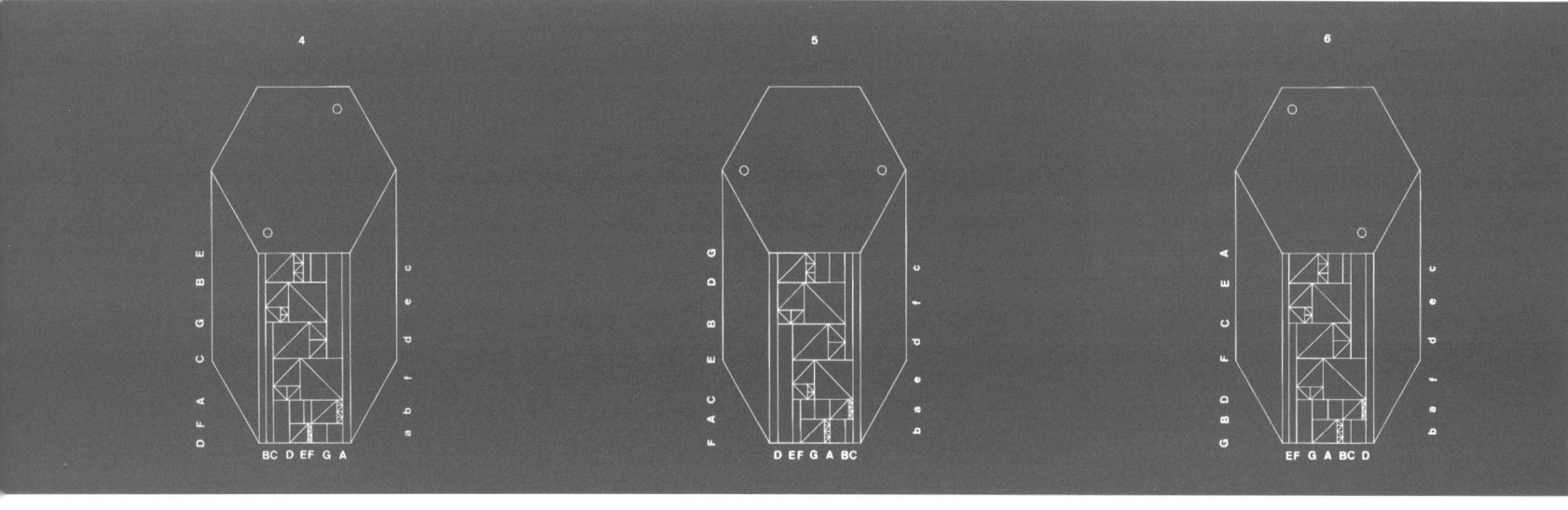

G6. MATHEMATICAL MEANS

Just as consonance in music is defined by simple intervals between pitches, so mathematical means refer to the simplicity of numerical relationship between terms.

These projects represent the arithmetic, geometric and harmonic means spatially as lines inscribed on the surfaces of boxes.

These boxes as well as the 'Music box' and the 'Diatonic box', can be described as ornamental objects. The objects are, to be sure, useful, usable, but the inscription of lines on the surfaces of the boxes adds nothing to their function. Instead, the purpose of these inscribed lines is to be understood as what Gombrich calls "explanatory articulation". In 'Boxes with golden means' and 'Four measures, six boxes', lines articulate and explain the proportion of the box itself, while in 'Boxes with consonant means' and 'Box with golden consonance', lines trace out certain mathematical relations.

Ornament should not be considered as a category of objects because there is no fixed set of properties which answers to the concept 'ornament'. What appears as ornament in one context may not be so in another context.

The aim is to unify ornament with the object ornamented so that ornament transcends itself and disappears.

P11. Boxes with consonant means

For the set of eight intervals consisting of the six consonant intervals 6/5, 5/4, 4/3, 3/2, 8/5, 5/3, the unison 1/1 and the octave 2/1, there are cases in which the arithmetic mean A and the harmonic mean H of a smaller interval S in the set and a larger interval L in the set are themselves intervals in the set:

(i) $L = 2/1$ $S = 1/1$ $A = 3/2$ $H = 4/3$
(ii) $L = 3/2$ $S = 1/1$ $A = 5/4$ $H = 6/5$
(iii) $L = 5/3$ $S = 1/1$ $A = 4/3$ $H = 5/4$
(iv) $L = 2/1$ $S = 6/5$ $A = 8/5$ $H = 3/2$
(v) $L = 2/1$ $S = 4/3$ $A = 5/3$ $H = 8/5$
(vi) $L1 = 5/3$ $S1 = 4/3$ $A1 = 3/2$
      $L2 = 3/2$ $S2 = 6/5$ $H2 = 4/3$

The mathematical relations (i) to (vi) are represented in the six boxes (I) to (VI)

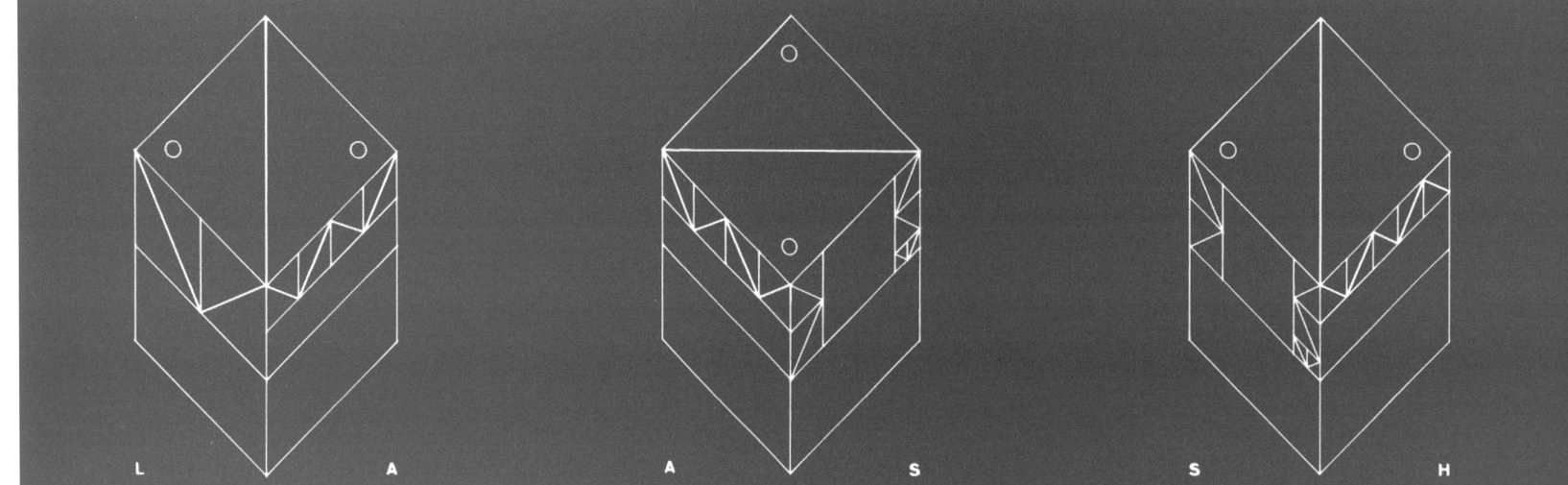

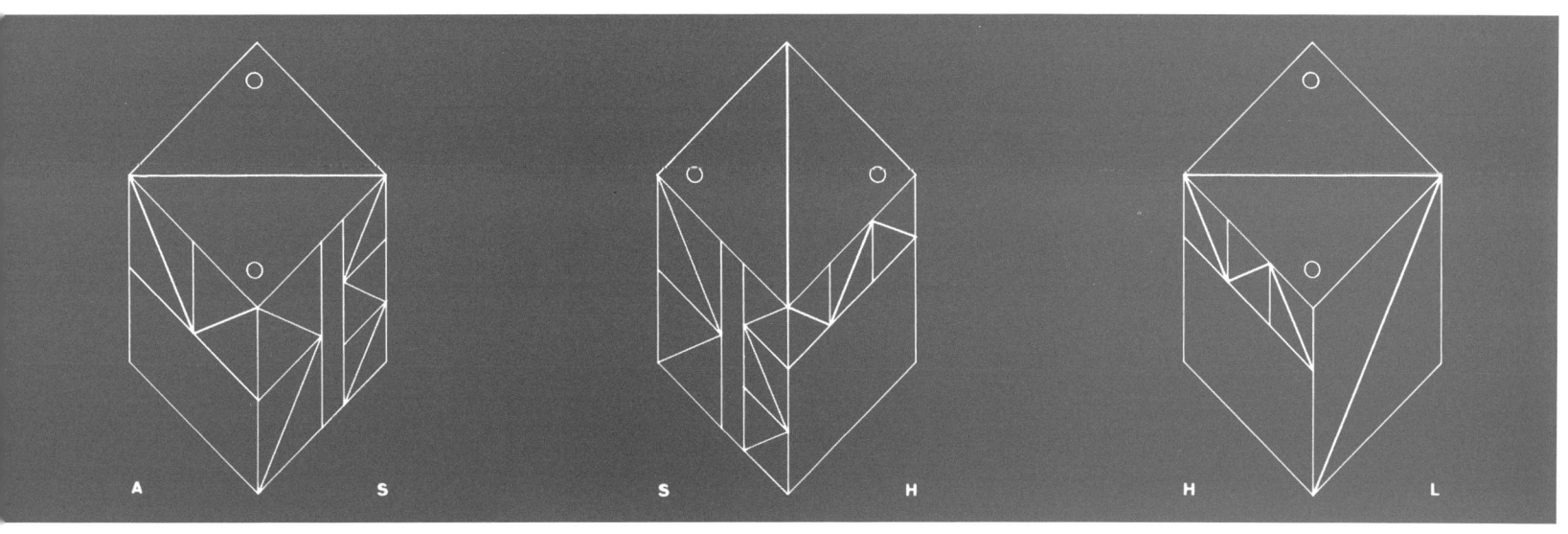

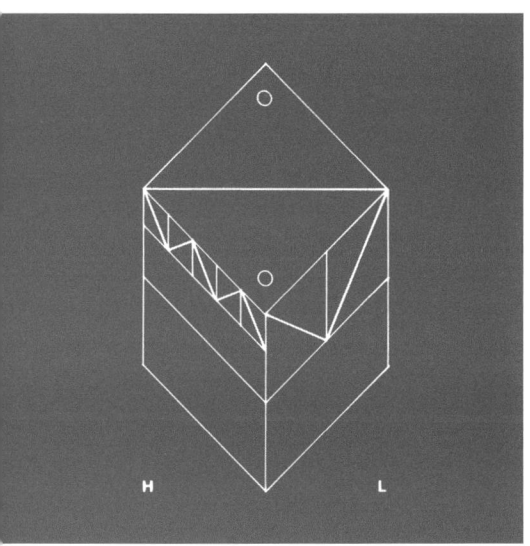

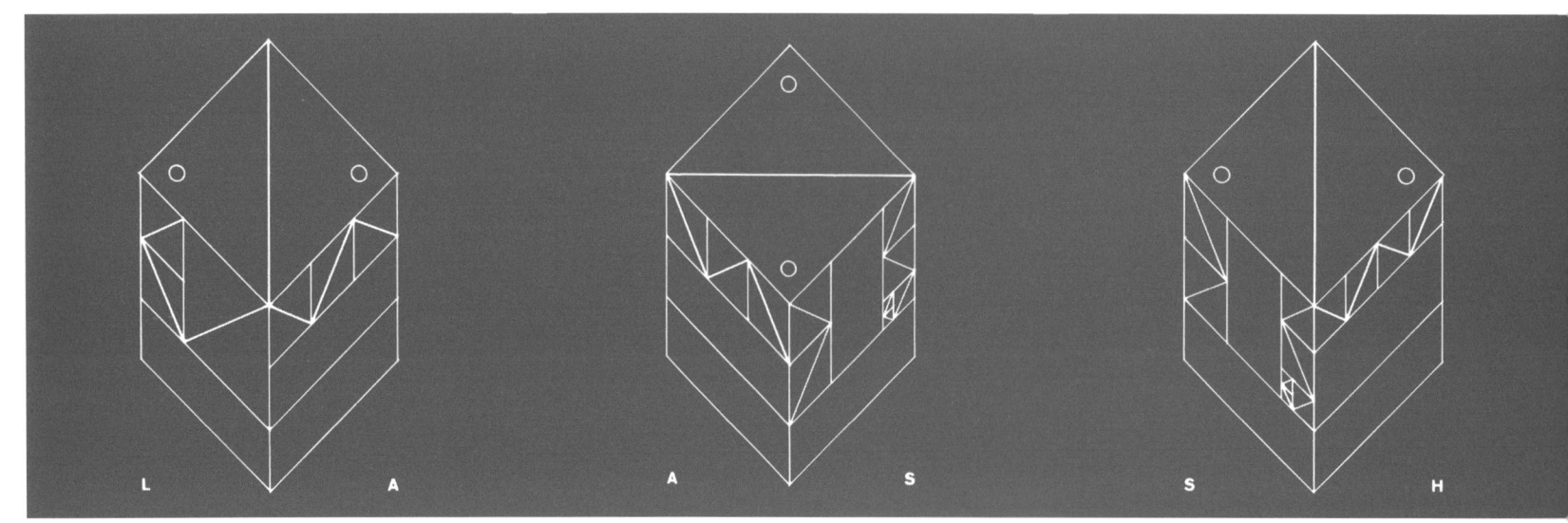

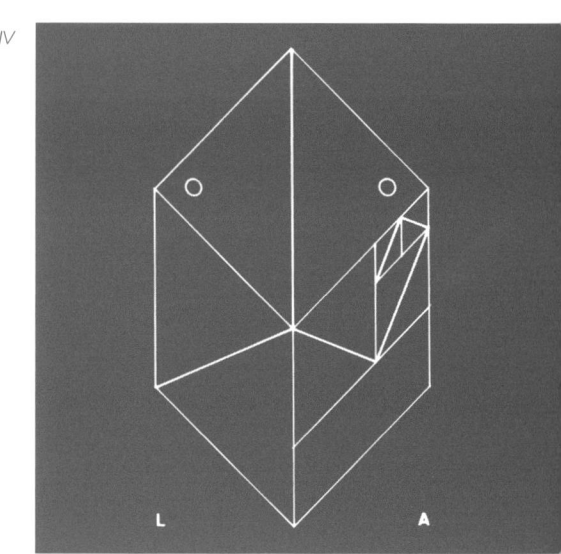

IV

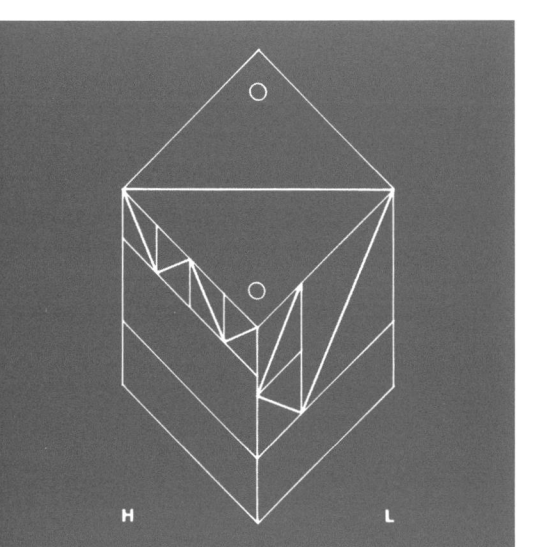

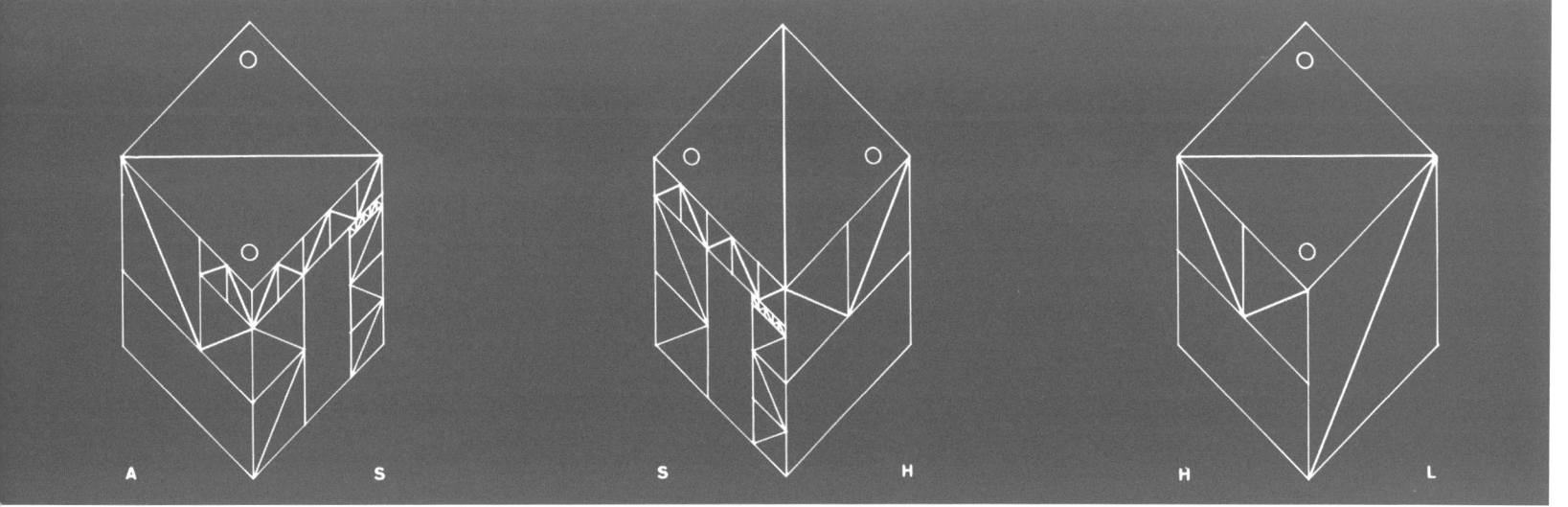

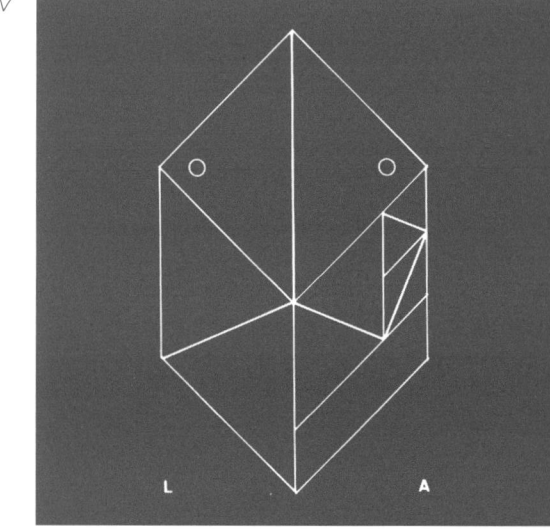

L   A

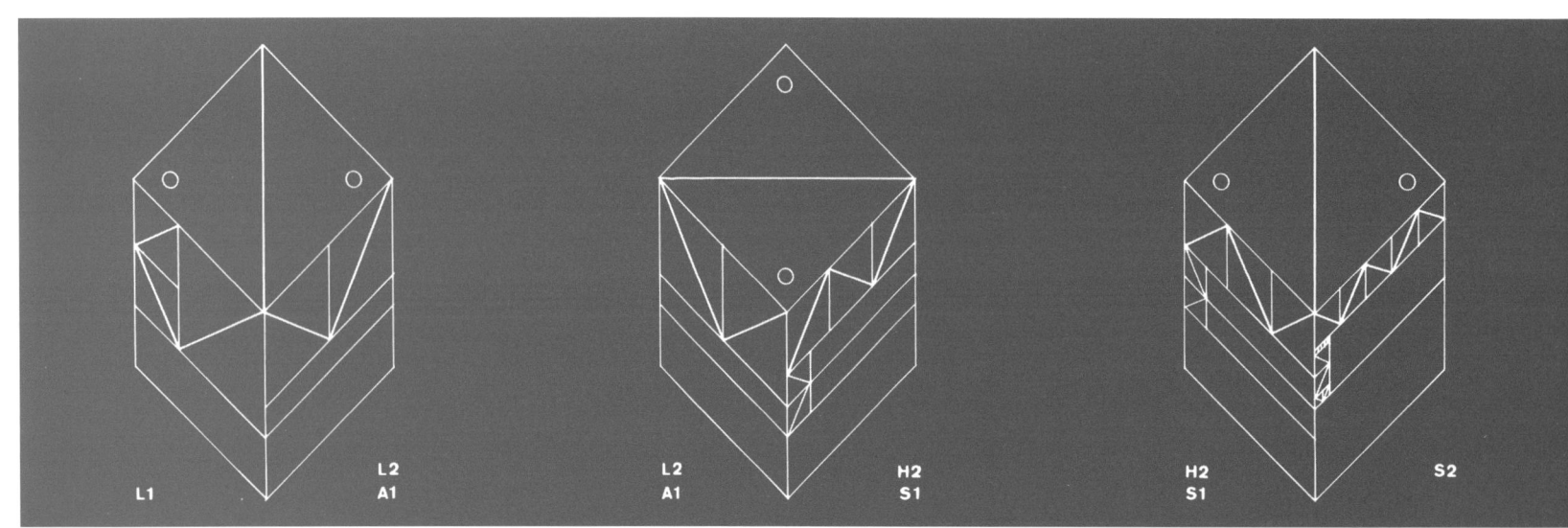

L1   L2
A1

L2   H2
A1   S1

H2   S2
S1

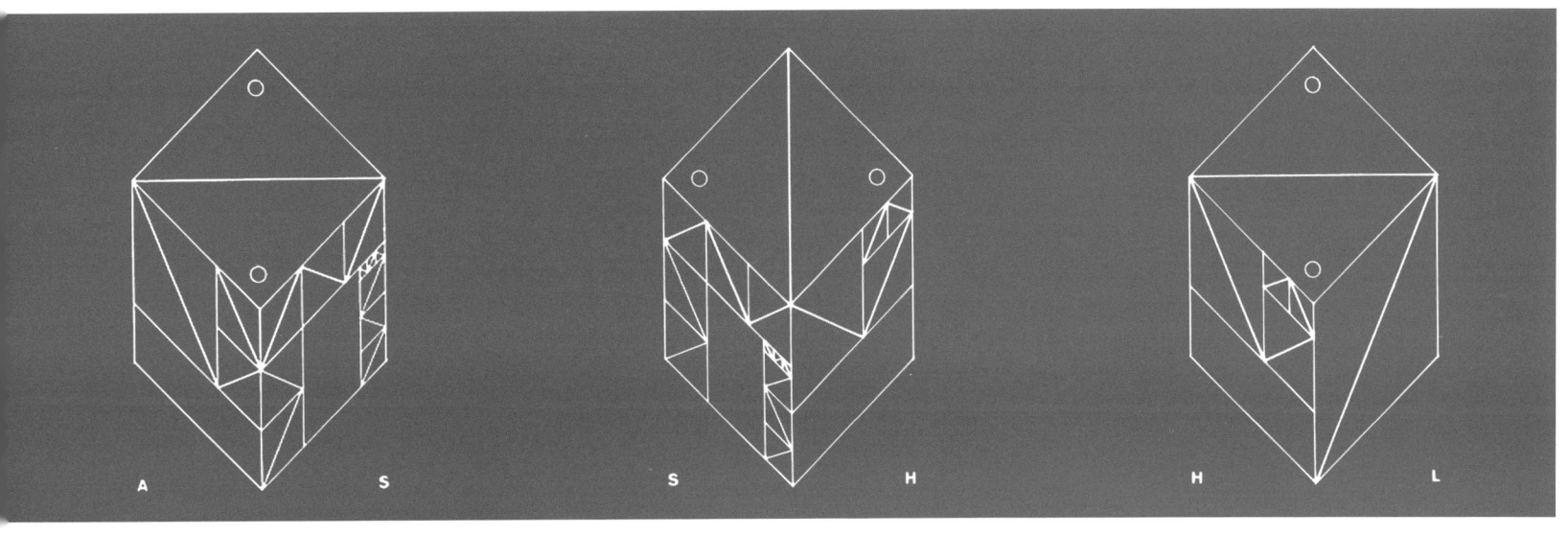

A   S   S   H   H   L

VI

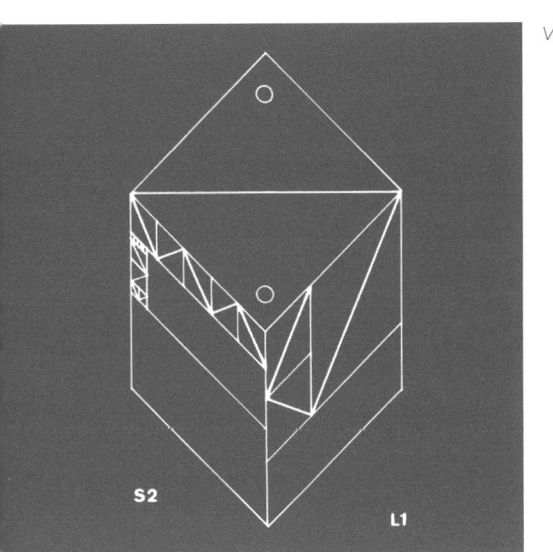

S2

L1

This project brings together the mathematics of the consonant intervals and the mathematics of the golden ratio.

The six consonant intervals a to f, the unison u and the octave v can be expressed as numerical ratios where $u = 1/1$, $a = 6/5$, $b = 5/4$, $c = 4/3$, $d = 3/2$, $e = 8/5$, $f = 5/3$, $v = 2/1$

The terms of the Fibonacci sequence, where adjacent terms approach the golden ratio, are $F_1 = 1$, $F_2 = 1$, $F_3 = 2$, $F_4 = 3$, $F_5 = 5$, $F_6 = 8$...

And then there is a visual paradox embodied in the object.

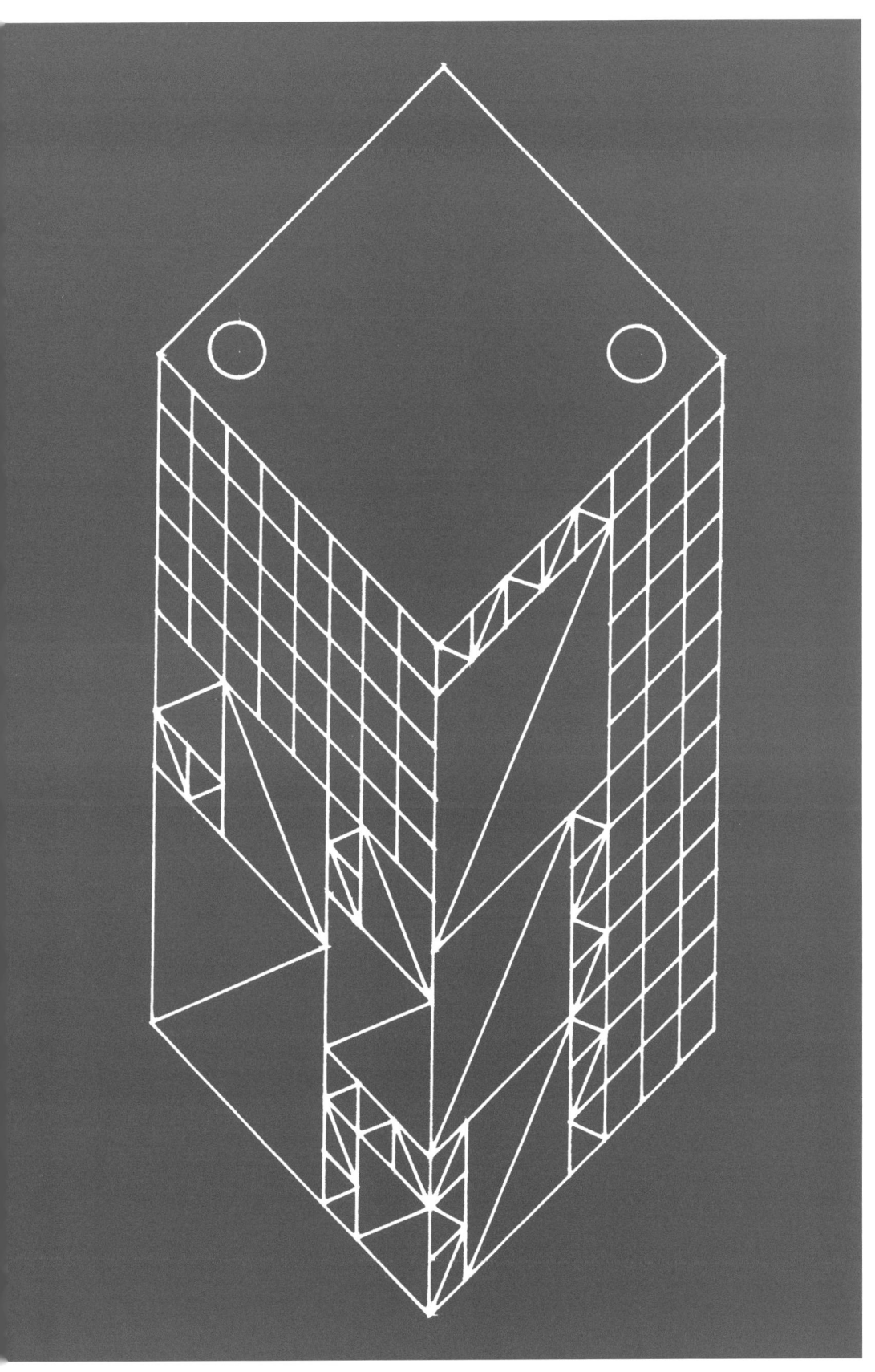

P13. Boxes with golden means

Just as 'Boxes with consonant means' makes use of the mathematics of two consonant intervals having another consonant interval as their mathematical mean, so this project makes use of the mathematics of two Fibonacci terms having another Fibonacci term as their mathematical mean.

Let the terms of the Fibonacci sequence be T_n, T_{n+1}, T_{n+2}, $T_{n+3}\ldots$, then the arithmetic mean of T_n and T_{n+3} is T_{n+2}, the geometric mean of T_n and T_{n+2} approaches T_{n+1}, and the harmonic mean of T_n and T_{n+3} approaches T_{n+1}.

Fibonacci terms and their means are represented on the three boxes I, II, III.

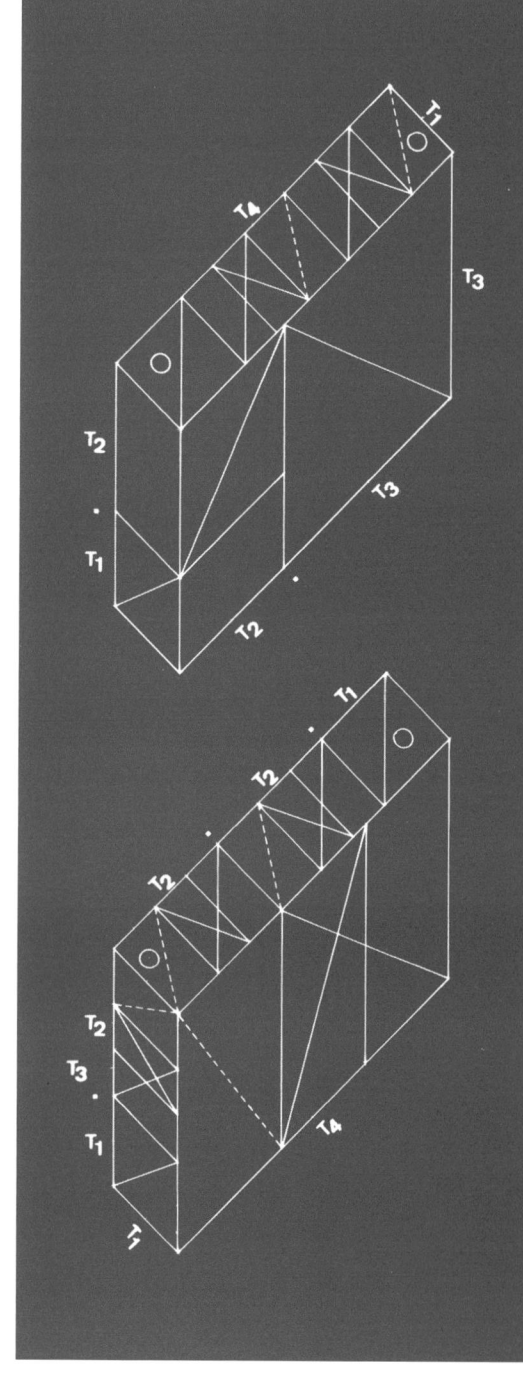

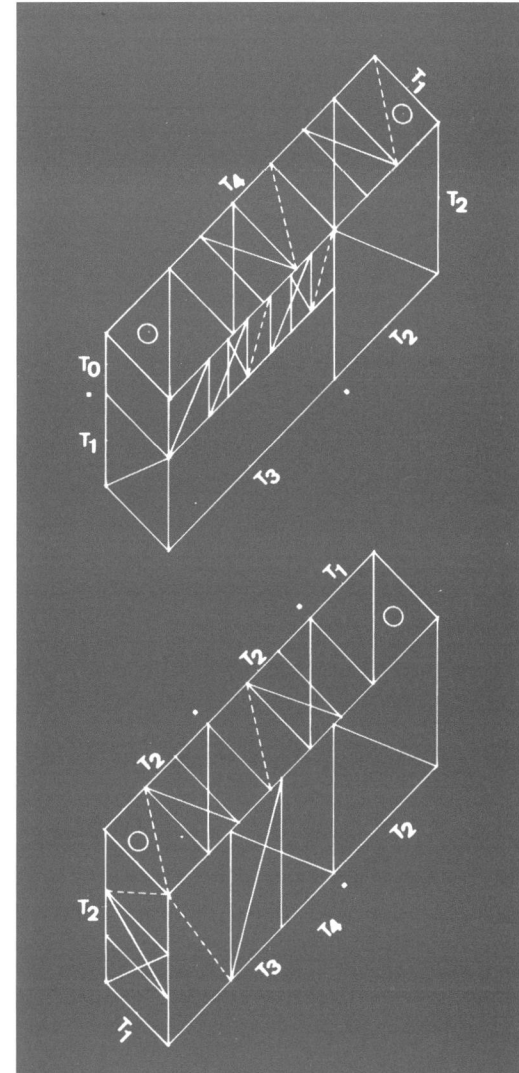

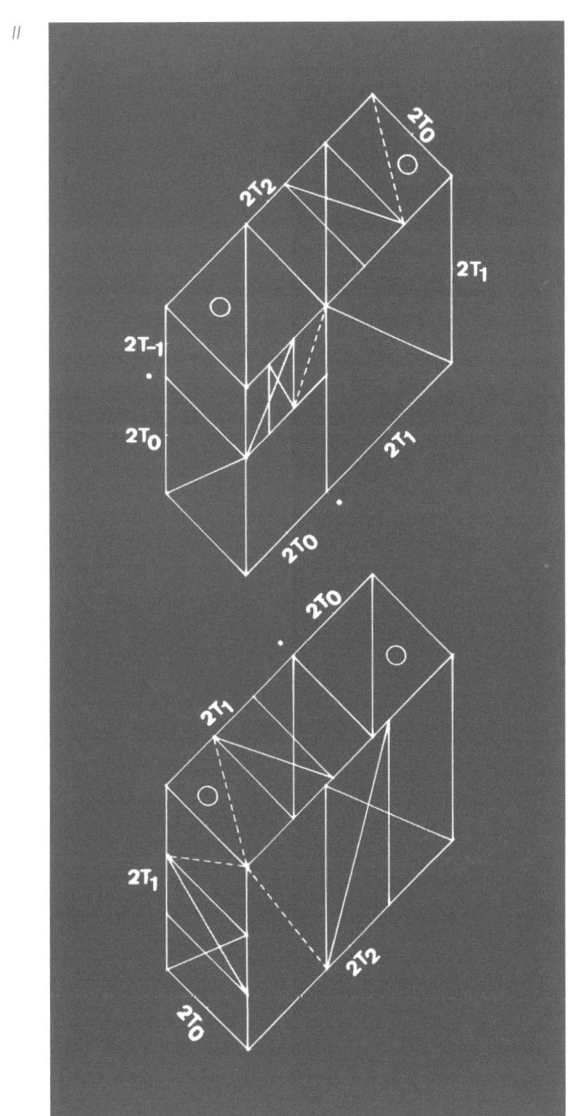

61

The shape and size of a rectangular volume can be described by three measurements.

Using four measures S, H, A, L, the form of six boxes I to VI are given as follows:

(i)   (S+H) X A X L
(ii) (S+A) X H X L
(iii) (S+L) X H X A
(iv) (H+A) X S X L
(v)   (H+L) X S X A
(vi) (A+L) X S X H

S being the smallest measure and L being the largest measure, H being their harmonic mean and A being their arithmetic mean, geometrical properties are inscribed on the surfaces of boxes I to VI.

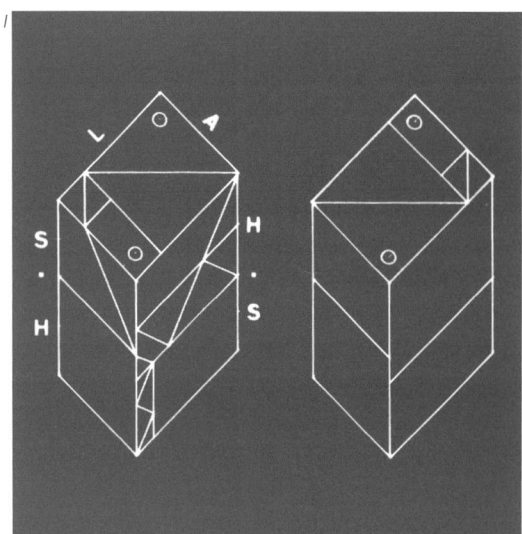

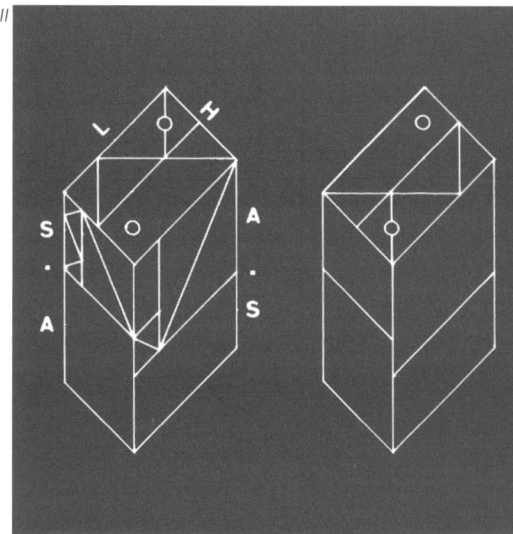

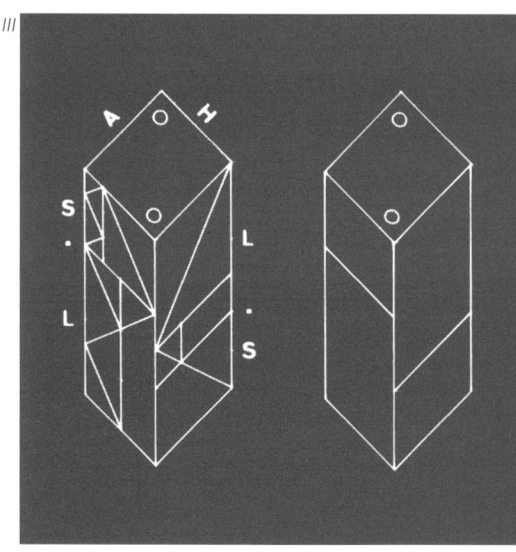

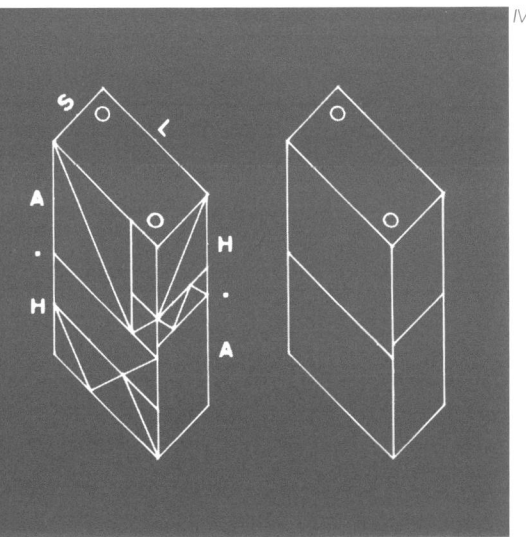

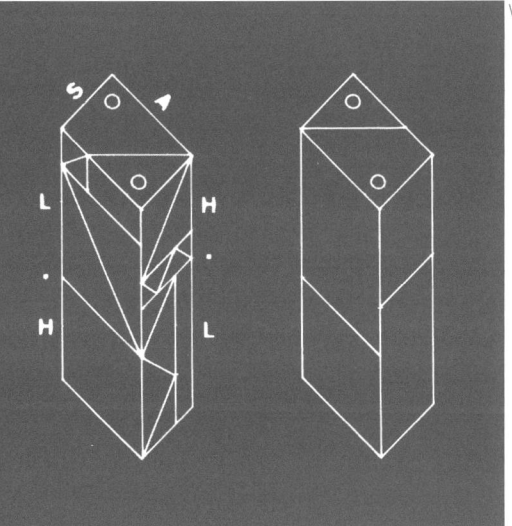

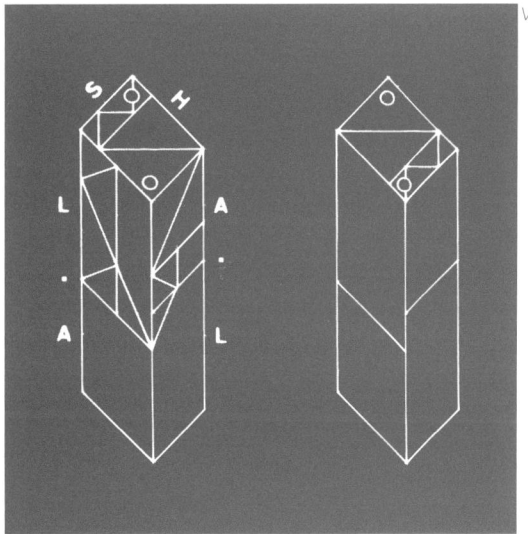

SCREENS...

G7. TRAVERSAL, DEFLECTION

The intricate patterns of these lattice screens are achieved by the traversal and deflection of lines diagonally across the panels of these screens according to invented rules, rules the sole purpose of which is to make complex patterns.

Wittgenstein recommended throwing away the ladder of logic after one has climbed up it. Likewise the generative rules for these projects have no further significance once the objects have been designed.

Therefore, rules are in these cases being used, made use of, used up.

P15. Screens with obstacles

Complex patterns are generated by diagonal lines which begin at each corner and end at a corner of each panel of the screen with the course of traversal being deflected by virtual obstacles placed along the way.

Virtual obstacles are positioned on the screen in order to achieve the desired density and degree of irregularity for the lattice pattern.

This requires two irregular series to position the virtual obstacles, one series for those obstacles oriented vertically and the other series for those obstacles oriented horizontally.

The first series is that in which the sum of two consecutive terms equals to the value of the subsequent term, while the second series consists of all the factors of those non-prime terms contained in the first series.

This generative method is applied to both objects, screens I and II.

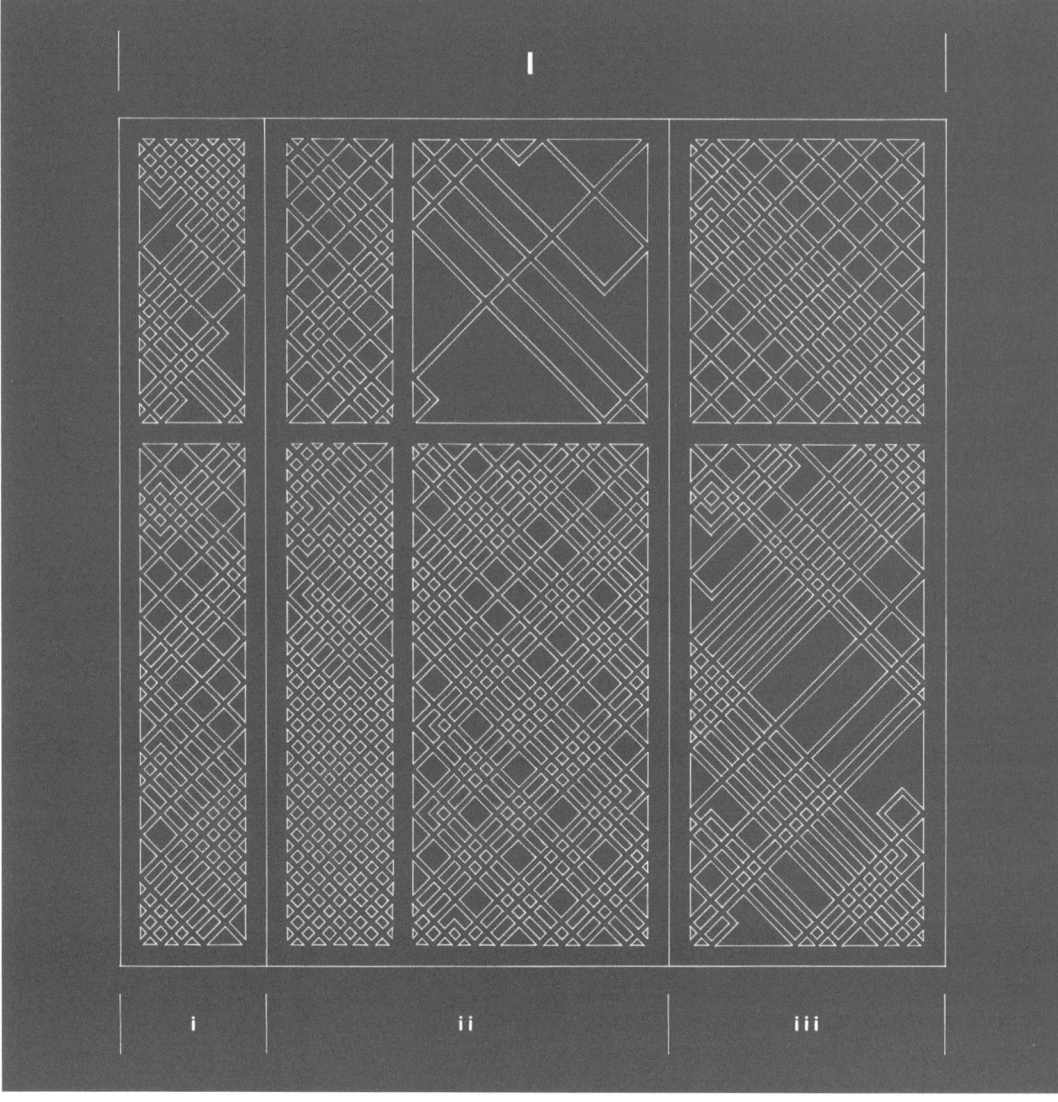

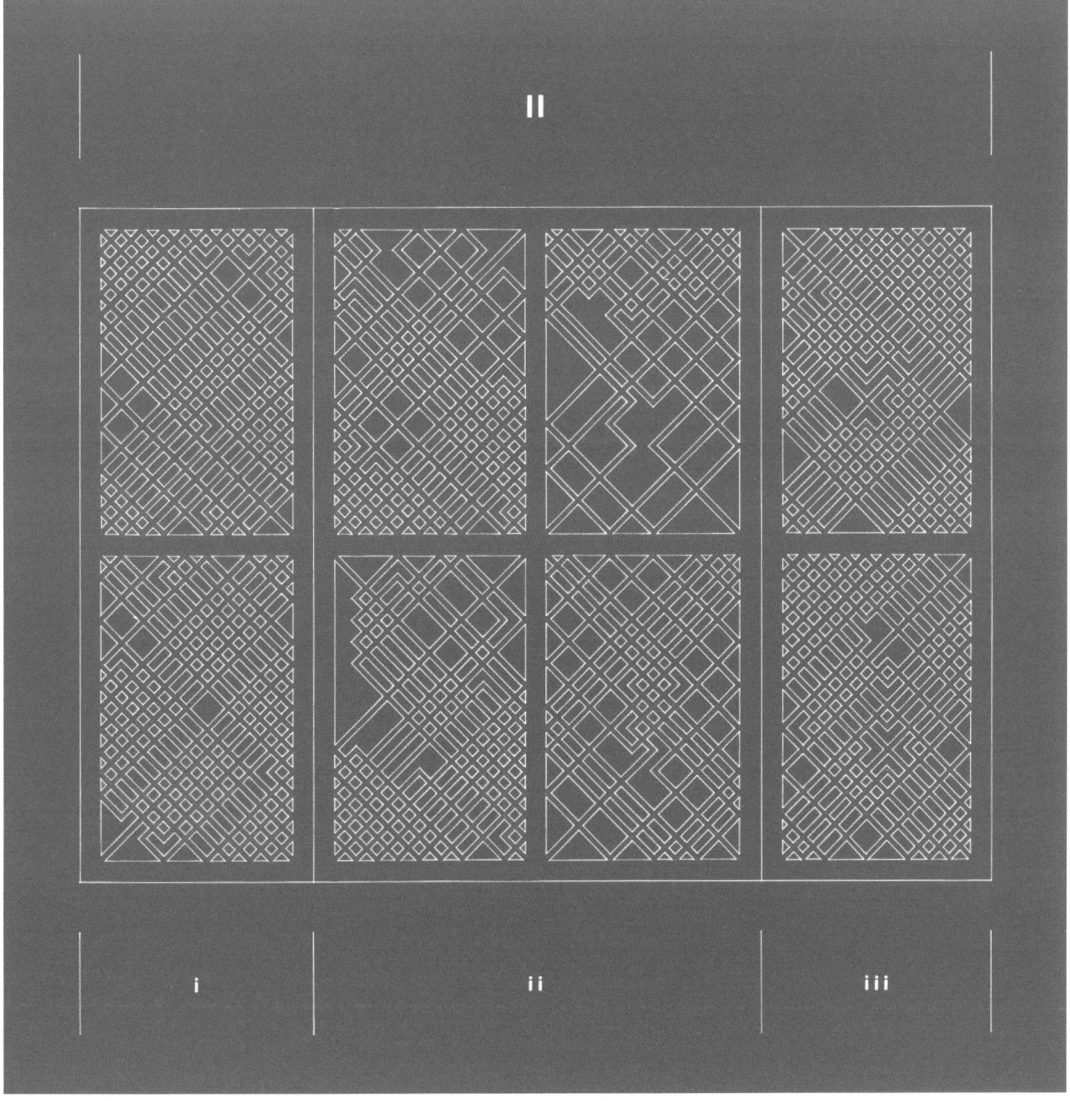

P16. Truncated screens

Complex patterns are generated by diagonal lines which begin at each corner and end at a corner of each panel of the screen with the course of traversal being deflected by the truncated outline of the panels.

A method is to be devised to give an irregular outline to each panel of each screen.

In order to achieve this, let a panel measure yXz where y = aXb = cXd... and z = eXf = gXh..., then those rectangles which measure aXb, cXd... will be removed from the top left corner of the panel, and those rectangles which measure eXf, gXh... will be removed from the top right corner of the panel.

This generative method is applied to both objects, screens I and II.

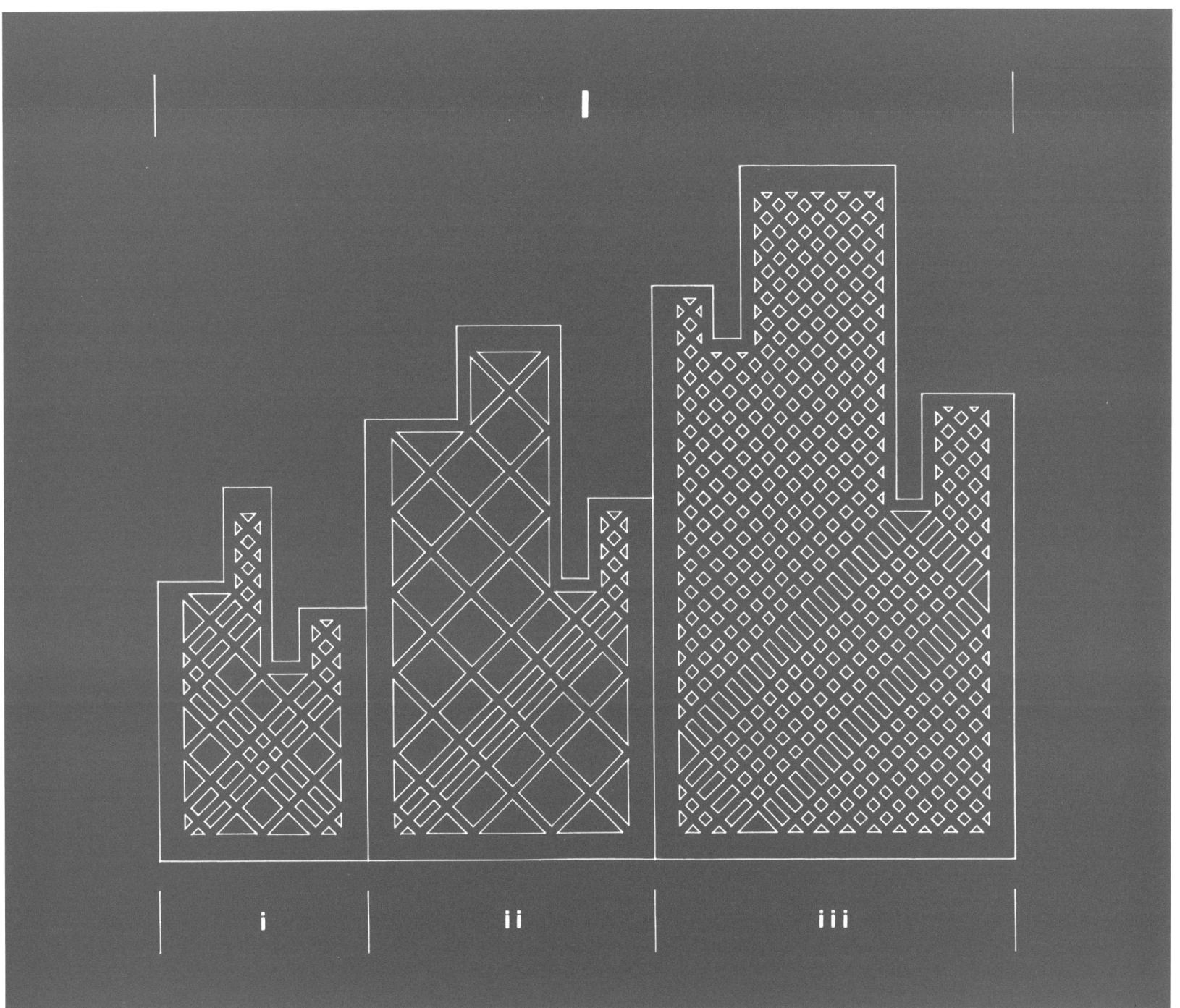

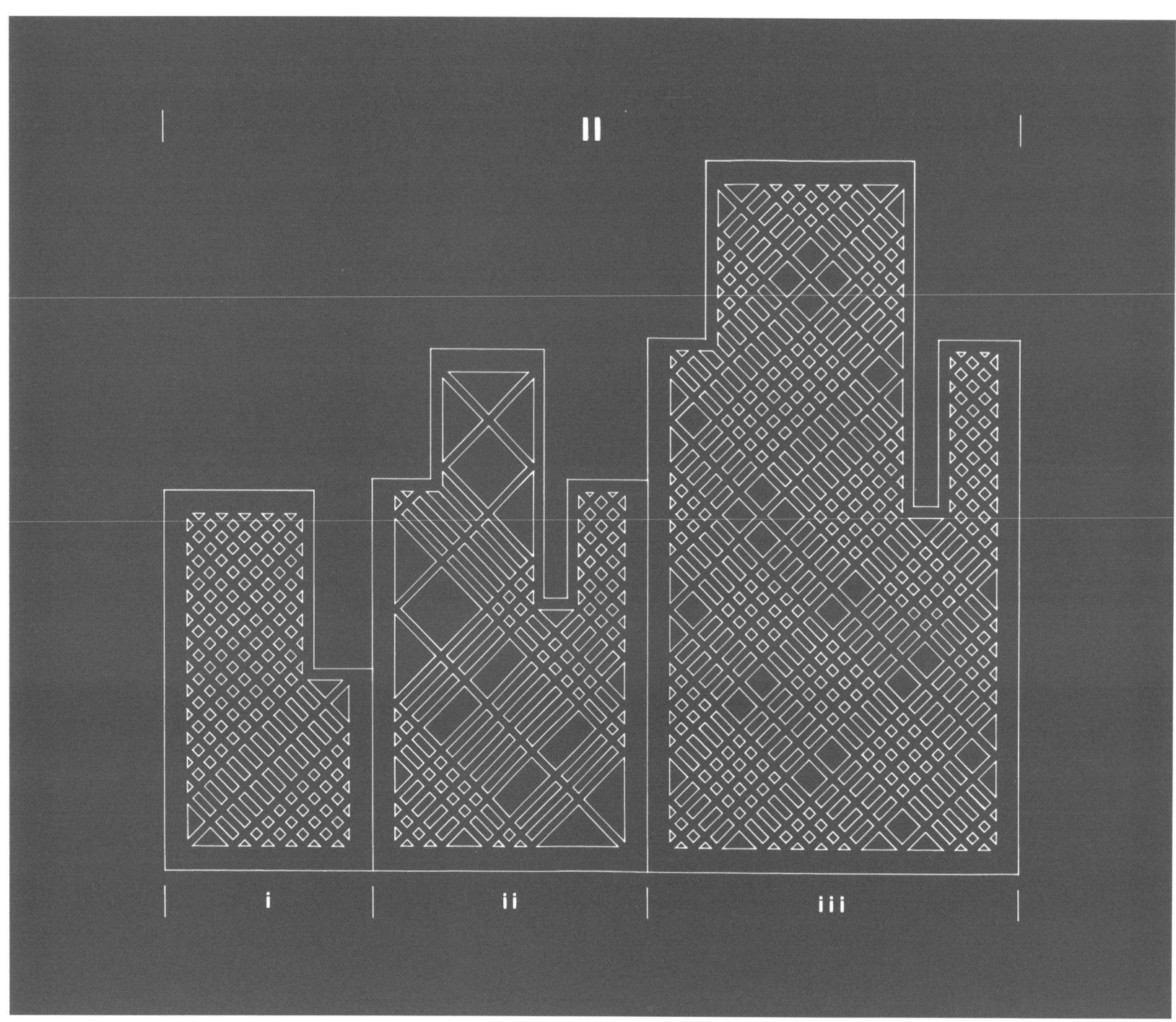

G8. CODE, INSCRIPTION

On the panels of these screens geometrical relations are inscribed and numerical relations are encoded.

As codes, the mathematical relations on these objects will not be directly readable. However, one could say that the aesthetics of the mathematical material have already been absorbed into the form of the screens, so that the visual and formal interests of the screens are maintained without reference to the generating mathematics.

Unlike the previous group of projects 'Traversal, deflection' in which the generative rules have no further significance once the objects have been designed, the generative material for the present group of projects possesses intrinsic worth, and yet objects must be able to justify themselves independent of their generative material.

The formal and conceptual structure of a creative work is not necessarily displayed, but without such formal and conceptual structure the work cannot have come into existence.

On the panels of each screen are inscribed geometrical figures in which mathematical relations are embodied.

The mathematics of the golden ratio, of the Pythagorean triangles and means: these are treasures to be mined.

Screen I consists of the geometrical construction of the golden ratio in which $a : b = b : a+b$ where a, b, $a+b$ are three consecutive terms in the Fibonacci sequence. The object also shows geometrically the algebraical properties of the golden ratio.

Screen II consists of the geometrical constructions of the Pythagorean triangles as well as geometric, arithmetic and harmonic means. The object also shows that the Pythagorean triangles geometrically constructed have integral sides.

Screen III gathers together the geometrical constructions of the golden ratio, the Pythagorean triangles and means. By combining geometrical constructions, algebraical properties can be extracted from these geometrical figures.

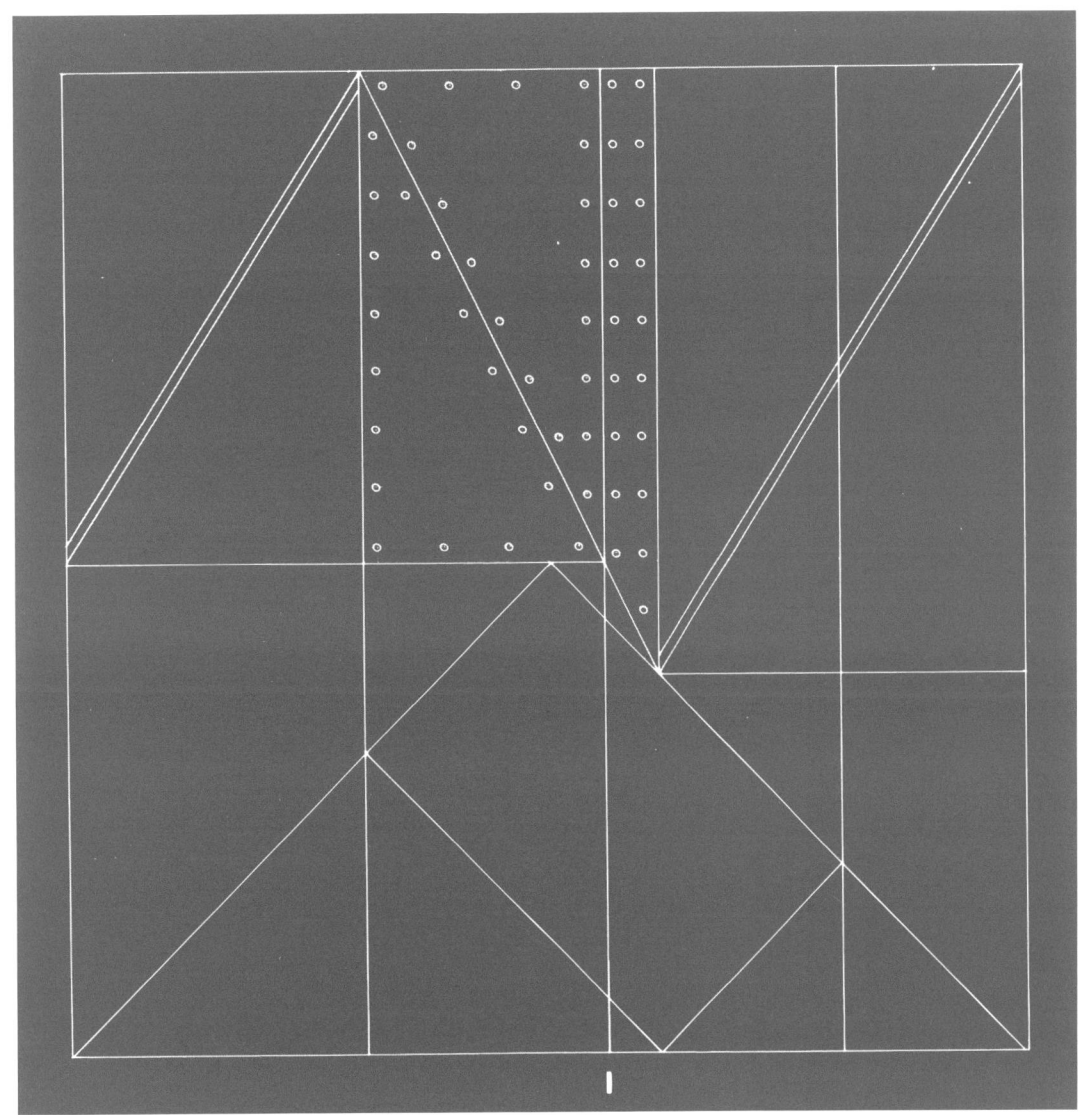

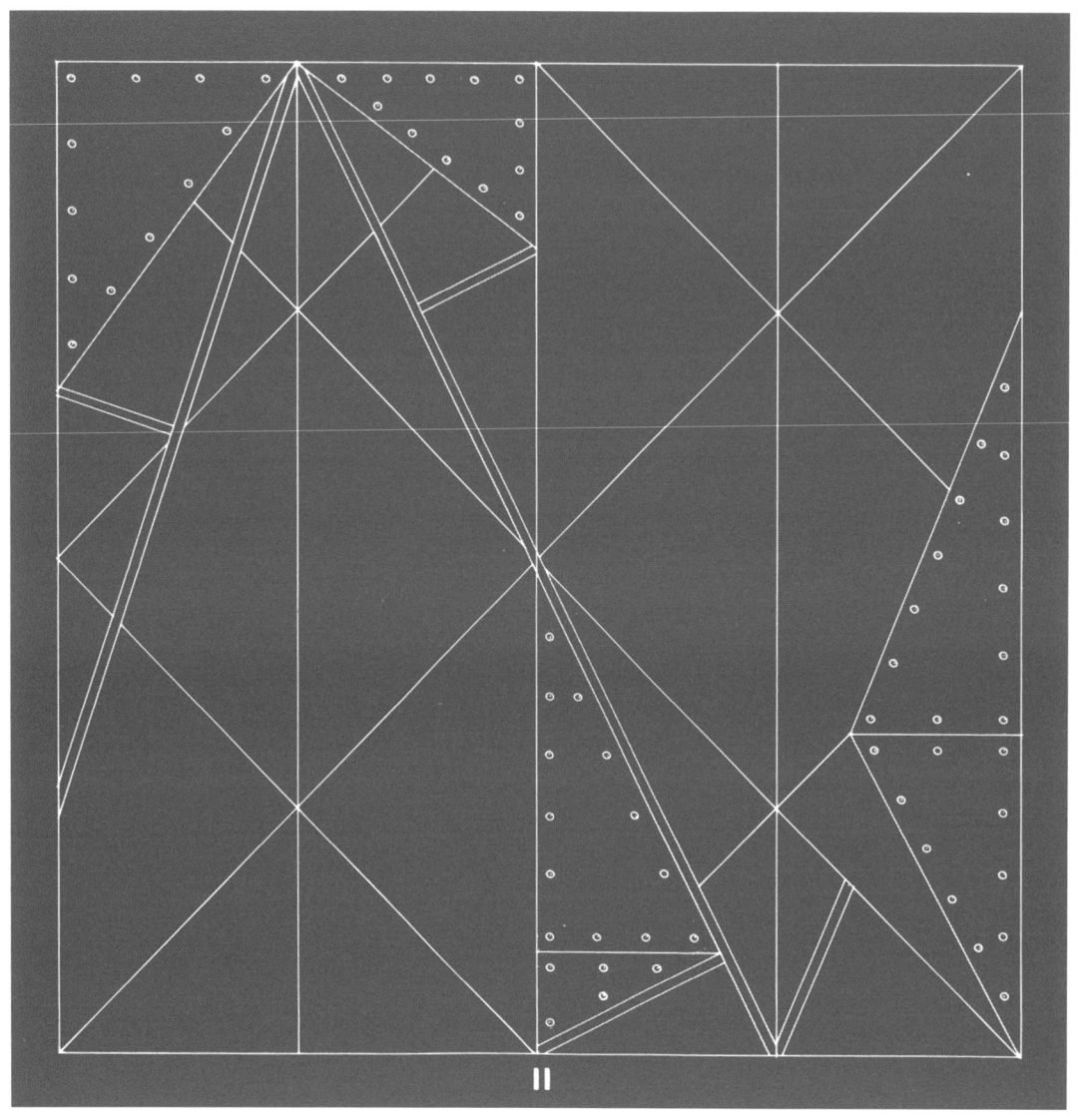

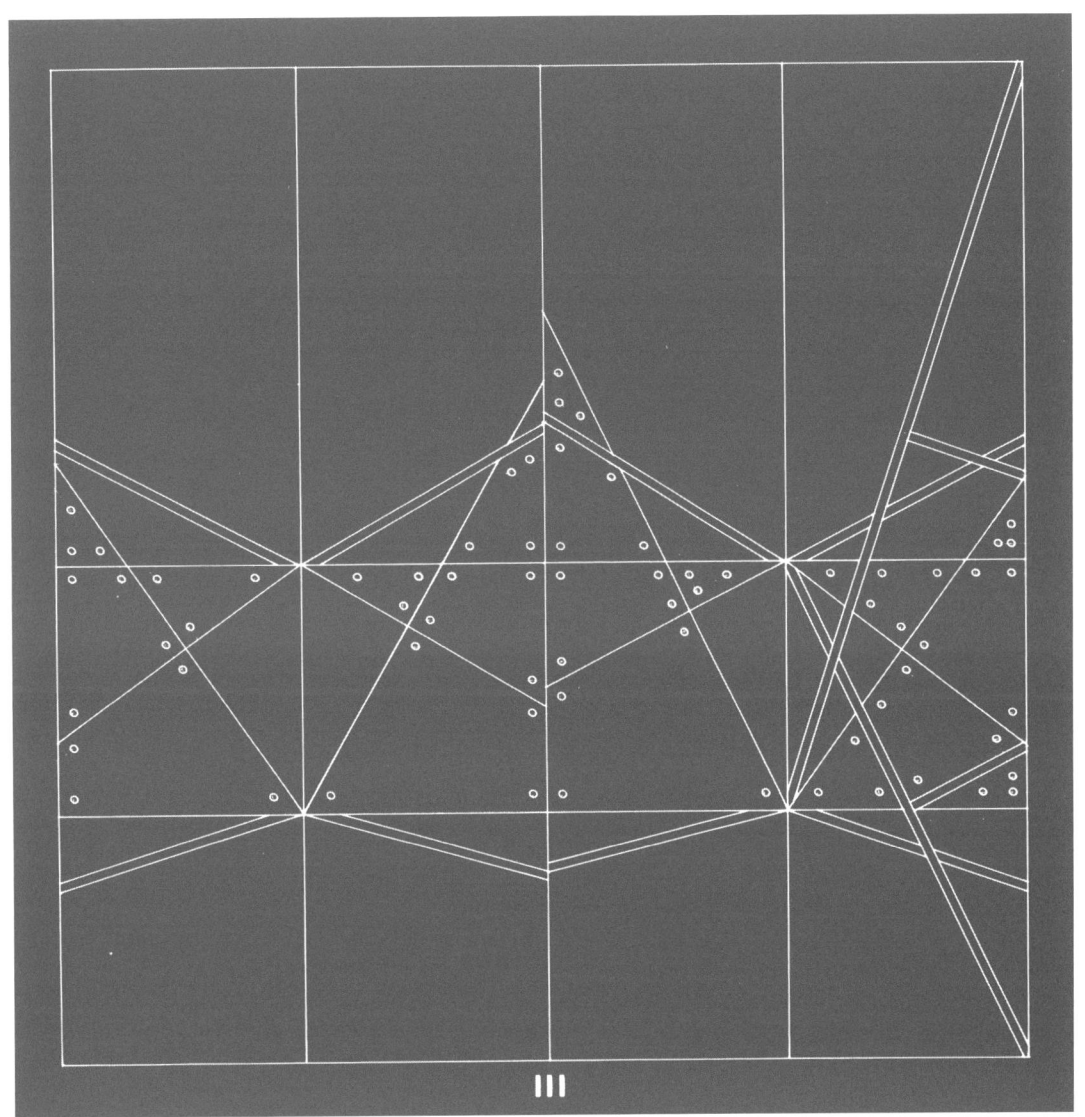

III

P18. Musico-mathematical screen

The composition of this screen relates the mathematics of the consonant intervals in music—6/5, 5/4, 4/3, 3/2, 8/5, 5/3—to the Pythagorean triangles—(3, 4, 5), (8, 15, 17), (5, 12, 13)—to the numerical series—(3, 5, 8, 13, 21, 34…), (2, 3, 4, 5, 7, 10 …), (4, 5, 6, 6 $\frac{1}{2}$, 8, 10)— and so on.

These relations are then inscribed in geometrical figures and encoded in symbols.

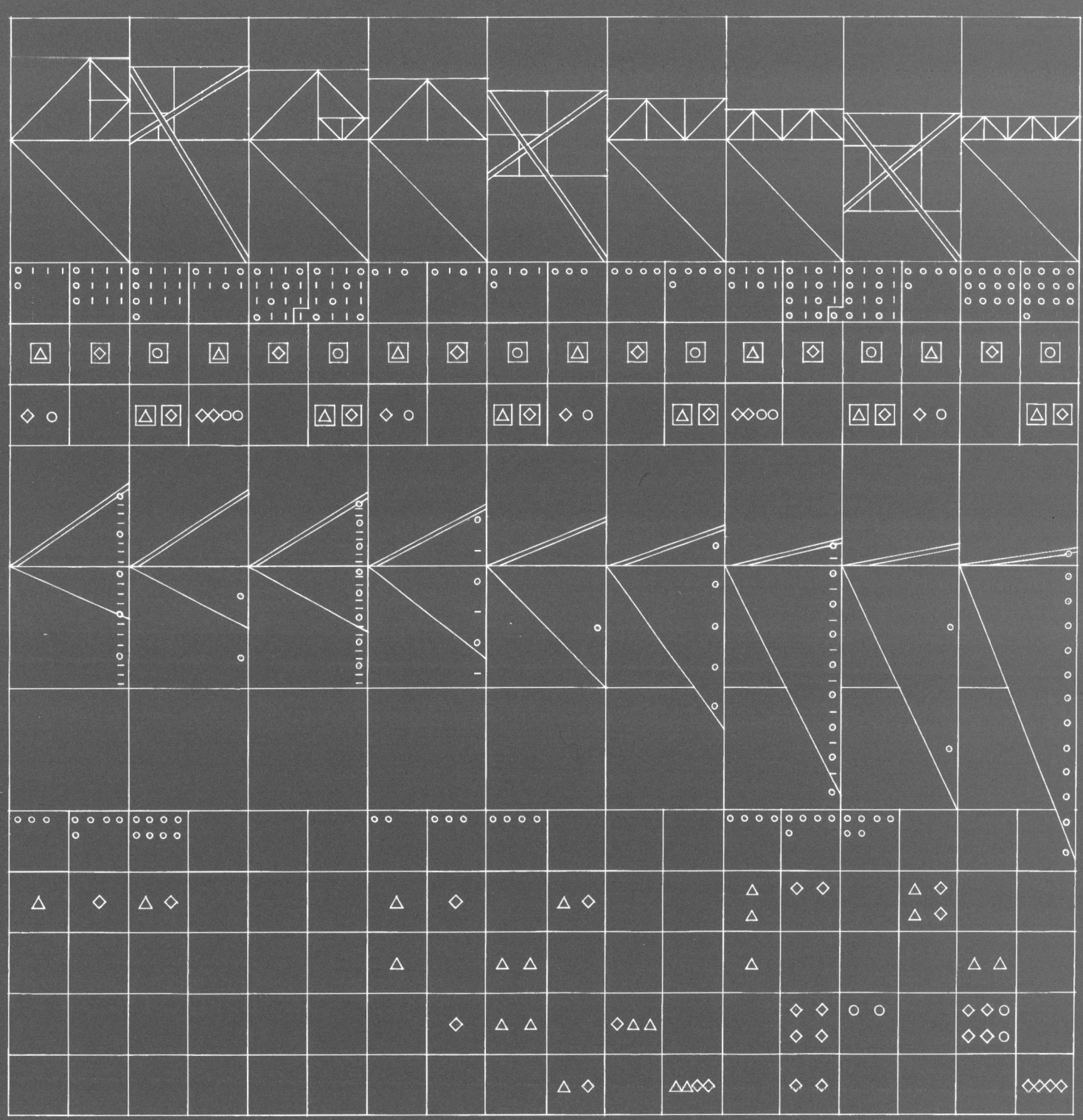

1
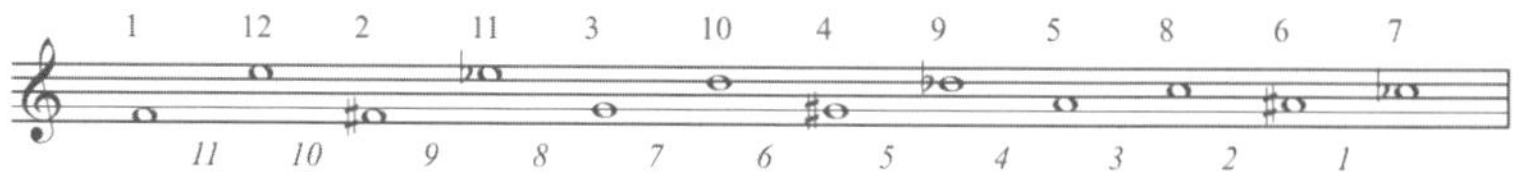
1 12 2 11 3 10 4 9 5 8 6 7
11 10 9 8 7 6 5 4 3 2 1

2
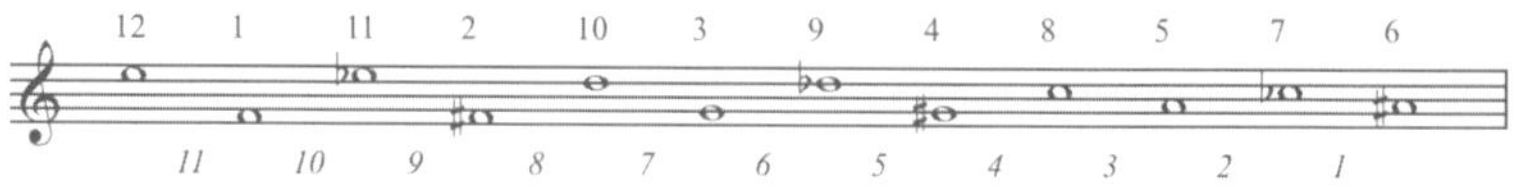
12 1 11 2 10 3 9 4 8 5 7 6
11 10 9 8 7 6 5 4 3 2 1

3
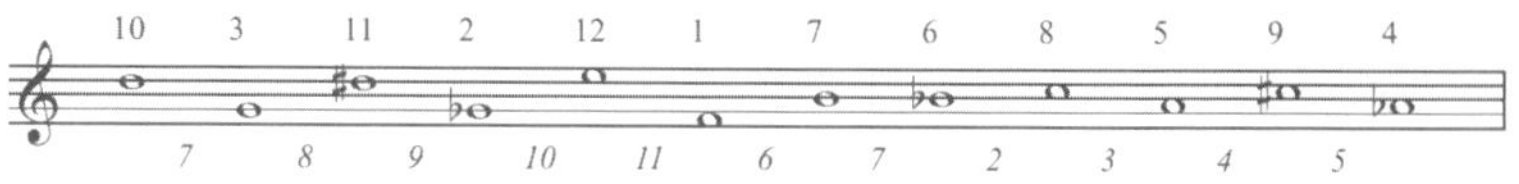
10 3 11 2 12 1 7 6 8 5 9 4
7 8 9 10 11 6 7 2 3 4 5

4
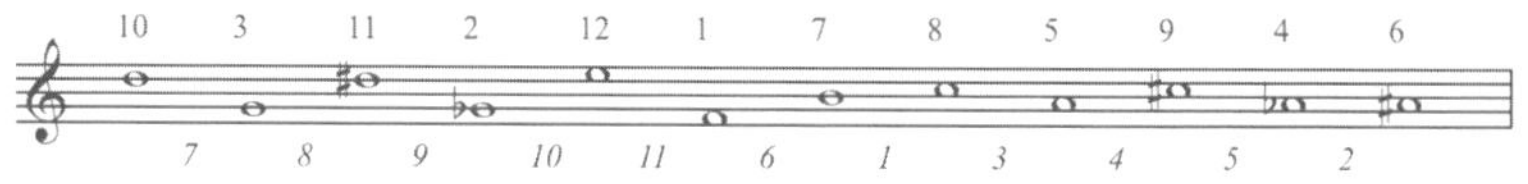
10 3 11 2 12 1 7 8 5 9 4 6
7 8 9 10 11 6 1 3 4 5 2

G9. ALL-INTERVAL ROWS

In twelve-note music the dissolution of the function of consonance and dissonance enables the composition to be organised by means of a note-row.

A note-row is a sequential arrangement of all the twelve notes within the octave without reference to tonality.

An all-interval note-row is a special case of the note-row. It is that arrangement in which not only each of the twelve notes within the octave is used exactly once in sequence but also each of the eleven intervals within the octave appears exactly once between adjacent notes.

Expressed in mathematics, an arithmetic progression can be arranged such that not only each of its n numbers is used exactly once in sequence but also, taking positive values, each of its n-1 differences appears exactly once between adjacent numbers.

All-interval rows of any length can be constructed as follows:

(a) The fundamental all-interval row of a certain length can be constructed by taking the smallest number followed by the largest number, then the next smallest number followed by the next largest number, and so on, until every number has been used up. Take the first six integers: 1 to 6 can be arranged to give the fundamental all-interval row (1 6 2 5 3 4).

(b) Separating any fundamental all-interval row of non-prime length into sections of equal length, reversing each section—denoted by r—will give another all-interval row. For the fundamental all-interval row (1 6 2 5 3 4), r(1 6 2)r(5 3 4) gives the all-interval row (2 6 1 4.3 5) and r(1 6)r(2 5)r(3 4) gives the all-interval row (6 1 5 2 4 3).

(c) Defining complementary numbers in an all-interval row as the pair of the smallest and the largest numbers, as the pair of the next smallest and the next largest numbers, and so on, substituting each number for its complement in an all-interval row—denoted by c—will give another all-interval row. For the all-interval row (2 6 1 4 3 5), c(2 6 1 4 3 5) gives the all-interval row (5 1 6 3 4 2).

(d) The difference between the first and the last numbers in any all-interval row is equal to the difference between certain two adjacent numbers in the row. Separating the row between these two adjacent numbers into two sections and reversing each section will give another all-interval row. For the all-interval row (2 6 1 4 5 3), r(2 6 1 4)r(5 3) gives the all-interval row (4 1 6 2 3 5).

(e) There are some all-interval rows in which separating the row into two sections and reversing one section will give another all-interval row. For the all-interval row (2 6 1 4 3 5), (2 6 1 4)r(3 5) gives the all-interval row(2 6 1 4 5 3) and r(2 6 1 4)(3 5) gives the all-interval row (4 1 6 2 3 5).

These are some all-interval rows and their transformational rules by which further all-interval rows can be generated.

Each of the all-interval rows on the left uses all the twelve notes of the chromatic scale.

P19. All-interval screens

On each panel of a screen an all-interval row is conceptually placed on one side and a transformed all-interval row is conceptually placed on the opposite side. Then connecting the same numbers on both sides following invented rules will give an intricate pattern.

The panels can be read as variants of one another.

Variants refer to the same rule being applied to different material so that one recognises similarity within the different as well as differences within the similar.

Screens I and II, with controlled differences, are recognisably related.

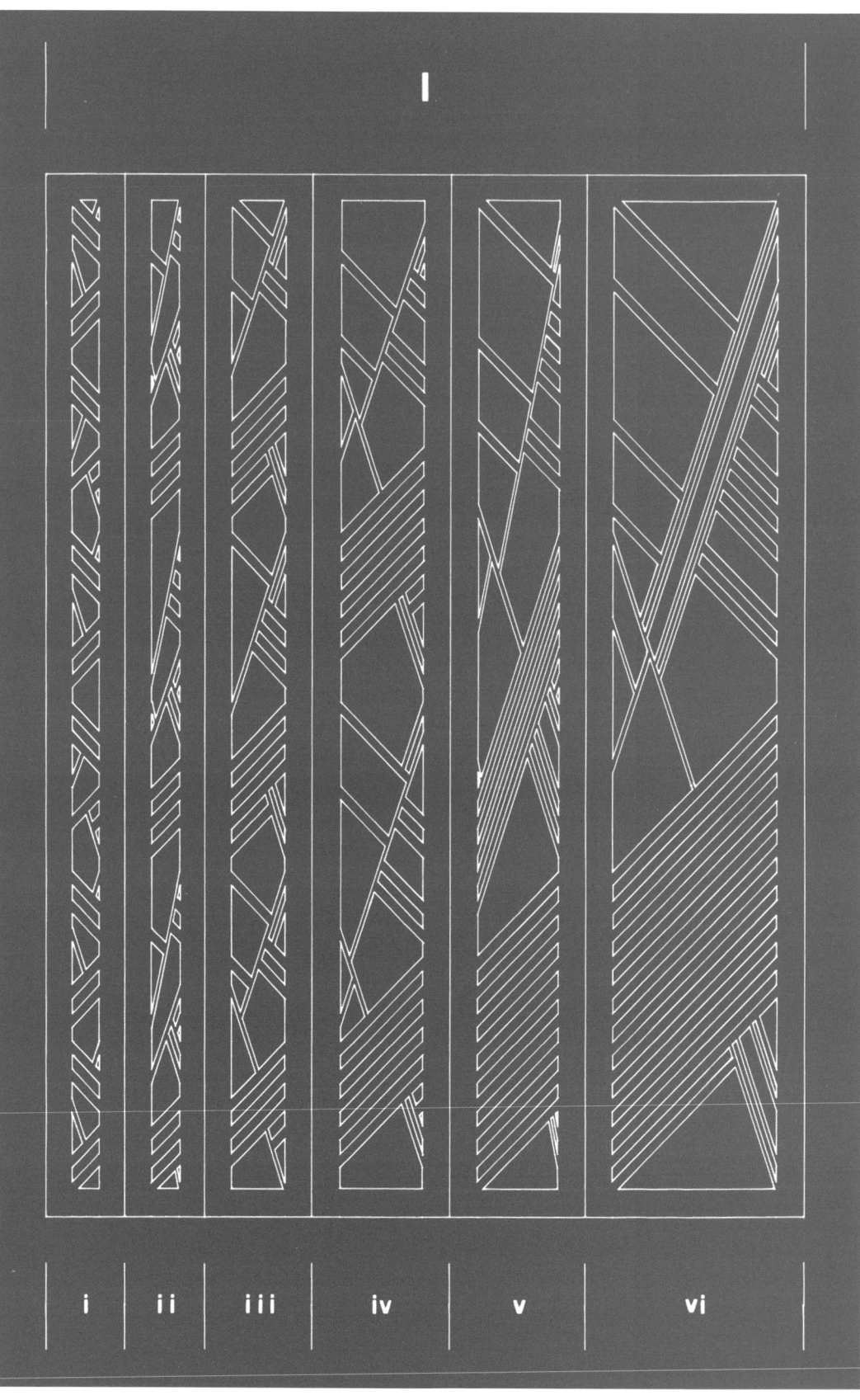

I

i   ii   iii   iv   v   vi

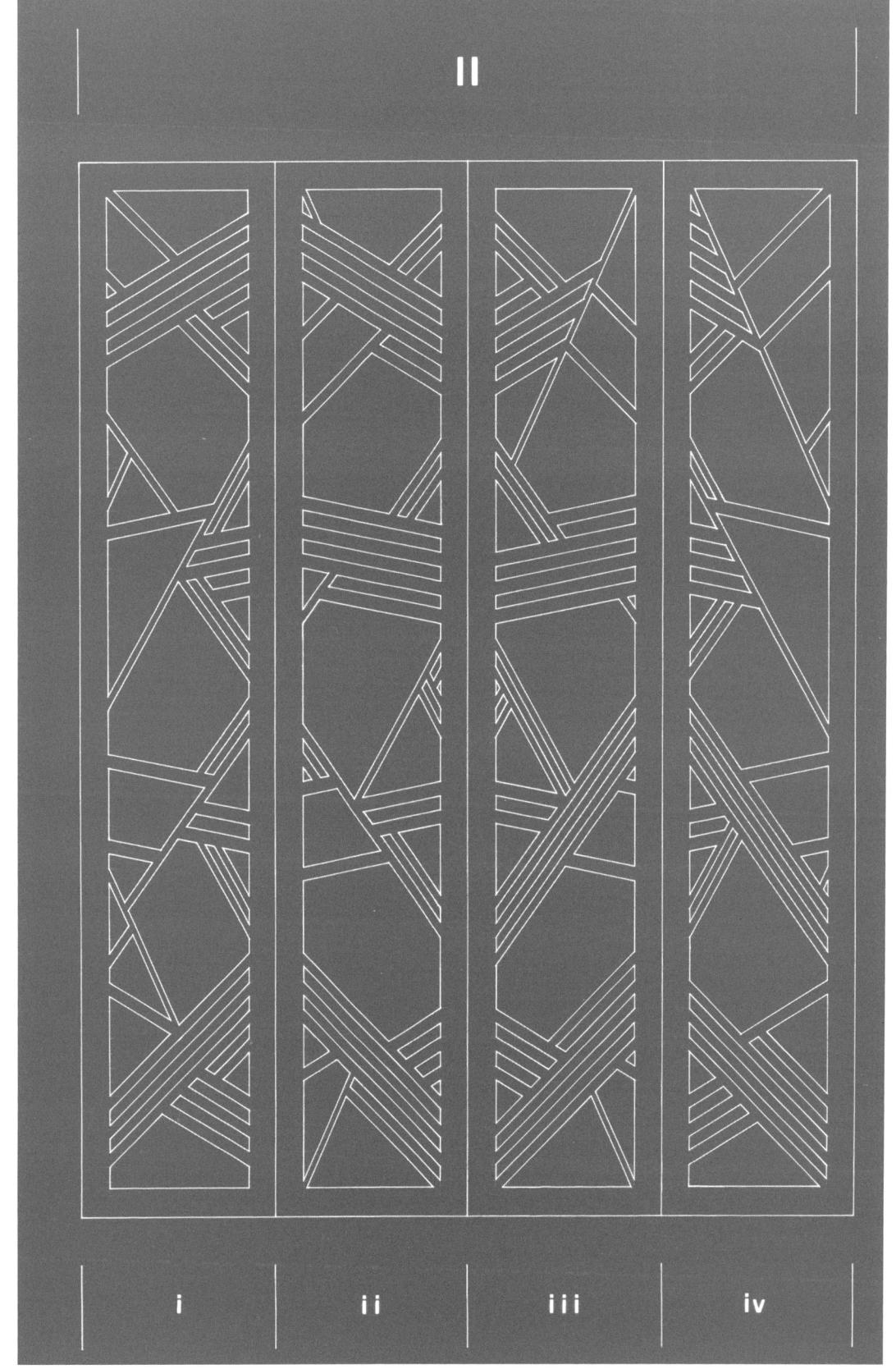

P20. Berg's Goldbach variations

While the panels in 'All-interval screens' can be read as variants of one another, the panels of this screen consist of a theme T and its variations V1 to V10.

While variants refer to the same rule being applied to different material so that one recognises similarity within the different as well as differences within the similar, variations refer to progressive departure from the original theme by means of introducing supplementary ideas for each variation.

This screen uses Goldbach's conjecture and adapts Berg's note-row for the composition of the theme and its variations.

Christian Goldbach conjectured that every even number greater than 2 is the sum of two primes.

Alban Berg, following Schoenberg's *Method of composition with twelve notes* and turning the screw, had works based on all-interval rows in which not only each of the twelve notes within the octave is used exactly once in sequence but also each of the eleven intervals within the octave appears exactly once between adjacent notes.

To construct the theme for the screen, let P be the sequence of odd primes 3, 5, 7, 11, 13, 17, 19... and let D be the sequence of even numbers 6, 8, 10, 12, 14, 16... each of which being the sum of two odd primes, then arranging the first terms of P such that each of the first terms of D appears exactly once between the adjacent terms of P as rearranged will, using the least number of terms, give the theme as (11, 3, 19, 5, 17, 7, 13) with the differences between adjacent terms as (8, 16, 14, 12, 10, 6):

```
11   3   19   5   17   7   13
   8   16   14   12   10   6
```

Each of the differences between two adjacent primes in the theme will be even which, being even, will, according to Goldbach, be the sum of two primes.

In general, the difference between two odd primes is the sum of two odd primes!

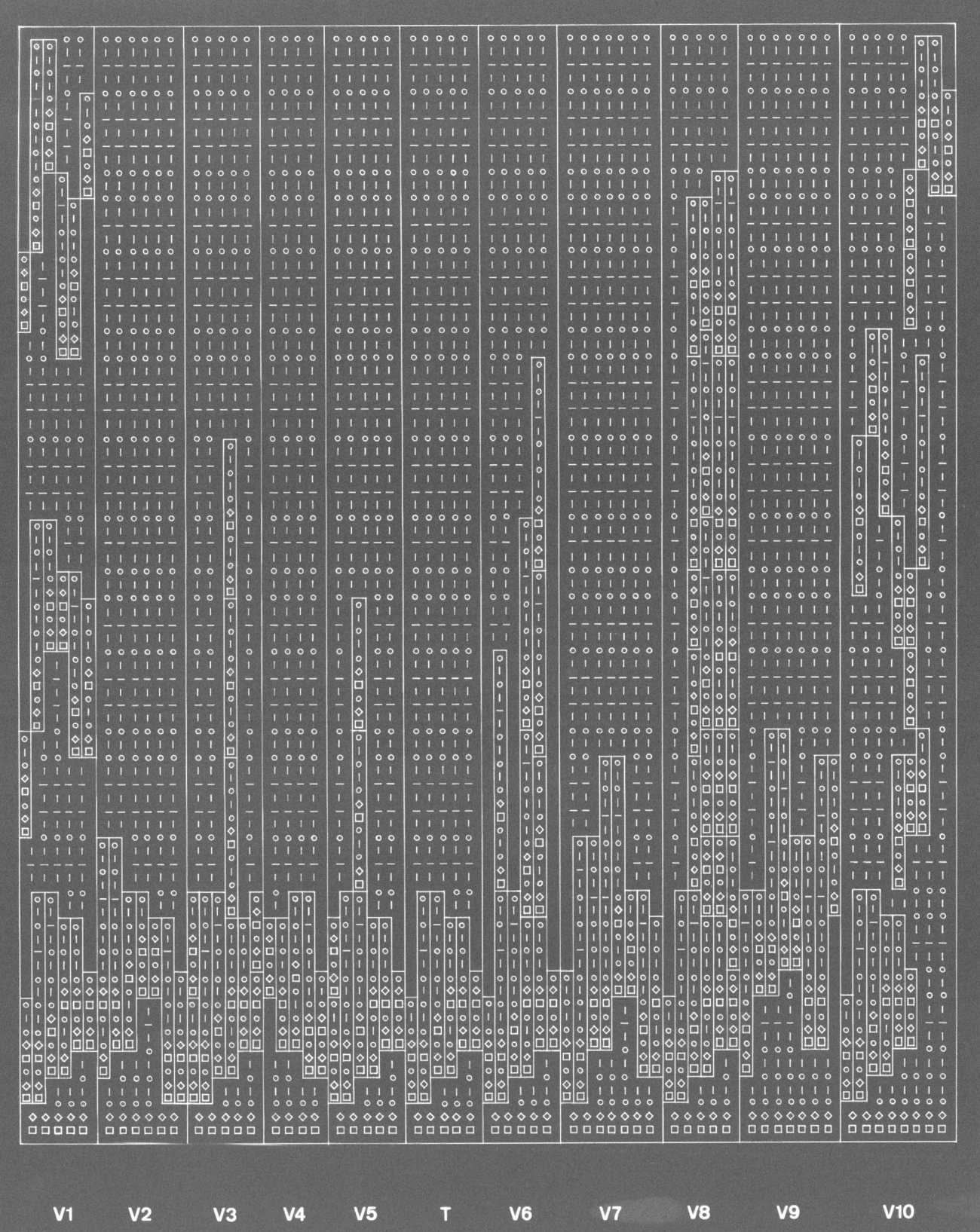

V1   V2   V3   V4   V5   T   V6   V7   V8   V9   V10

P21. Stars and constellations

Divine order, celestial harmony, cosmic rules: this is the Classical description of the world.

These two objects continue the Classical tradition of relating music, mathematics, and the heavenly bodies.

Each object uses an all-interval row to locate the light points.

The all-interval row used is simply the fundamental row of length 6 (1 6 2 5 3 4) which determines the relative distances between light points.

Light points are located on a disc suspended from the ceiling as if they were stars in the sky, and light points are joined up as if they were constellations.

Stars are represented by holes cut into the disc and are lit from behind the disc, and constellations are represented by slits cut into the disc.

Objects 1 and 2 use the same material, and also the same method of organisation but with one single difference. The two objects are therefore mutations of each other.

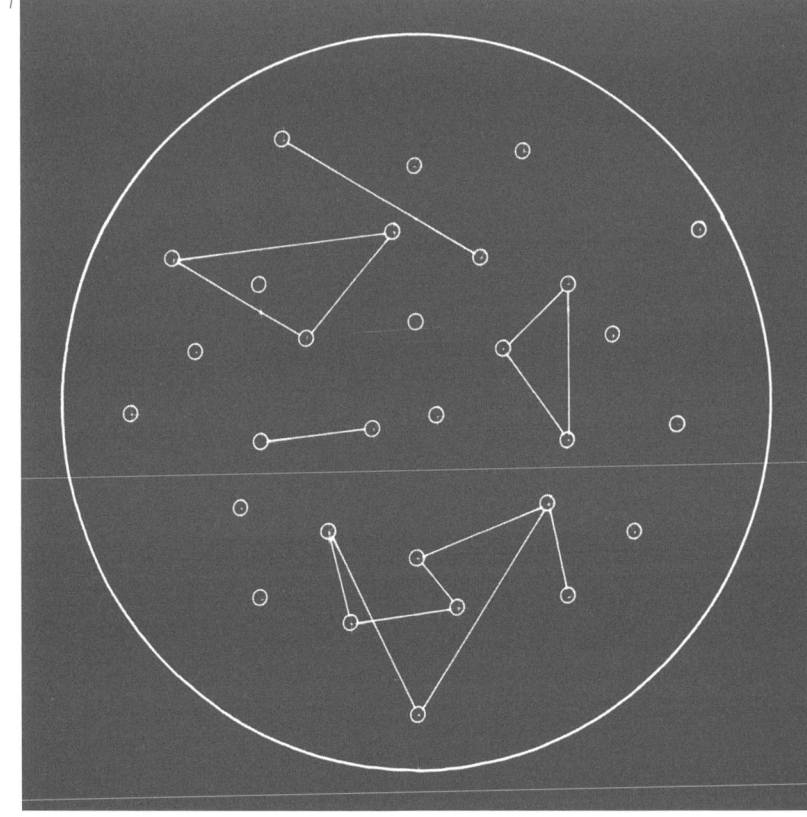

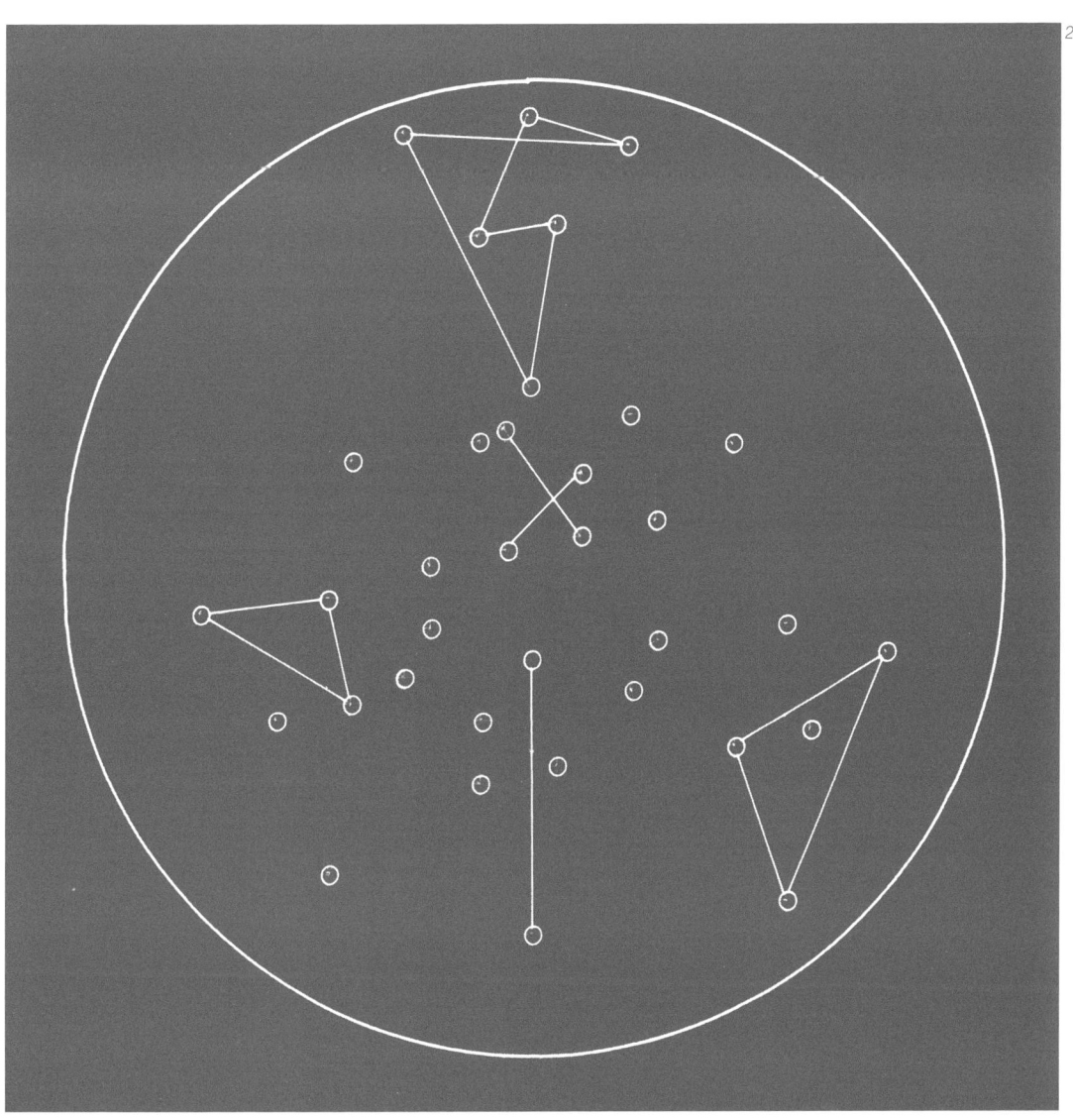

This clock uses twelve linear all-interval rows of lengths from 1 to 12.

These 12 rows—D=10, E=11, T=12—are (1), (1 2), (2 3 1), (2 3 1 4), (3 4 2 5 1), (3 4 2 5 1 6), (4 5 3 6 2 7 1), (4 5 3 6 2 7 1 8), (5 6 4 7 3 8 2 9 1), (5 6 4 7 3 8 2 9 1 D), (6 7 5 8 4 9 3 D 2 E 1), (6 7 5 8 4 9 3 D 2 E 1 T)

All these rows are such that the difference between adjacent numbers increases by one each time and that, considering alternate pairs of consecutive rows, for one pair, from the shorter to the longer row, add the largest number to the end of the shorter row, and for the other pair, from the shorter to the longer row, add one to all the numbers in the shorter row and then add the number 1 to the end of the shorter row.

These twelve linear all-interval rows, arranged in a certain order, are placed radially on the clock face.

The object also uses a circular all-interval row of length twelve which arranges the twelve linear all-interval rows on the clock face by the number of terms in a linear row being that number in the circular row.

This row – D=10, E=11, T=12 – is (D 3 E 2 T 1 7 8 5 9 4 6)

It adds irregularity by having a sequence of rising intervals (1 7 8) within a pattern of alternate rising and falling intervals.

Then the same numbers in each linear all-interval row are connected by bars to form an intriguing pattern on the clock face, spinning the web of time.

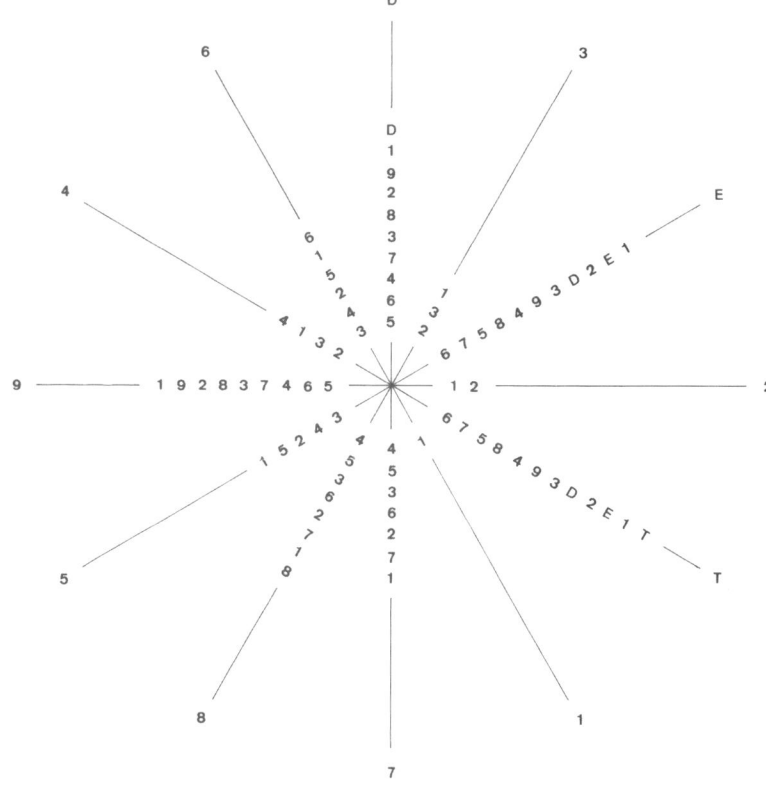

Diagram showing the twelve linear all-interval rows and the circular all-interval row

P22. All-interval hourglass

This hourglass uses all-interval rows on the three sides of its lower and upper triangular frames.

These rows are A = (4 3 1 6 2 5), B = (2 6 1 4 5 3), C = (5 3 2 6 1 4), iA = (3 4 6 1 5 2), iB = (5 1 6 3 2 4), iC = (2 4 5 1 6 3)

Each of these rows has a sequence of either rising or falling intervals within a pattern of alternate rising and falling intervals so that irregularity is added to the overall pattern.

Then the same numbers in each row on the same side of the lower and upper frames are connected by bars, making a stable structure for the object.

An hourglass is represented in Durer's *Melencolia I*. As an implement for measuring time, the hourglass is complementary to the tools of geometry, geometry being the technique for measuring space. Panofsky thought of the melancholic artist as he who is gifted in geometry, he who applies in his work the rules of mathematics. The melancholic artist is therefore not the subjective artist who invents but the contemplative artist who searches. He is therefore not the subjective master who wills the work into existence but the slave who is subject to the material, to the rules of mathematics, to the self-imposed rules for the work, and so also to the time taken up by, and given over to, the work, and to the interval in which the work will not progress. For the melancholic artist who is entangled in a creative impasse of a work in progress, neither will the work give in, nor can the worker give up. Meanwhile the hourglass continues to beat time.

Diagrams showing the six all-interval rows with the same numbers connected

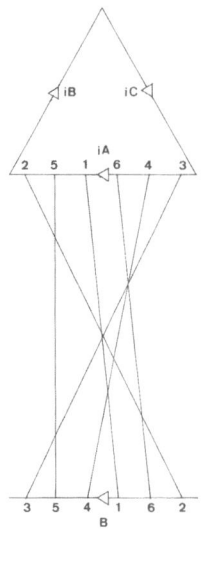

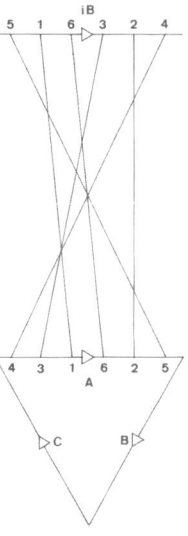

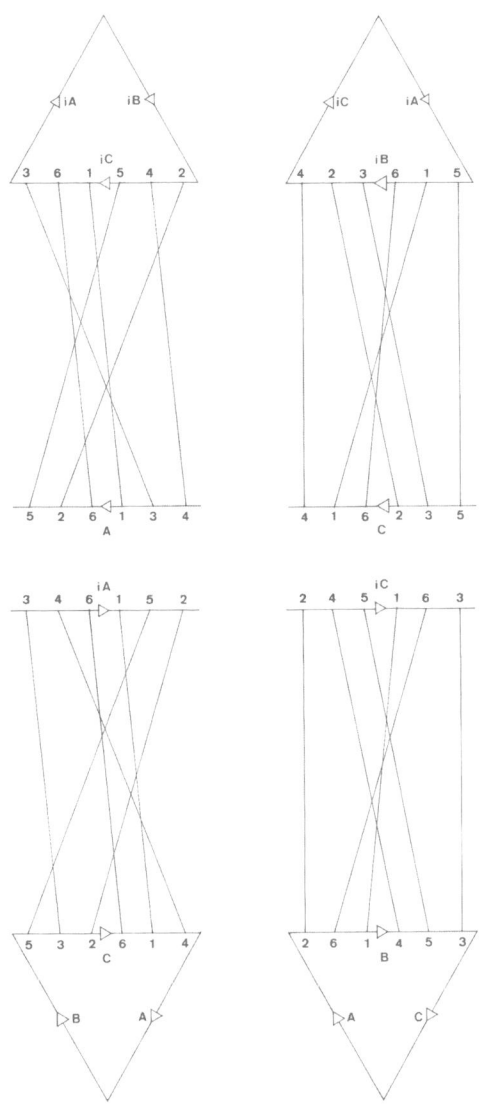

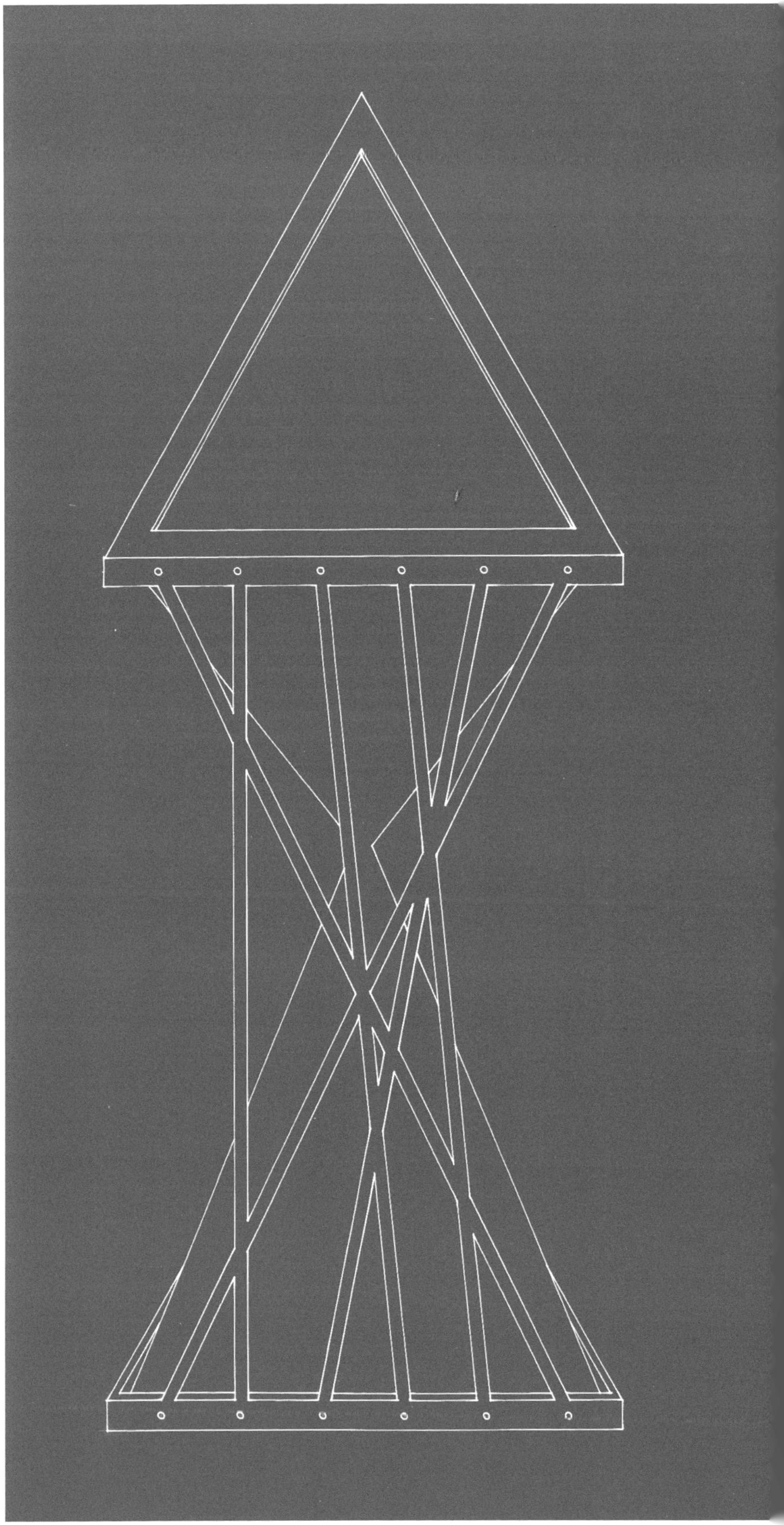

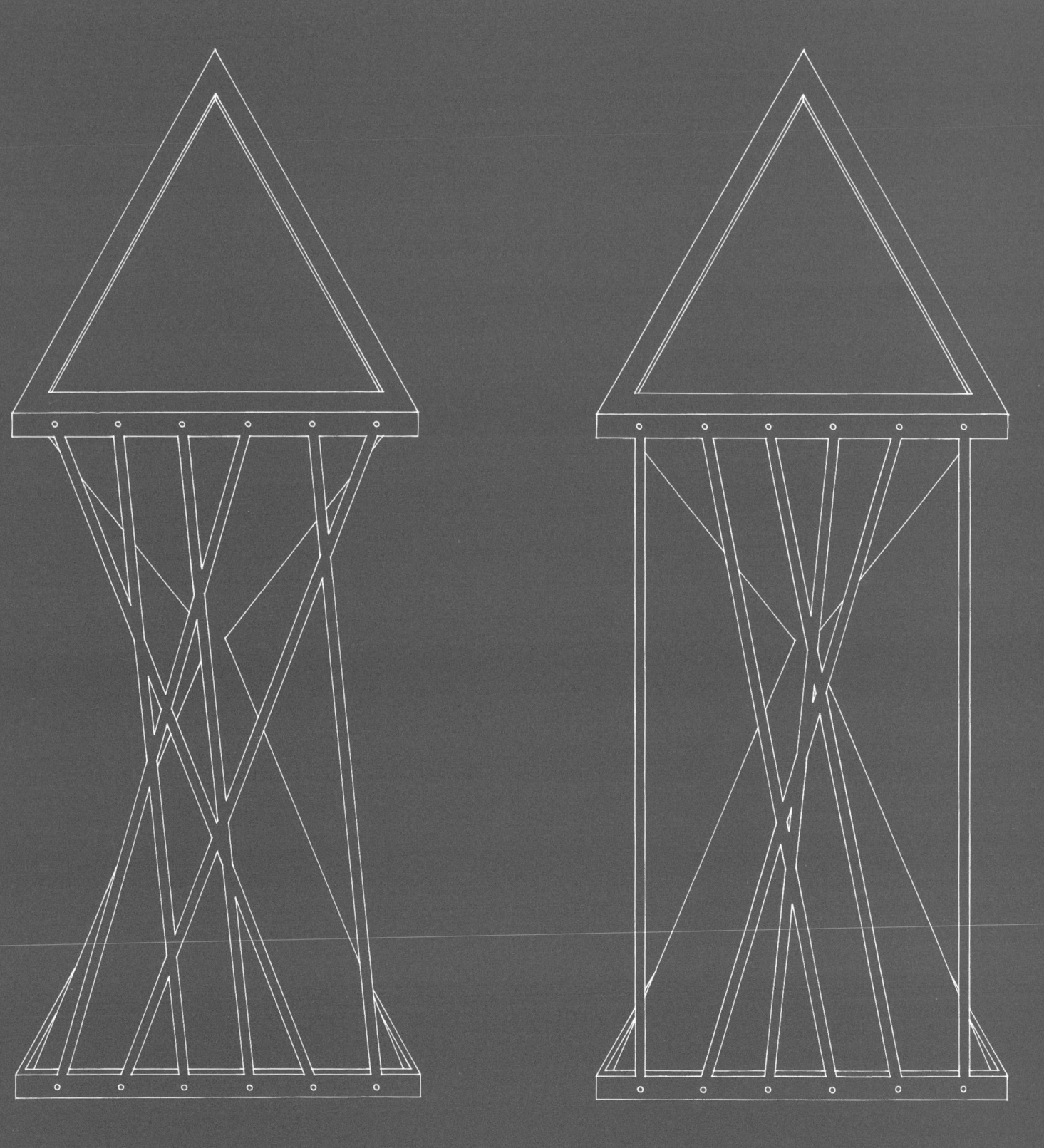

G10. FORM AND TEXT

In Classical thought, it is the designed object that is the final reality, the signified, while postmodern thought enables the deconstruction of such reality, the marginalisation of the signified.

In this spirit, Eisenman moves away from traditional architecture where the signified, the built object, has always been distinct from its signifier, the model and the drawings, to the architecture of House X, House El Even Odd, and so on, in which the built object, the model and the drawings are all entangled in a chain of signification.

The following project can be described as narrative furniture in which the visual (perceptual), formal (geometrical) and textual (conceptual) aspects of the objects are structurally interlocked.

Hors d'oeuvre

Two objects

Each object is composed of three related parts—the mirror piece (M) and the gold frame (G) superposed on the silver frame (S).

Each object appears to be square—until further attention discloses its geometrical irregularities.

In one object there are angular deviations and in the other proportional deviations.

Mirror 1 with angular deviations:
On one side of the object the gold and silver frames appear to be parallel, but on each of the other three sides the frames appear to be tilted relative to each other in such a way that the frames as a whole cannot merely be tilted relative to each other, and the following possibilities remain:

If one frame is square (in the sense that all angles are right angles) then the other frame cannot also be square.

If one frame is not square (in the sense that at least one angle is a non-right angle) then the other frame may or may not be square.

(The mirror piece, being the portion which shows itself and which is bounded by the silver frame, will have the same geometrical properties as the silver frame.)

Mirror 2 with proportional deviations:
On one side of the object the gold frame appears to be placed centrally on the silver frame, but on each of the other three sides the frames appear to be shifted relative to each other in such a way that the frames as a whole cannot merely be shifted relative to each other, and the following possibilities remain:

If one frame is square (in the sense that all sides are the same length) then the other frame cannot also be square.

If one frame is not square (in the sense that at least one side is a different length) then the other frame may or may not be square.

(The mirror piece, being the portion which shows itself and which is bounded by the silver frame, will have the same geometrical properties as the silver frame.)

Each object teases first our eyes and then our minds.

The privilege of the frame:
Our attention has been drawn from the centre, the mirror piece, the intrinsic, the essential, the ergon, to the edges, the frames, the extrinsic, the ornamental, the parergon.

The mirror piece is framed by the silver frame. If the silver frame is the parergon to the mirror piece, is the superposed gold frame then the frame of the frame, the parergon to the parergon?

And yet, in the absence of the gold frame, geometrical irregularities do not appear—the mirror piece itself, each frame by itself, and even the mirror piece framed by the silver frame, appear to be square.

So the gold frame (Kant's bad parergon), the frame of the frame, the parergon to the parergon, is that which enables geometrical irregularities to appear.

Not therefore merely the frame of the frame, the parergon to the parergon, the gold frame fills the lack in the mirror piece, it fills the lack in the silver framed mirror.

Without parerga, Derrida writes, "the lack within the work would appear or, what amounts to the same, would not appear.... The lack of the ergon is the lack of a parergon".

This is the privilege of the gold frame.

Impasse/Bypass:

The gold frame enables geometrical irregularities to appear. But where are the geometrical irregularities? In the mirror piece? In the silver frame? In the gold frame itself?

If the mirror piece is to be measured against the gold frame, then the gold frame must be a neutral transcendental measure. But is the gold frame a transcendental measure, a neutral square? Or is the gold frame itself geometrically irregular?

From the possibility of the gold frame being non-square another frame is required to measure the gold frame. From the possibility of this other frame being non-square....

An infinite regression.

Lacking the certitude of a neutral transcendental measure, what is the measure and what is being measured are thoroughly confused, and nothing is measured.

Have we reached an impasse?

Do we not want to resolve the possible states of affair given by deduction into the actual state of affair? Do we not desire the truth?

For the sake of truth, let us create a bypass.

The impasse of deduction in its inability to assert the actual state of affair is grounded in logic, It is, therefore, a necessary limit. But the inadequacy of perception from which deduction is called upon is only a contingent limit.

It is, therefore, in principle possible to overcome the contingent inadequacy of perception by inferring the existence, in principle possible, of a superior being who is endowed with perfect spatial intuition, so that he has a perfect grasp of the geometrical properties of things.

In this way the superior being is able to grasp, naturally and spontaneously, the actual geometries of the object and the process of deduction is bypassed.

We have the truth, but at what cost?

The superior being, with his perfect spatial intuition, with his perfect grasp of the geometrical properties of things, will have neutralized, in his perfection, the pleasures of the ambiguous and the depths of the enigmatic.

Not only this object, this type of objects, but also perspective and illusionistic art of all kinds, in their geometrical transparency for the superior being, will have bypassed the attention of the superior being.

The project has reached its goal of truth, which is also the end of its significance.

The truth lacks significance, and the project can no longer sustain itself.

Let us turn round and retrace our path.

Let us recreate the impasse of perceptual inadequacy, identifying it not as an unsurpassable obstacle but as a protective wall, as that optimal metaphorical 'frame' along which the project is sustained, the pleasures of the ambiguous and the depths of the enigmatic are preserved.

Located at the limit of deduction, structured upon the inadequacy of perception, the 'frame' sustains the project, preserves the ambiguous and the enigmatic by occluding the ultimate geometrical truth of the object which is 'outside' the 'frame'.

What is the status of this text?

The text is not 'outside' the 'frame'. It does not disclose the object's geometrical truth, but explains why the object's geometrical truth must not be disclosed.

A text which reads an object, even being the authorial/authorised/authentic reading, is to be displaced to the margin, the 'frame', the parergon in relation to the ergon, the work, the object itself.

And yet, this text also structures the object—it gives those formal conditions which the object must fulfil, those geometrical properties which the object must embody. The text must, therefore, be interior to, anterior to, the object.

Not, therefore, an *hors d'oeuvre* in the sense of being outside the work, the text is an *hors d'oeuvre* in the sense of that dish which is served before the meal.

Hence temporal priority for the text.

There are in fact many possible objects which fulfil the formal conditions and have the geometrical properties given in the text.

The text prefigures a set of perceptual/conceptual objects, but it is itself not yet a formal/geometrical figure in which the perceptual/conceptual properties can reside.

Therefore, an object from the set of possible objects is a necessary exemplification of the text—but any particular object from this set of possible objects is merely a contingent example, one which can be substituted by any other object from the set of possible objects.

So that the particular object which is made, the contingent example, is being displaced to the margin, the 'frame', the parergon.

And yet, this displacement is not a detachment—even though one example can be substituted by another, exemplification cannot be done without.

Therefore the text and the object are necessarily interlocked contingently.

The text and the object mutually fill each other's lack: without the possibility of the text, of linguistic formulation and expression, the object remains unstructurable and unintelligible, and without the actualisation of the object, of formal/geometrical expression, the ideas in the text remain unproven.

In fact, the visual (perceptual), formal (geometrical) and textual (conceptual) aspects of the object are structurally interlocked.

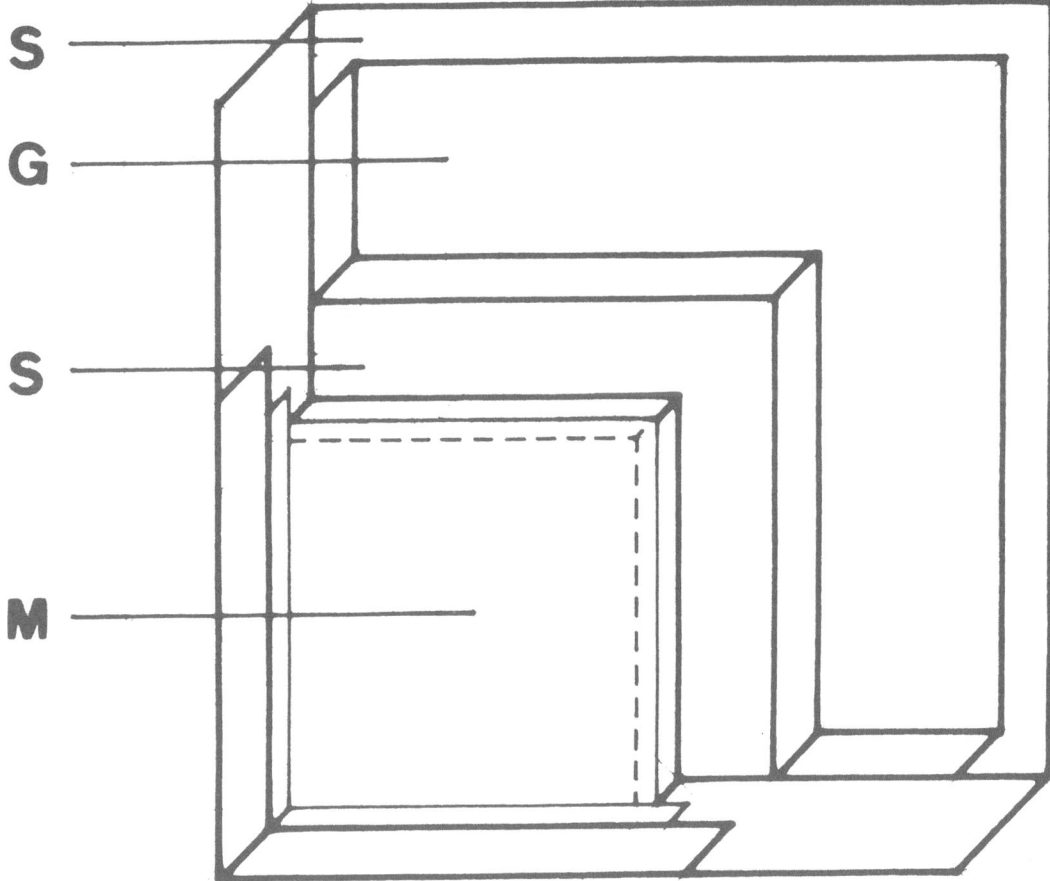

Sectional drawing to show the mirror piece M, the gold frame G and the silver frame S

S

G

S

M

1

CABINETS

G11. TABULATION OF ELEMENTS

In these designs, elements are collected and classified, then selected and combined to form objects.

In these cases, all the compositional elements are already present and ordered, where the totality of possibilities is displayed, before selection and combination take place.

To collect in order to accumulate things is uninteresting, but to collect in order to classify, to arrange and to categorise things in the collection is already an act of organisation that points towards the creative act of selecting, combining, and transforming the elements.

P25. Non-square towers

Each object is a stack of boxes.

The boxes are slightly different from the square and from one another.

A box is non-square in the sense that at least one angle is a non-right angle.

The boxes are not the same in the sense that every box has a different configuration of non-right angles.

A box in isolation, its angular deviations being so slight that they cannot be perceived, will appear square.

But by stacking the boxes, and examining those sides of a box which are discontinuous with the corresponding sides of the boxes immediately below and above, angular deviations will be shown up.

How many non-square forms and groups of non-square forms are there?

A form is grouped together with its rotations, inversion and complement, and for the 81 forms 13 groups are required.

The 81 forms and the 13 groups are tabulated from which individual forms are selected using invented rules to give shape to a tower of boxes.

Tower 1 with thirteen boxes is a freestanding object, tower 2 with nine boxes is to be placed against a wall, and tower 3 with four boxes is to be placed against a corner.

*Tabulation of the 81 forms in
13 groups A to M*

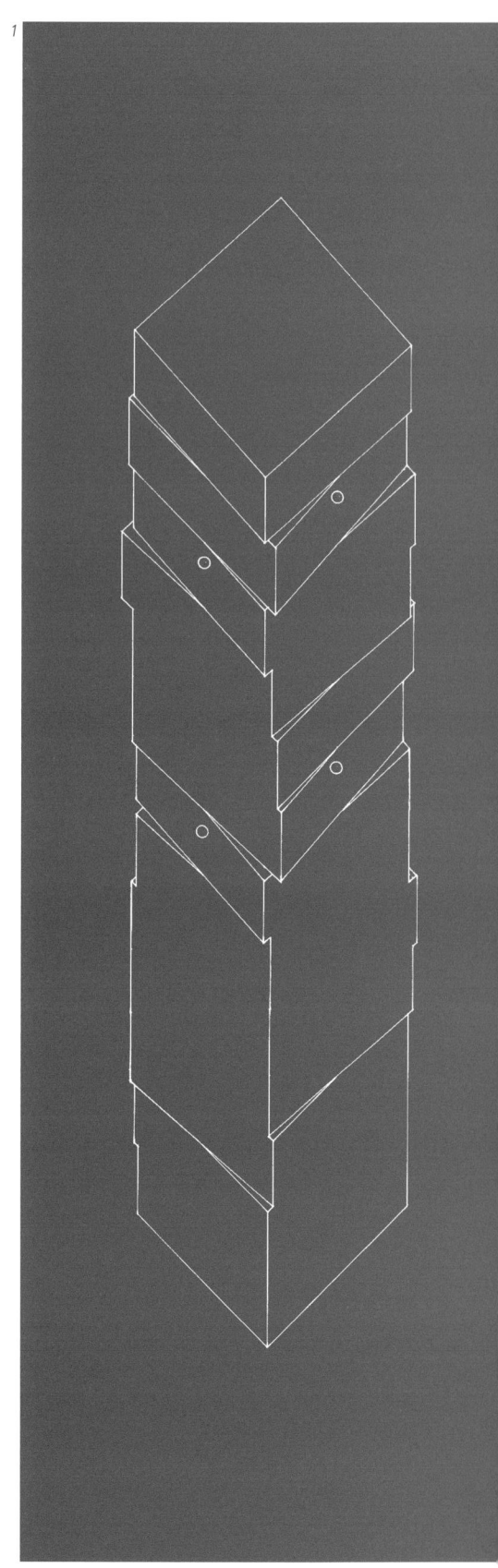

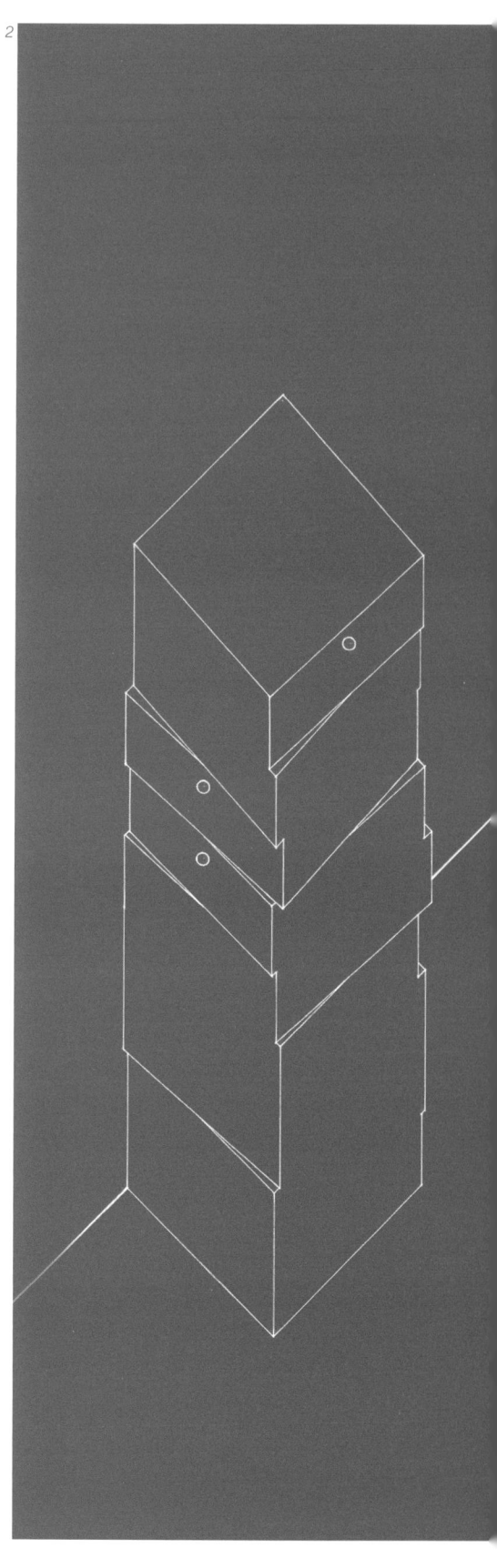

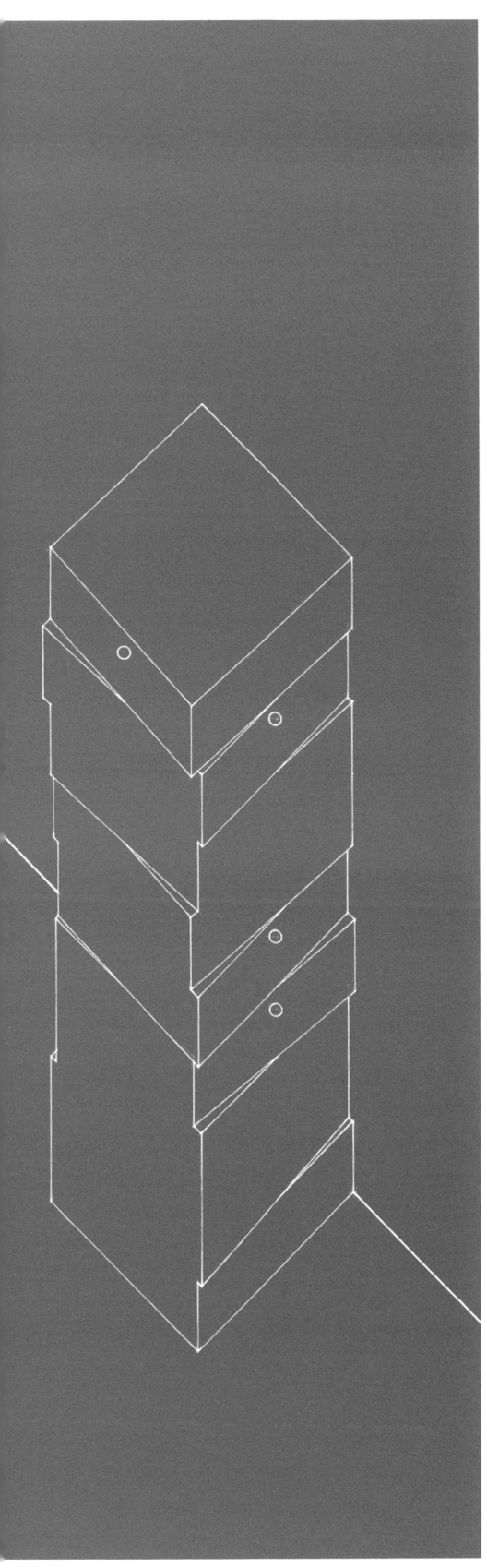

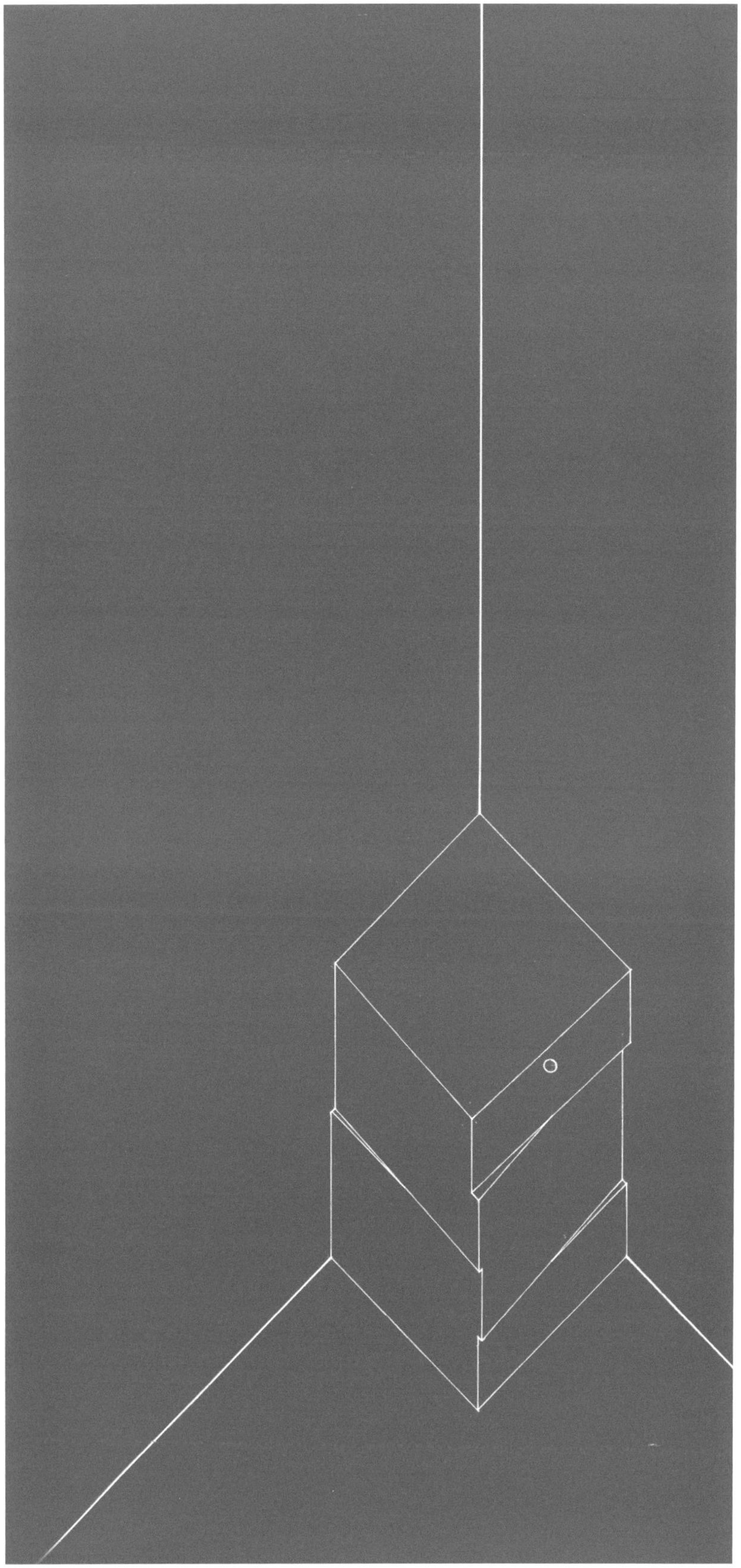

2

'Derangement' is a term in mathematics which refers in this project to the distribution of forms without two forms being adjacent more than once.

Forms are separated out into classes, types, sets and groups, and for each form its 'density' is calculated and a 'mass number' is given.

The kinds of forms and their 'mass numbers' are tabulated from which individual forms are picked out following invented rules to structure the object.

Object W requires three forms, one from each of the three classes I to III, to fill a 2x2 square. Object X requires six forms, one from each of the six types i to vi, to fill a 3x3 square. Object Y requires twelve forms, one from each of the twelve sets a to m, to fill a 5x5 square. And object Z requires twenty-one forms, one from each of the twenty-one groups A to V, to fill an 8x8 square.

Derangement? There is indeed order in madness!

Tabulation of all the forms in three classes I to III, six types i to vi, twelve sets a to m, twenty-one groups A to V

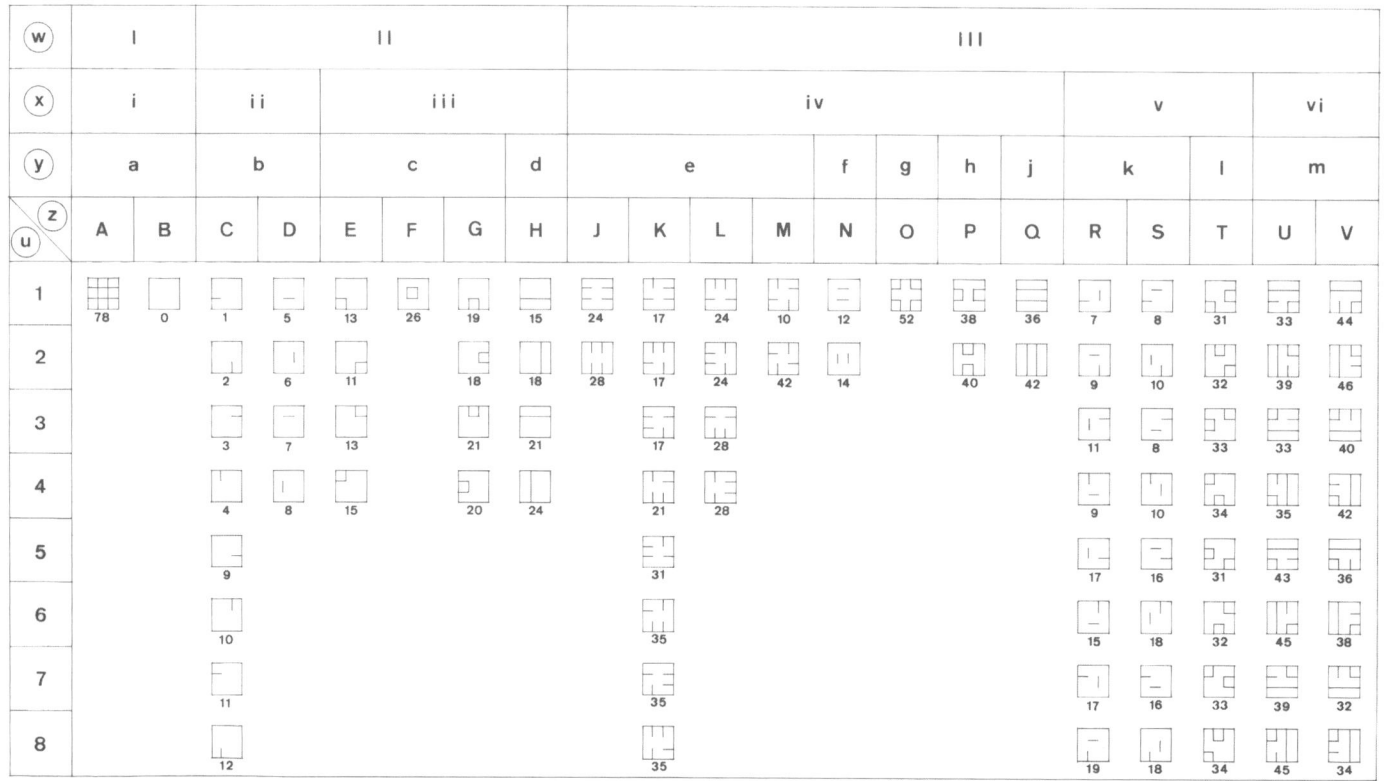

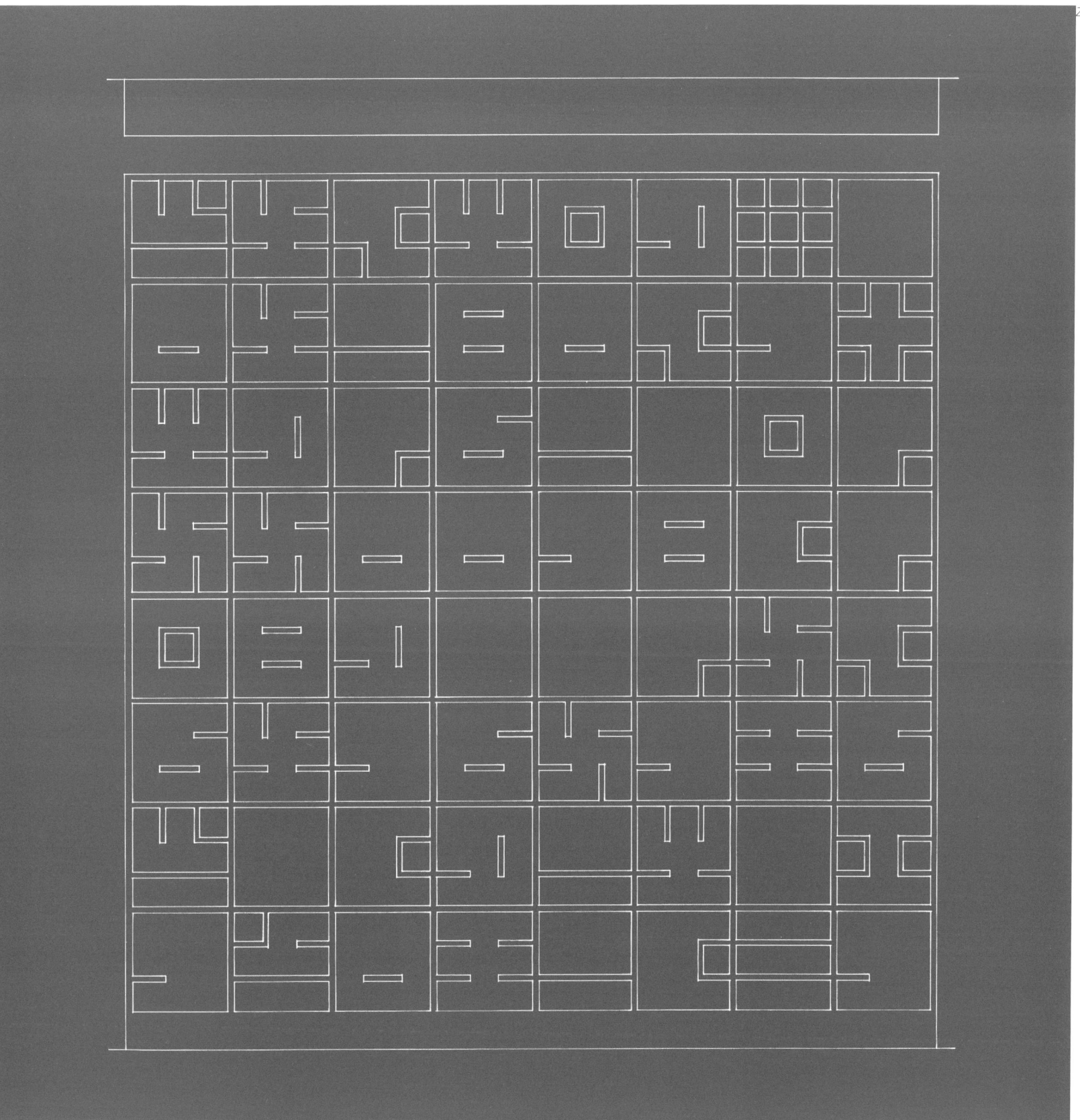

4	7	5	9	1
6	3	3	2	8
8	4	1	1	7
10	2	5	6	2
1	11	4	9	12

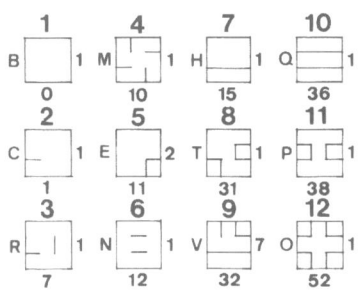

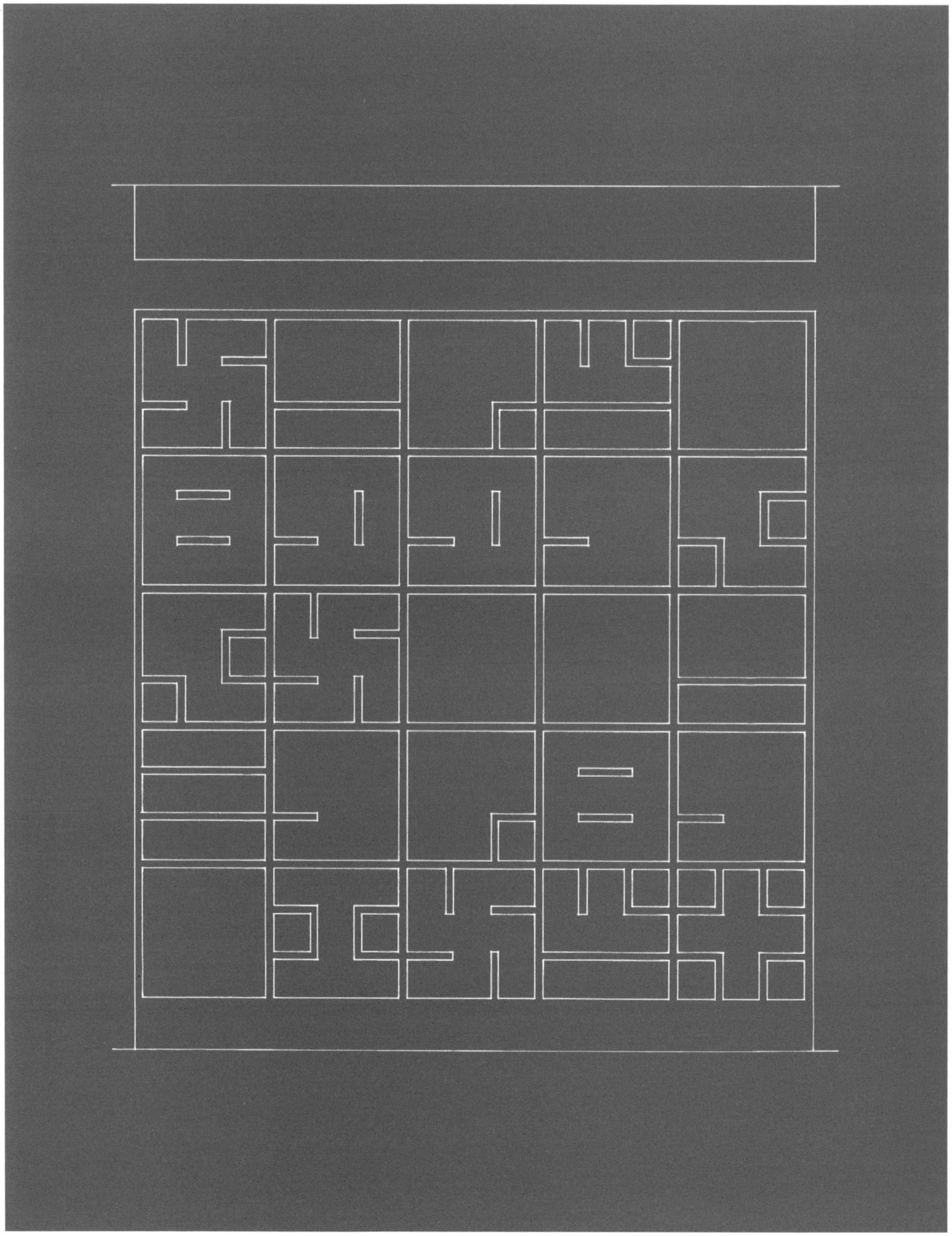

3	3	2
4	1	1
2	5	6

X

1
B ___ 1
0

4
M ___ 1
10

2
C ___ 1
1

5
E ___ 2
11

3
R ___ 1
7

6
V ___ 7
32

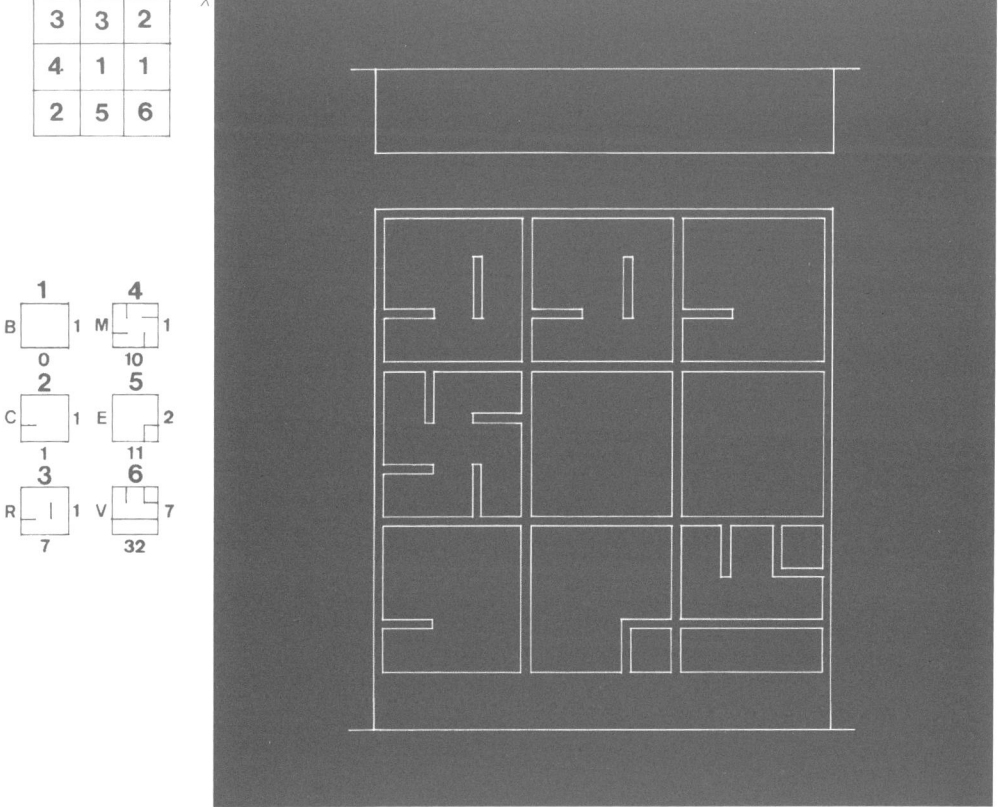

3	2
1	1

r
z ☐ u
s
1
B ☐ 1
0
2
C ☐ 1
1
3
R ☐ 1
7

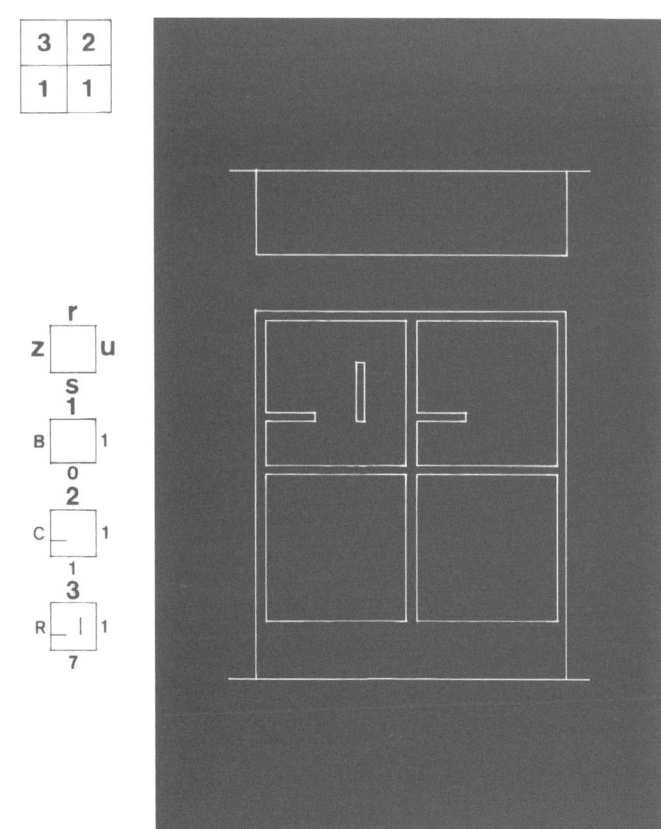

G12. RULES OF COMBINATION

In these as in many other designs, self-imposed rules are invented in order to open up possibilities, in order to set in motion the design process.

It is the *Oulipo—Ouvroir de Littérature Potentielle*—participants who have contributed greatly to the inventive use of self-imposed rules and formal constraints in writing.

In Georges Perec's two lipogrammatical novels, *La Disparition* is written entirely without the letter e while its complement *Les Revenentes* uses the letter e as the only vowel in the book.

Even though the imposition of formal constraints define the scope of a delimited world, the process of world-making will still require choices and decisions.

A fully automated process of world-making is illustrated by John Conway's game called Life. In Life, simple rules are applied recursively to an initial configuration, which develops and either stabilises into a final configuration or settles into an oscillating state.

'(Ana(gram)matical) shelves' follow Life in the recursive application of simple rules to an inititial configuration. This is, therefore, a process of generating objects without subjective intervention once the initial conditions have been established.

In Life as in '(Ana(gram)matical) shelves', a simple object is transformed in time into different but related objects in a closed system within which everything has relational necessity.

This temporal unfolding of generations of objects, from simpler to more complex objects, from more regular to less regular objects, suggests the priority of teleology over ontology.

Encountering an object, instead of the question "What is it?" one asks "What can be done to it?" "What destiny does it fulfil?" In teleology, the end is always already immanent in the origin.

In 'Arrangement/rearrangement', complexity of form is achieved by means of combination of elements. And unlike '(Ana(gram)matical) shelves' where the objects are given diachronically by transformation, the objects in 'Arrangement/rearrangement' are given synchronically by combination.

P27. Arrangement/rearrangement

Typically, shelving and storage systems are made up of a module or a group of modules repeated vertically and horizontally any number of times. This means that neither the vertical nor the horizontal extent of the object can be determined by the module or the group of modules.

The following method of organising material will internally determine both the vertical and the horizontal extents of the object:

Let the object have a repeating group of z modules on one column, a repeating group of y modules on a second column, a repeating group of x modules on a third column… and let the vertical number of modules, that is the height of the object, be the least common multiple of z,y,x…, then a different conjunction of modules will appear on each row, and all the possible conjunctions of modules will appear on all the rows.

Objects A,B,C,D arrange/rearrange different groups of material.

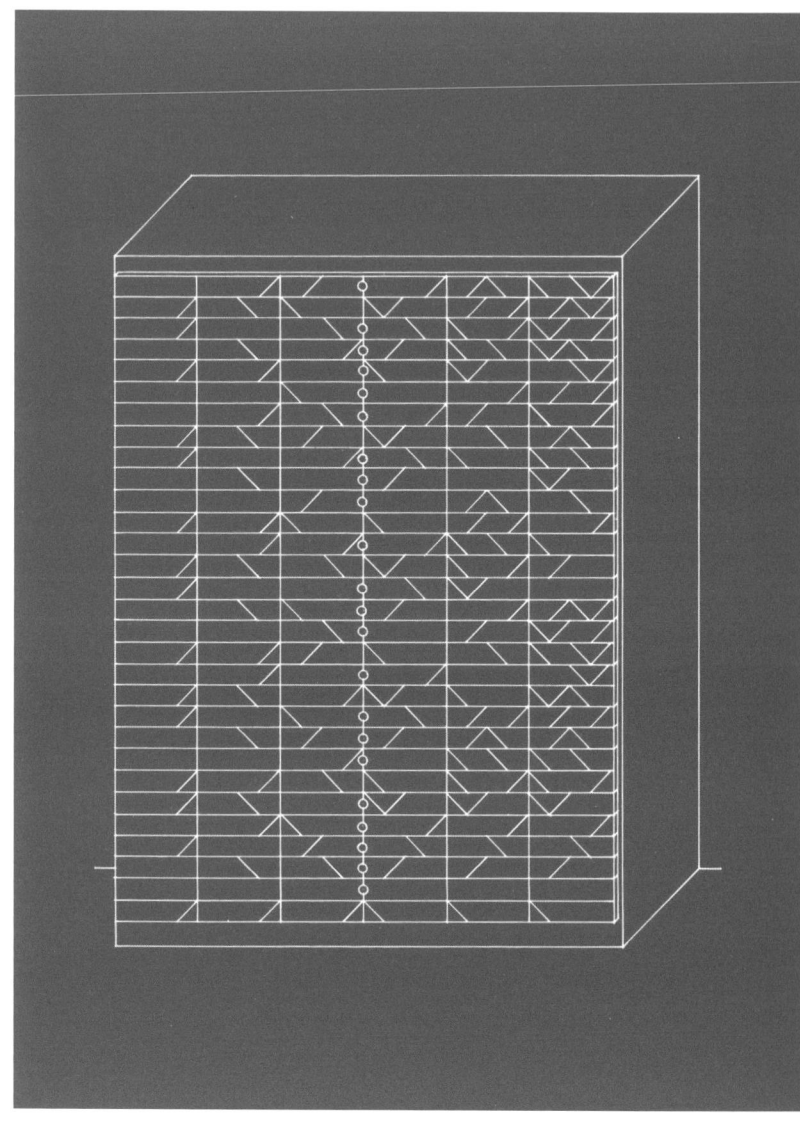

Object A – Juxtapositions of different combinations of elements a, b, c, d to give 30 modules vertically

d c b a   a b c d

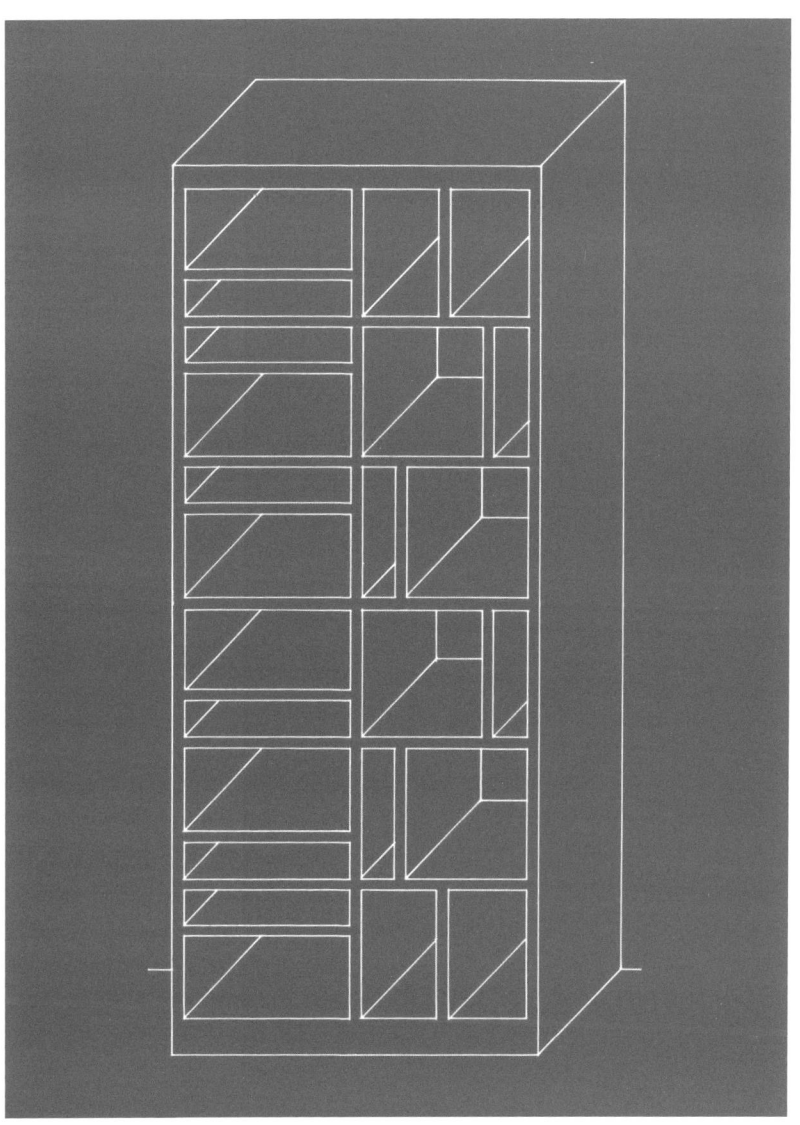

Object B – 2 modules a, b
juxtaposed with 3 modules c, d, e
to give 6 modules vertically

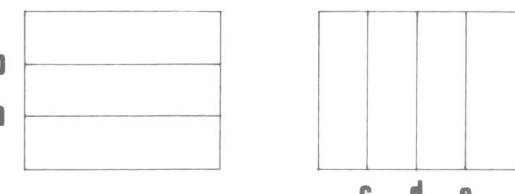

Object C – 2 modules a, b
juxtaposed with 3 modules c,
d, e to give 6 modules vertically

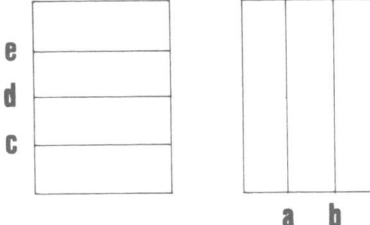

e

d

c

a   b

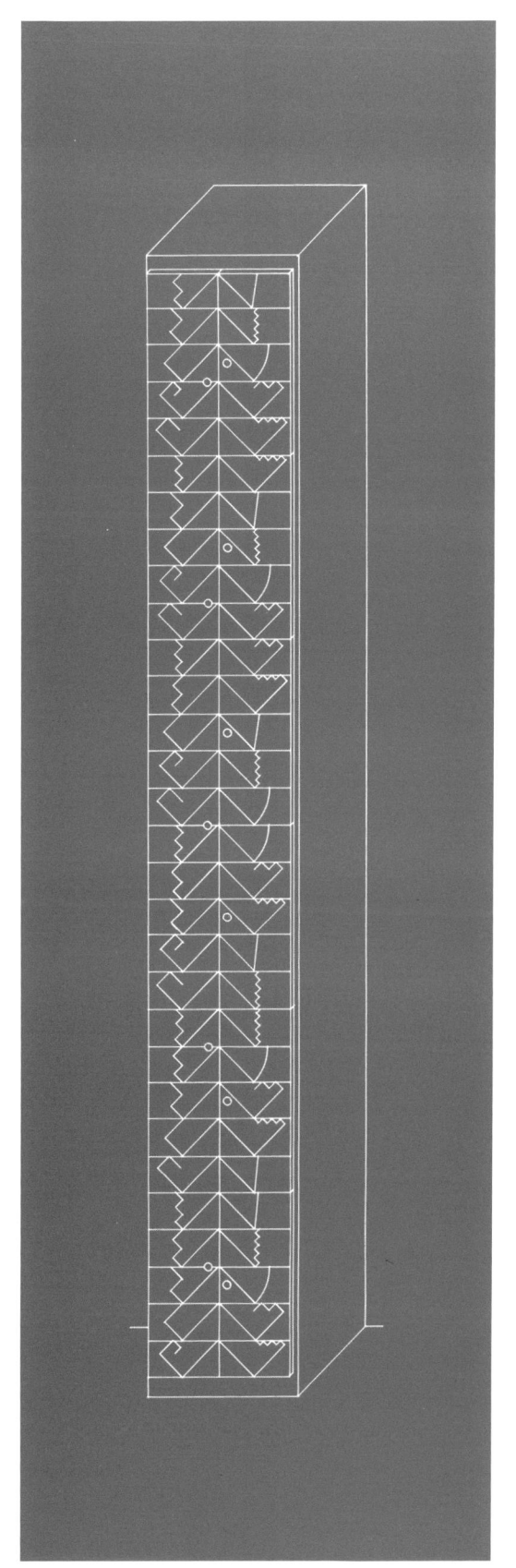

Object D – 6 modules a to f
juxtaposed with 5 modules g
to k to give 30 modules vertically

f

e

d

c

b

a

k

j

i

h

g

P28. (Ana(gram)matical) shelves

These shelves are not vertical repetition of horizontal planes, but grammatical arrangements of vertical and horizontal planes as well as their anagrammatical rearrangements.

Let a plane be present or absent on each of the four sides of a unit square, then there are 16 permutations of planes to give 16 forms:

Let each of the 16 forms be used exactly once, and let the 16 *forms* be arranged on a 4x4 grid of 16 unit squares as a possible *configuration*, then, following transformational rules, a collection of configurations will be generated.

Just as a sentence is a grammatical arrangement of words, so a configuration is a grammatical arrangement of forms.

And just as some words are anagrammatical rearrangements of the letters of some other words, and some sentences are anagrammatical rearrangements of the words of some of the other sentences, so configurations are anagrammatical rearrangements of the forms of other configurations.

The fourteen structurally continuous objects 1, 2, 3, 4, 5, 8, 9, 10, 11, 12, 15, 19, 22, 23 are to be realised.

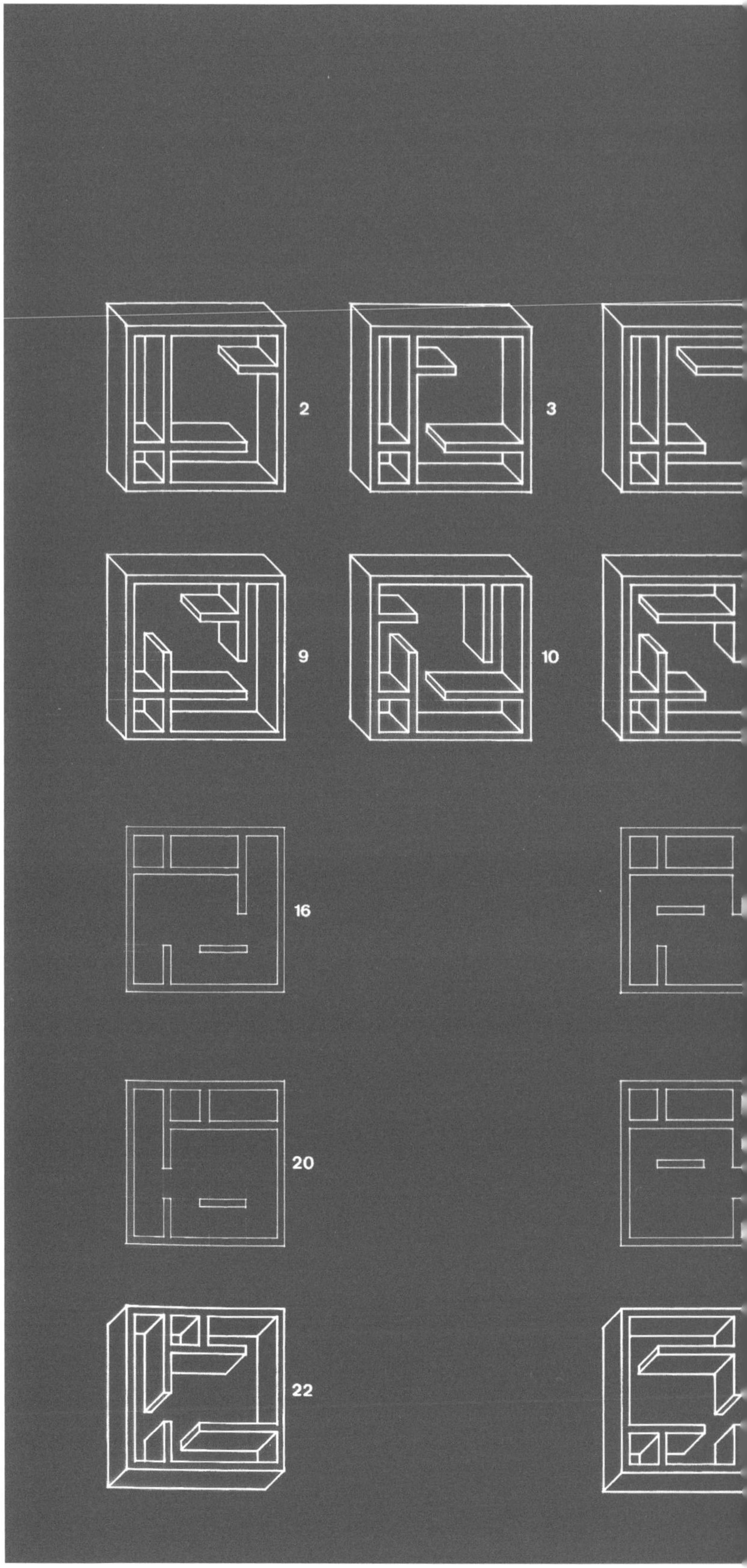

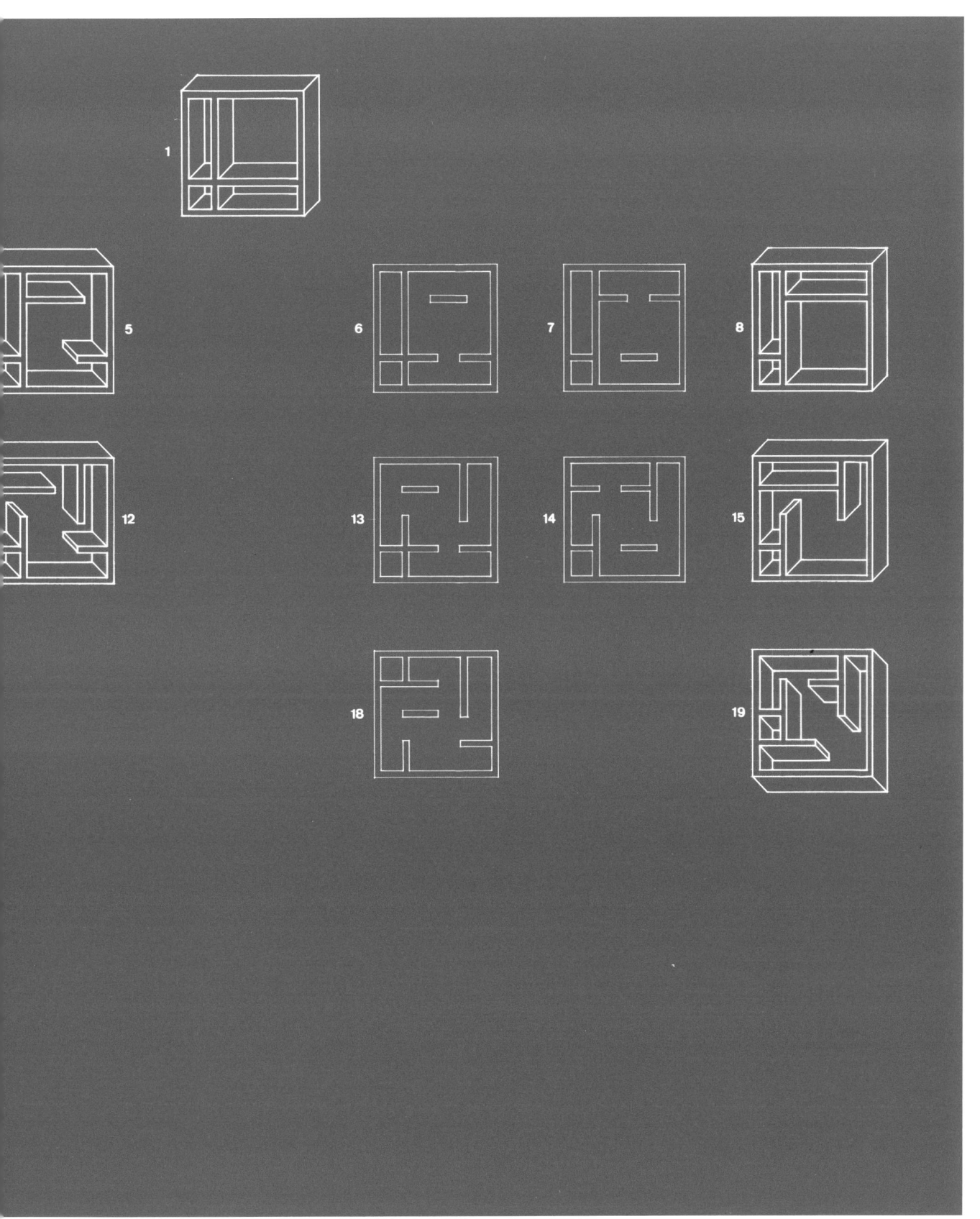

Diagram which records the
transformational sequence from
one configuration to another

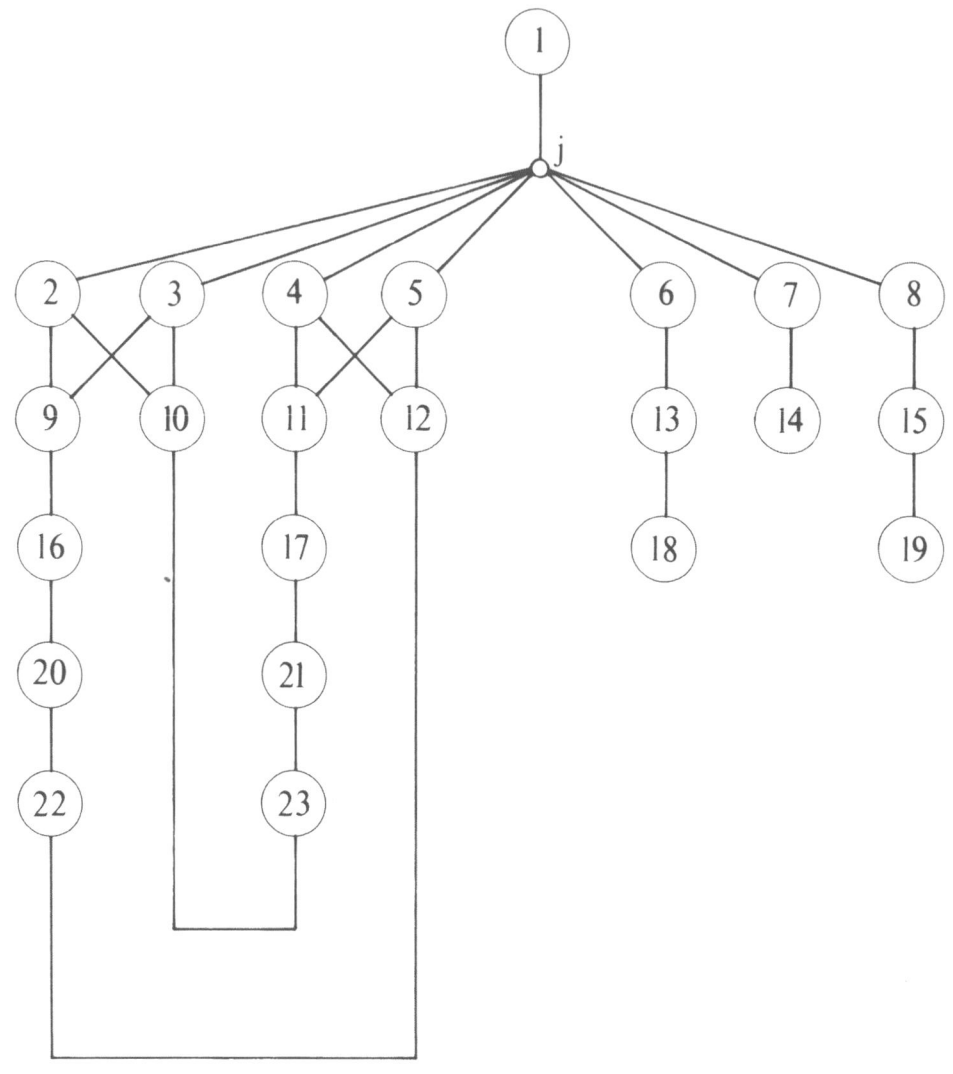

G13. MUSICAL FORMS

Composers have a repertoire of musical forms to choose, develop and deviate from. Not so the furniture maker.

These furniture designs are derived from musical forms, being spatial applications of the outline of the fugue, the passacaglia, and the sonata form.

Just as musical forms organise musical material in time, so the derived musical forms, which have been taken out of their cultural context and reduced from their historical references, are to be used to structure formal material in space.

Space, not time, is the superior mode of organisation, representation and comprehension. Spatial and pictorial truth is placed above temporal and discursive reason. Plato in *Phaedo*' raised the immediacy of ocular knowledge, where the whole of truth is made known purely, directly, instantaneously.

In this spirit Walter Benjamin in writing and Anton Webern in music wished to say and understand everything at once. Even though literature and music are narrative arts which are presented in time, ideally narrative art points to the organisation of its material in space.

There are composers who put to use what Xenakis called "Outside-Time" composition. There are cases in which all the material and its organisation have already been determined before "In-Time" composition begins, as in Messiaen's *Mode de valeurs et d'intensités*, and there are extreme cases in which not only all the material and its organisation but also the temporal order of the appearance of the notes are fixed in space, as in Boulez's *Structure Ia*.

'Quasi una passacaglia', like '(Ana (gram) matical) shelves', like Boulez's *Structure Ia*, like John Conway's Life, are generated without subjective intervention after the material and the generative rules have been determined. But while the following fugal and sonata pieces present material in space, decisions are required at each and every stage of the composition. As such, 'Quasi una fuga' and 'Quasi una sonata' cannot be described as being generated by rules.

In works that are generated by rules, the same rule or the same set of rules must be applied to the material at any stage of transformation. Where different instructions are issued to the material at different stages of transformation, then the work will have to achieve its sense of unity and its appearance of necessity through the rhetoric of narrative force.

These eleven objects I to XI are based on the outline of the fugue.

Analogous to the fugue, each object consists of successive entries of voices after which the thematic material is transformed and rearranged.

Even though these are spatial objects, their reading must be directional and temporal, from left to right and from beginning to end, as music scores are read and as music is listened to. Thus there is always a residue temporality in these spatial objects.

The titles of objects I to XI give some idea to their structure:

(i) Simple Fugue, (ii) Monothematic Fugue, (iii) Stretto Fugue, (iv) Rotation Fugue, (v) Retrograde-Inversion Fugue, (vi) Topological Fugue, (vii) Squares-in-Four-Rows Fugue, (viii) Squares-in-Four-Quarters Fugue, (ix) Augmentation Fugue, (x) Permutation Fugue, (xi) Minimal Fugue

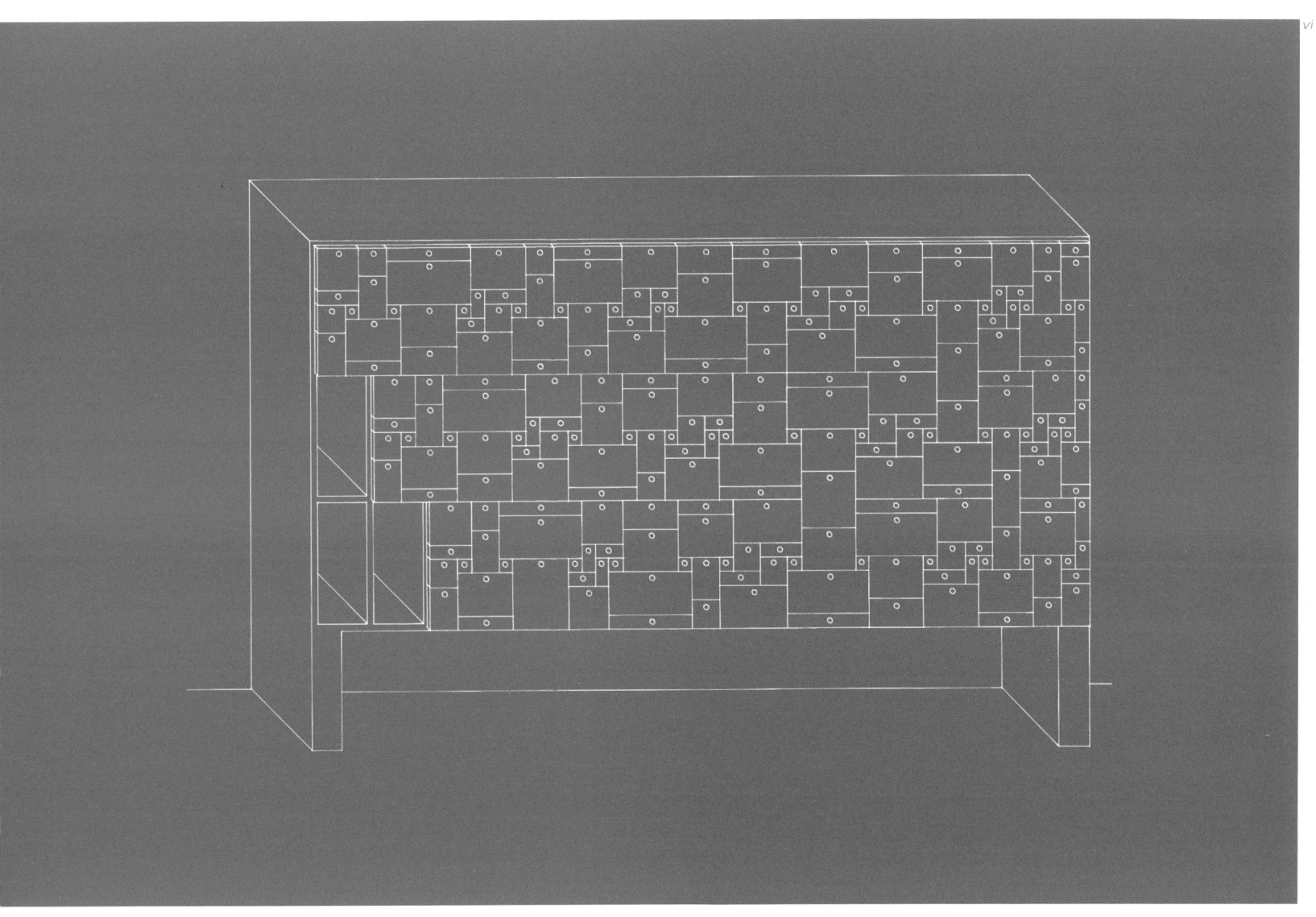

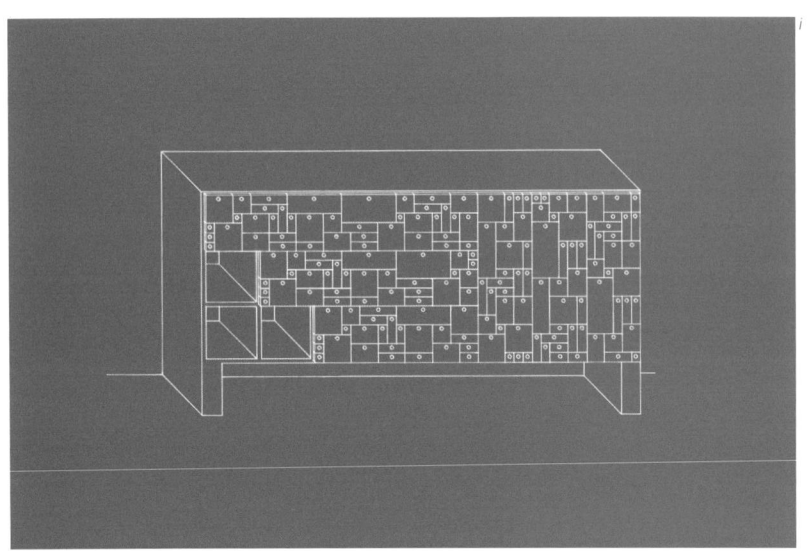
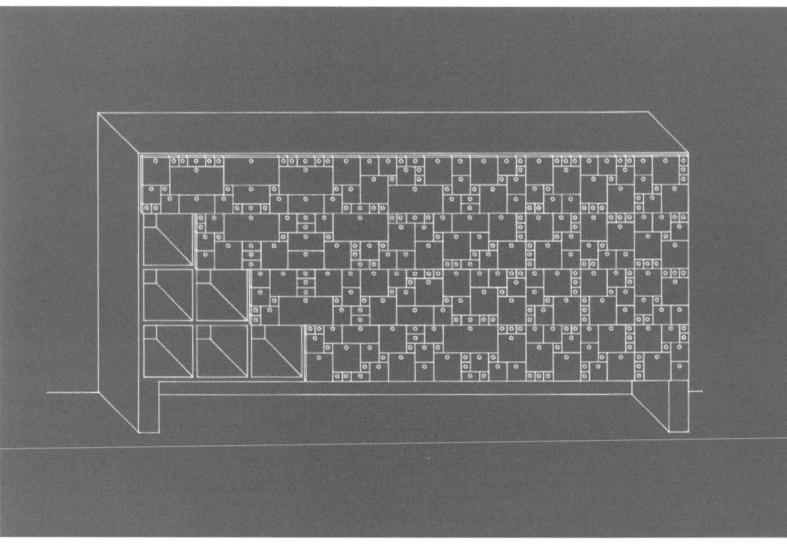
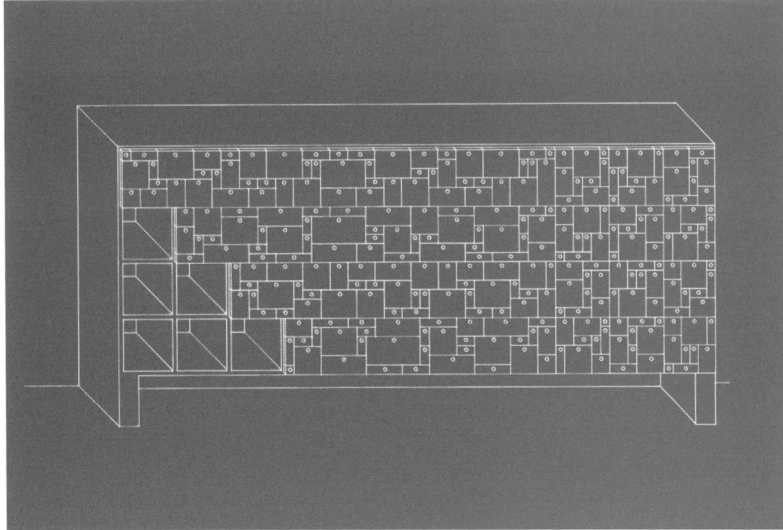
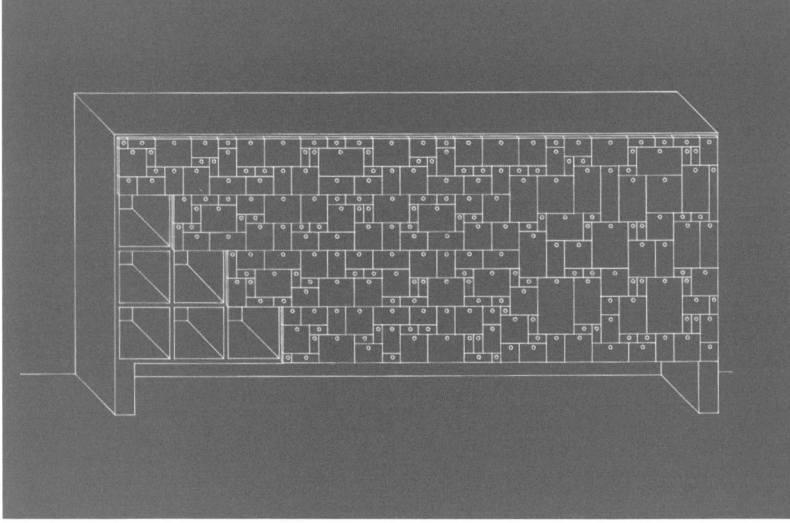

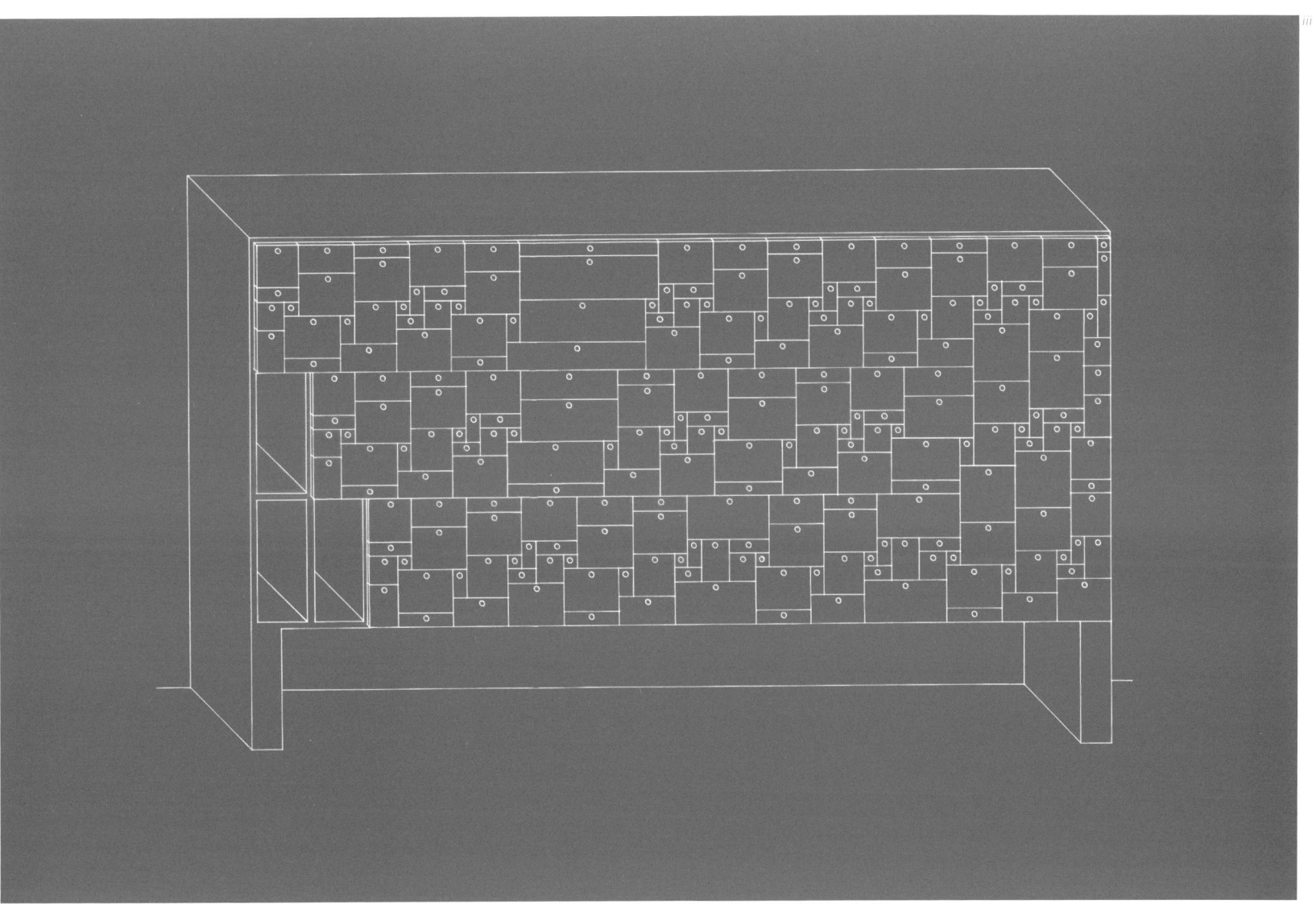

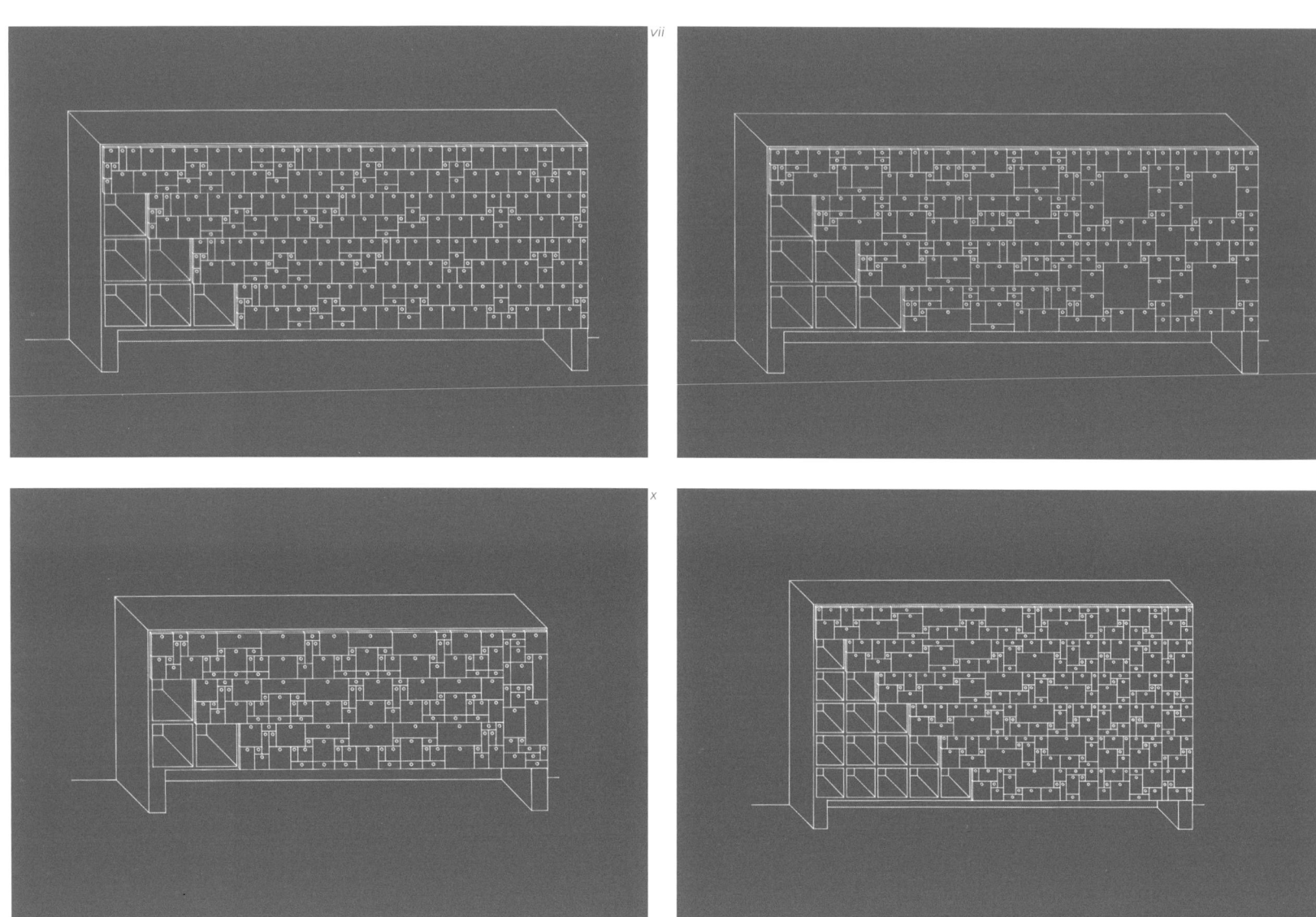

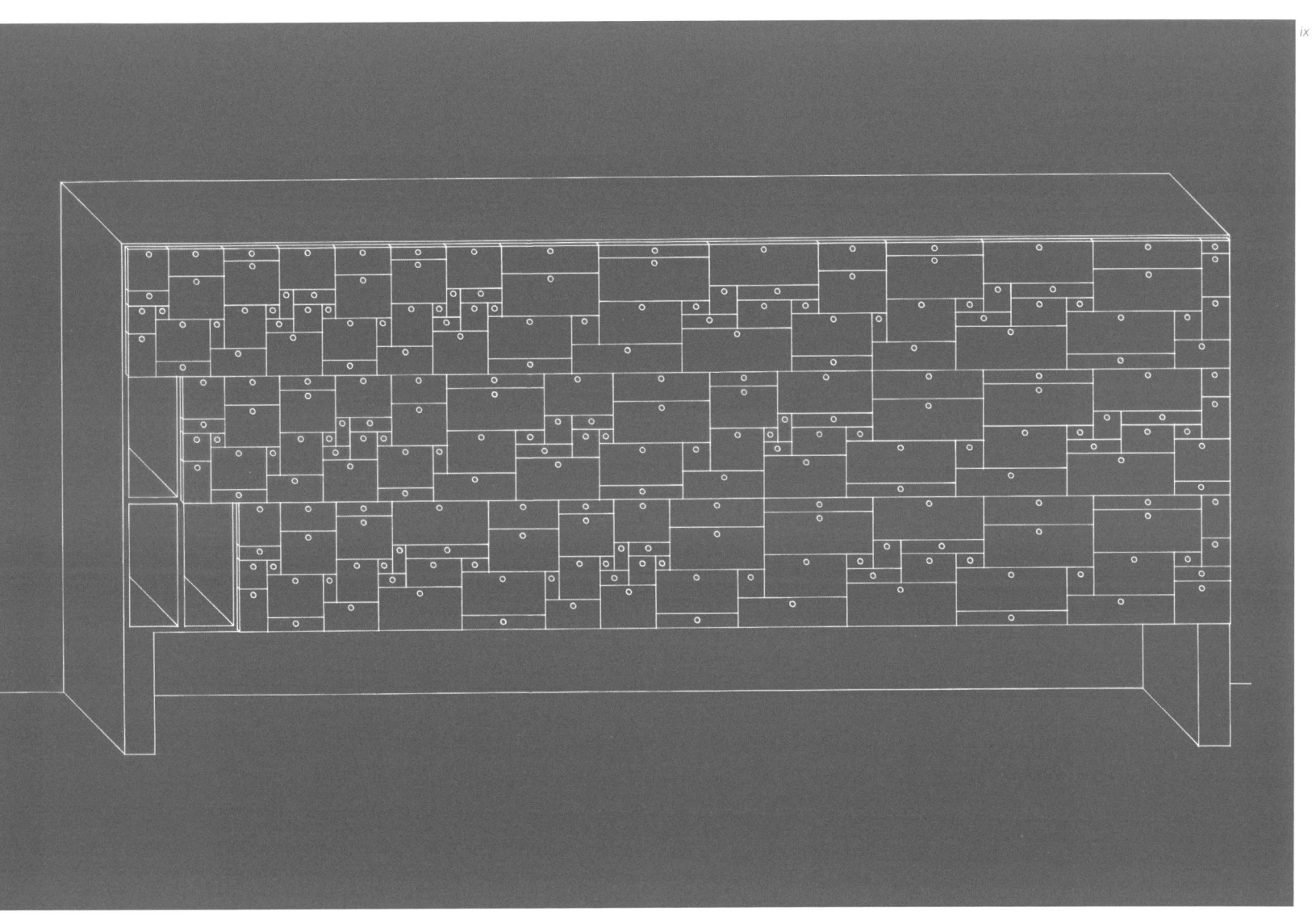

This project is a tribute to Purcell, Shostakovich, Britten, and their great passacaglias.

Repetition is in itself superfluous, but the repetition of the passacaglia bass, its insistent obsessive recurrence, over which transforming and developing material is superposed, is a powerful and profound device in musical composition.

A passacaglia consists of a superposed set of variations over a repeating ground *bass*, while each object in this collection consists of a superposed set of variations over a *base* with differently spaced vertical planes.

The number of objects in this collection is determined by the number of ways the vertical planes in the base can be spaced.

Applying invented rules to the individual way the vertical planes in the base is spaced will generate the variations over the base.

These objects are related as follows:

An arrangement of vertical planes in the base of one object is a *variant* of another arrangement of vertical planes in the base of another object.

Invented rules generate *variations* in each object.

The same invented rules are applied to all the objects so that every object is a *variant* of every other object.

There are ten objects A to J.

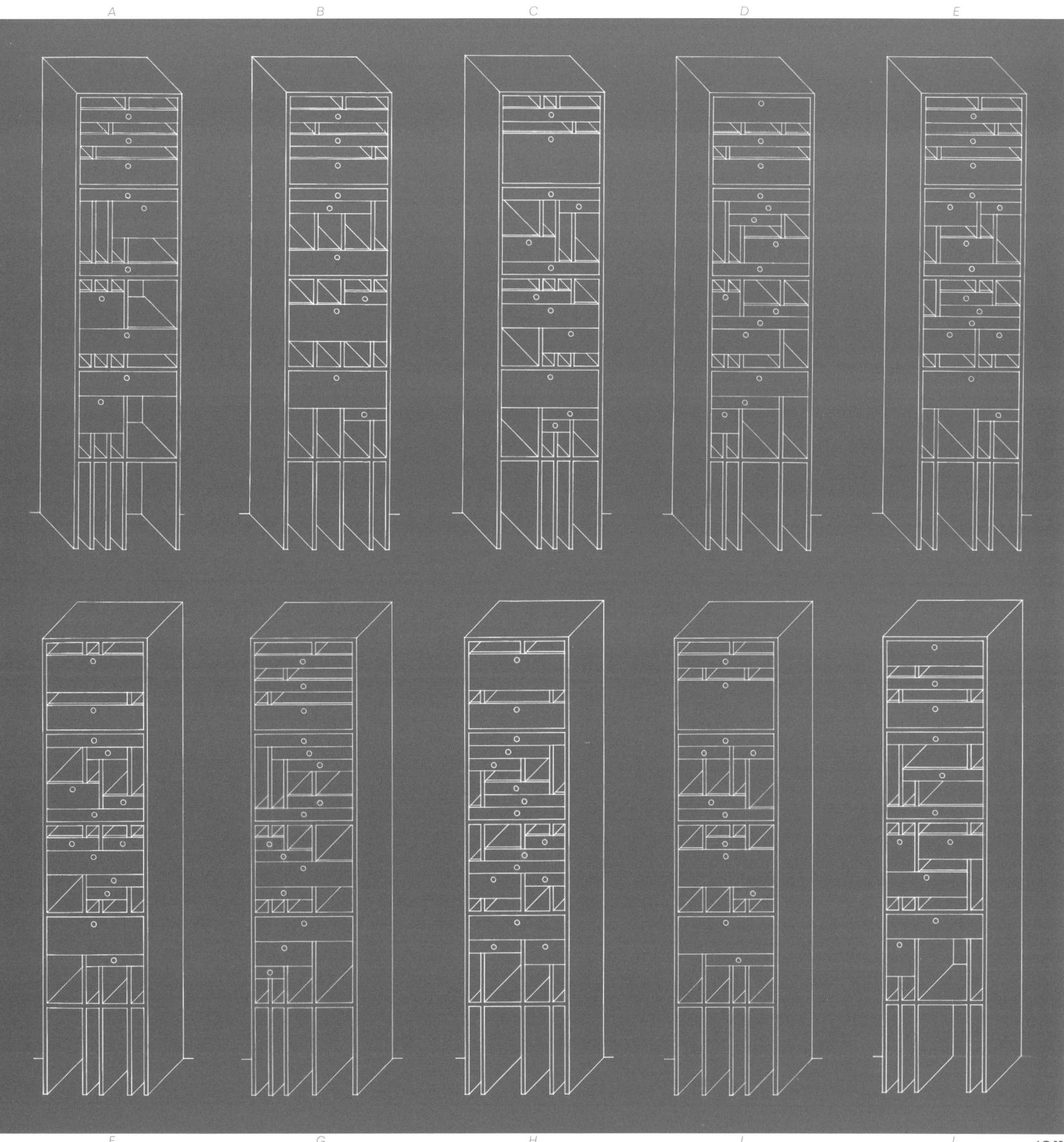

These three objects C1,C2,C3 are based on the outline of the sonata form.

Analogous to the sonata form, each object consists of the three parts of exposition, development and recapitulation in which the thematic material is reflected, rotated, reduced and elongated.

While sonatas unfold in time, these objects present themselves in space.

And while the outline of the sonata is a *sequential* tripartite form, its spatial transcription will simply be a *symmetrical* tripartite form. But in order to overcome the superfluity of symmetry, the sequential tripartite form is combined with the symmetrical tripartite form in these objects as follows:

Let the first subject in the exposition and its reappearance in the recapitulation be a symmetrical (reflected) pair, and let the second subject in the exposition and its reappearance in the recapitulation be an identical (non-reflected) pair, then the spatial relation between the two subjects in the recapitulation will be different from the spatial relation between the two subjects in the exposition. This is analogous to the sonata movement where in the exposition the first subject is in the tonic while the second subject is in the dominant but in the recapitulation both subjects are to be in the tonic.

To be sure, while the recapitulation in music is experienced as an event *after* the exposition and the development, the recapitulation in a spatial object is to be considered as an event not after but *other than* the exposition and the development. In this way, temporal experience of music is replaced by the spatial reading of these objects.

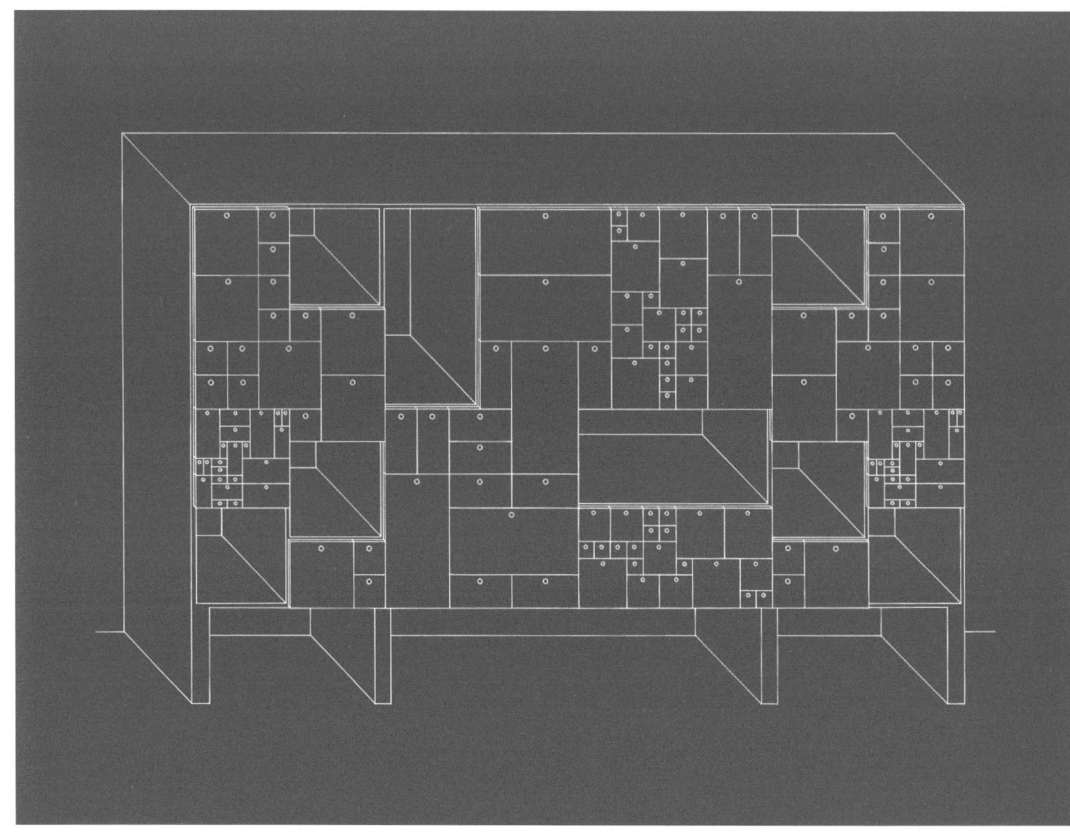

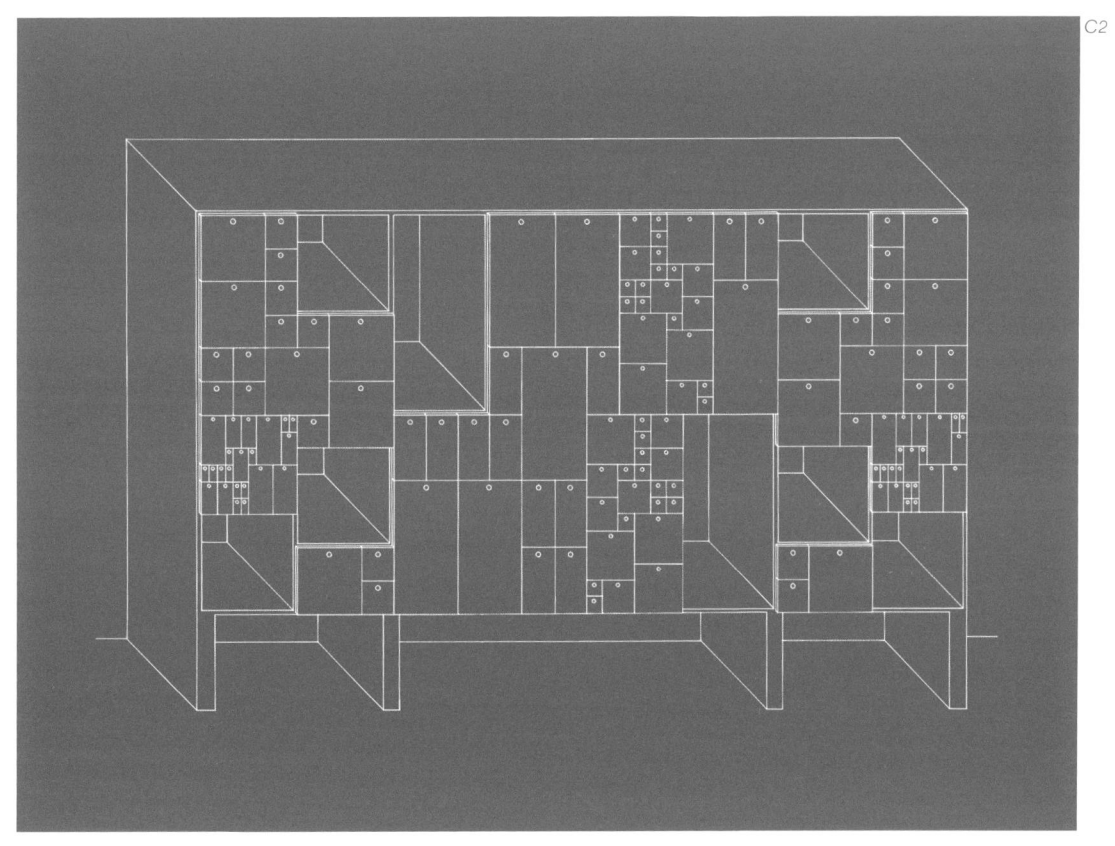

C2

127

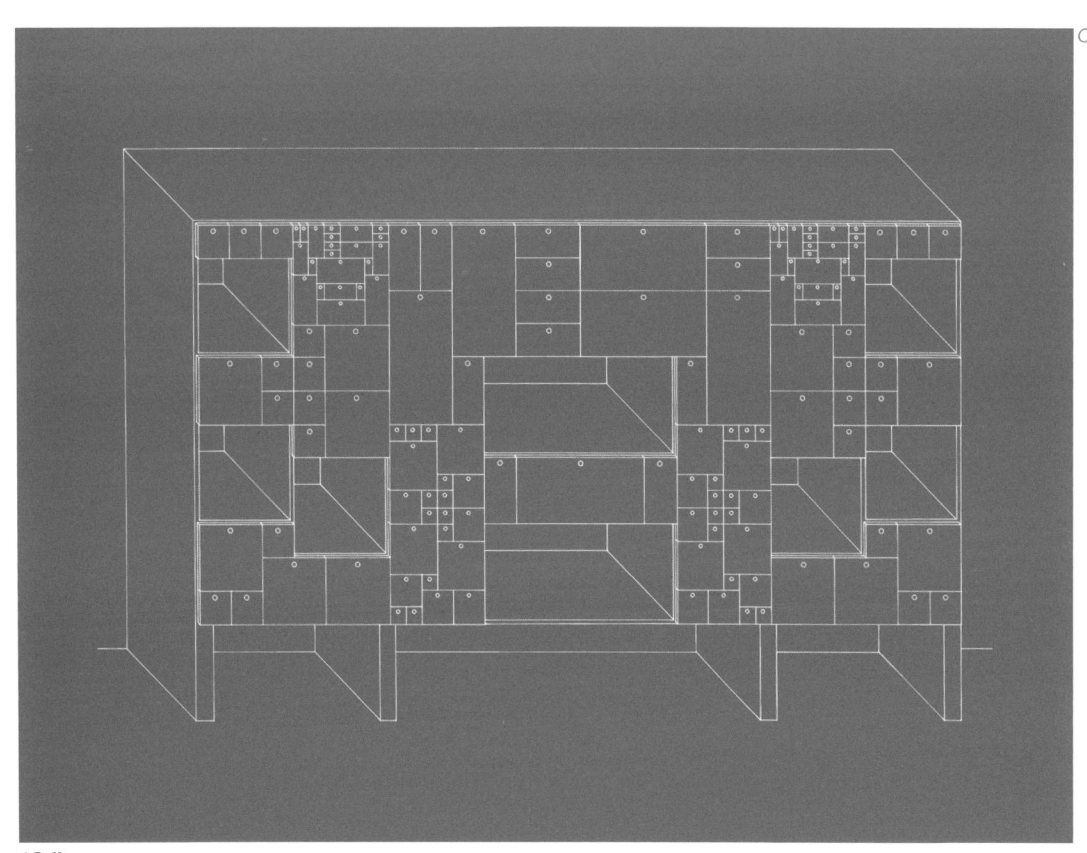

G14. COMPOSING NUMBERS

Every number has its unique properties.

GH Hardy told this story about his fellow mathematician Ramanujan. Hardy remarked that the number of the taxicab, 1729, he took to visit Ramanujan was a rather dull number, to which Ramanujan countered by showing the very interesting property of 1729 as the smallest number expressible as the sum of two cubes in two different ways. In fact, 1729 = 13 + 123= 93 +103. To mathematicians, each number has its own character, which can be directly apprehended like concrete objects.

The properties of certain numbers are material to be presented and developed using the outline of the sonata form.

The sonata form is capable of gathering together different contents into a coherent whole. It encompasses diversity within unity.

Like 'Quasi una sonata', 'Invention on a number' and 'Invention on a numerical relation' are not generated by rules but are composed of different but related material, all of which is organised like a sonata which gives articulation to each element and cohesion to different elements.

P32. Invention on a number

The number 36 is the smallest number discounting 1 which is both square and triangular.

Properties of the number 36 are spatialised and represented in this object.

Being a square number, 36 can be expressed as
(a) the sum of the first odd numbers, so that 36 = 1 + 3 + 5 + 7 + 9 + 11
(b) the sum of two consecutive triangular numbers, so that 36 = 15 + 21
(c) the sequence 1 + 2 + 3 + 4 + 5 + 6 + 5 + 4 + 3 + 2 + 1.

Being a triangular number, 36 can be expressed as
(d) the sum of the first integers, so that 36 = 1 + 2 + 3 + 4 + 5 + 6 + 7 + 8
(e) the sum of a square and two triangular numbers, this being possible for alternate triangular numbers, so that 36 = 16 + 10 + 10
(f) the sum of two consecutive triangular numbers, their sum and their difference in which their sum is a square number and their difference is the integral root of that square number, this being possible for alternate triangular numbers, so that 36 = 6 + 10 + 16 + 4.

And so on.

The object resonates with the number 36.

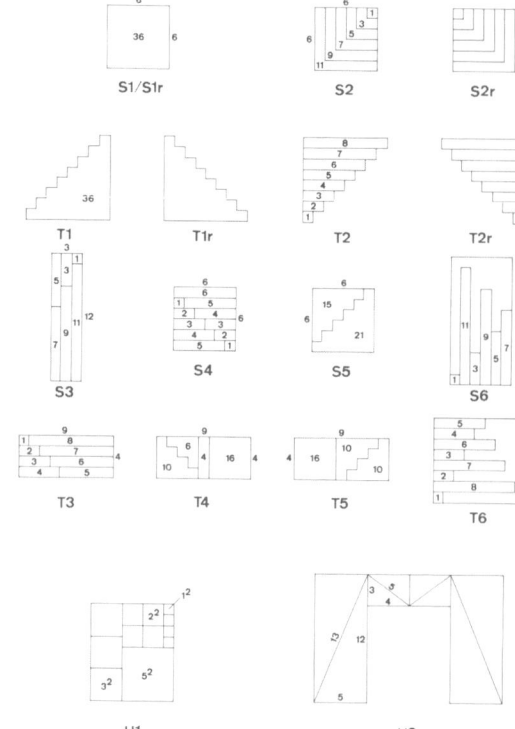

Spatial representations of properties of the number 36

*Organisation of the material
by referring to the outline
of the sonata form with
exposition E, development
D, recapitulation R*

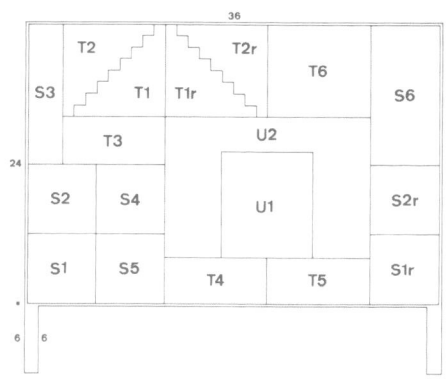

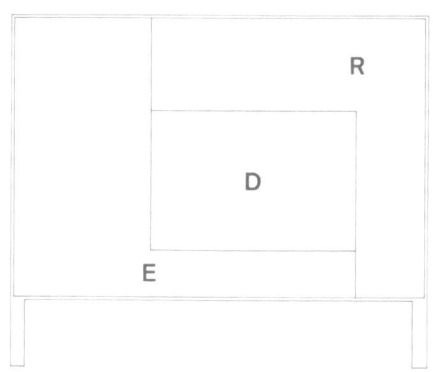

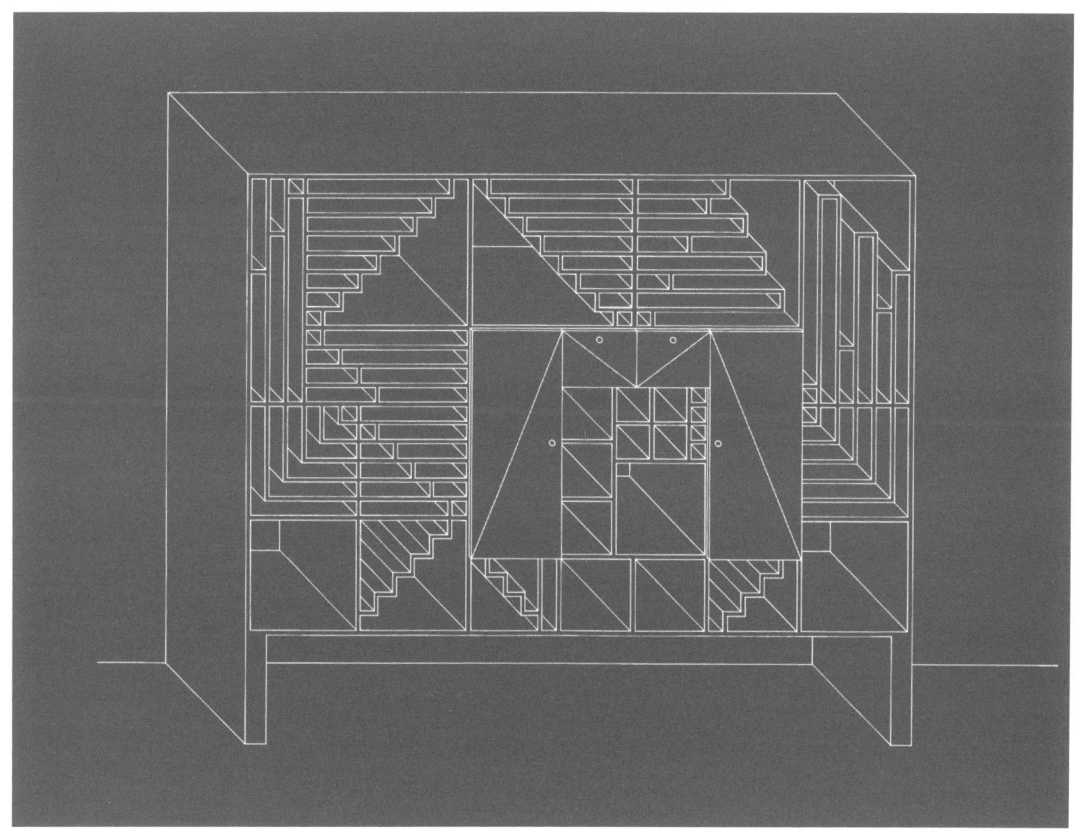

The triangular number $55 = 1^2 + 2^2 + 3^2 + 4^2 + 5^2$ is the smallest possibility, and the triangular number $91 = 1^2 + 2^2 + 3^2 + 4^2 + 5^2 + 6^2$ is the next possibility, in which a triangular number is equal to the sum of the first square numbers.

Properties of the numbers 55 and 91, and their difference 36 which is both square and triangular, are spatialised and represented in this object.

Being a triangular number, 55 can be expressed as
(a) the sum of the first integers, so that $55 = 1 + 2 + 3 + 4 + 5 + 6 + 7 + 8 + 9 + 10$

Being a triangular number, 91 can be expressed as
(b) the sum of the first integers, so that $91 = 1 + 2 + 3 + 4 + 5 + 6 + 7 + 8 + 9 + 10 + 11 + 12 + 13$

Being a square number, 36 can be expressed as
(c) the sum of the first odd numbers, so that $36 = 1 + 3 + 5 + 7 + 9 + 11$

Being a triangular number, 36 can be expressed as
(d) the sum of the first integers, so that $36 = 1 + 2 + 3 + 4 + 5 + 6 + 7 + 8$.

And so on.

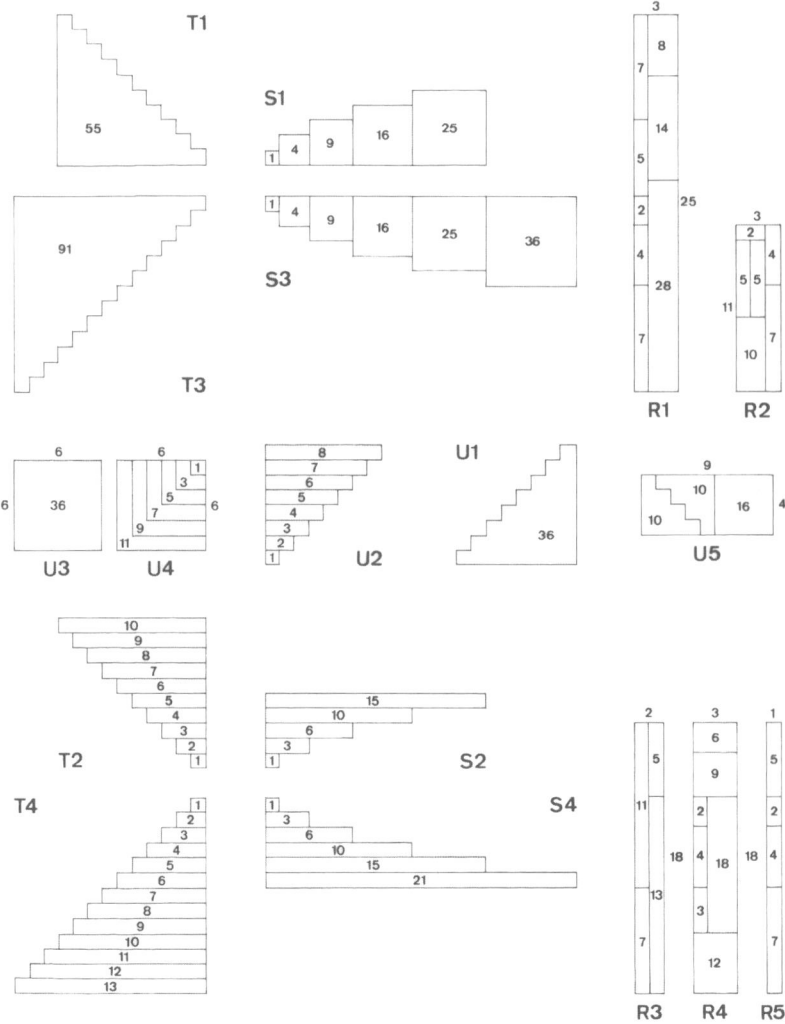

Spatial representations of properties of the numbers 55, 91, and their difference 36

Organisation of the material by referring to the outline of the sonata form with exposition E, development D, recapitulation R, and a supplementary introduction / coda Z

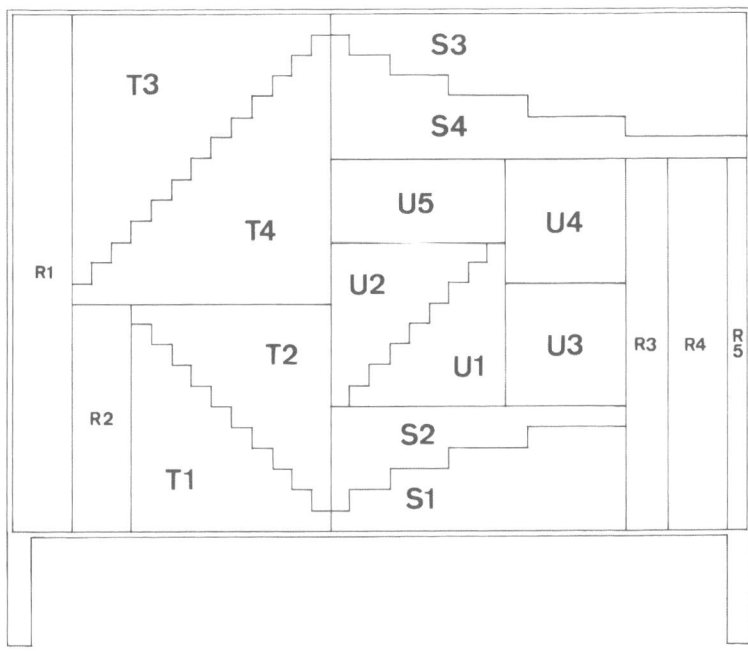

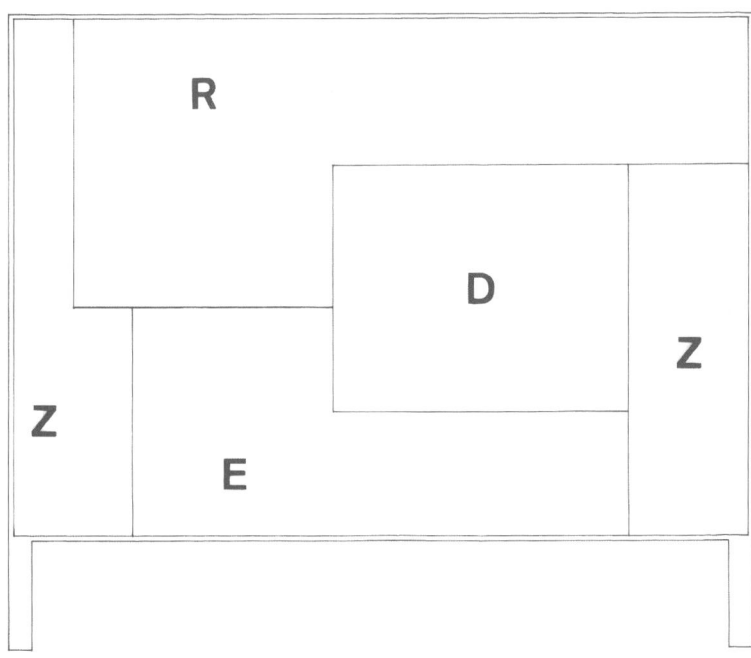

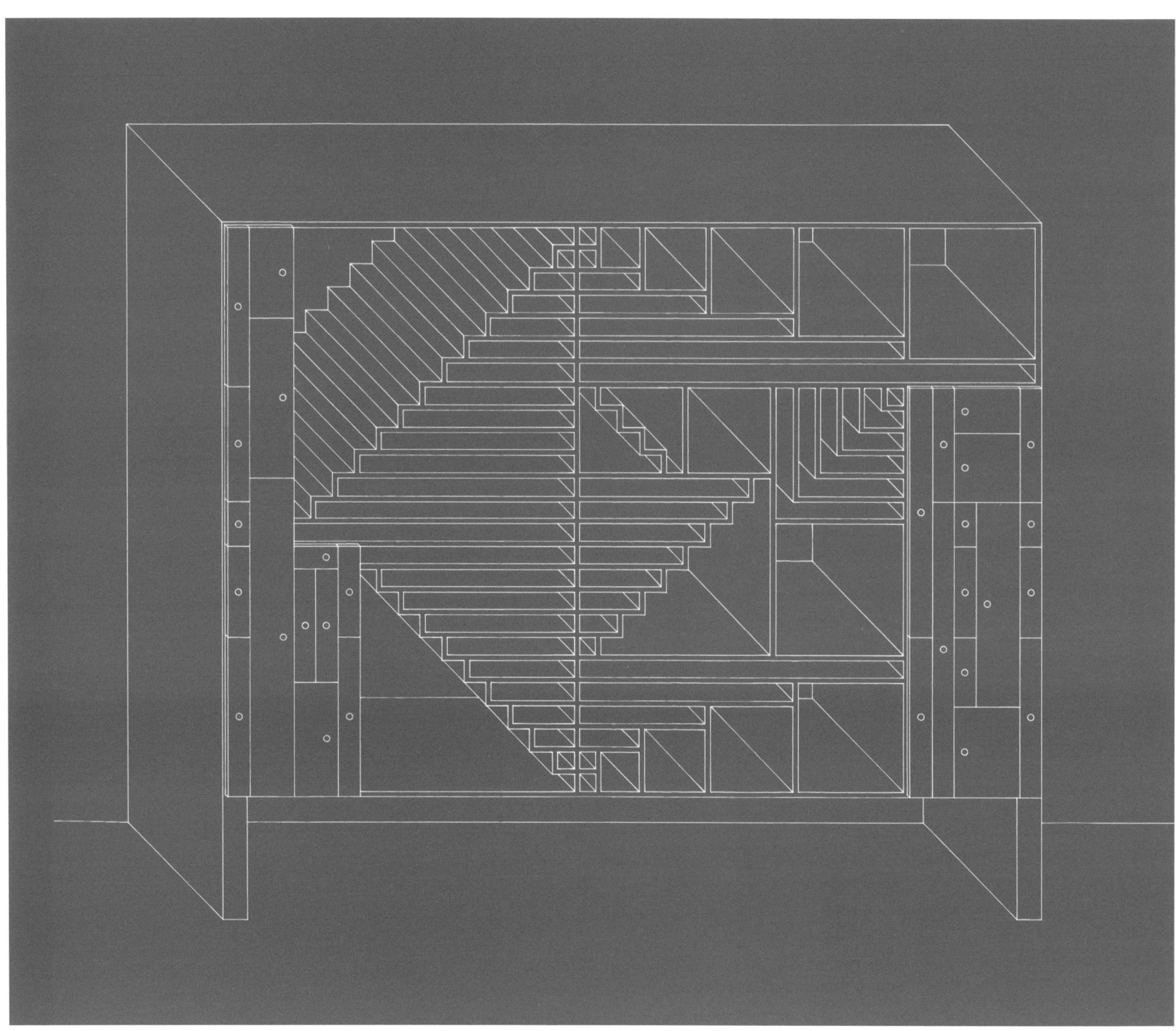

G15. PRIME NUMBERS

Prime numbers are the basic building blocks in mathematics.

Because the distribution of primes is irregular, the use of prime number sequences and related ideas in the following projects produces intriguing results.

And because the distribution of primes is irregular, the series of primes will have an ever evolving pattern. Designs which use primes as its material will therefore be 'open' projects in the sense that what is represented in the object is merely one segment of the potentially infinite series of primes, so that the lower and upper limits of the represented segment must be determined and justified by certain properties they possess.

P34. Paired odd primes, isolated odd non-primes

For the sequence of odd numbers,
(a) paired primes are (11, 13), (17, 19), (29, 31), (41, 43) …
(b) isolated non-primes are 9, 15, 21, 39, 45 …

From (a), the sum of paired odd primes is always a multiple of 12, and the mean of paired odd primes is always a multiple of 6.

These mathematical relations are spatialised in object A where the shelving grid measures 12 units horizontally and 6 units vertically, so that the sum of paired odd primes represented horizontally can be read as a multiple of 12, and the mean of paired odd primes represented vertically can be read as a multiple of 6.

From (b), the value of an isolated odd non-prime is always a multiple of 3, and the value of an isolated odd non-prime ± 3 is always a multiple of 6.

These mathematical relations are spatialised in object B where the shelving grid measures 3 units horizontally and 6 units vertically, so that the value of an isolated odd non-prime represented horizontally can be read as a multiple of 3, and the value of an isolated odd non-prime ± 3 represented vertically can be read as a multiple of 6.

Object B – the 3 x 6 grid shows the value of an isolated odd non-prime to be 3n and the value of an isolated odd non-prime ± 3 to be 6n

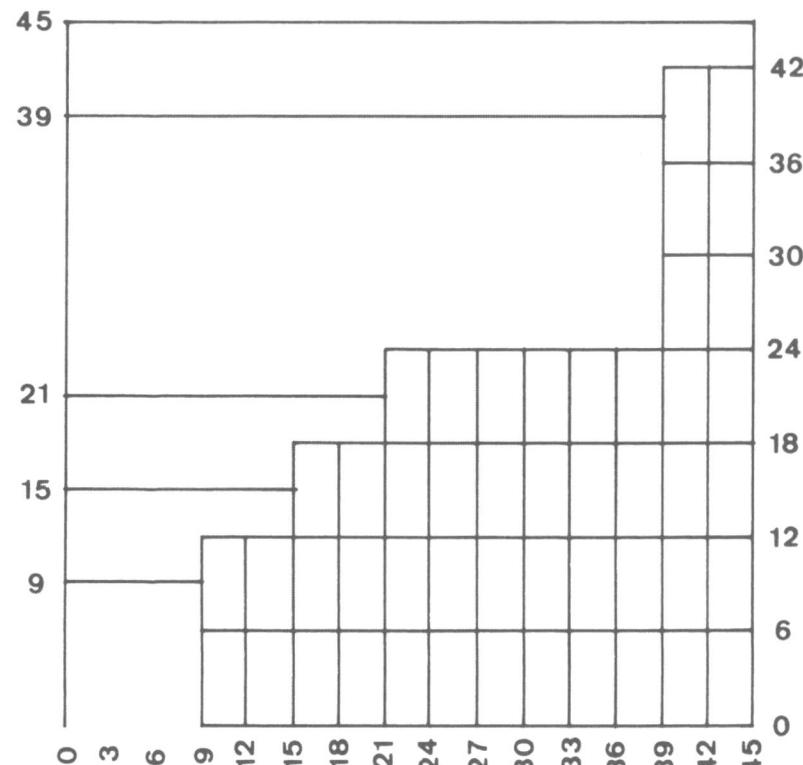

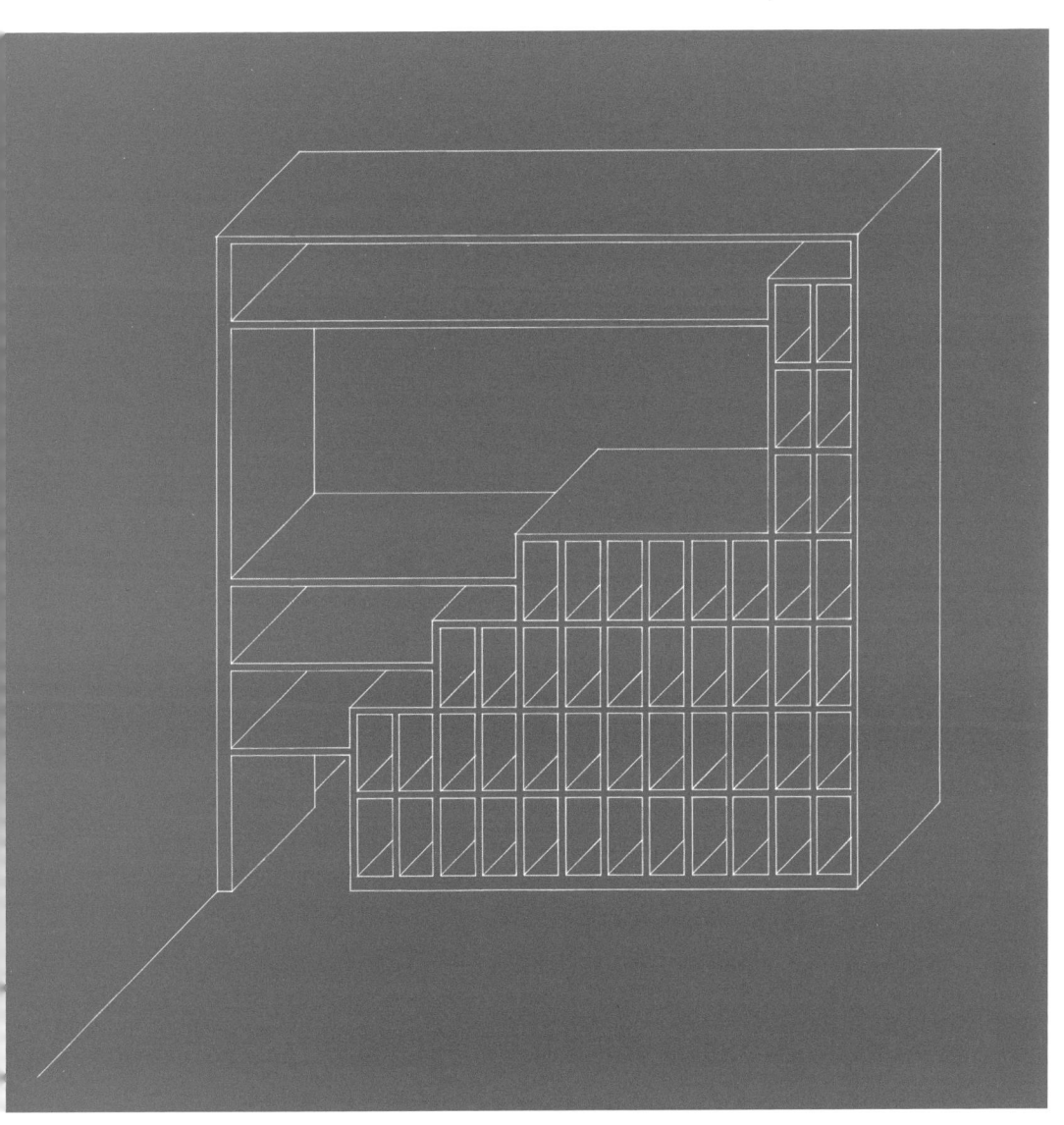

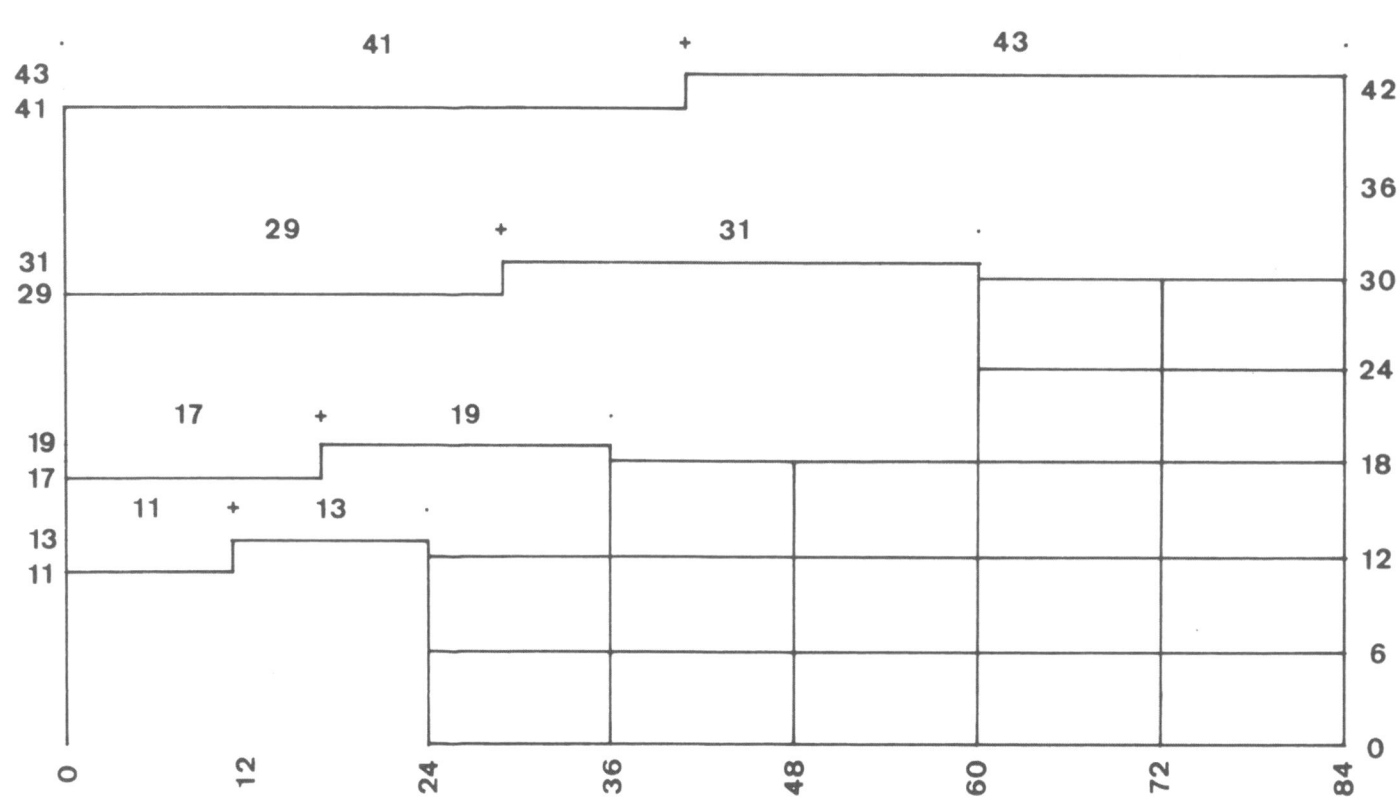

Object A – The 12 x 6 grid shows the sum of paired odd primes to be 12n and the mean of paired odd primes to be 6n

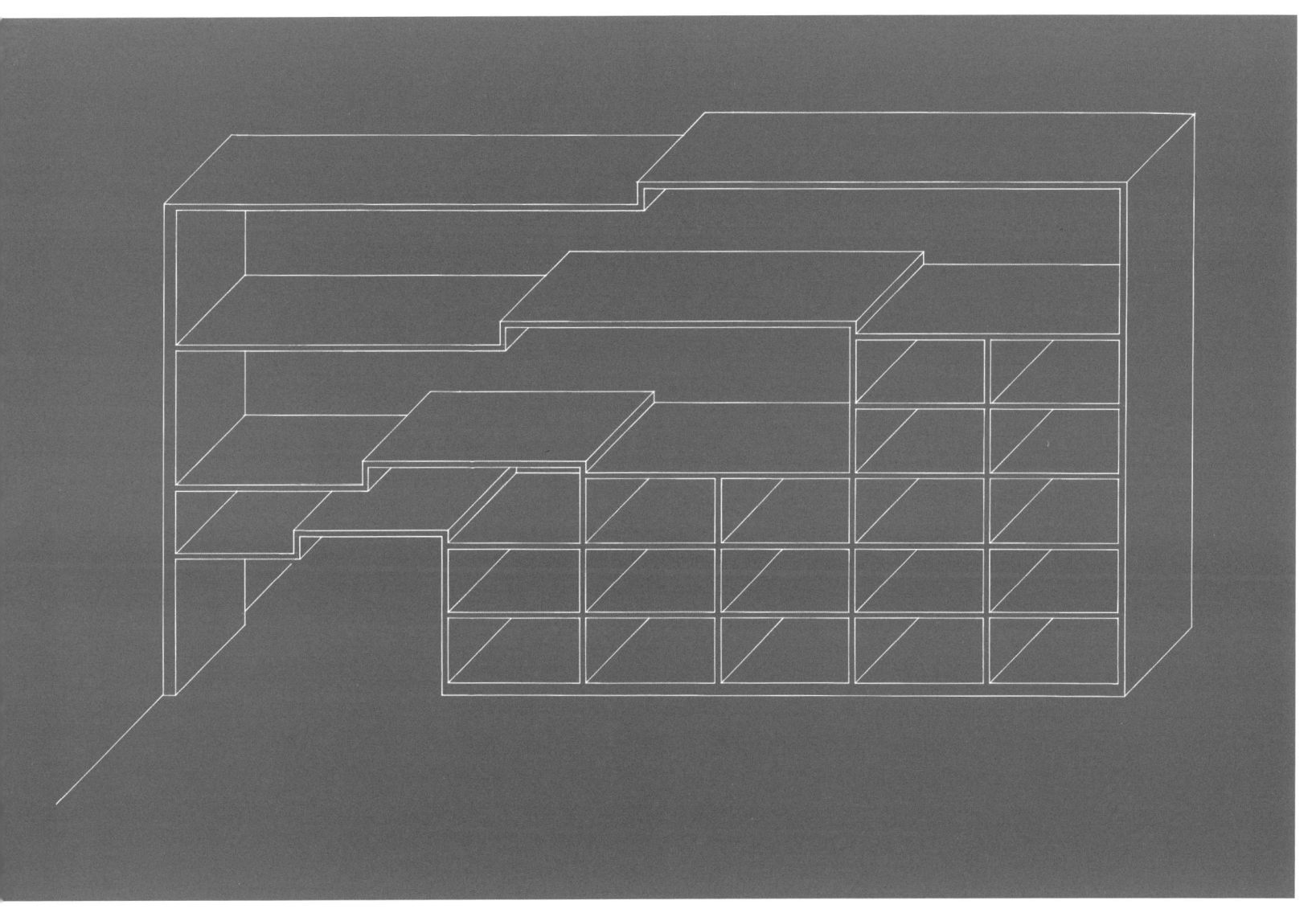

139

P35. Odd numbers, primes and non-primes, paired and isolated

For the sequence of odd numbers,
(a) paired primes are (11, 13), (17, 19), (29, 31), (41, 43) …
(b) isolated primes are 23, 37, 47, 53 …
(c) paired non-primes are (25, 27), (33, 35), (49, 51) …
(d) isolated non-primes are 9, 15, 21, 39, 45 …

From (a), the mean of paired odd primes can always be expressed as $6n$, and from (b), the value of an isolated odd prime can always be expressed as $6n\pm1$ or its equivalent $6n\pm5$.

These mathematical relations are spatialised in object V where the shelving grid measures 6 units both horizontally and vertically, so that the mean of paired odd primes represented vertically can be read as a multiple of 6, and the value of an isolated odd prime represented horizontally will show up as a unit deviation from $6n$.

From (c), the mean of paired odd non-primes can always be expressed as $6n\pm2$ or its equivalent $6n\pm4$, and from (d), the value of an isolated odd non-prime can always be expressed as $6n\pm3$.

These mathematical relations are spatialised in object W where the shelving grid measures 6 units both horizontally and vertically, so that the mean of paired odd non-primes represented horizontally will show up as a two-unit deviation from $6n$, and the value of an isolated odd non-prime represented vertically will show up as a three-unit deviation from $6n$.

Object V – The 6 x 6 grid shows the mean of the paired odd primes to be $6n$ and the value of an isolated odd prime to be $6n\pm1$

Object W – The 6 x 6 grid shows the mean of paired odd non-primes to be $6n\pm2$ and the value of an isolated odd non-prime to be $6n\pm3$

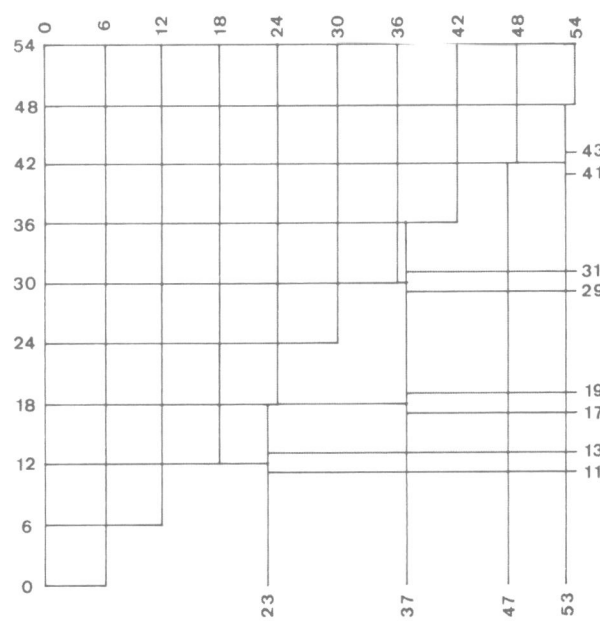

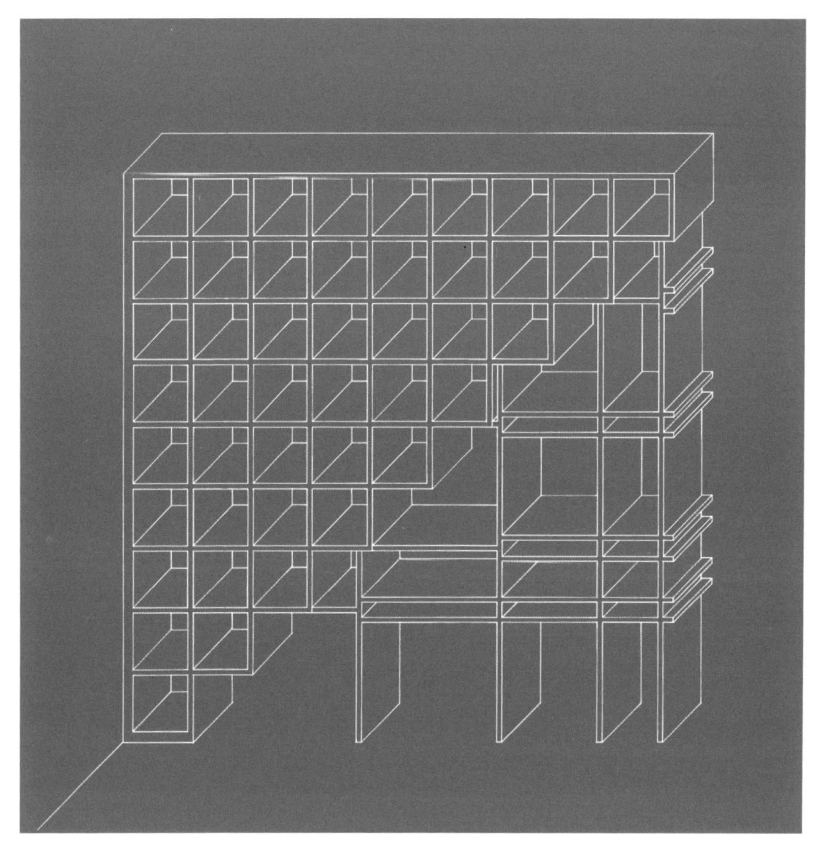

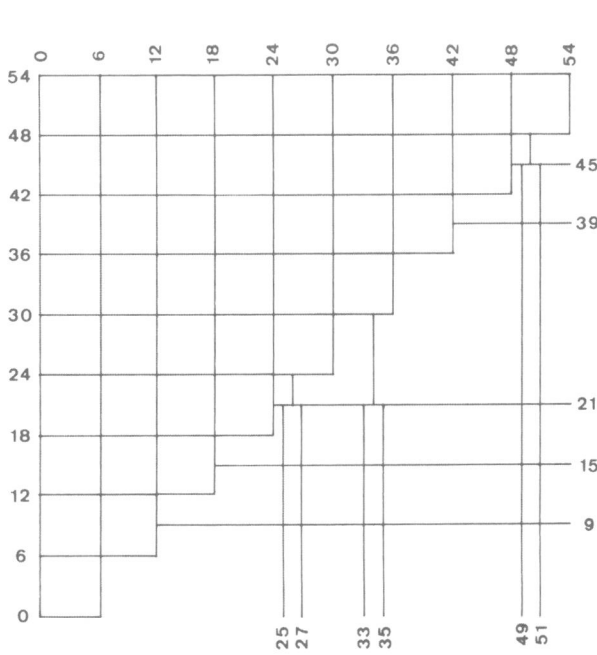

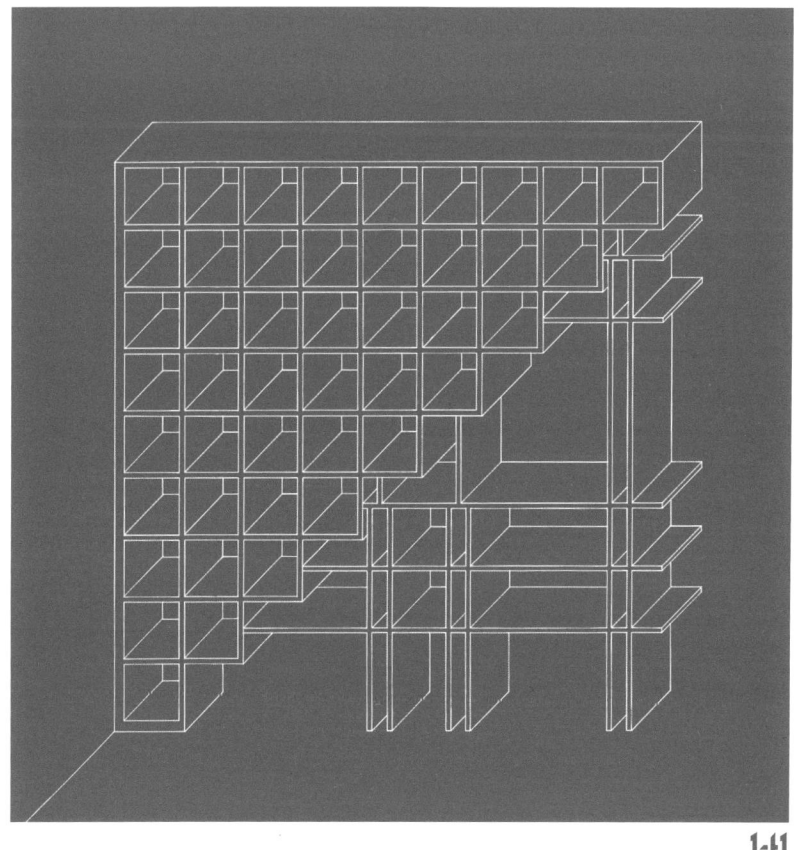

Let a sequence of numbers be represented by each number being one unit high and prime numbers being expressed as drawers, then the sequence of numbers is separated into columns of consecutive numbers by the smaller prime of a prime pair determining the top drawer of one column and the larger prime of the same prime pair determining the bottom drawer of the next column.

This object with drawers and shelves is a spatial representation of the distribution of prime numbers.

Spatial representation of the distribution of prime numbers. Of a prime pair, the smaller prime ends one column and the larger prime begins the next column.

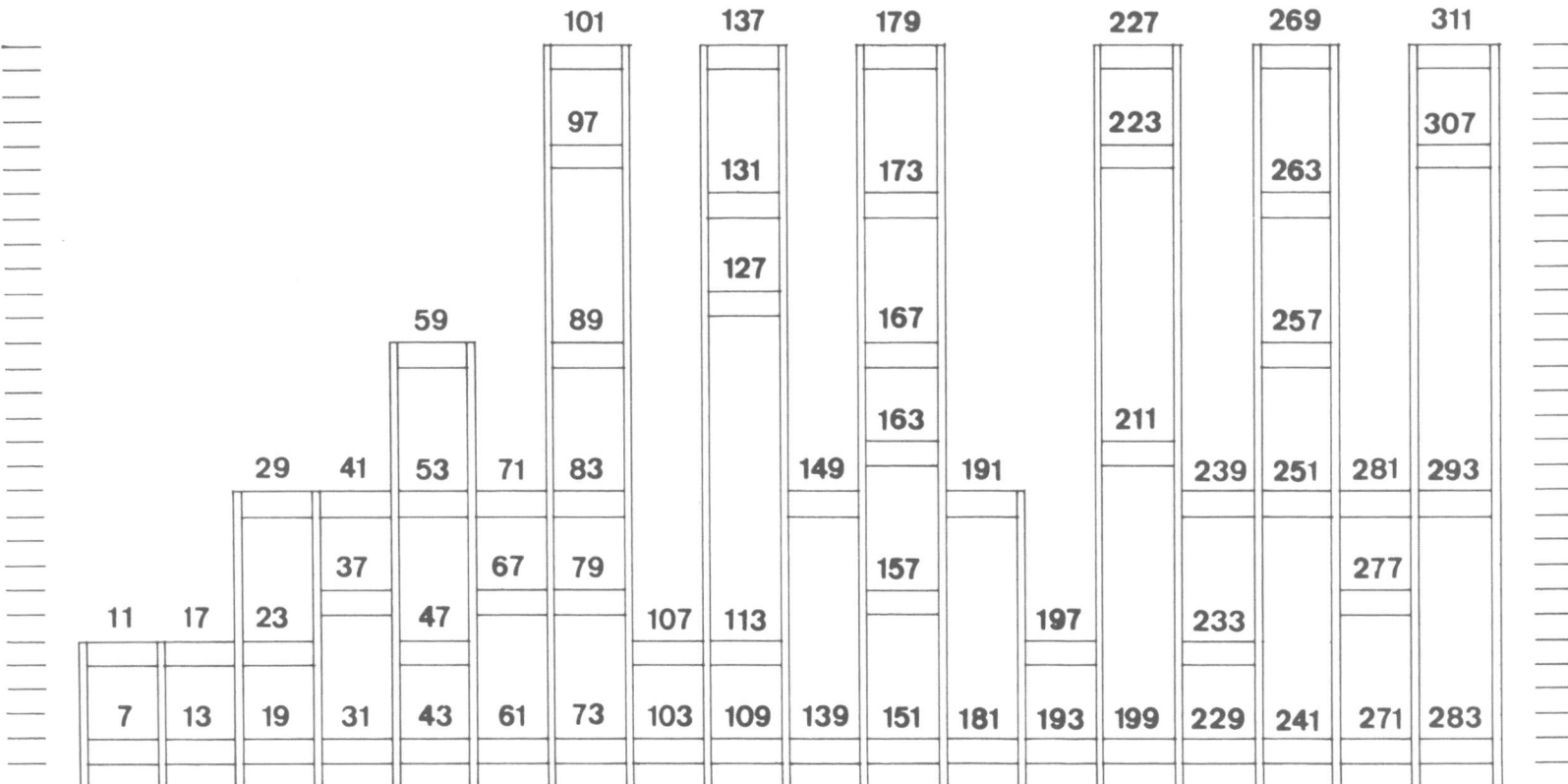

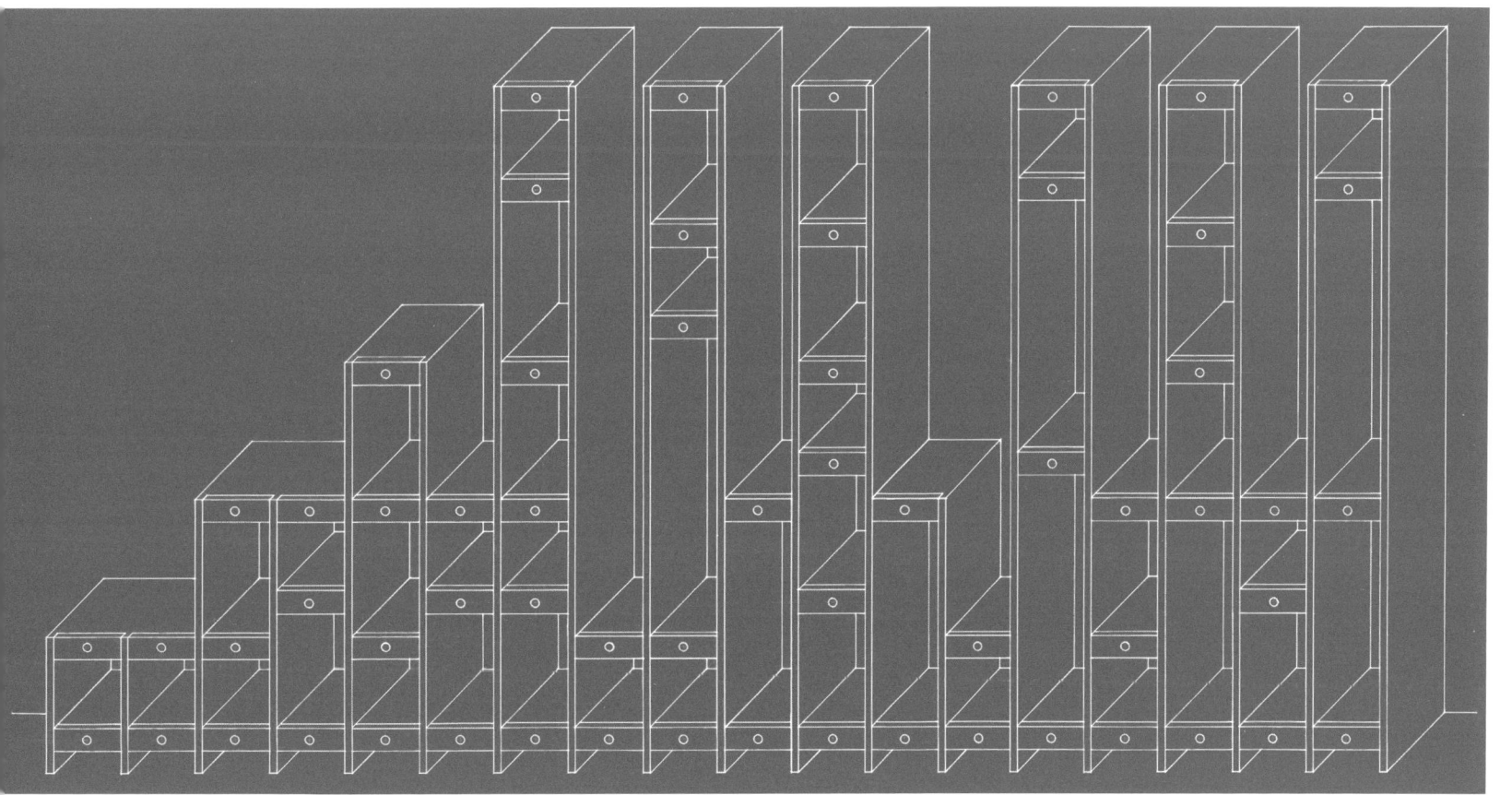

P37. Primes as sum and difference of squares

Every odd prime can be expressed in the form of $4n+1$ or $4n-1$.

Every $4n+1$ prime can be expressed as the sum of two squares.

Every $4n-1$ prime can be expressed as the difference between two squares. This is from the general formulation in which every odd number can be expressed as the difference between two successive squares.

This project consists of shelves and storage compartments where shelves represent prime numbers.

Each $4n+1$ prime is represented by the combined area of two juxtaposed squares where the combined area becomes shelves.

Each $4n-1$ prime is represented by the remaining area of two superposed squares where the remaining area becomes a shelf and the superposed area becomes a storage compartment.

This object represents spatially the range of odd primes up to 23 as the sum of two squares and as the difference between two squares:

The $4n+1$ primes represented are
$5 = 1^2 + 2^2$, $13 = 2^2 + 3^2$, $17 = 1^2 + 4^2$

The $4n-1$ primes represented are
$3 = 2^2 - 1^2$, $7 = 4^2 - 3^2$, $11 = 6^2 - 5^2$, $19 = 10^2 - 9^2$, $23 = 12^2 - 11^2$

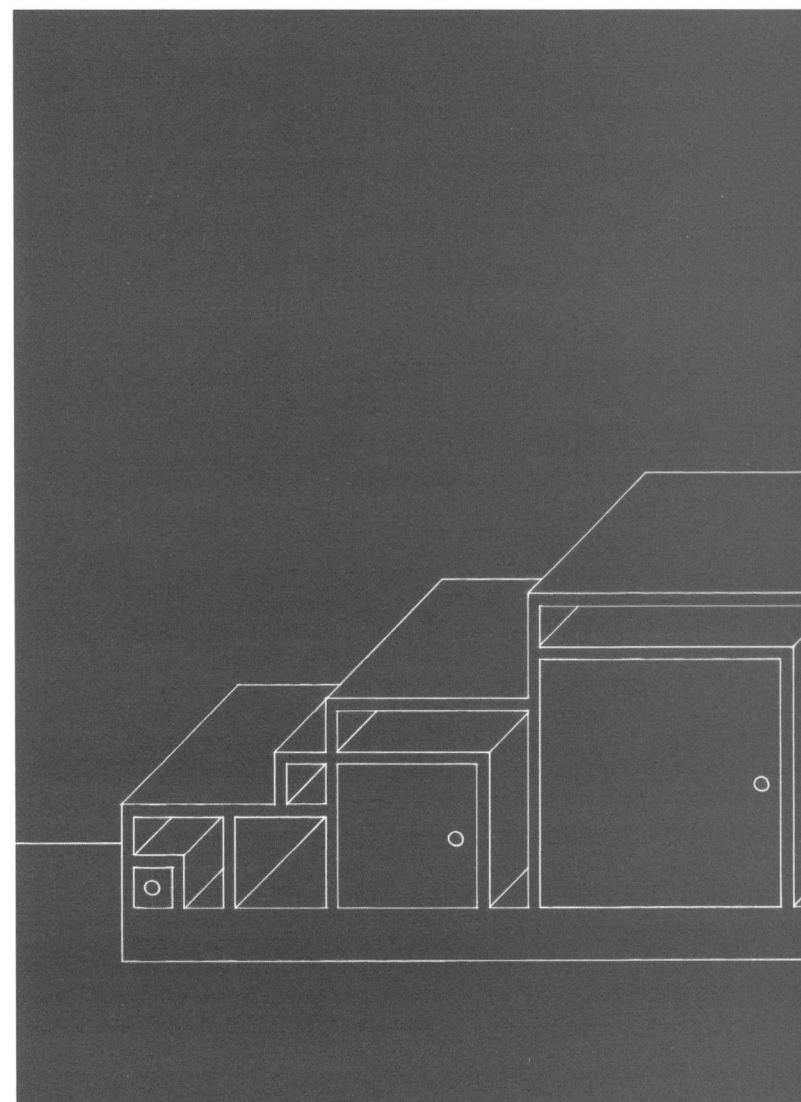

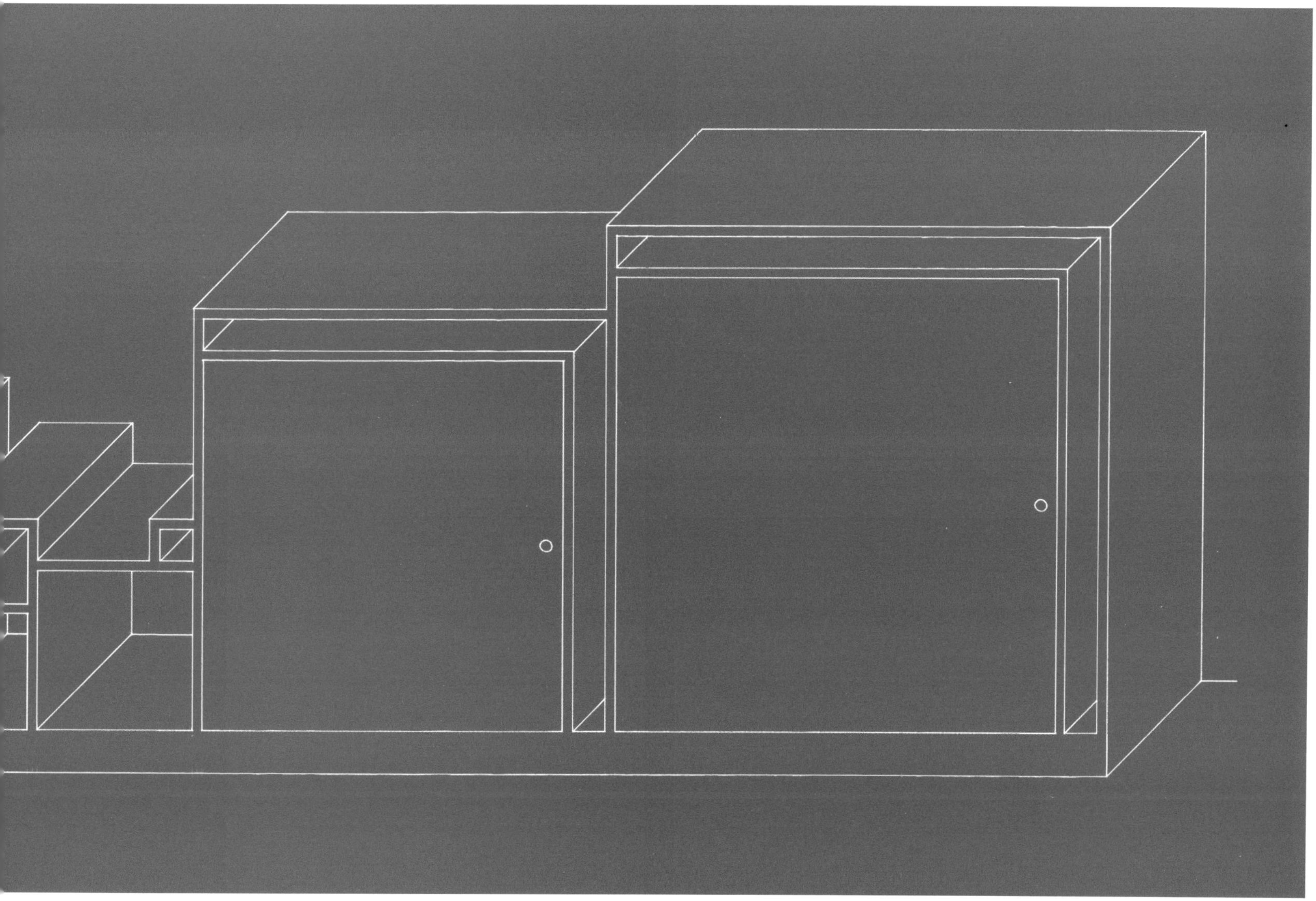

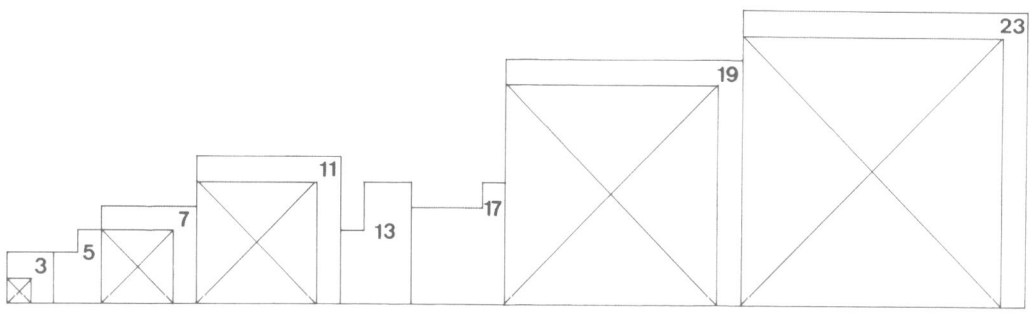

Spatial representation of 4n+1 primes as the sum of two squares and the 4n-1 primes as the difference between two squares

Two integers P and Q being prime to each other, their sum R will be prime to P and Q.

P, Q, R are a relatively prime triplet.

Working forwards, Q and R being prime to each other, their sum S will be prime to Q and R

Working backwards, P and Q being prime to each other, their difference N, as a positive integer, will be prime to P and Q.

And so on.

The sequence… N, P, Q, R, S… consists of terms such that… N + P = Q, P + Q = R, Q + R = S…

This is a sequence in which, for any three consecutive terms, the sum of the first two terms is the value of the third term.

The Fibonacci sequence is such a sequence.

Each object in this project is structured by the properties of a relatively prime triplet.

Objects i, ii, iii/II form a set of three objects of increasing size but similar arrangement.

Objects I, iii/II, III, IV, V form a set of five objects of the same size but different arrangement.

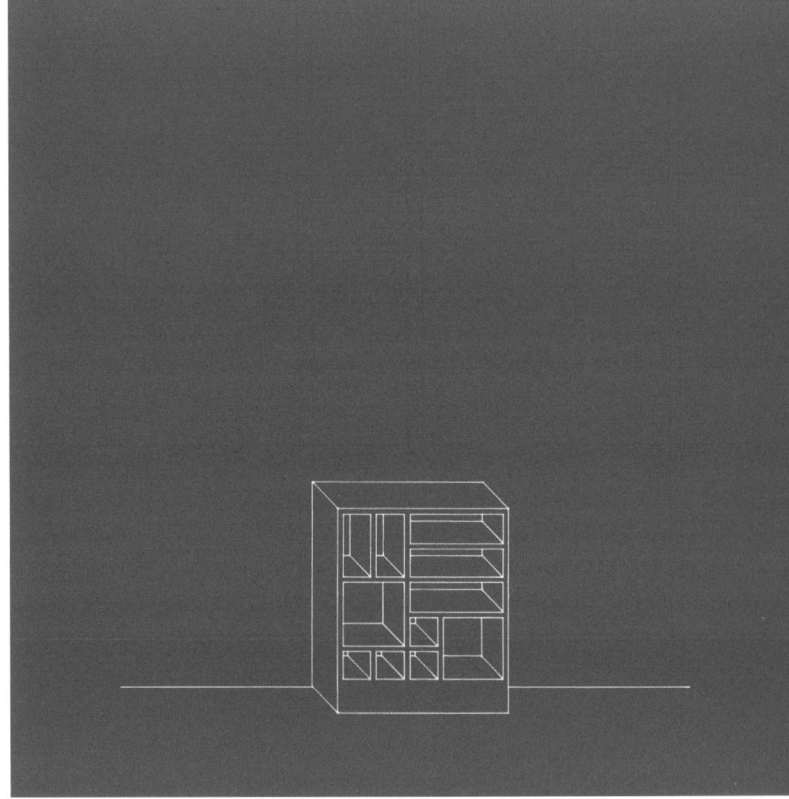

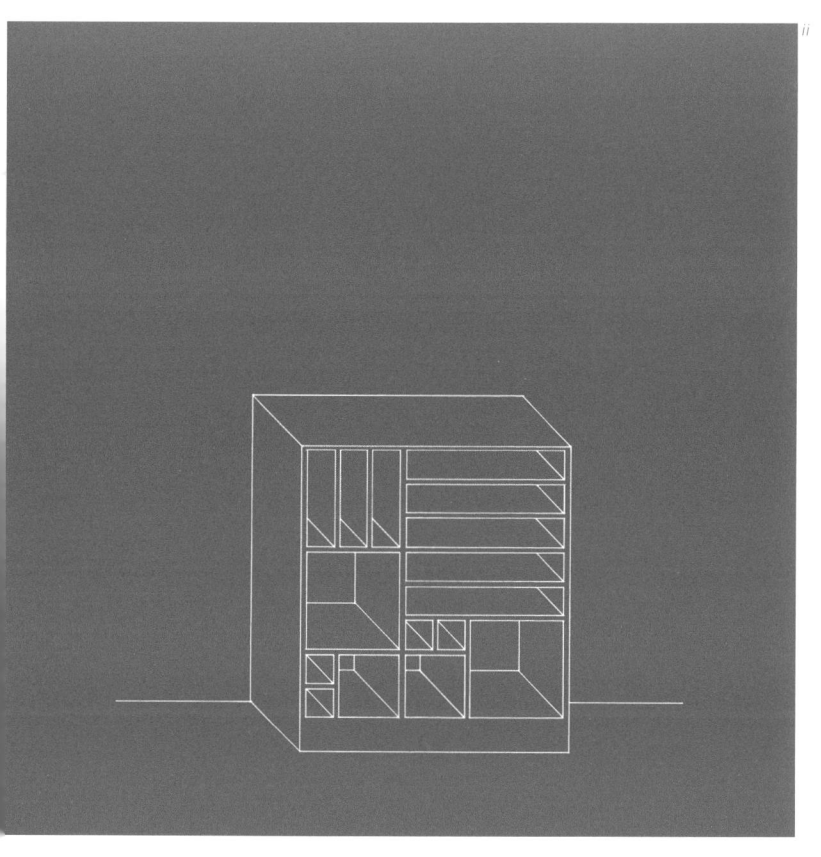
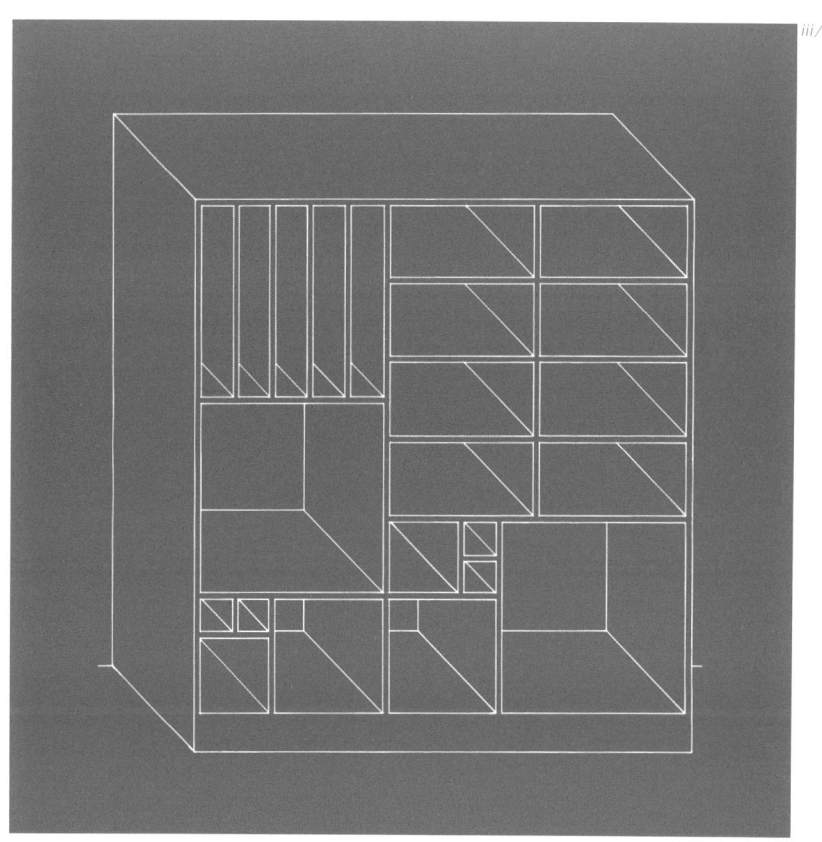

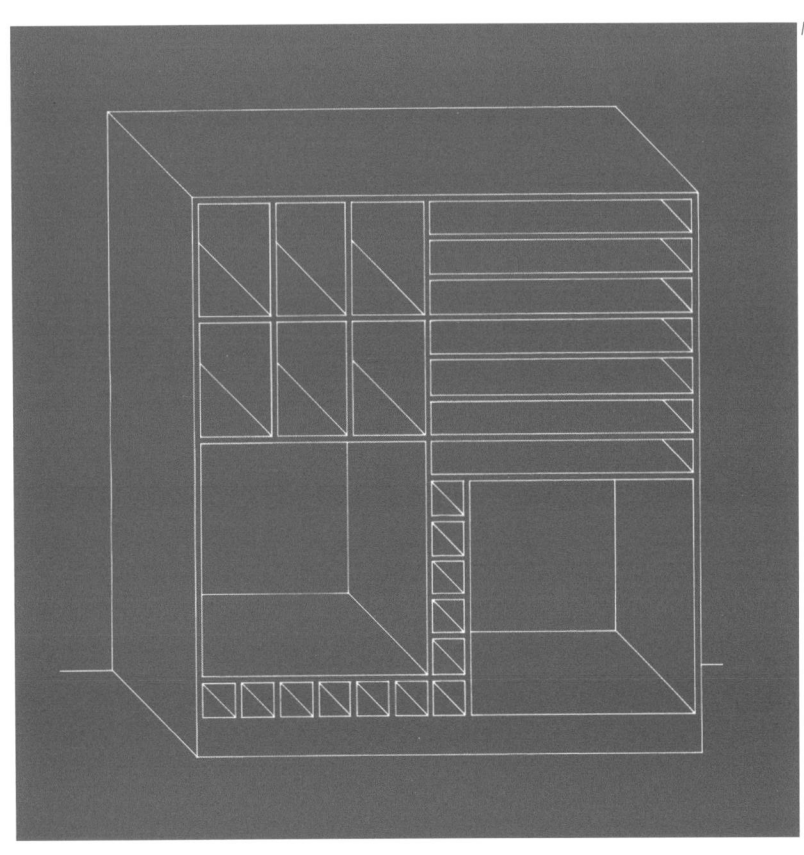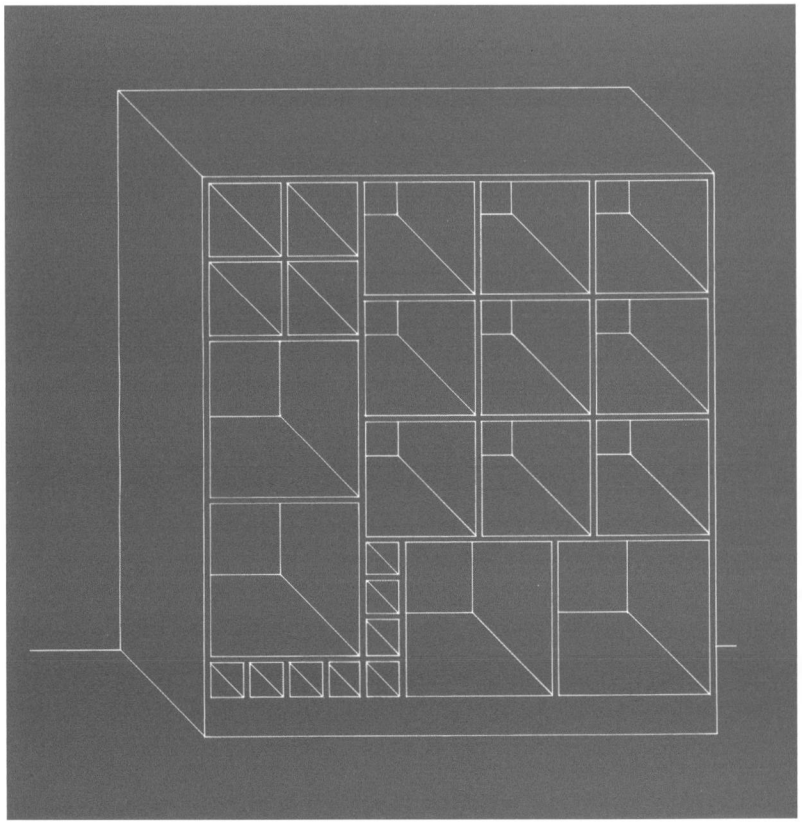

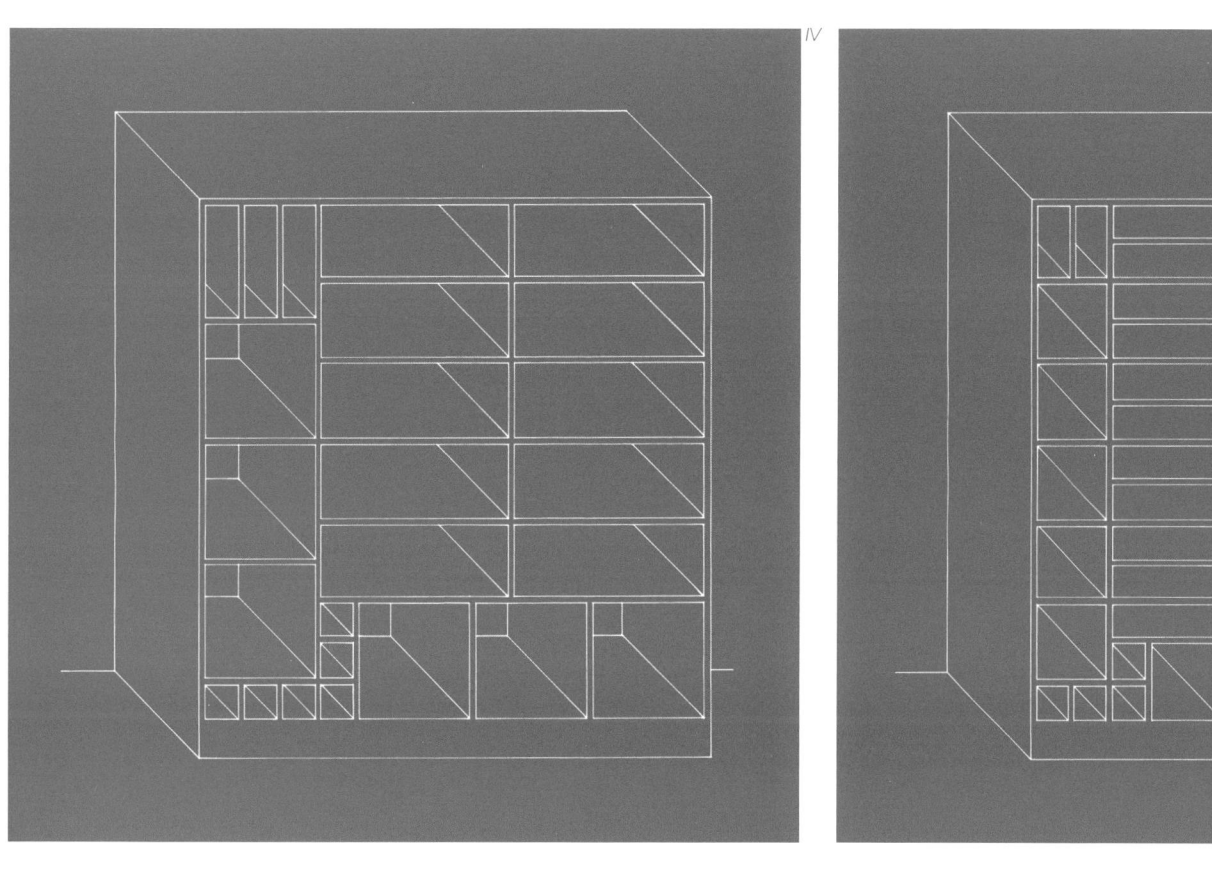
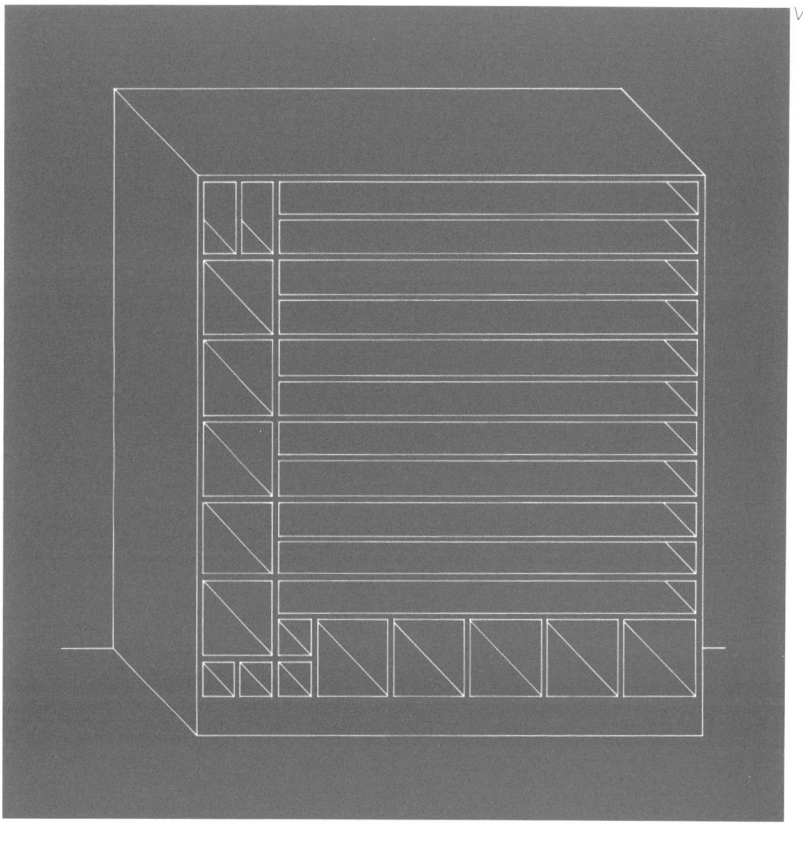

Two integers are prime to each other for
(i) any pair of successive natural numbers
(ii) any pair of successive odd numbers
(iii) any odd number d and any power of two 2^n
(iv) d and $(d + 2^n)$.

Each object in this project is structured by the properties of a relatively prime pair.

Objects i, ii, iii, iv represent the mathematical relations i, ii, iii, iv.

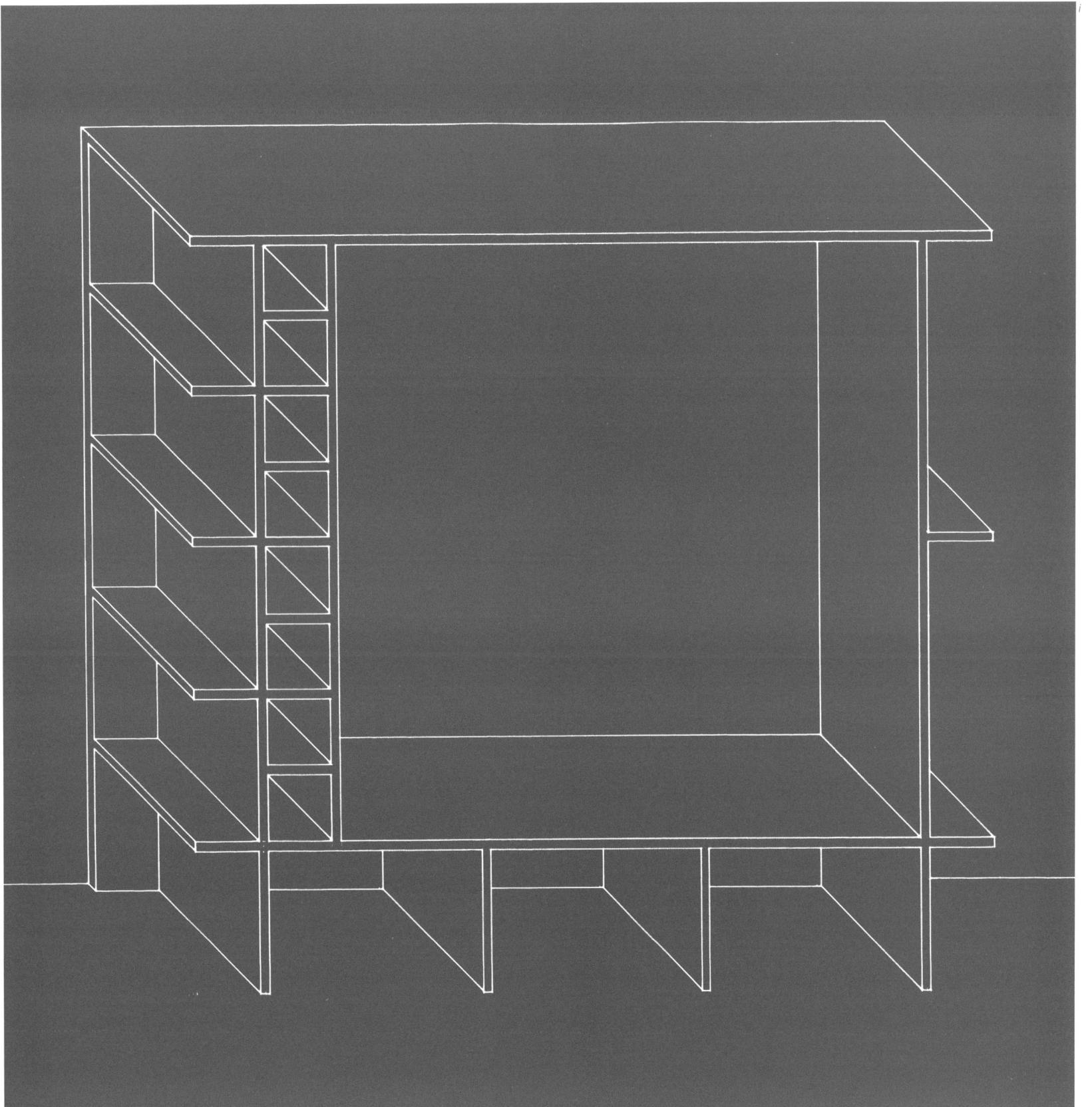

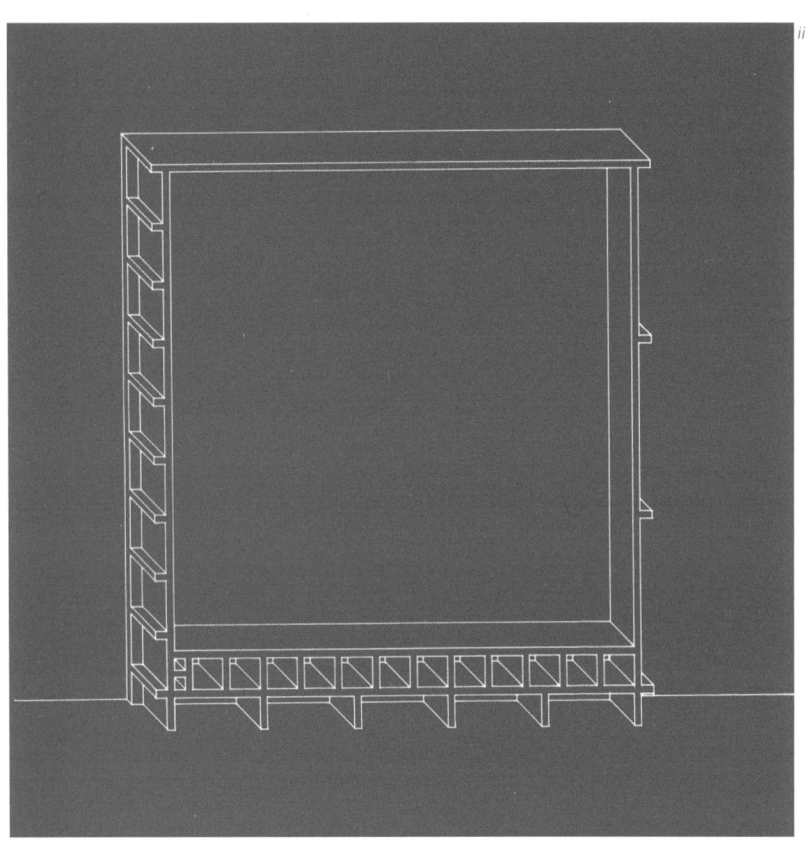

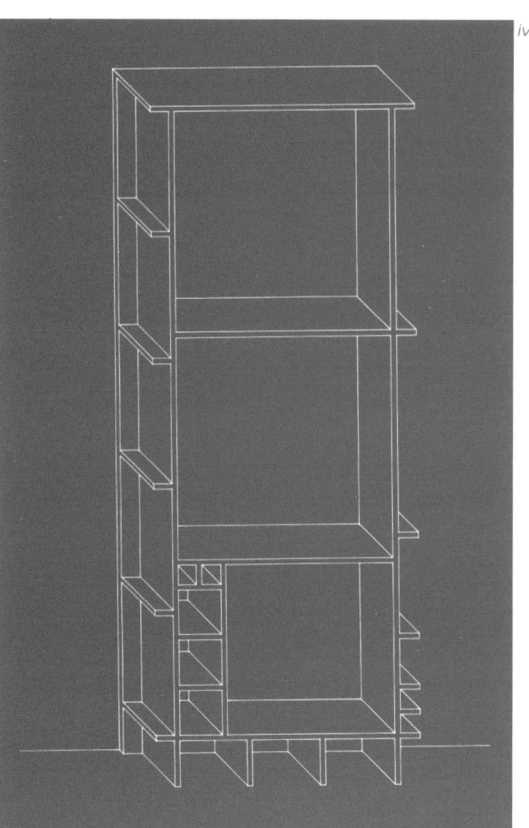

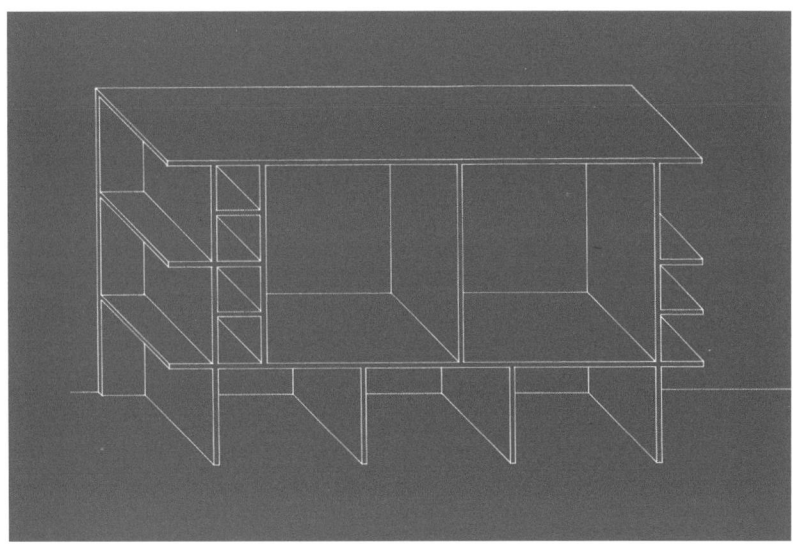

G16. MATHEMATICAL SQUARES

The square is a recurring figure in mathematical diversions.

'Spatialisation of the magic-square' develops the mathematical construction of the magic-square, in which numbers in an arithmetic progression are arranged in a square to give a meaningful mathematical structure.

'Rectangle of distinct squares and its other' develops the mathematical construction of squared rectangles, in which squares of different sizes are arranged to fill an overall rectangle.

Just as numbers can be represented by their shape—and this is the subject of the two groups of projects 'Natural, odd, triangular and square numbers' and 'Shaping numbers' —so numbers can also be represented by their extension or position in space—and this is the subject of the following two projects.

P40. Spatialisation of the magic-square

It is known that numbers in arithmetic progression can be arranged in the form of a square such that the horizontal, vertical and diagonal sums are the same.

The smallest magic-square arranges the numbers 1 to 9 in a 3x3 square.

Each number is represented by that geometrical square each side of which measures that number of units.

The nine squares are positioned and transferred by means of invented rules, and each square with non-prime sides will be articulated as rectangular pieces with integral sides, to give objects J and K.

Each square with non-prime sides articulated as rectangular pieces with integral sides will be separated, these pieces and the squares with prime sides are fitted within a larger square less a smaller square to give object M and within a rectangle to give object N.

For objects J, K, M, N, 1^2, 2^2, 3^2, 5^2, 7^2 are expressed as shelves and the rectangular pieces are expressed as drawers.

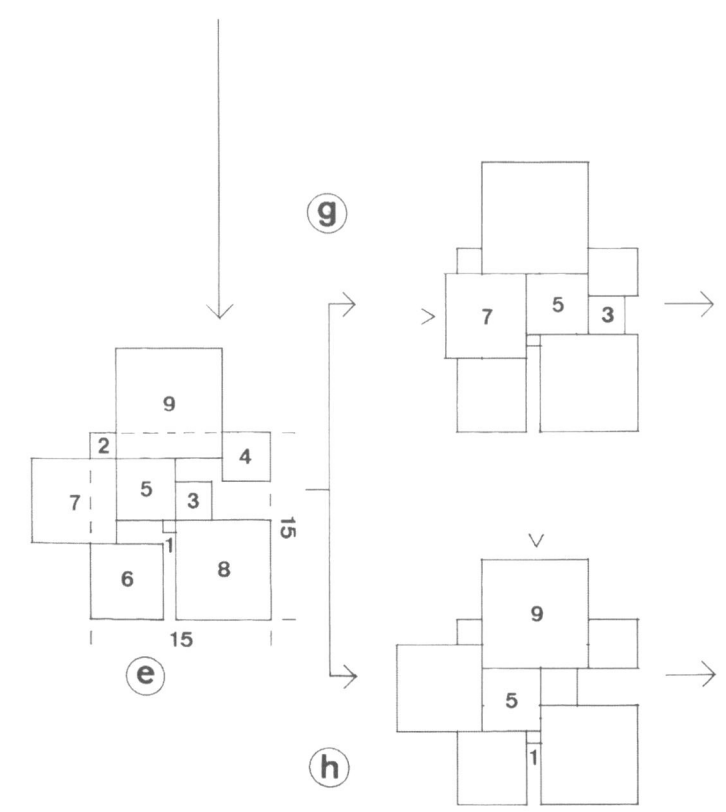

15-4

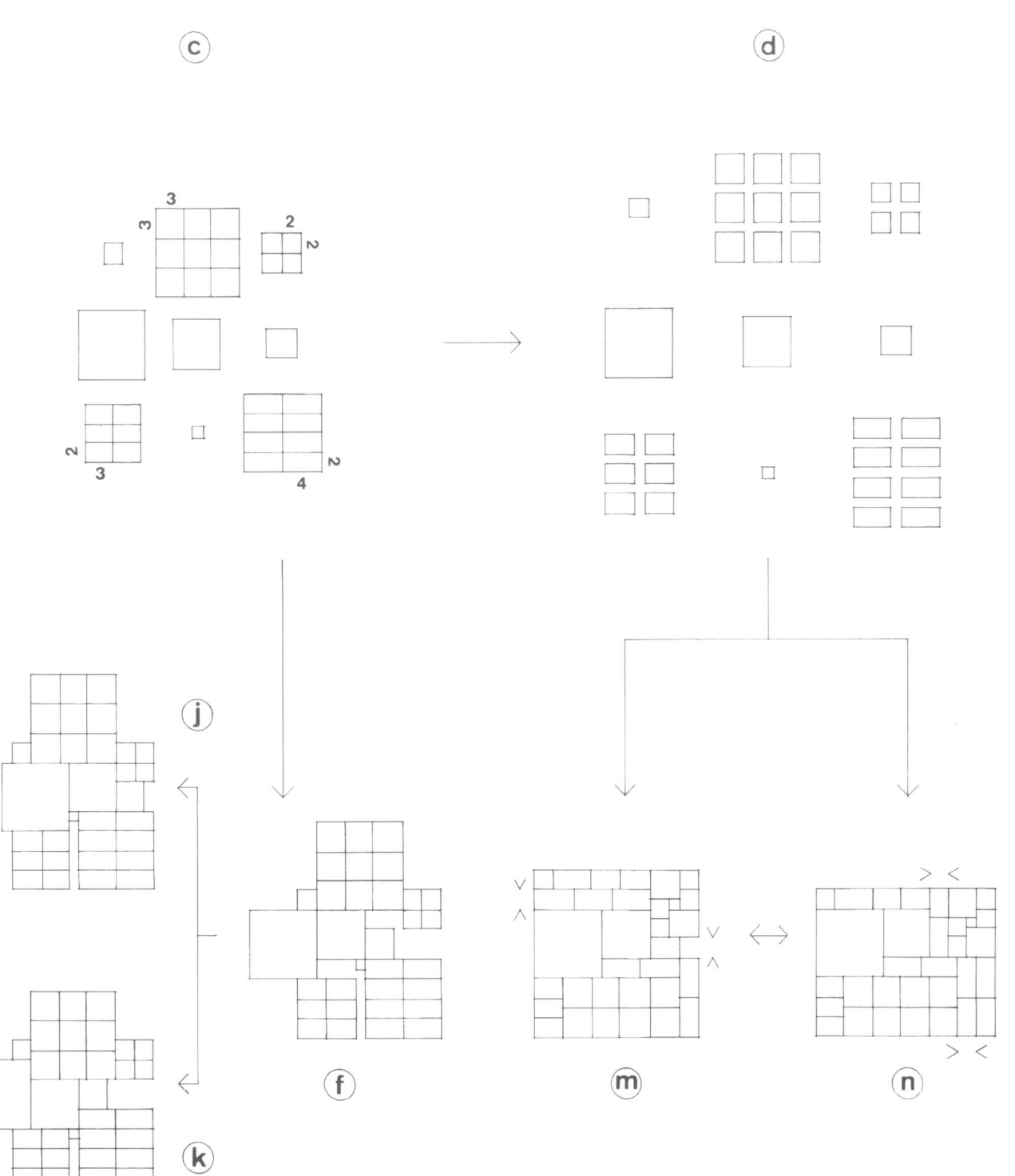

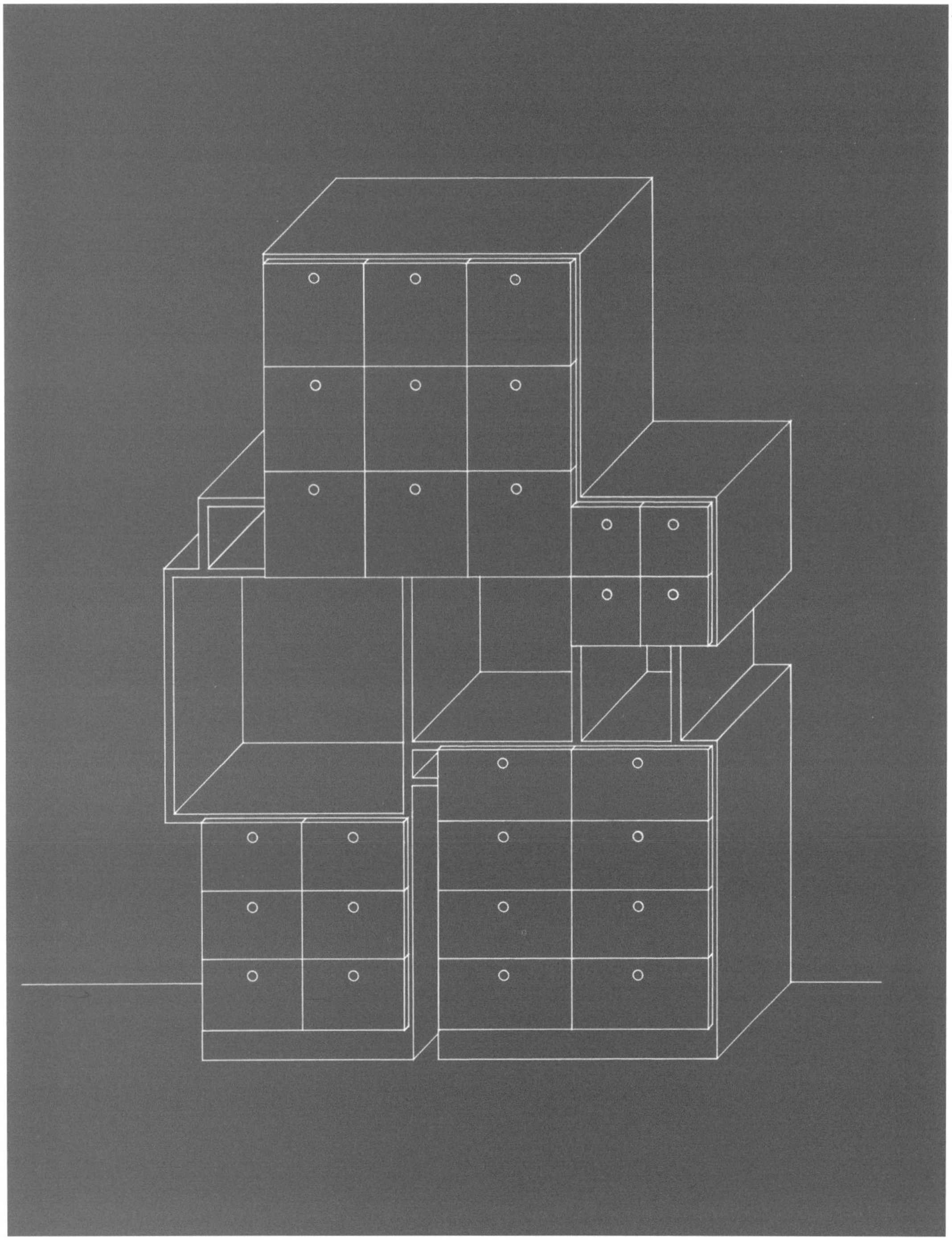

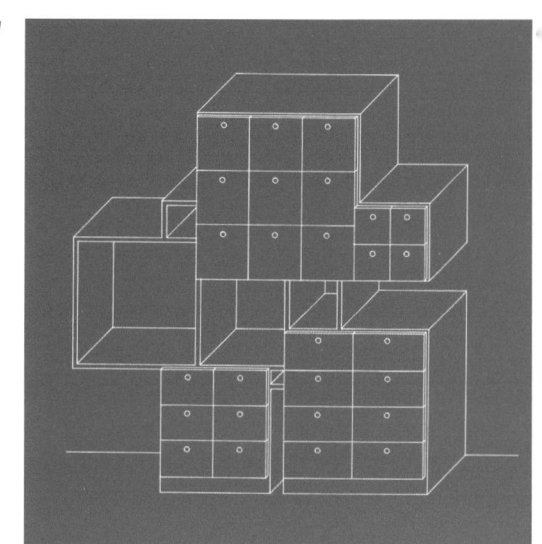

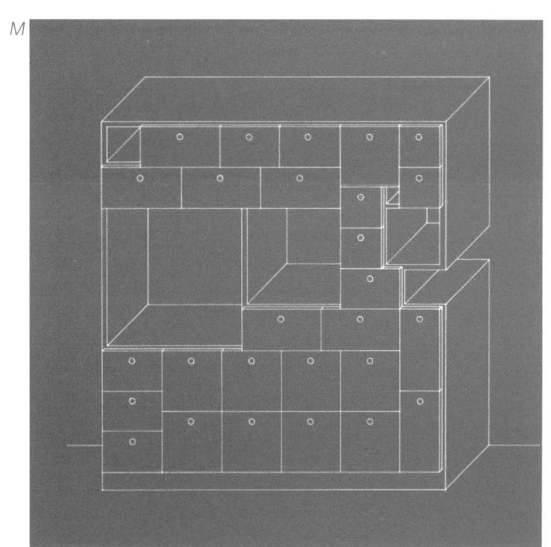

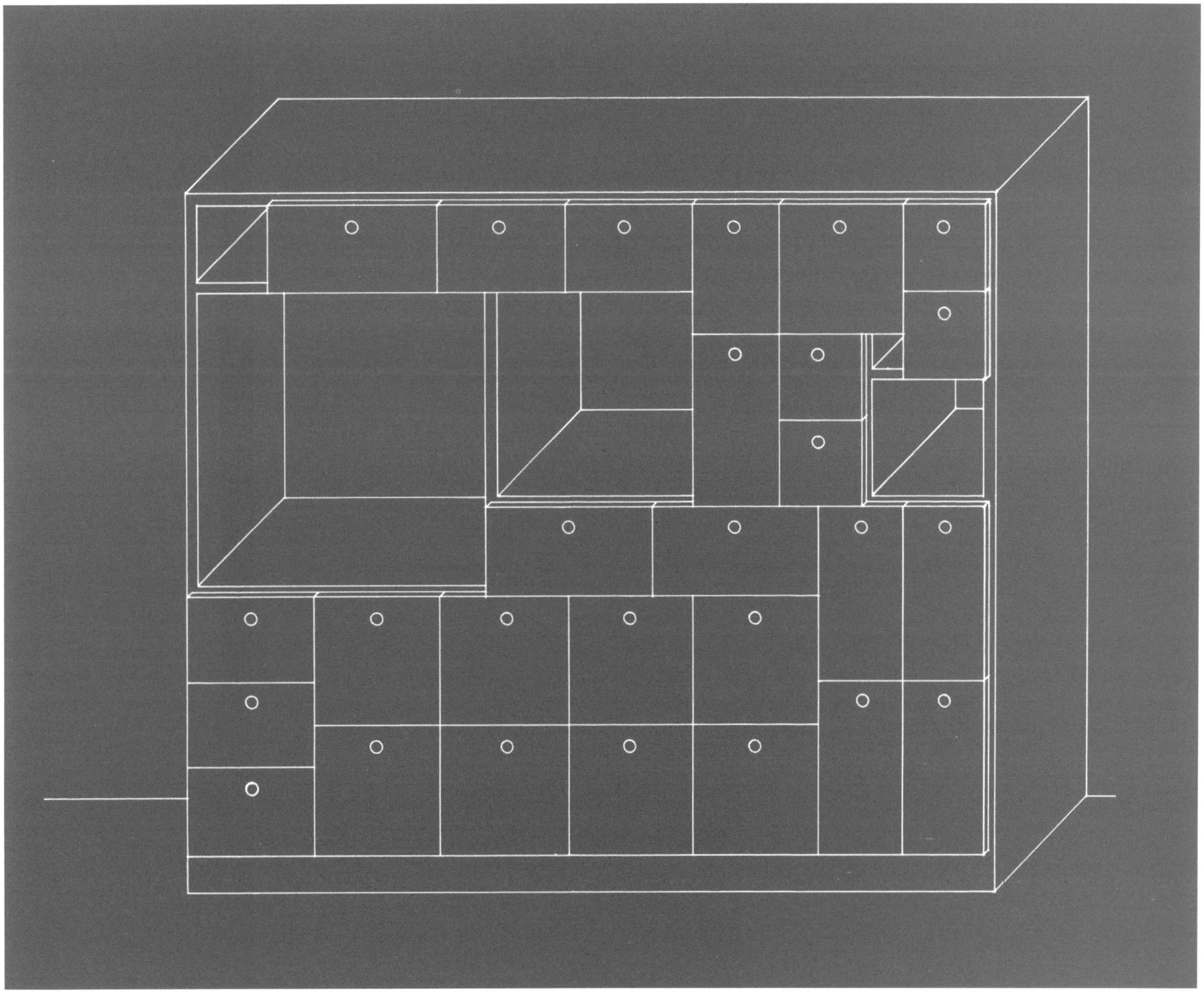

It is known that distinct squares can be fitted within a rectangle.

The smallest possibility consists of the squares of 1, 4, 7, 8, 9, 10, 14, 15, 18 fitted within a rectangle measuring 32x33.

It is found that the squares of the remaining integers between 1 and 18, that is the squares of 2, 3, 5, 6, 11, 12, 13, 16, 17, can be fitted within a rectangle measuring 27x39 given that each square with non-prime sides is separated into rectangular pieces with integral sides.

Similarly, let each square with non-prime sides within the rectangle measuring 32x33 be articulated as rectangular pieces with integral sides.

Then for object B, within the 32x33 rectangle, 1^2 and 7^2 are expressed as shelves and the rectangular pieces are expressed as drawers.

And for object F, within the 27x39 rectangle, 2^2, 3^2, 5^2, 11^2, 13^2, 17^2 are expressed as shelves and the rectangular pieces are expressed as drawers.

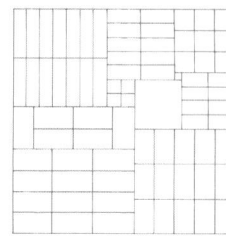

Diagram showing the design process from the simplest squared rectangles (a) to the final form (b) for the object B

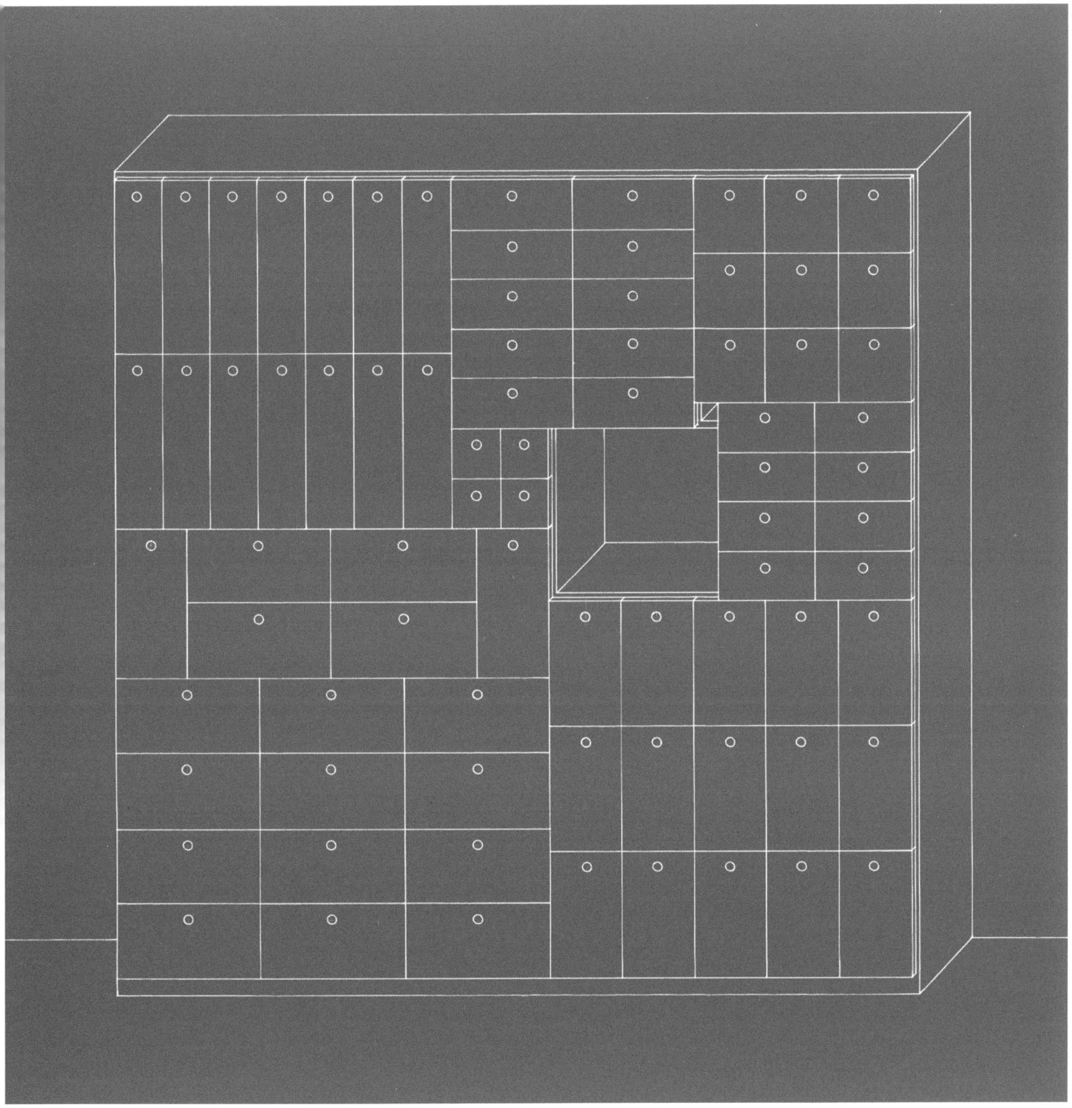

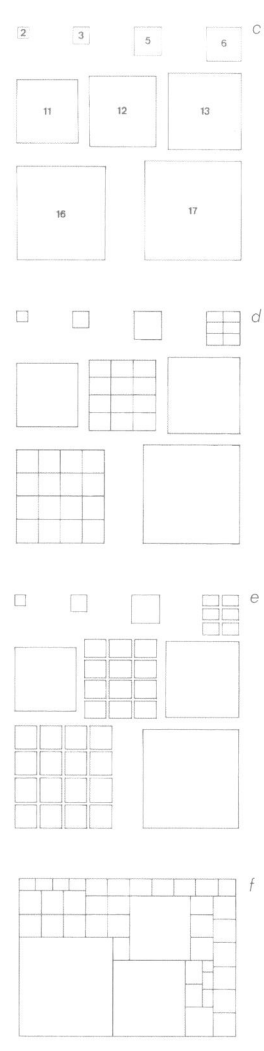

Diagram showing the design
process from (c), which
consists of those squares
unused in (a), to the final form
(f) for object F

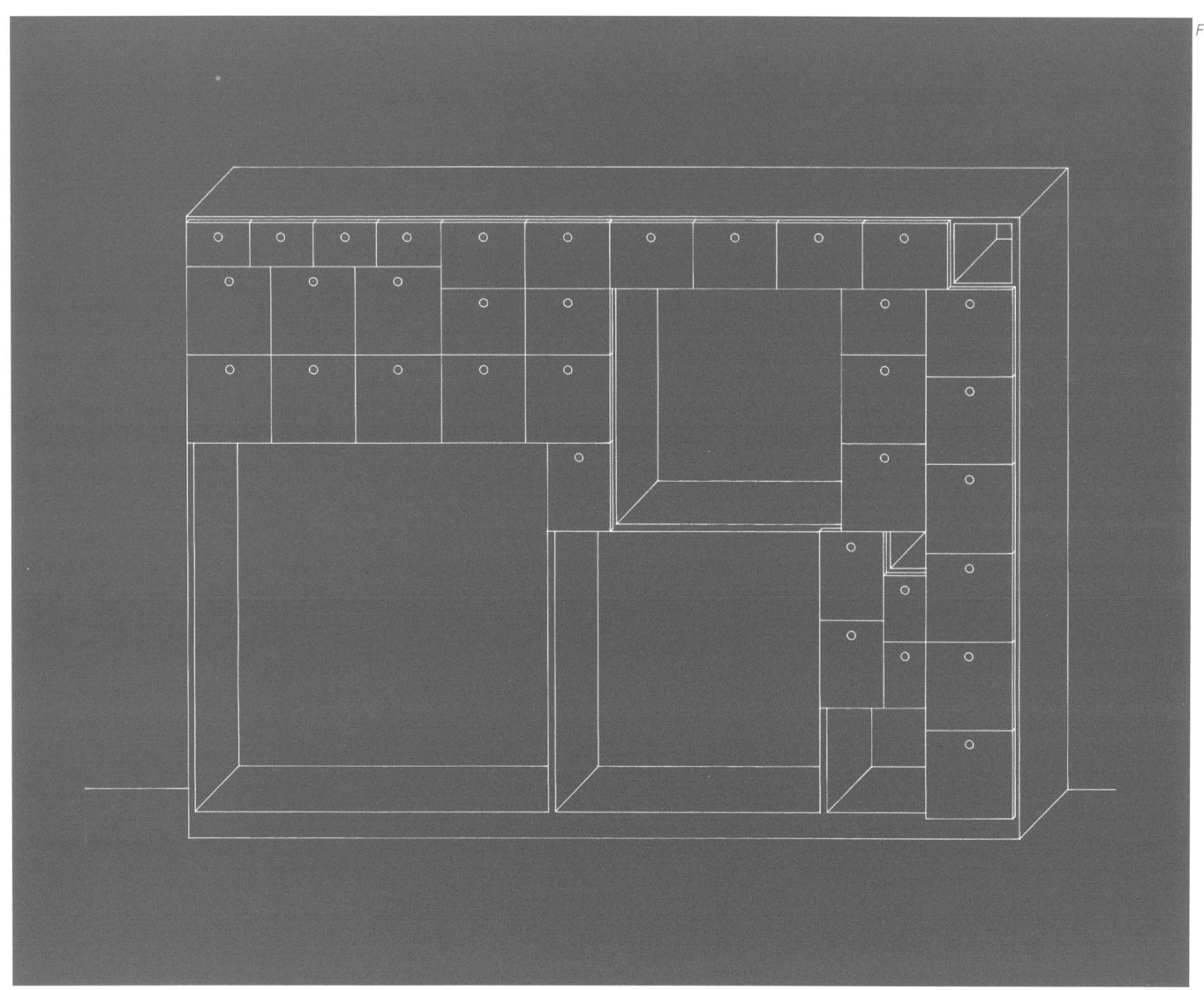

F

G17. SHAPING NUMBERS

Each type of number can be represented by its own shape, and each number within a type of number will be represented by its own size of that shape.

Every number is represented by its shape and size, the area of which in units is that represented number.

In these projects, numerical relations, translated into combinations of shapes, are used to make the form of cabinets.

Using natural, odd, triangular and square numbers as material, putting these types of number in certain mathematical relations, spatialising numbers by their shape and size, and further distinguishing different types of number by means of shelves and drawers, then two sets of objects are invented.

For each object in the pair of objects Y and ZA, the number of shelves is equal to the number of drawers.

For each object in the set of thirteen objects ZA to N, the total frontal area of shelves will be the same as the total frontal area of drawers.

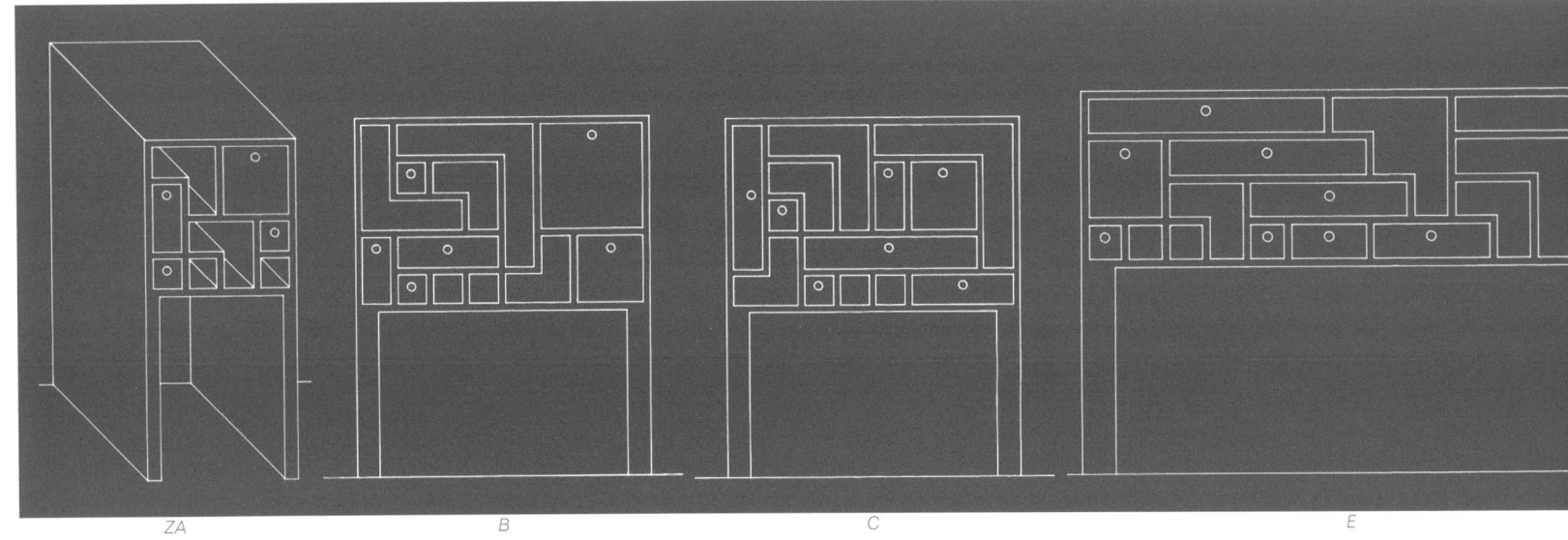

ZA   B   C   E

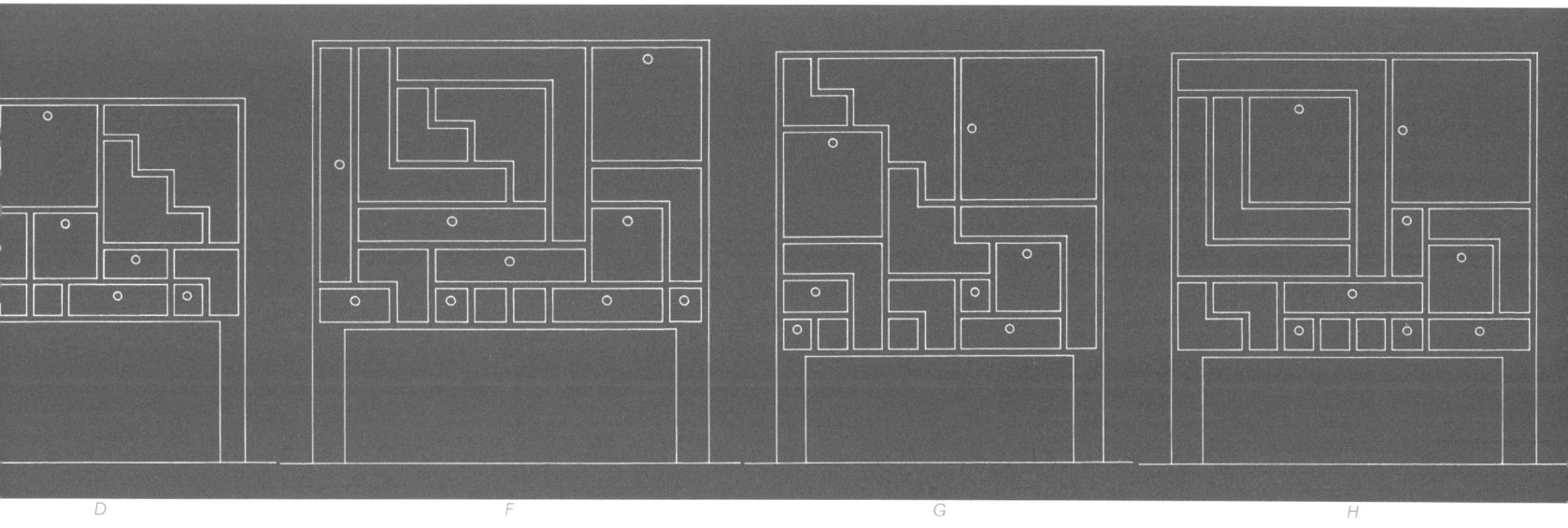

D   F   G   H

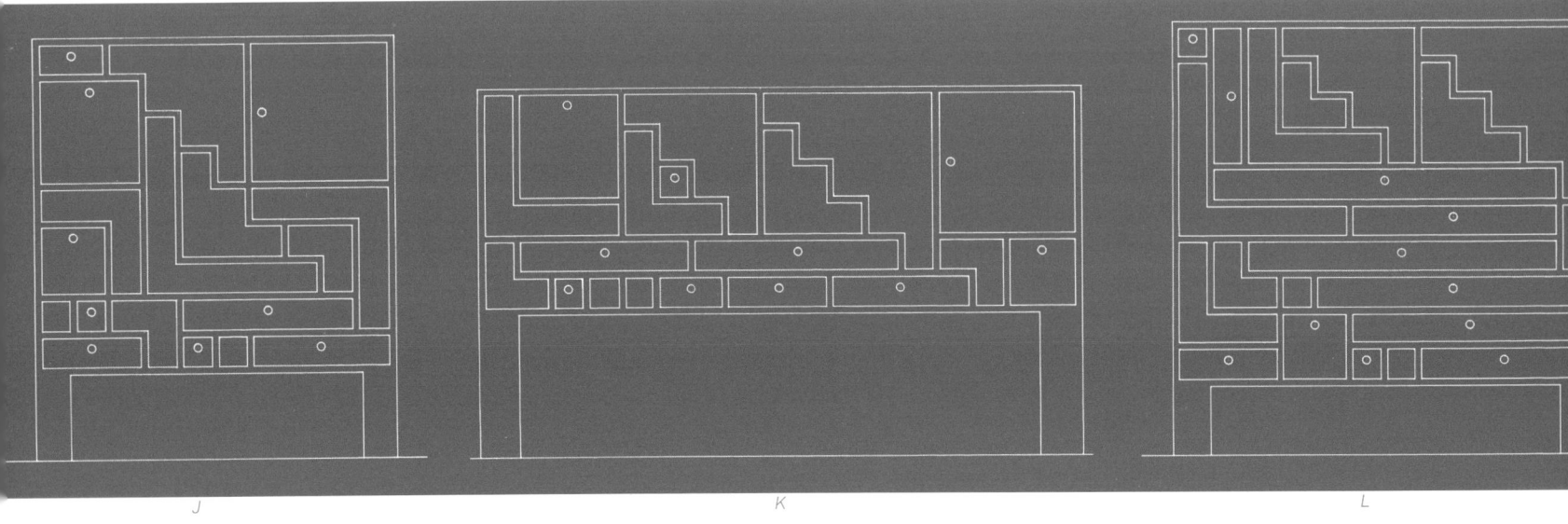

J   K   L

16-4

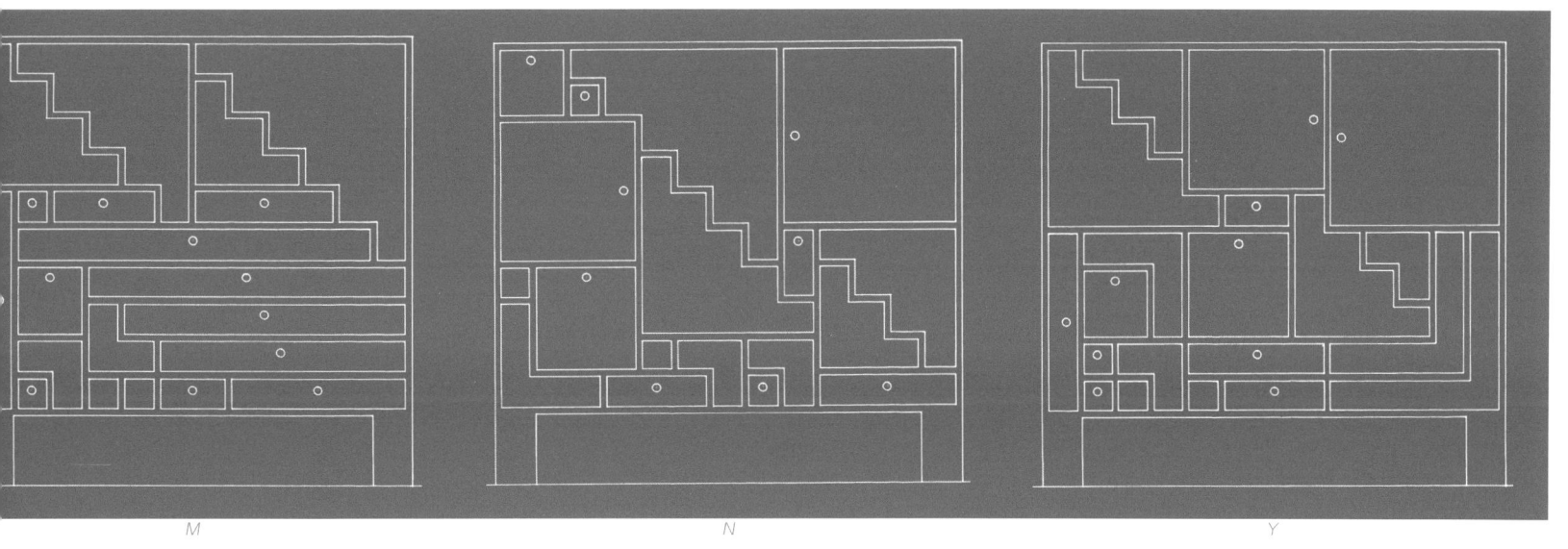

M   N   Y

P43. The shape of numbers

Each number can be represented by its unique combination of shape and size, by its unique figure.

The figures which represent the first terms of a number sequence are arranged to fill that figure which represents the sum of these first terms.

The number sequences used are
(a) the sequence of natural numbers N
(b) the sequence of odd numbers O
(c) the Fibonacci sequence where $F_n + F_{n+1} = F_{n+2}$
(d) the sequence where $G_n + G_{n+1} = G_{n+3}$
(e) the sequence where $H_n + H_{n+2} = H_{n+3}$
(f) the sequence where $I_n + I_{n+1} + I_{n+2} = I_{n+3}$.

Each object arranges the shapes of the first terms of a number sequence to fit the shape of their sum.

(1) Object Nr arranges the shapes of the first seven natural numbers to fill the shape of their sum 28.

Likewise, using the shape of numbers,
(2) Ns fits the first eight natural numbers into their sum 36
(3) Nt fits the first ten natural numbers into their sum 55
(4) Or fits the first three odd numbers into their sum 9
(5) Os fits the first four odd numbers into their sum 16
(6) Ot fits the first five odd numbers into their sum 25
(7) Fr fits the first four Fibonacci terms into their sum 11
(8) Fs fits the first five Fibonacci terms into their sum 19
(9) Ft fits the first six Fibonacci terms into their sum 32
(10) Gr fits the first four terms of G into their sum 9
(11) Gs fits the first six terms of G into their sum 20
(12) Gt fits the first eight terms of G into their sum 39
(13) Hr fits the first five terms of H into their sum 16
(14) Hs fits the first six terms of H into their sum 25
(15) Ht fits the first ten terms of H into their sum 126
(16) Ir fits the first four terms of I into their sum 12
(17) Is fits the first five terms of I into their sum 23
(18) It fits the first six terms of I into their sum 43.

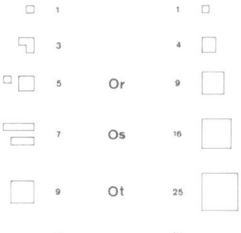

Diagram showing the shape of odd numbers O, and the shape of the sum EO of the first terms of O

O		EO	
□	1	1	□
	3	4	□
	5	Or	9 □
	7	Os	16 □
	9	Ot	25 □
	...		...

Nr

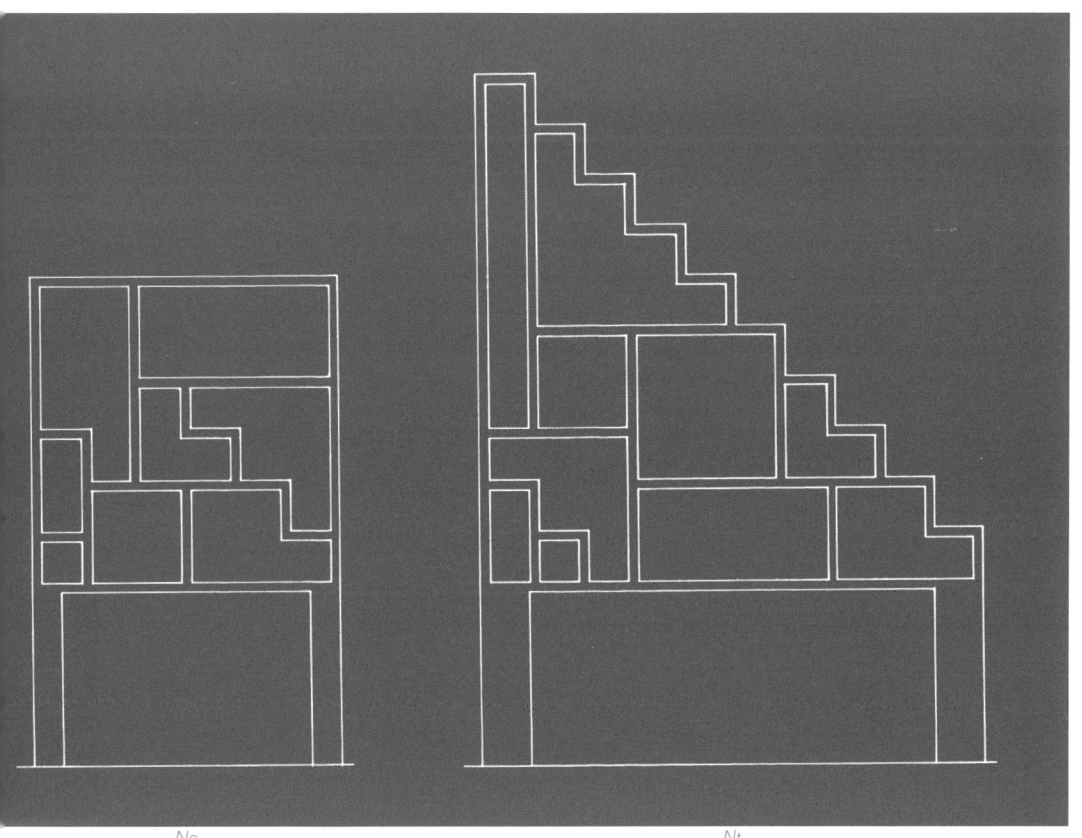

Or

Os

Ot

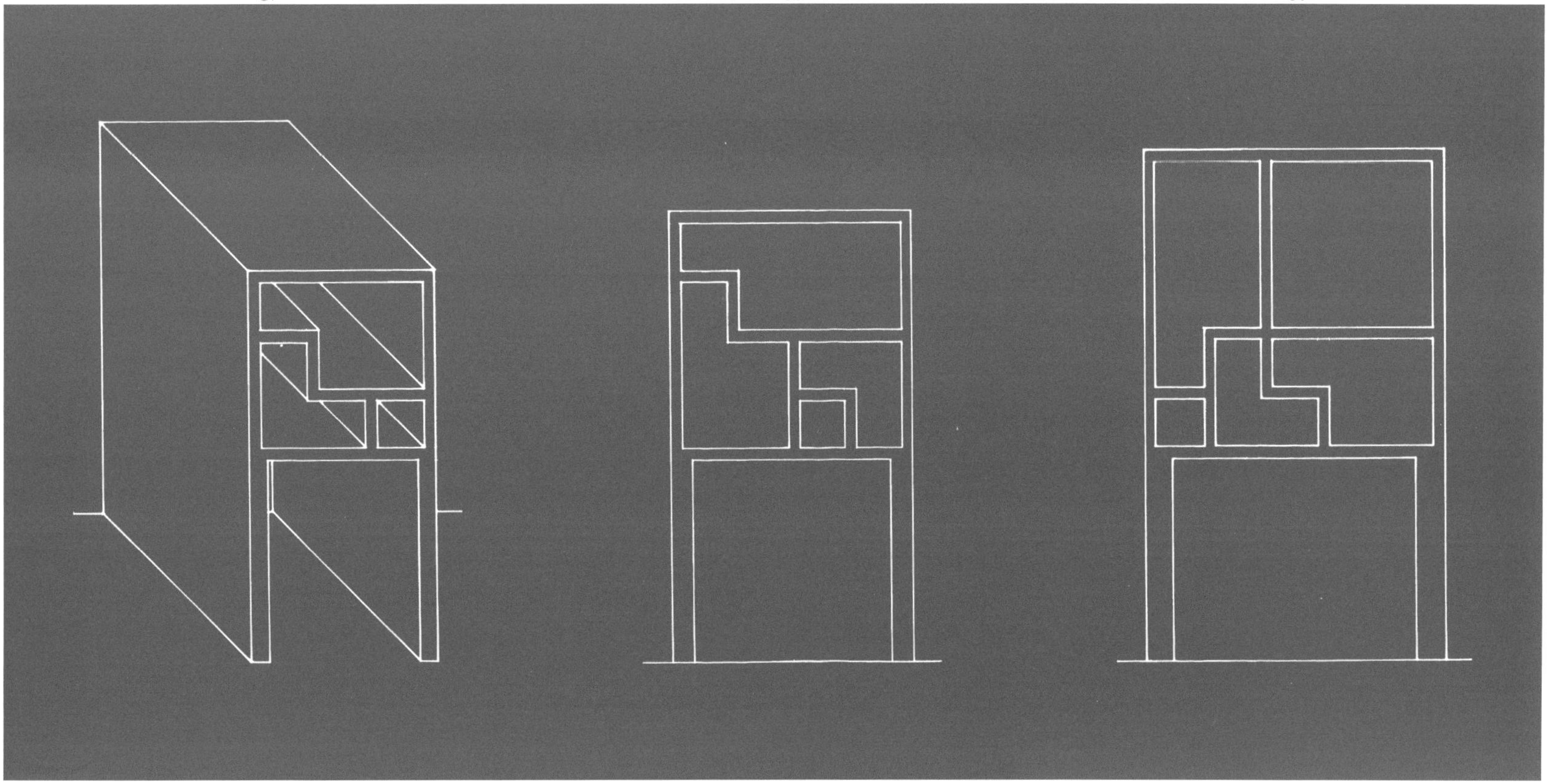

Ns

Nt

Diagram showing the shape
of natural numbers N, and the
shape of the sum EN of the
first terms of N

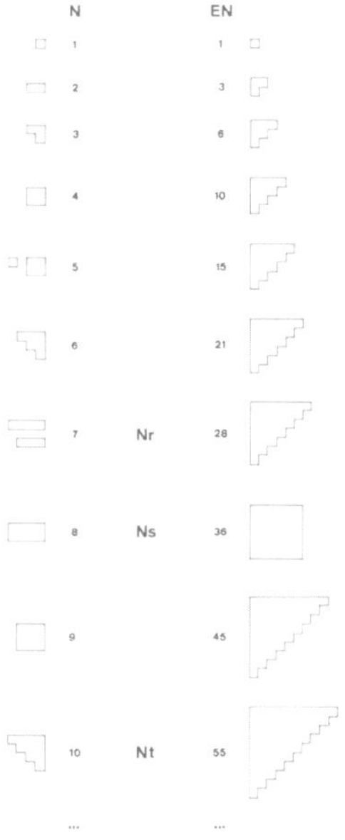

	N		EN
	1		1
	2		3
	3		6
	4		10
	5		15
	6		21
	7	Nr	28
	8	Ns	36
	9		45
	10	Nt	55
	...		...

167

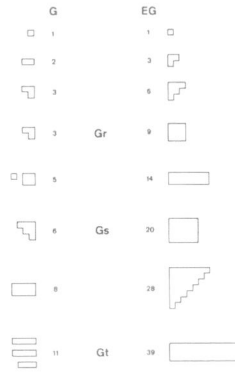

Diagram showing the shape
of terms G in the sequence
where $G_n + G_{n+1} = G_{n+3}$,
and the sum EG of the first
terms of G

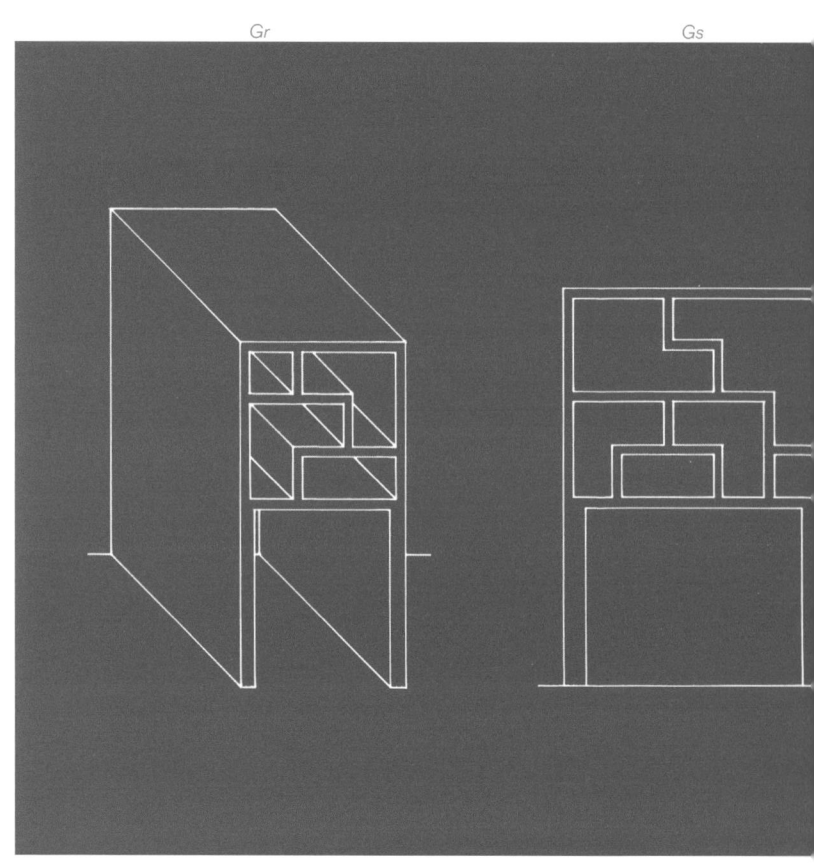

Gr

Gs

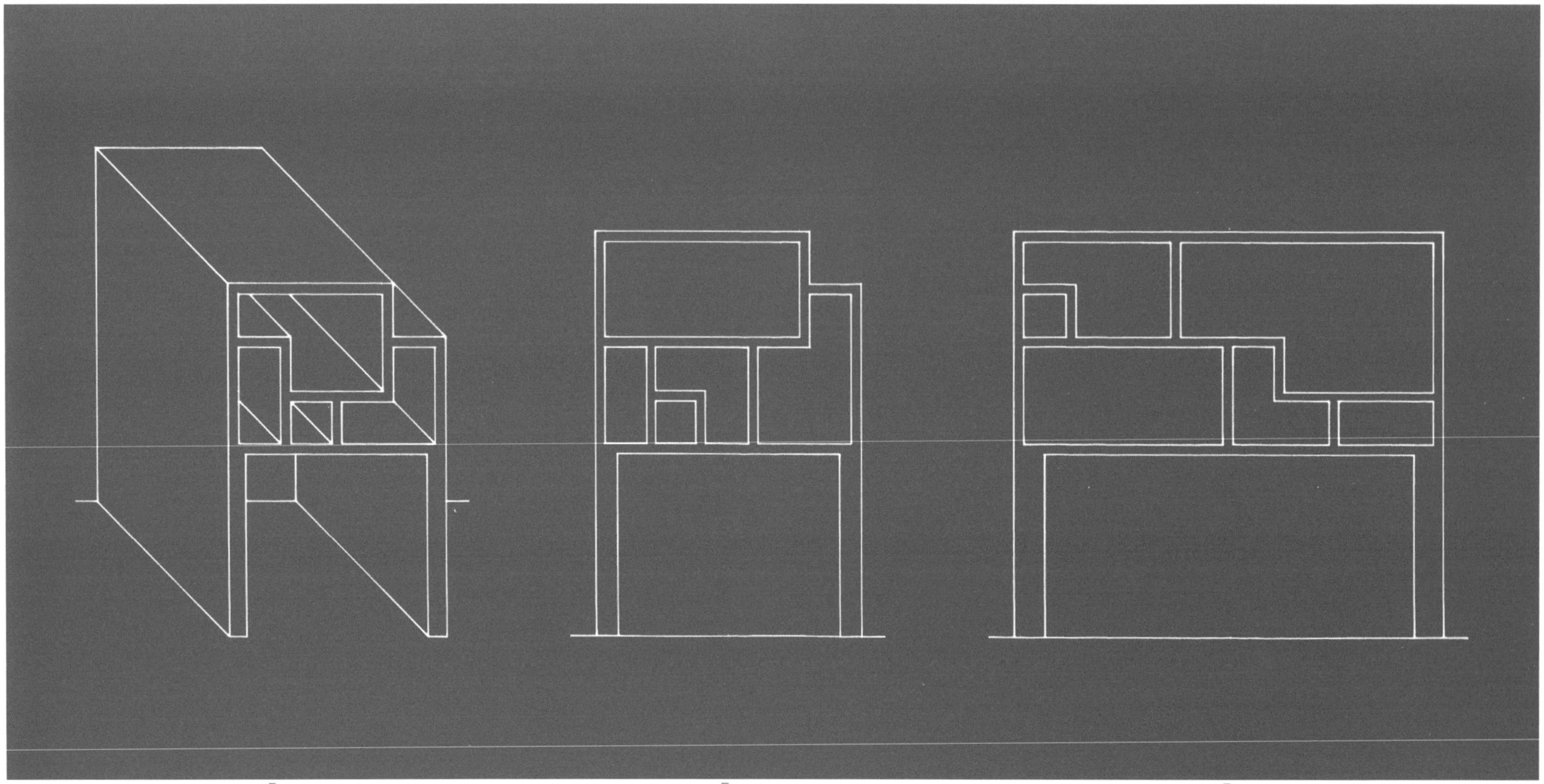

Fr

Fs

Ft

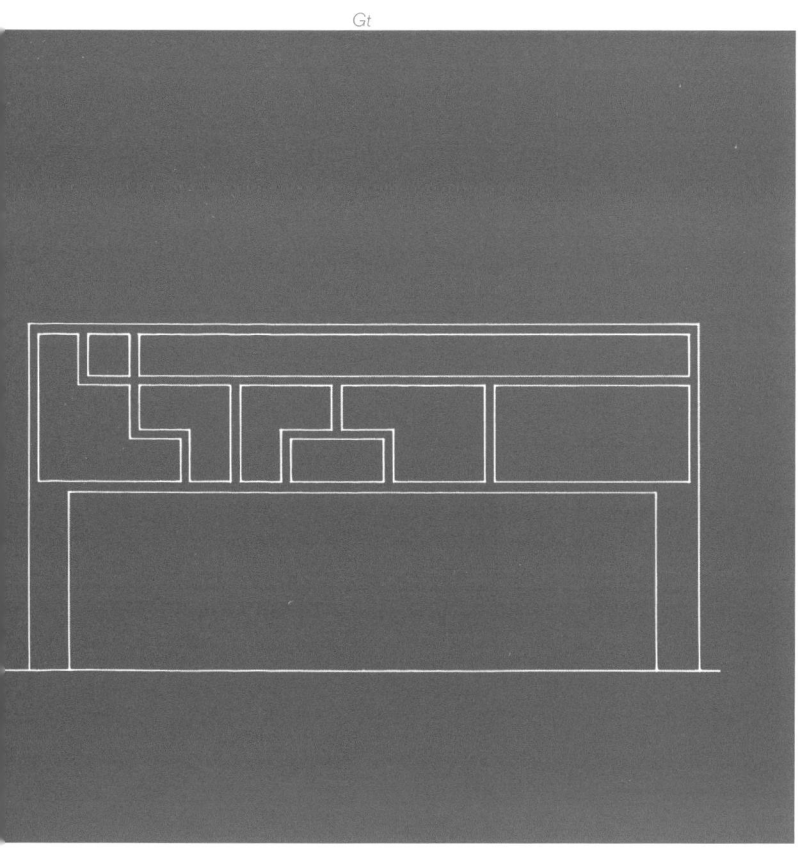

Diagram showing the shape
of Fibonacci terms F, and the
shape of the sum EF of the
first terms of F

Diagram showing the shape of terms H in the sequence where $H_n + H_{n+2} = H_{n+3}$, and the sum EH of the first terms of H

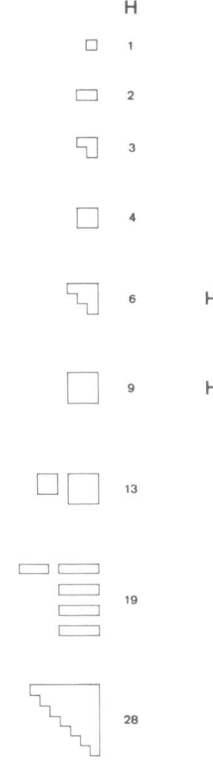

H

1

2

3

4

6   Hr

9   Hs

13

19

28

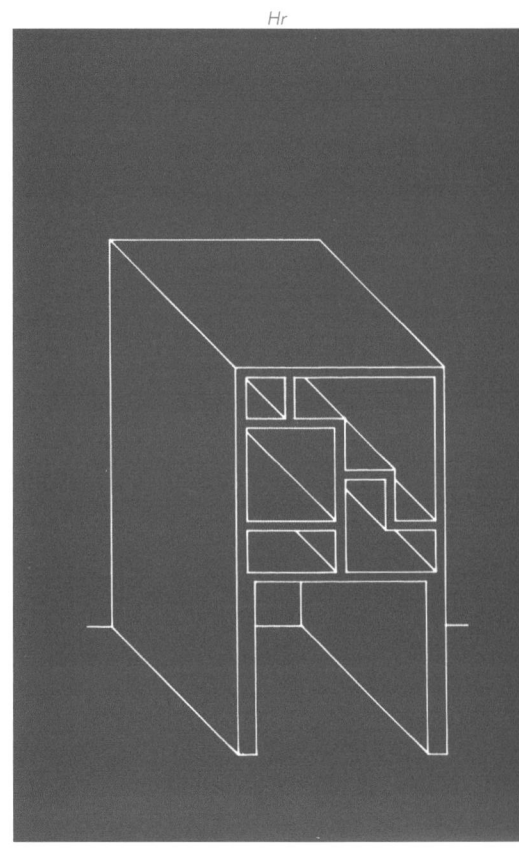

Diagram showing the shape of terms I in the sequence where $I_n + I_{n+1} + I_{n+2} = I_{n+3}$, and the sum EI of the first terms of I

I		EI	
1		1	
2		3	
3		6	
6	Ir	12	
11	Is	23	
20	It	43	
…		…	

Hs

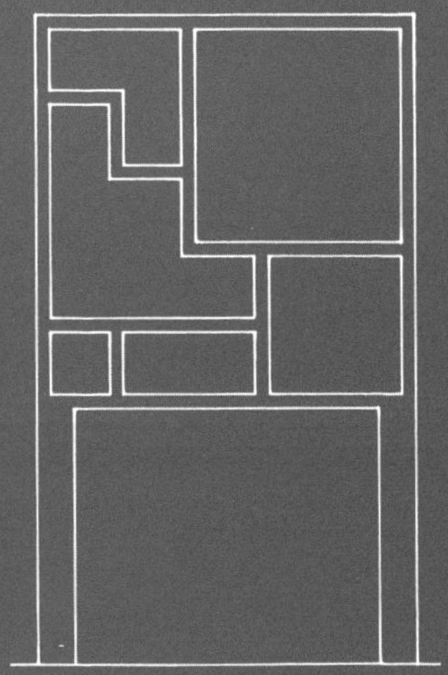

Ht

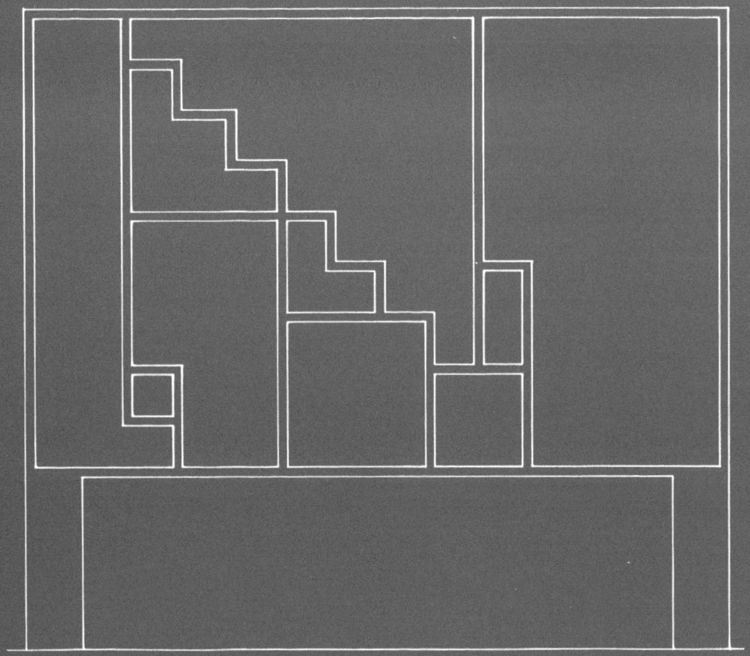

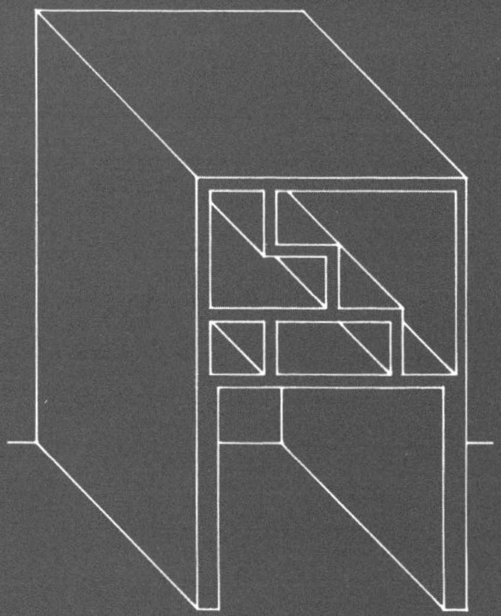

Ir

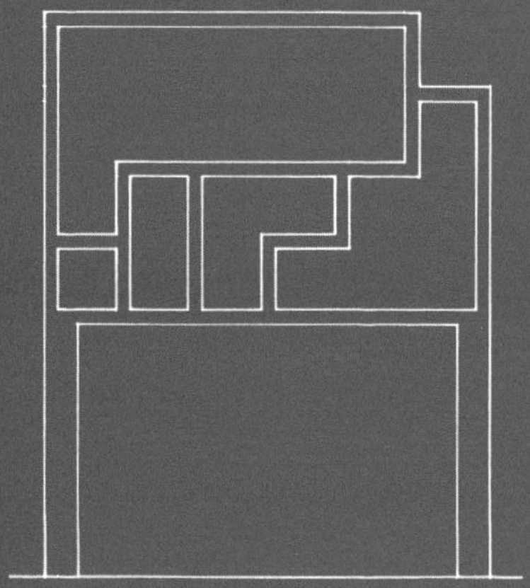

Is

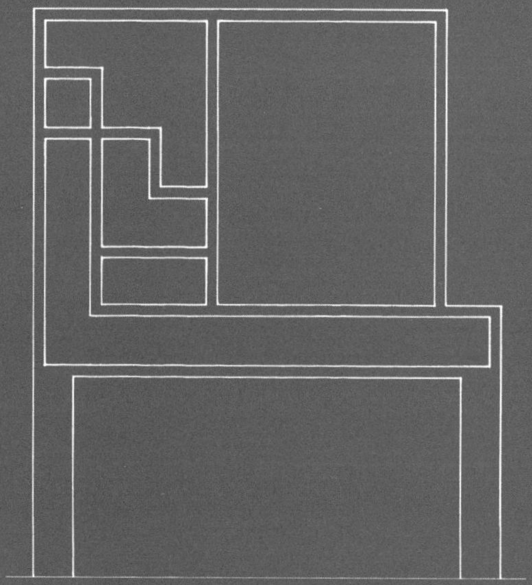

It

P44. Picking out types of number

From one number n to its double 2n
(a) there is always at least one prime P between n and 2n where n is 2 or greater
(b) there is always at least one square number S between n and 2n where n is 5 or greater
(c) there is always at least one triangular number T between n and 2n where n is 4 or greater.

From one square number S_n to its successor S_{n+1}
(d) there is always at least one prime P between S_n and S_{n+1}.
(e) there is always at least one triangular number T between S_n and S_{n+1}.

From one triangular number T_n to its successor T_{n+1}
(f) there is always at least one prime P between T_n and T_{n+1}.

Each object in this project expresses the fact that within a certain range of numbers there is always present a certain type of number.

To express this idea, each number is represented by its unique combination of shape and size, by its unique figure, and the figures which represent all the numbers within a range of numbers are arranged to fill that figure which represents the sum of all the numbers within this range, and the figures representing the numbers of that type which is always present within the range are picked out as drawers while the figures representing the remaining numbers are shelves.

(1) Object NP1 uses the range of numbers from one number to its double, 5 to 10, within which the prime number 7 is picked out.

Likewise, using n to 2n to pick out prime numbers,
(2) NP2 uses 6 to 12 to pick out 7 and 11
(3) NP3 uses 7 to 14 to pick out 11 and 13.

Using n to 2n to pick out square numbers,
(4) NS1 uses 5 to 10 to pick out 9
(5) NS2 uses 6 to 12 to pick out 9
(6) NS3 uses 7 to 14 to pick out 9.

Using n to 2n to pick out triangular numbers,
(7) NT1 uses 5 to 10 to pick out 6
(8) NT2 uses 6 to 12 to pick out 10
(9) NT3 uses 7 to 14 to pick out 10.

Using S_n to S_{n+1} to pick out prime numbers,
(10) SP1 uses 1 to 4 to pick out 2
(11) SP2 uses 4 to 9 to pick out 5 and 7
(12) SP3 uses 9 to 16 to pick out 11 and 13.

Using S_n to S_{n+1} to pick out triangular numbers,
(13) ST1 uses 1 to 4 to pick out 3
(14) ST2 uses 4 to 9 to pick out 6
(15) ST3 uses 9 to 16 to pick out 10 and 15.

Using T_n to T_{n+1} to pick out prime numbers
(16) TP1 uses 1 to 3 to pick out 2
(17) TP2 uses 3 to 6 to pick out 5
(18) TP3 uses 6 to 10 to pick out 7.

Three diagrams to show three ranges of numbers – 1 to 4, 4 to 9, 9 to 16 – where all the integers between two successive square numbers fill an overall rectangle

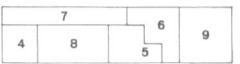

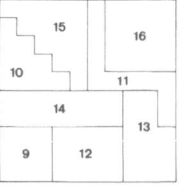

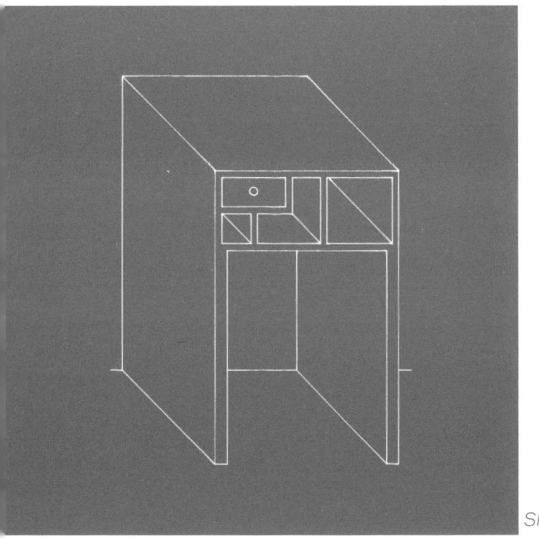

SP1

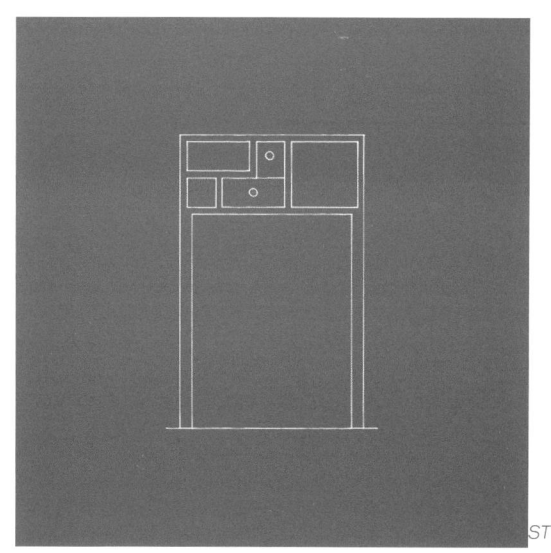

ST1

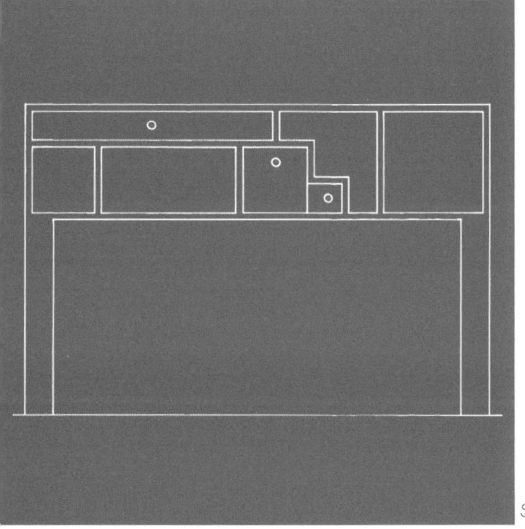

SP2

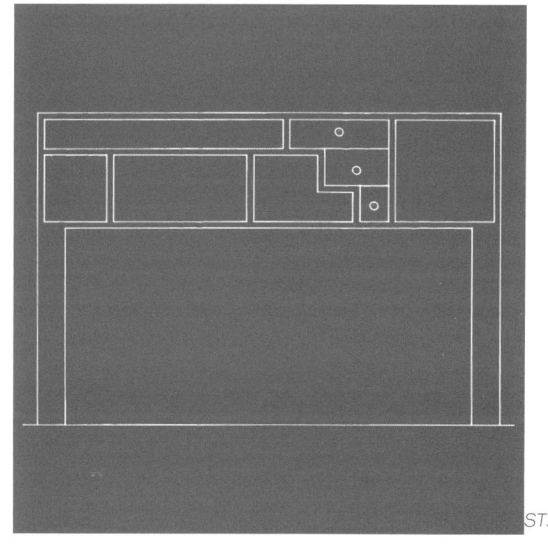

ST2

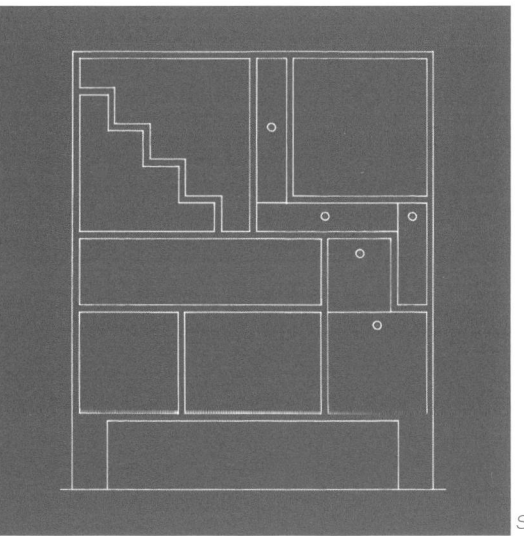

SP3

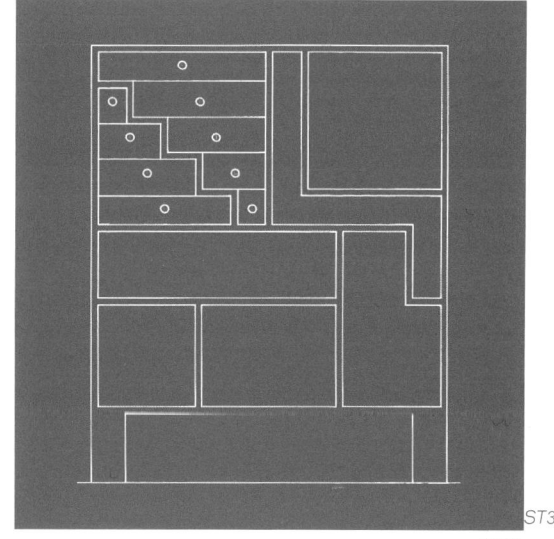

ST3

Three diagrams to show three ranges of numbers – 5 to 10, 6 to 12, 7 to 14 – where all the integers between a number and its double fill an overall rectangle

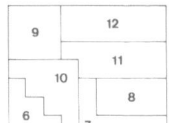

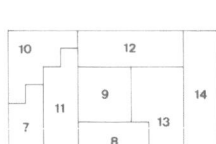

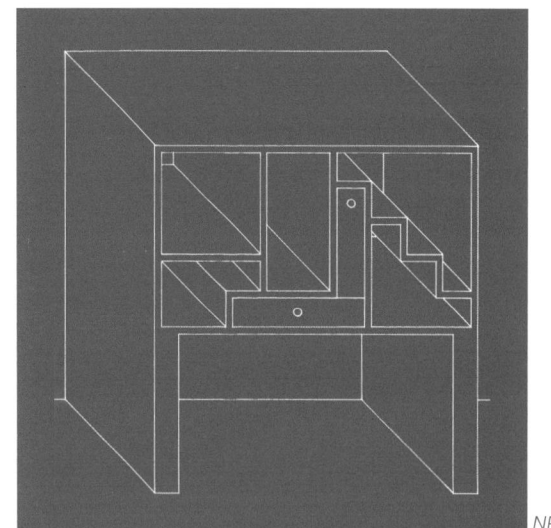

NP1

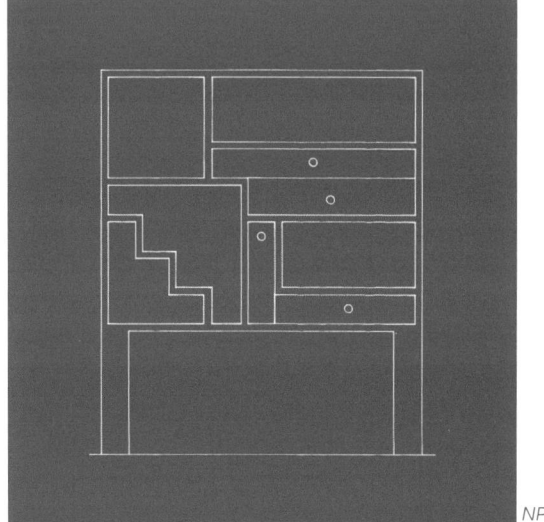

NP2

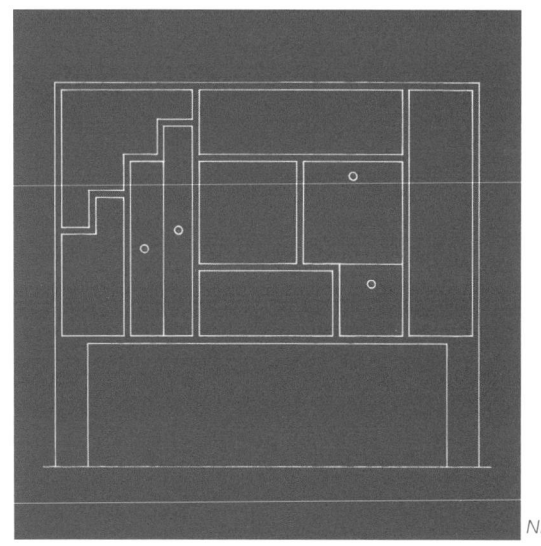

NP3

17·4

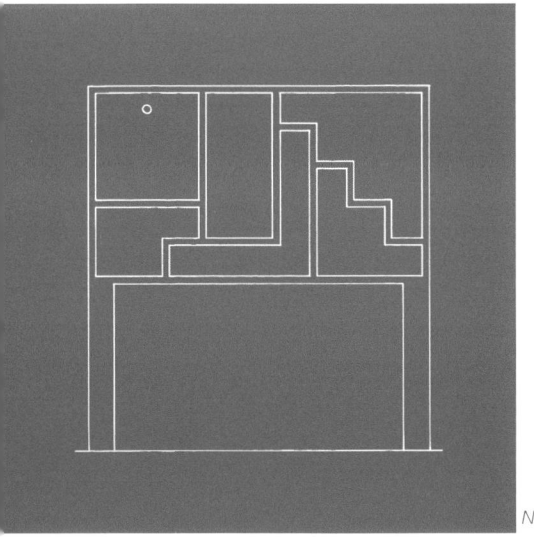

NS1

NT1

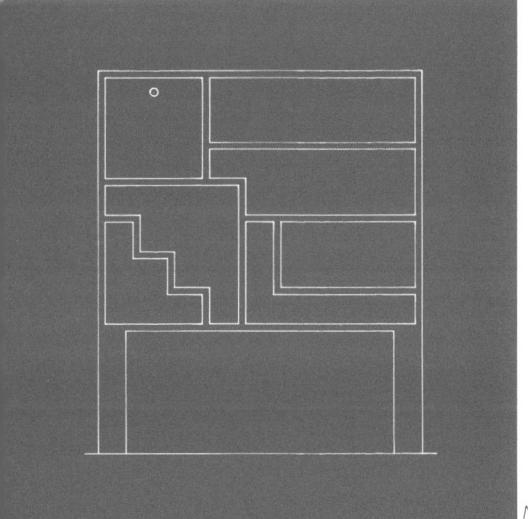

NS2

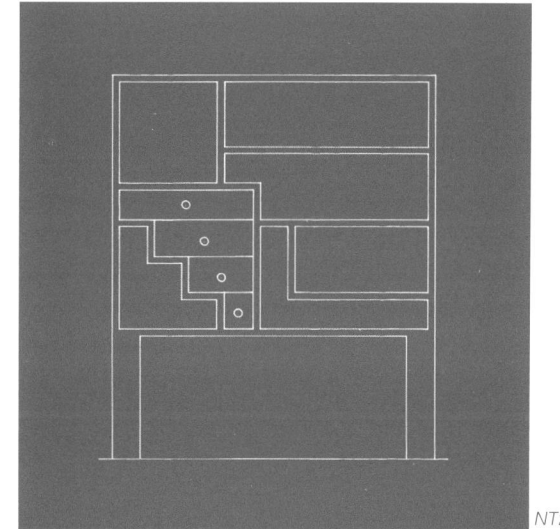

NT2

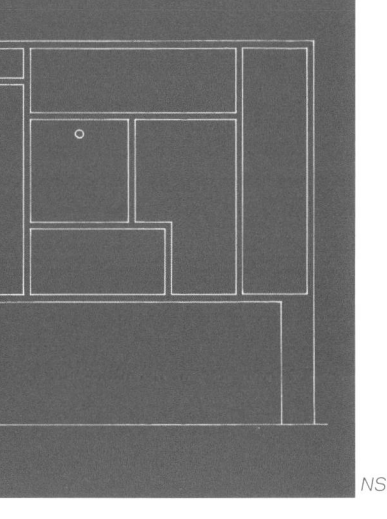

NS3

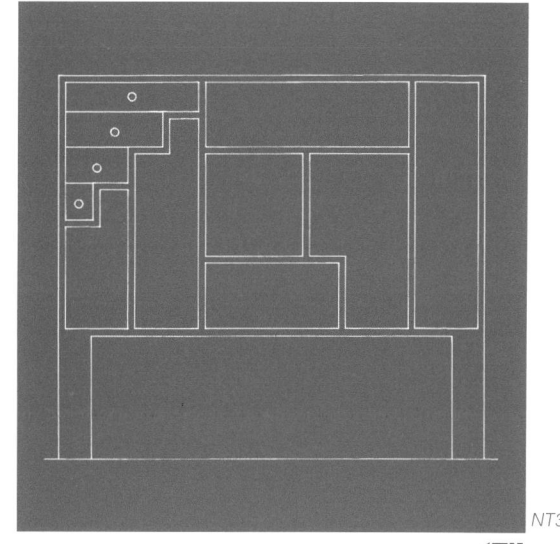

NT3

Three diagrams to show three ranges of numbers – 1 to 3, 3 to 6, 6 to 10 – where all the integers between two successive triangular numbers fill an overall rectangle

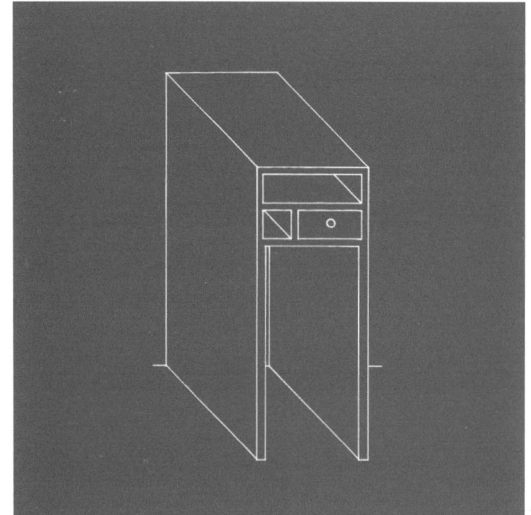

TP1

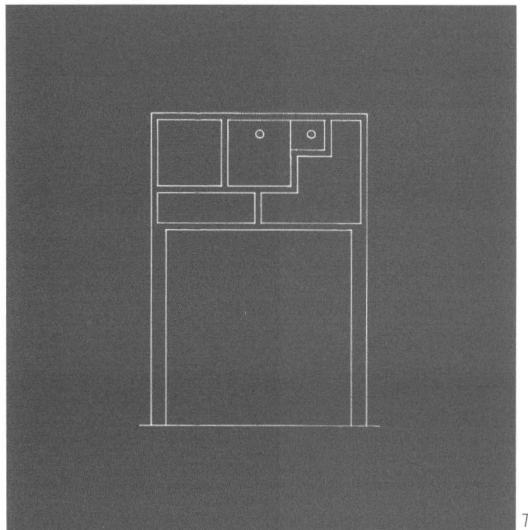

TP2

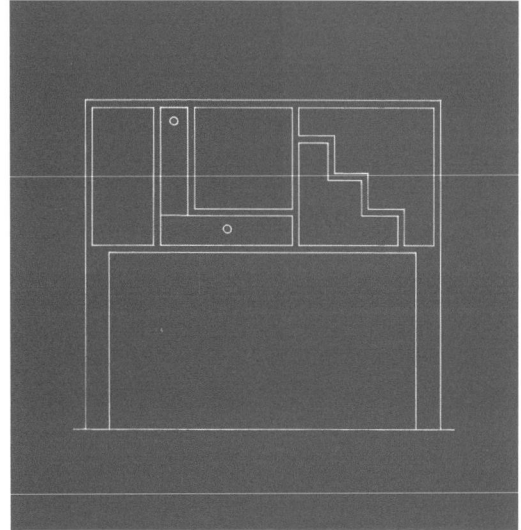

TP3

G18. NUMBERS AS THE SUM OF ...

One dreams of a machine that generates art.

The defining property of an art-generating machine is its automated process of production without subjective intervention once the initial conditions have been established and the generative rules given. This marginalises the subjective creative act and universalises the objective generative process.

Another property of such a machine is its capability to produce a quantity of different but related objects. This satisfies man's totalising and unifying desire that can only be realised in a delimited world within which nothing is superfluous, nothing can be different and everything is necessary. In this delimited world, profusion is justified by relatedness, totality transcends the fragment and unity overcomes the fragmented.

Each of these projects consists of a cornucopia of objects given by invented rules applied to mathematical material.

Here one experiences an *embarras de richesses*!

From Goldbach, every even number greater than 2 is the sum of two primes.

Every odd prime is either a 4n+1 prime or a 4n-1 prime.

And every even number being a multiple of 4 is the sum of one 4n+1 prime and one 4n-1 prime.

From Fermat, every 4n+1 prime is the sum of two squares.

Therefore, every even number being a multiple of 4 can be expressed as the sum of two squares and one 4n-1 prime.

A 4n-1 prime can be represented by a certain number of 1x4 strips and one 1x3 strip.

This means that every even number being a multiple of 4 can be represented by two squares, a certain number of 1x4 strips and one 1x3 strip.

Each object in this project consists of two squares made as shelves, 1x4 strips and one 1x3 strip made as drawers, which are fitted within a rectangle the area of which in units is that multiple of 4 being represented.

33 objects are generated until a supplementary rule stops the process.

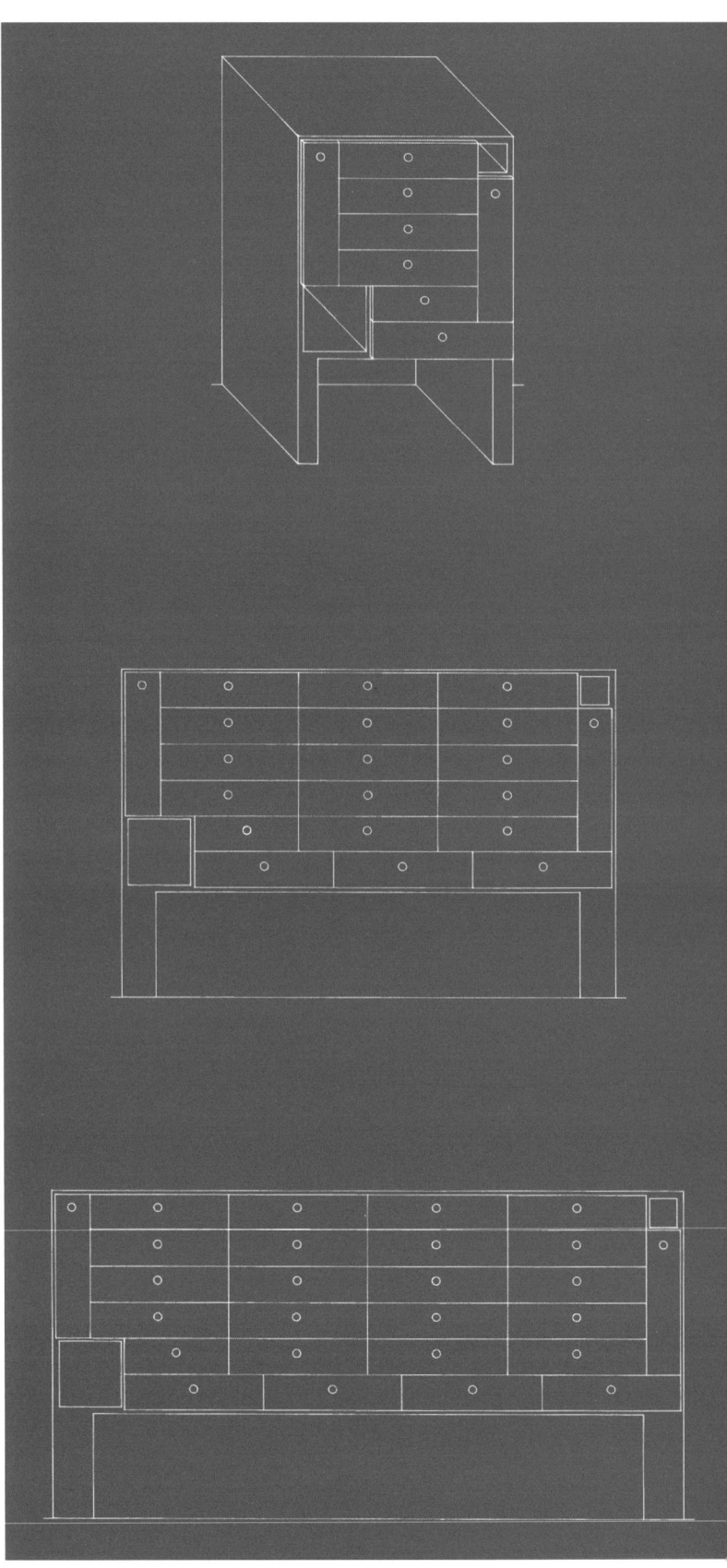

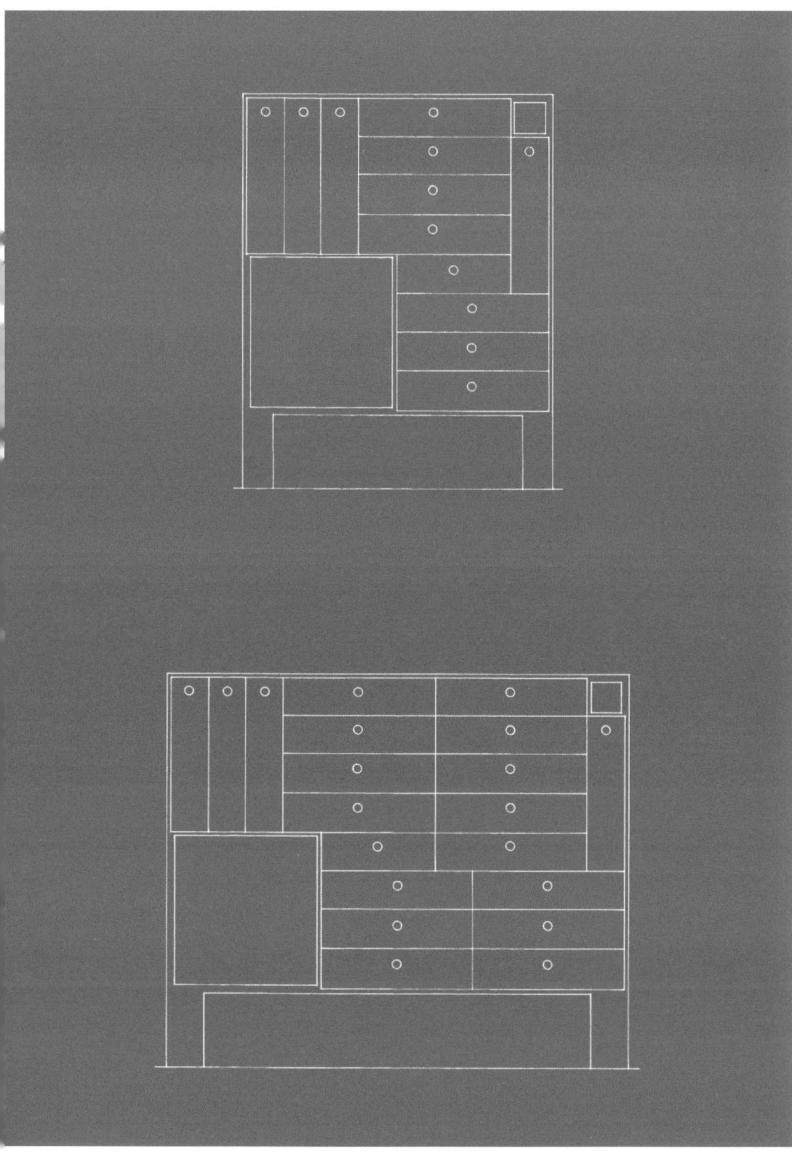

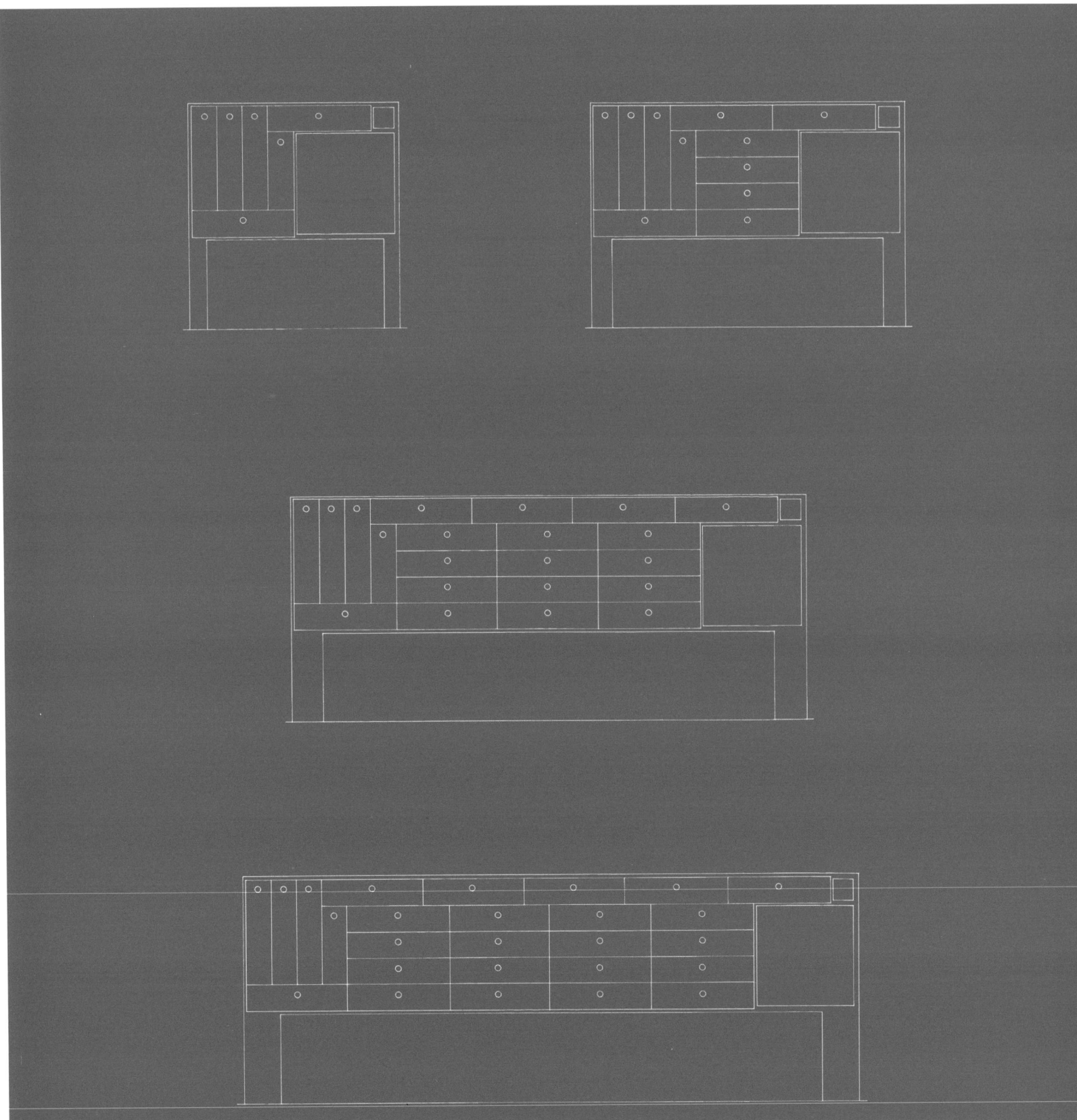

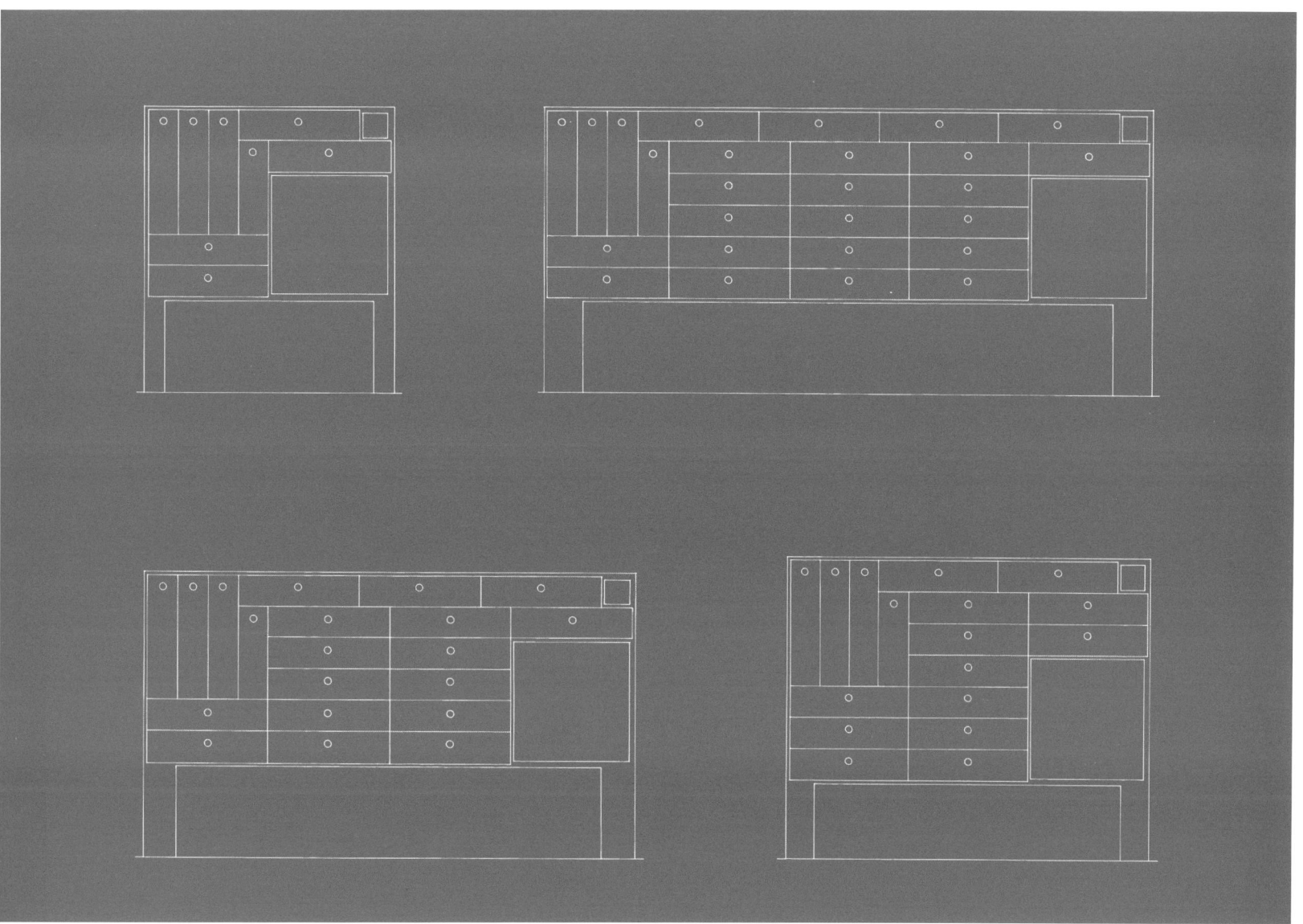

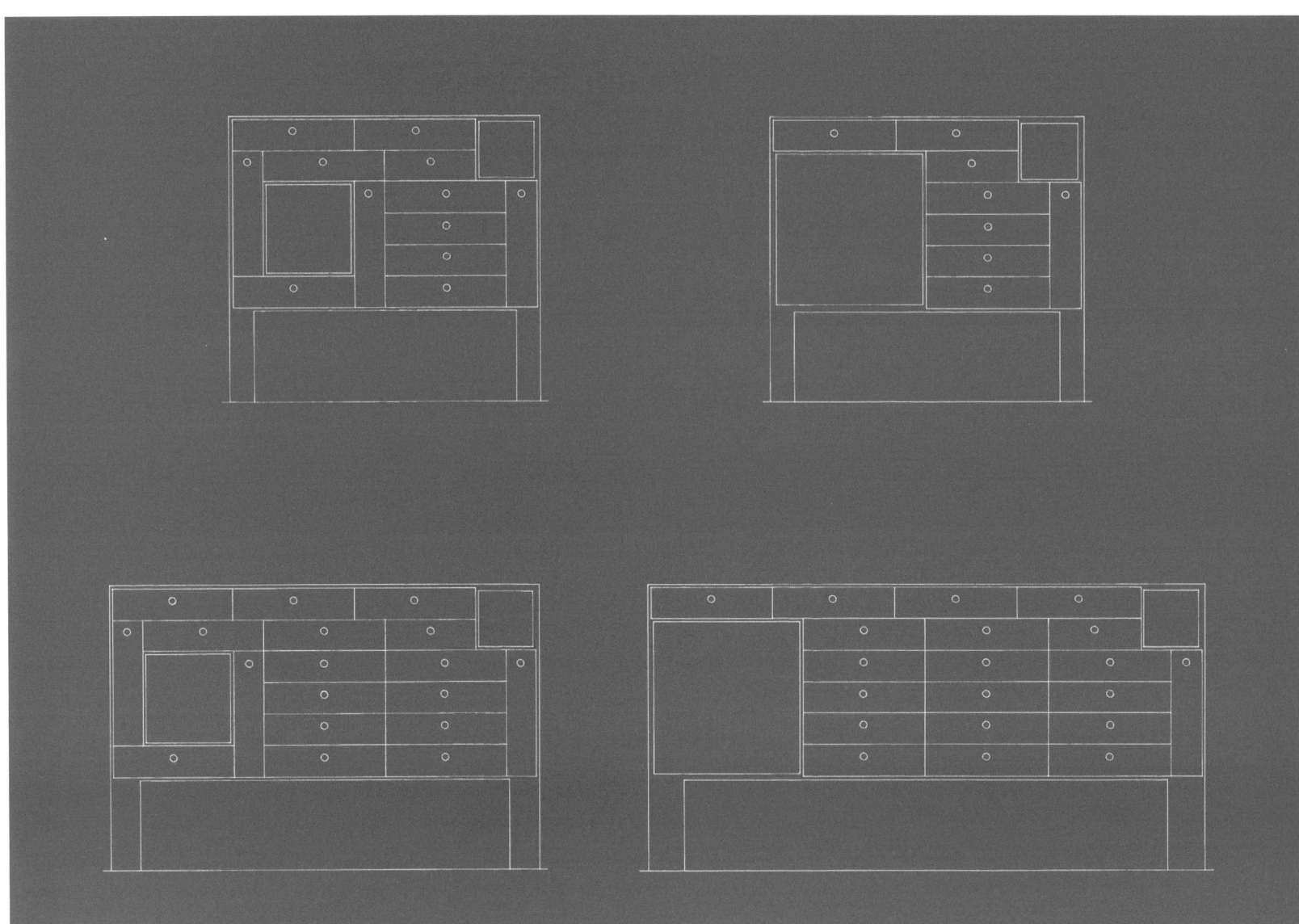

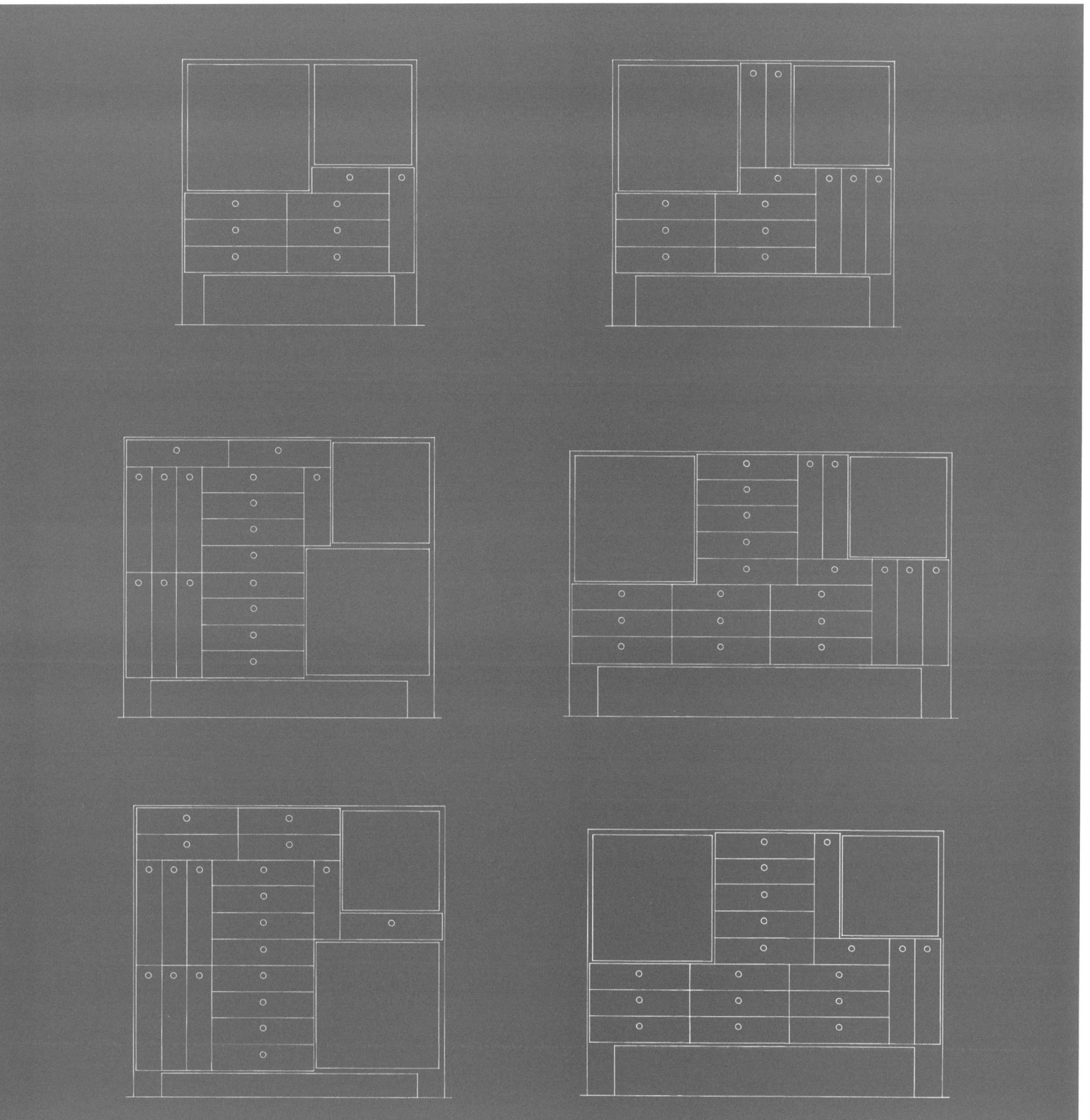

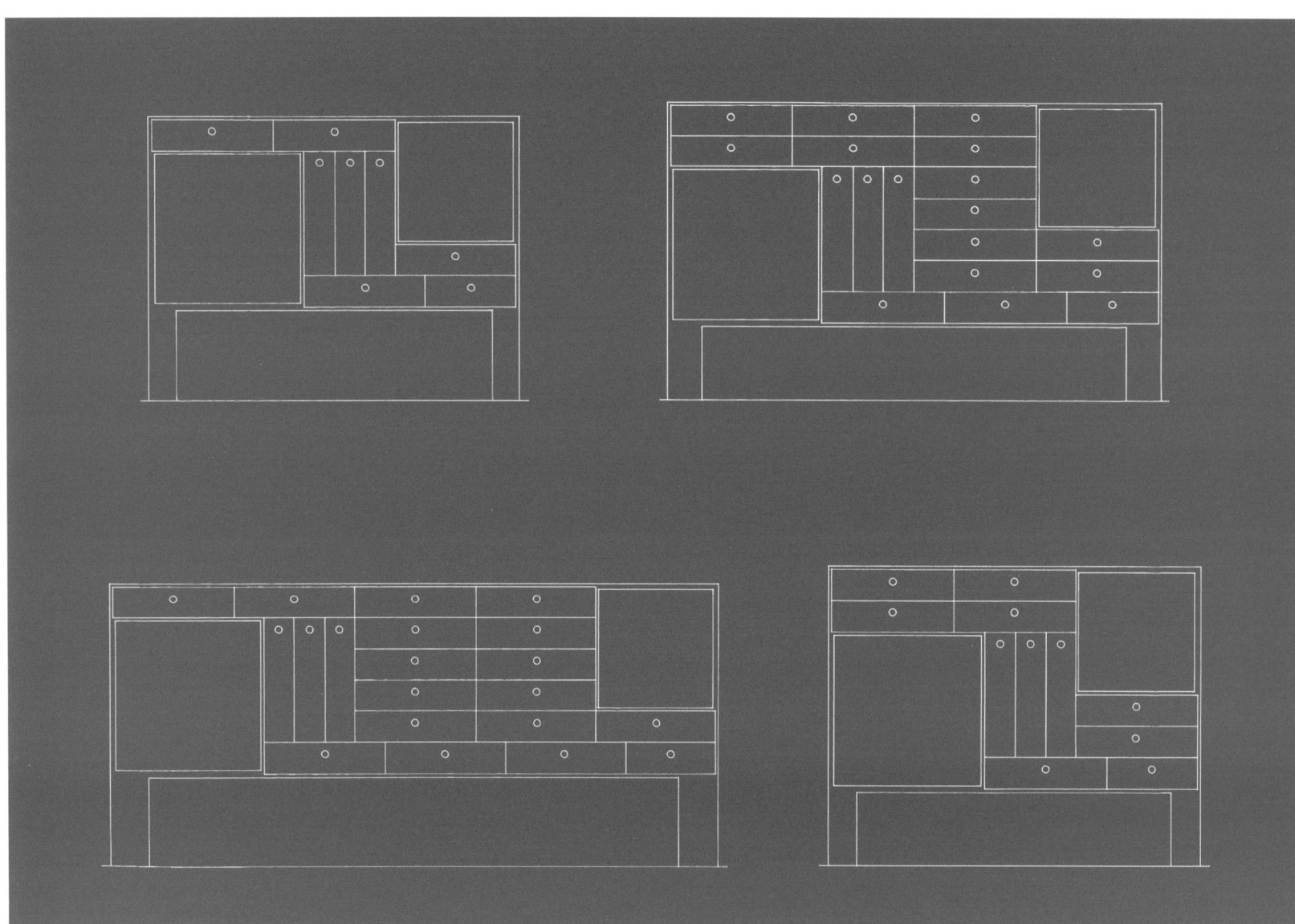

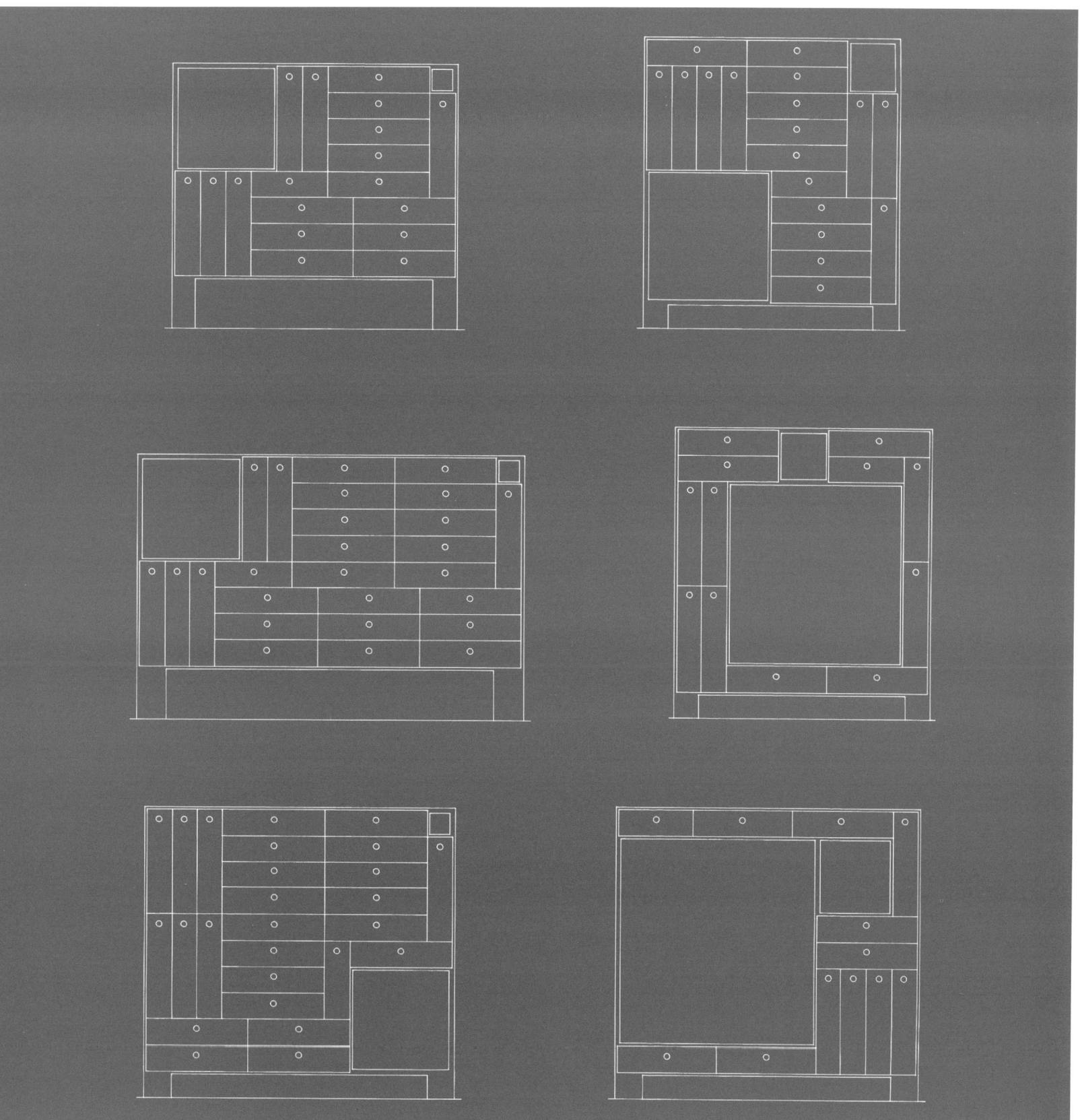

P46. Odd number, prime, power of two

Many odd numbers can be expressed as the sum of a prime and a power of two.

Specifically, every odd number from 3 to 125 is the sum of a prime and a power of two.

Furthermore, there are odd numbers from 3 to 125 being the sum of a 4n-1 prime and a power of two.

A 4n-1 prime can be represented by a certain number of 1x4 strips and one 1x3 strip.

A power of two can be expressed as the sum of the first terms of the series (1, 1, 2, 4, 8, 16, 32, 64...) so that a power of two can be represented by a collection of squares and double-squares.

This means that every odd number from 3 to 125 being the sum of a 4n-1 prime and a power of two can be represented by a certain number of 1x4 strips and one 1x3 strip, and a collection of squares and double-squares.

Each object in this project consists of a collection of squares and double-squares made as shelves, 1x4 strips and one 1x3 strip made as drawers, which are fitted within a rectangle the area of which in units is the number represented.

40 objects are generated.

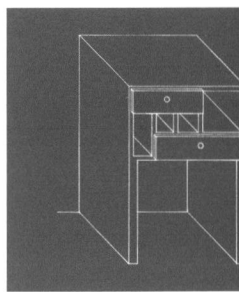

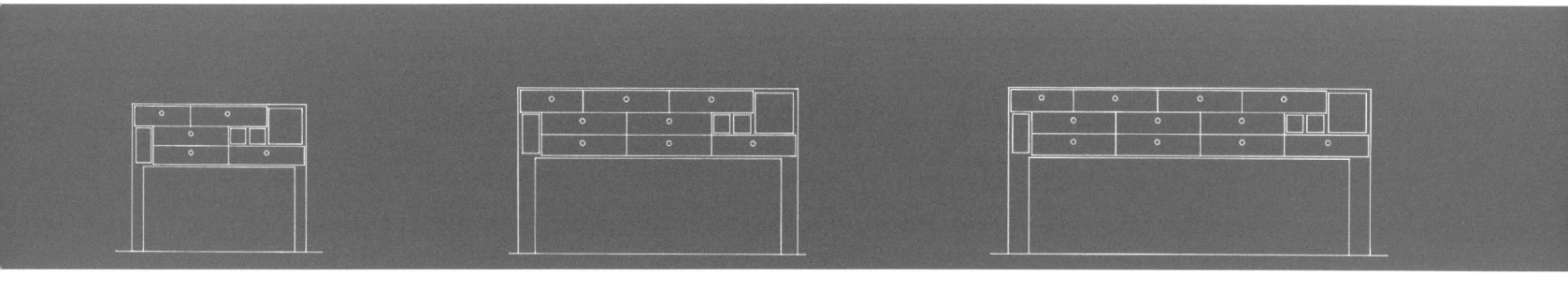

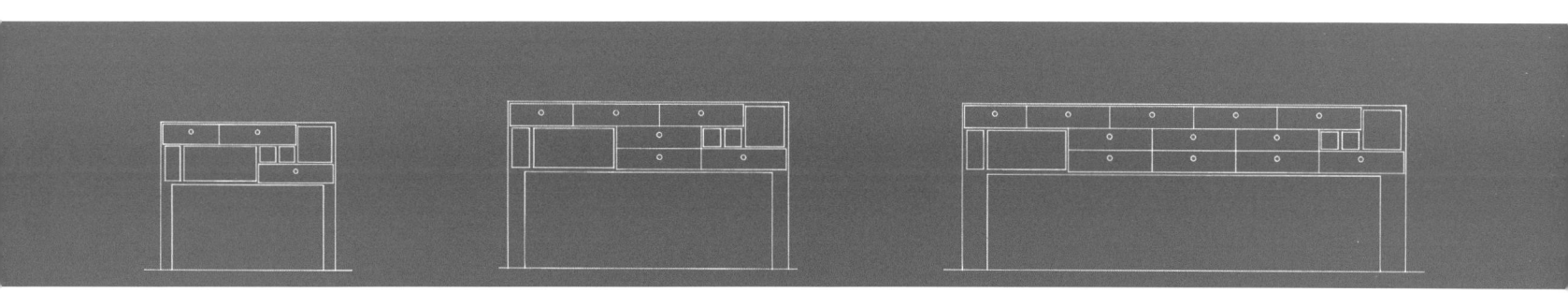

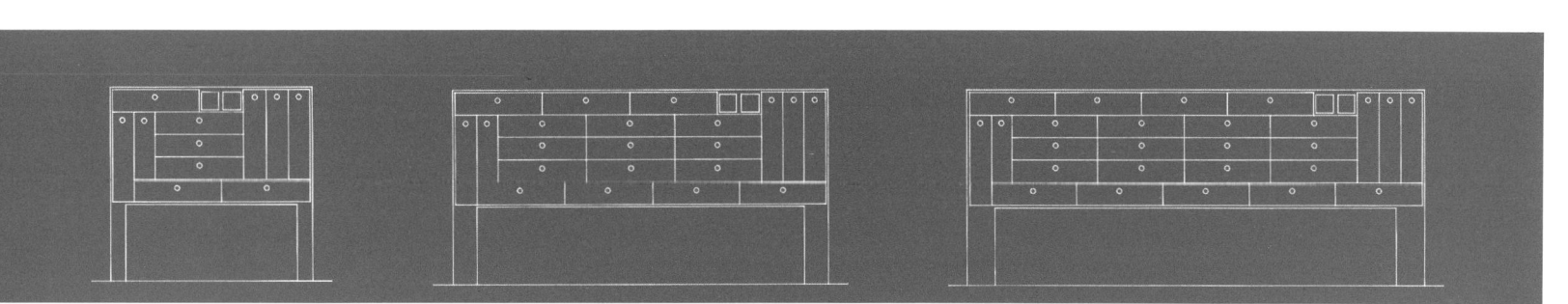

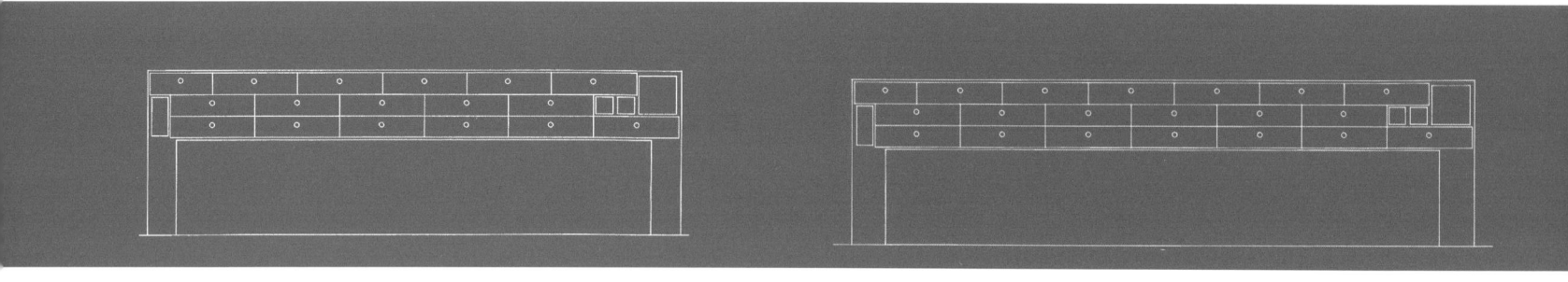

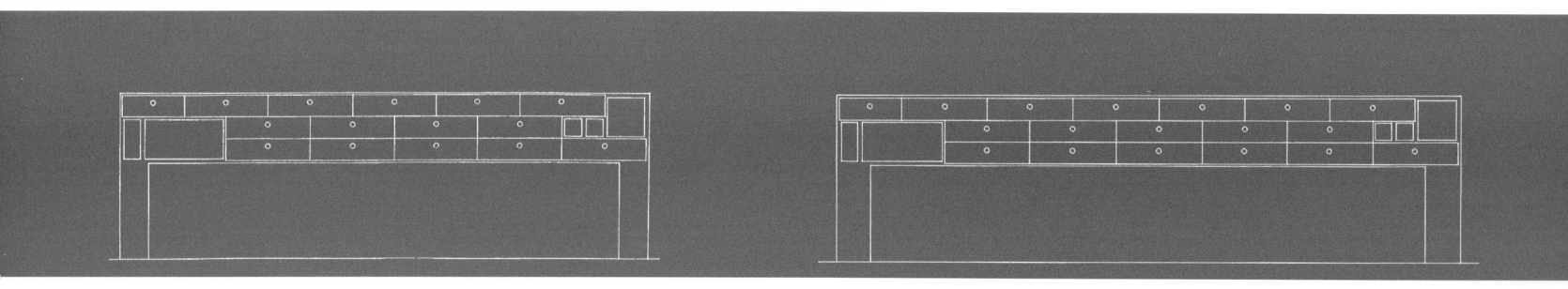

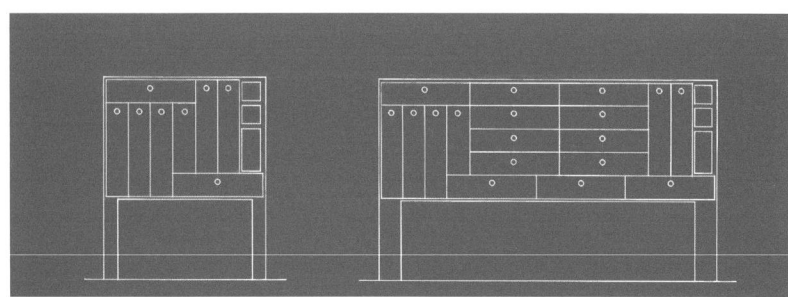

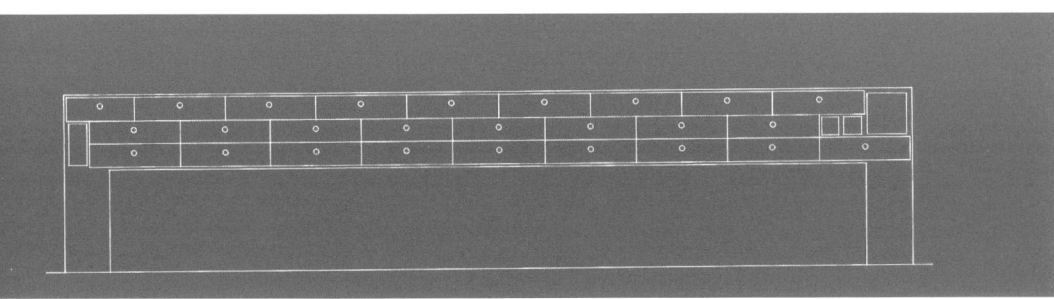

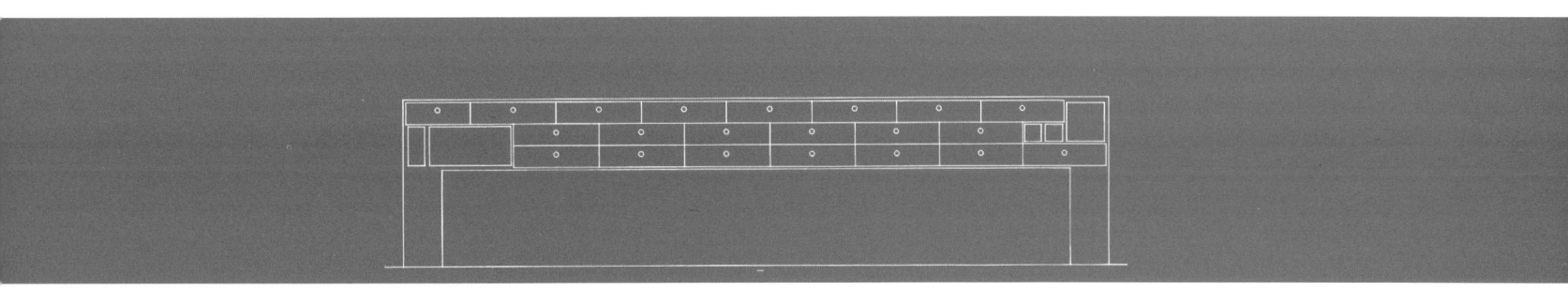

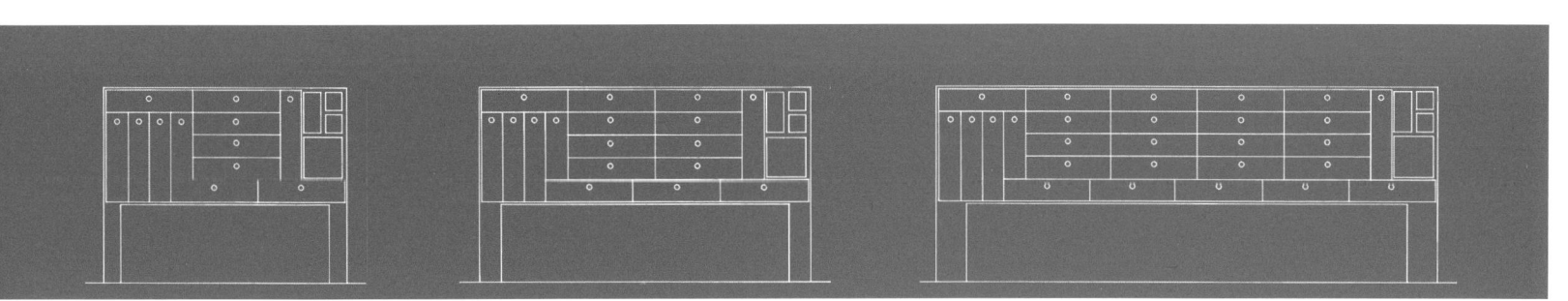

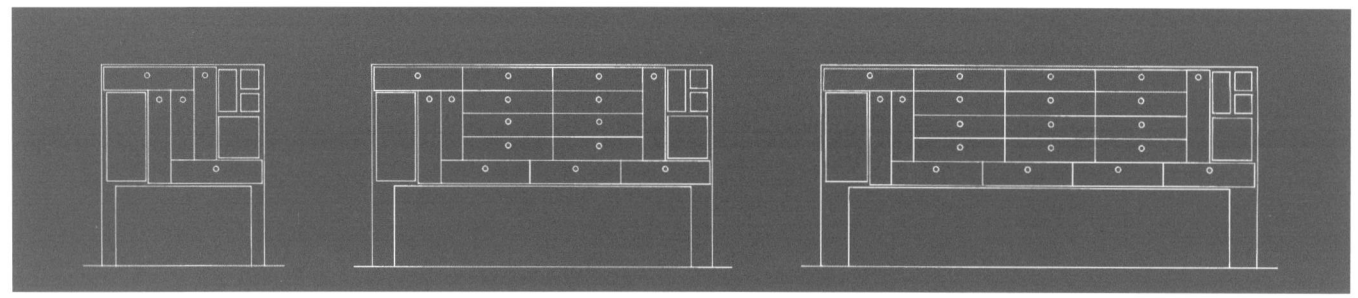

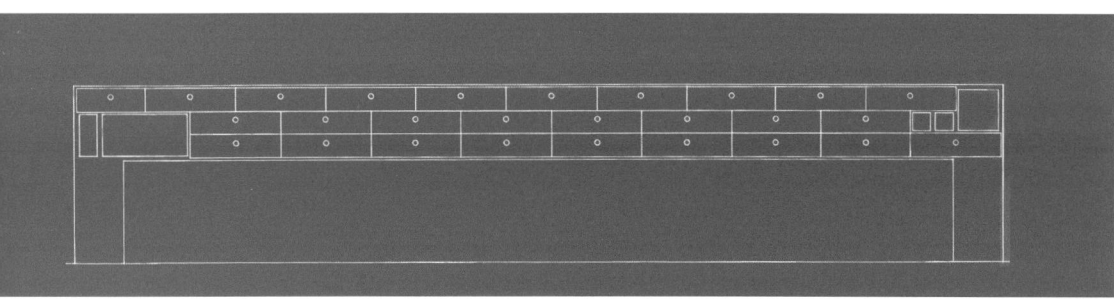

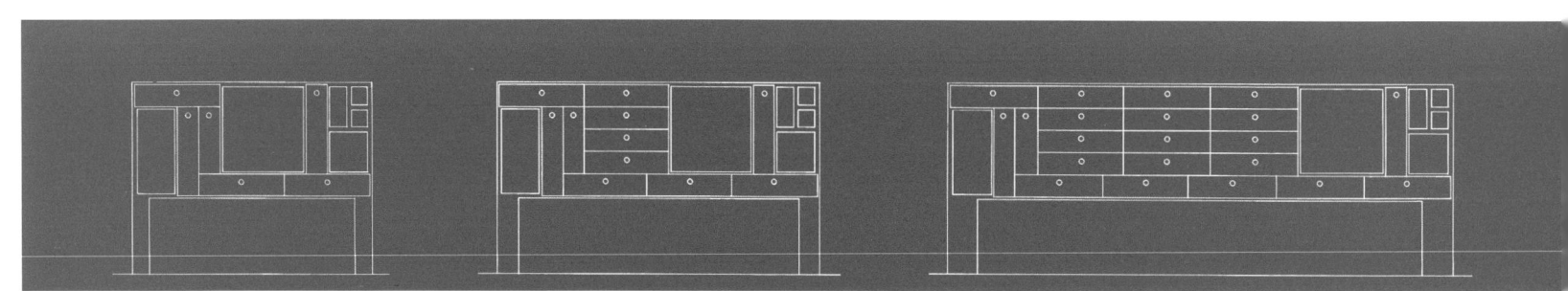

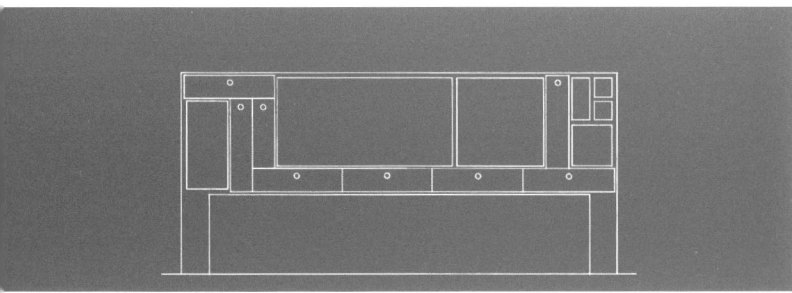

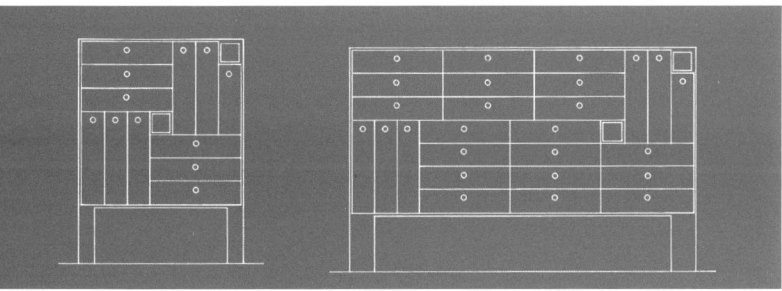

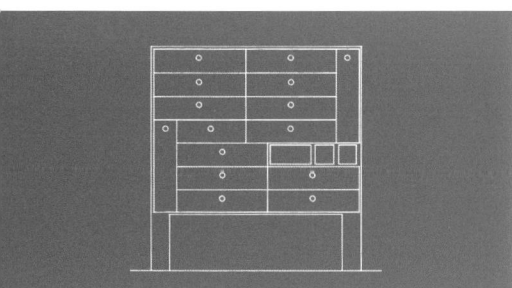

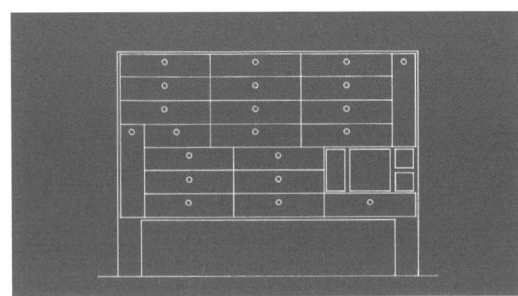

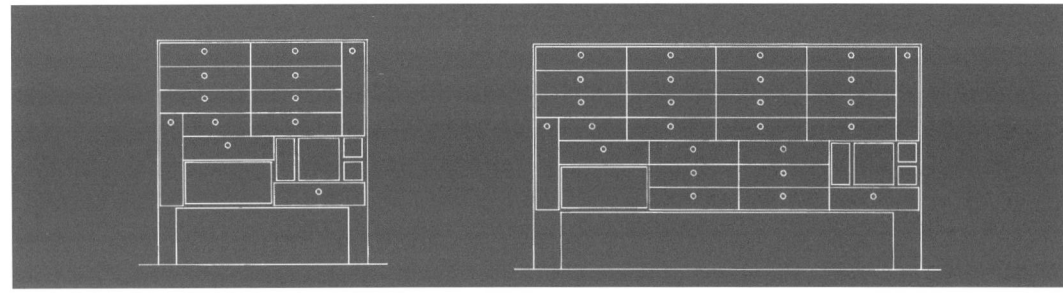

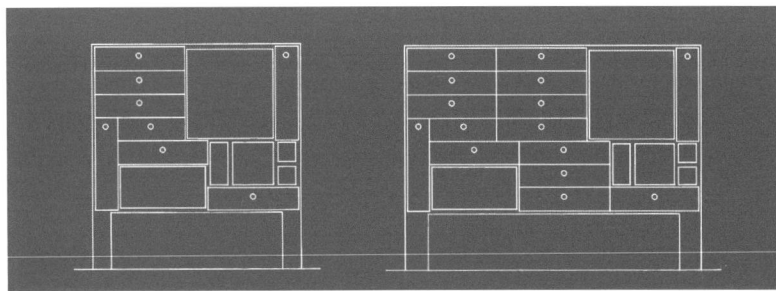

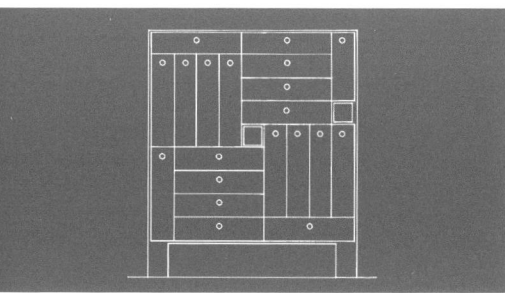

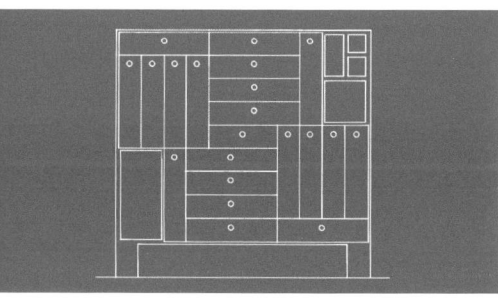

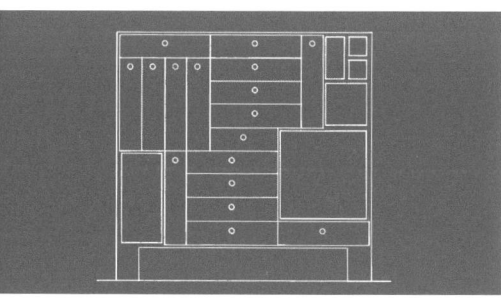

Many odd numbers can be expressed as the sum of a prime and a double-square.

Specifically, every odd number from 19 to 5775 is the sum of a prime and a double-square.

Furthermore, there are odd numbers from 19 to 5775 being the sum of a 4n-1 prime and a double-square.

A 4n-1 prime can be represented by a certain number of 1x4 strips and one 1x3 strip.

This means that every odd number from 19 to 5775 being the sum of a 4n-1 prime and a double-square can be represented by a certain number of 1x4 strips and one 1x3 strip, and a double-square.

Each object in this project consists of a double-square made as a shelf, 1x4 strips and one 1x3 strip made as drawers, which are fitted within a rectangle the area of which in units is the number represented.

The number of objects generated is determined by a supplementary rule.

22 objects are generated.

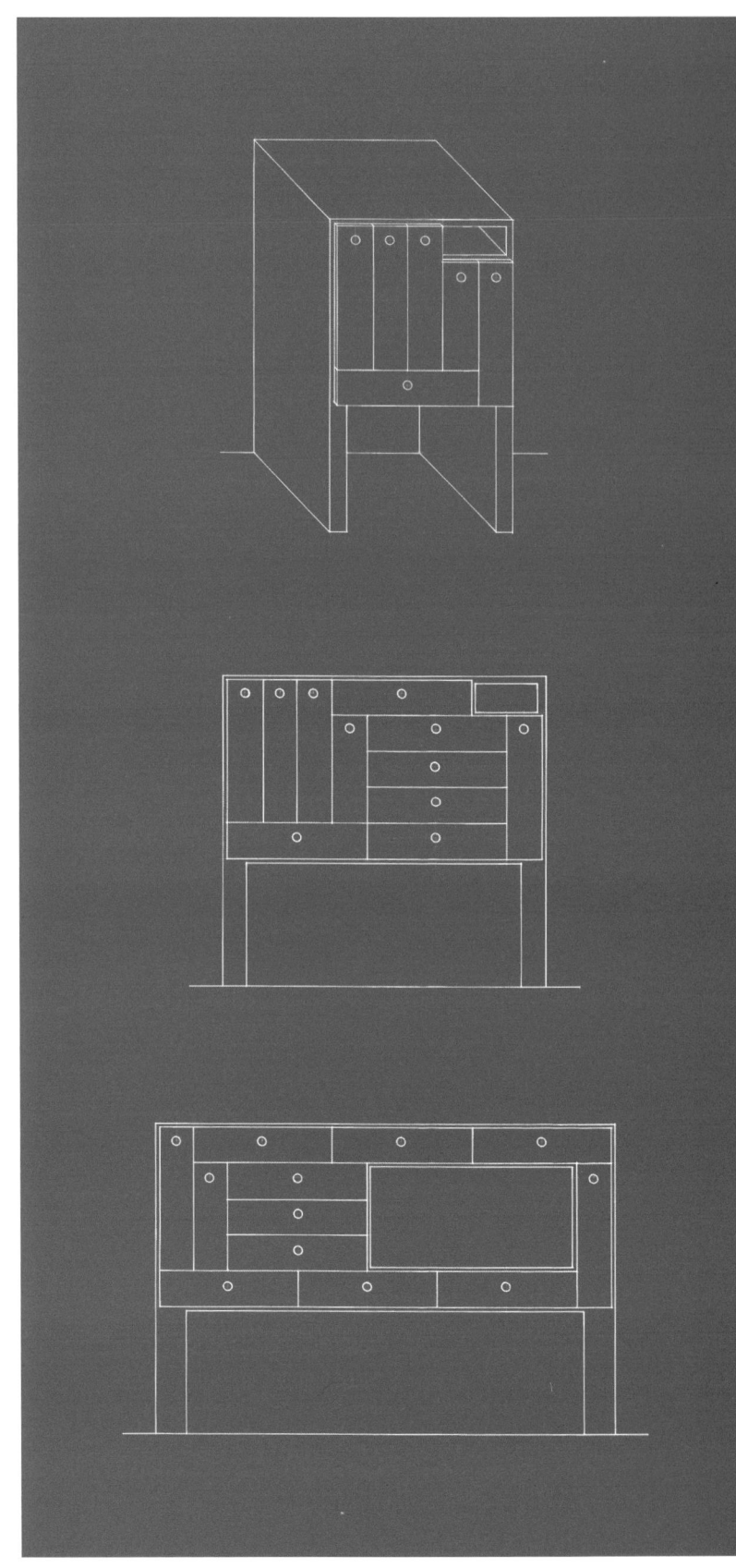

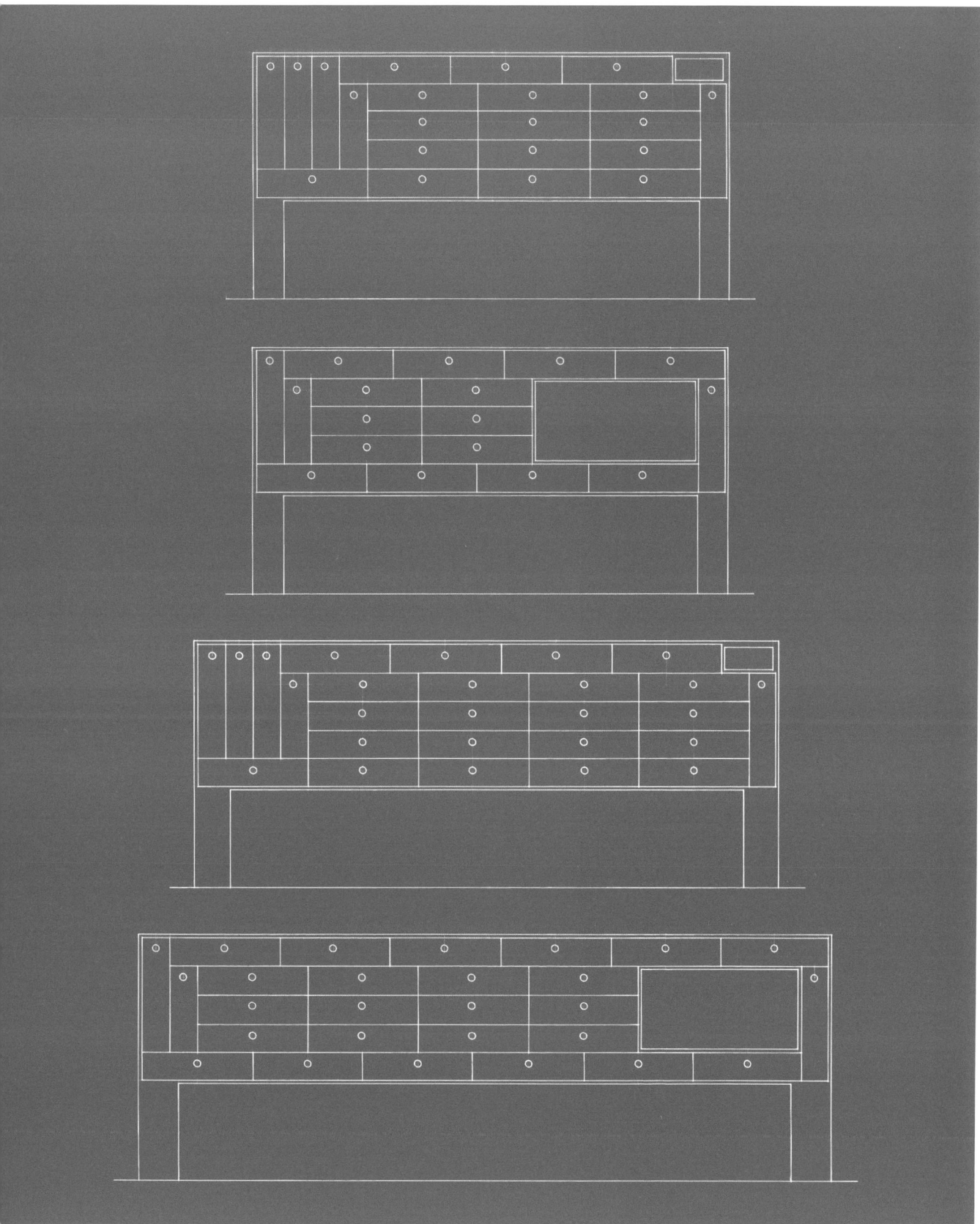

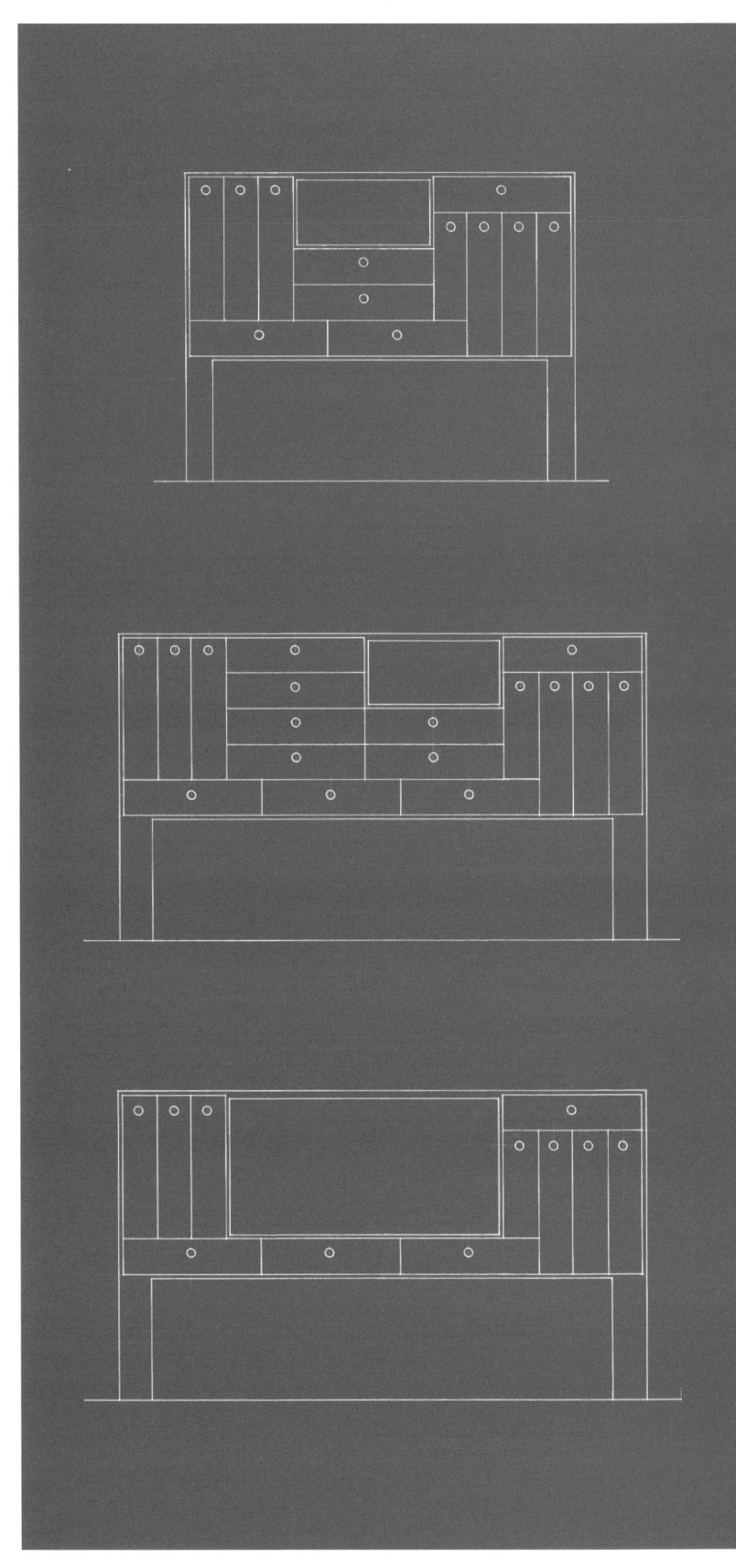

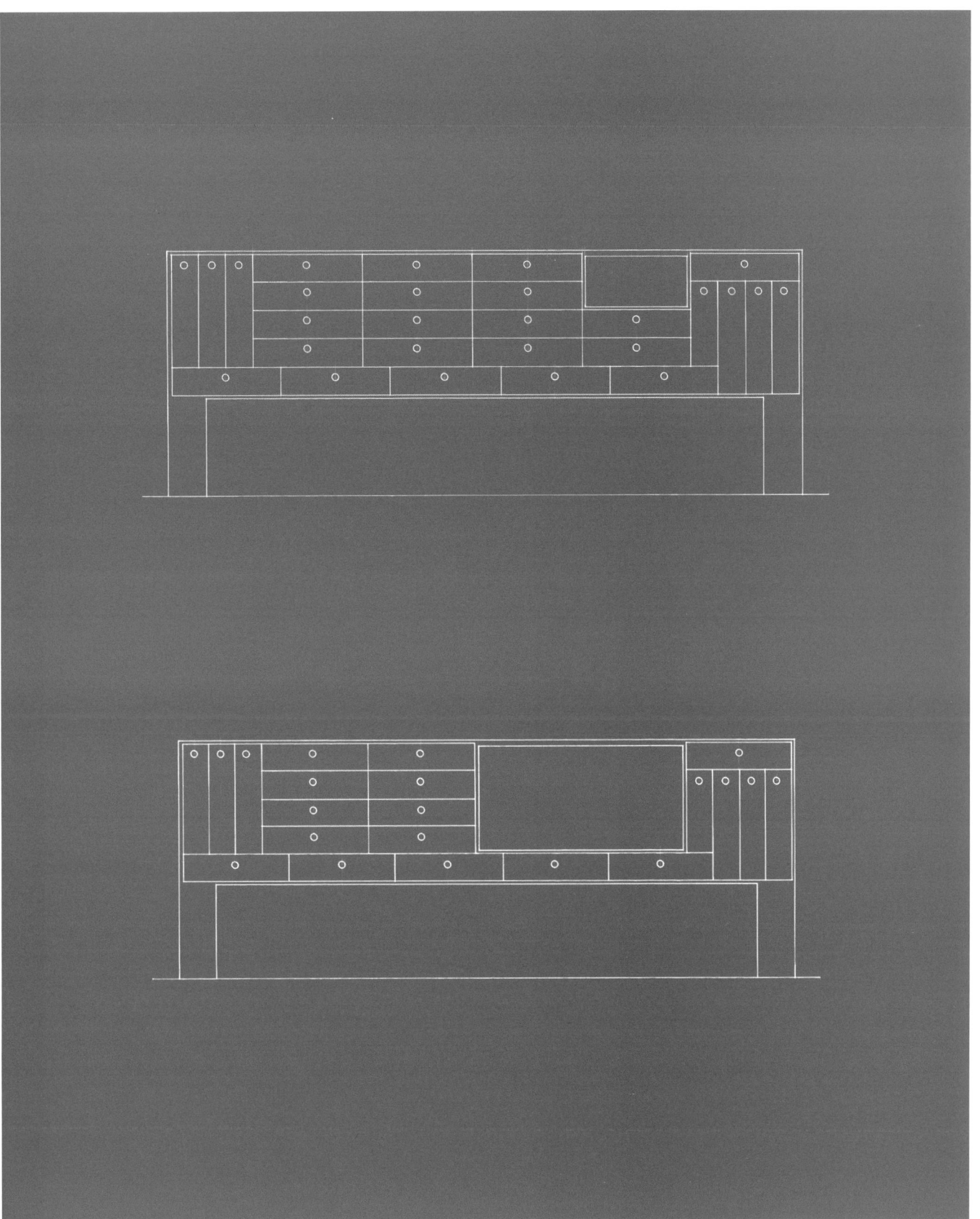

197

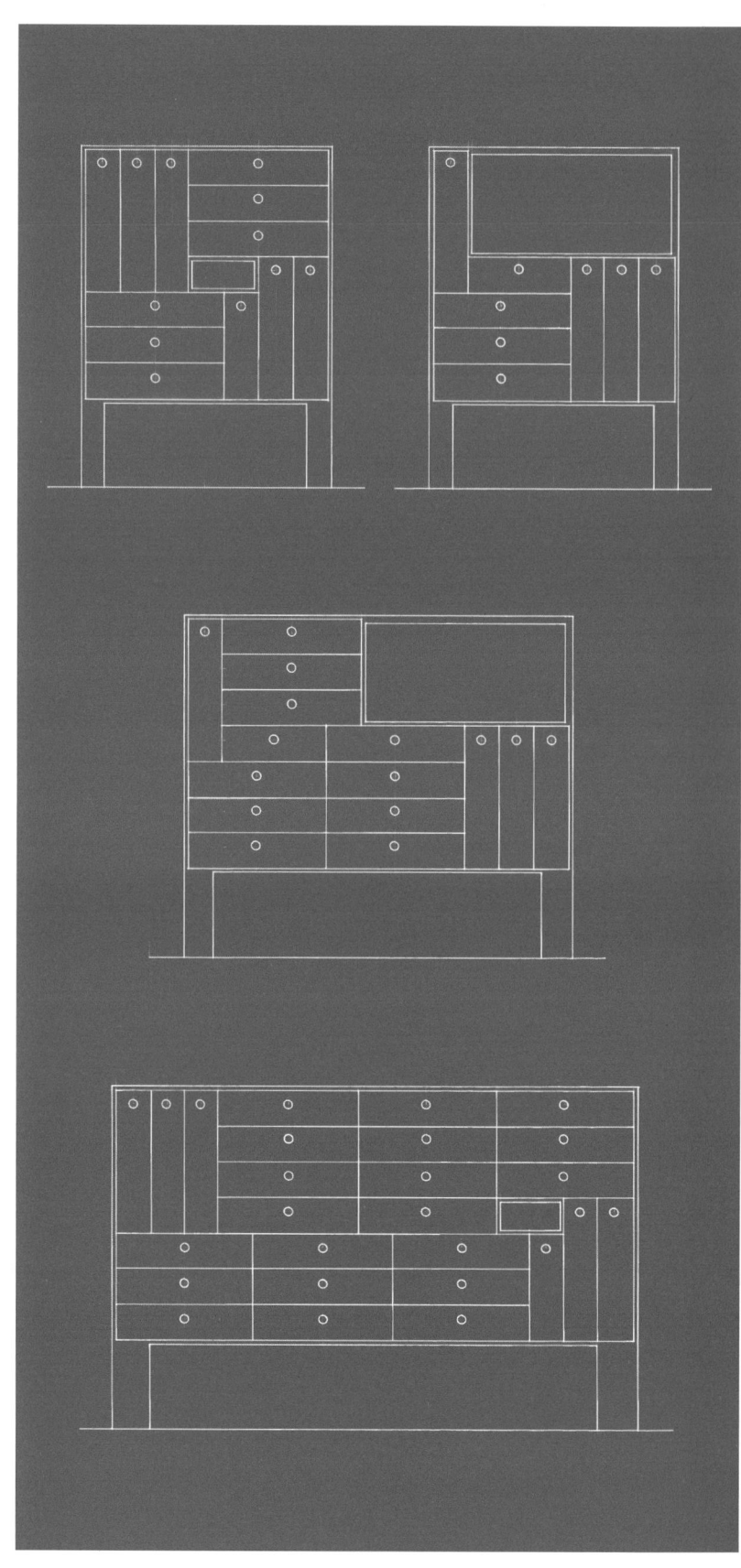

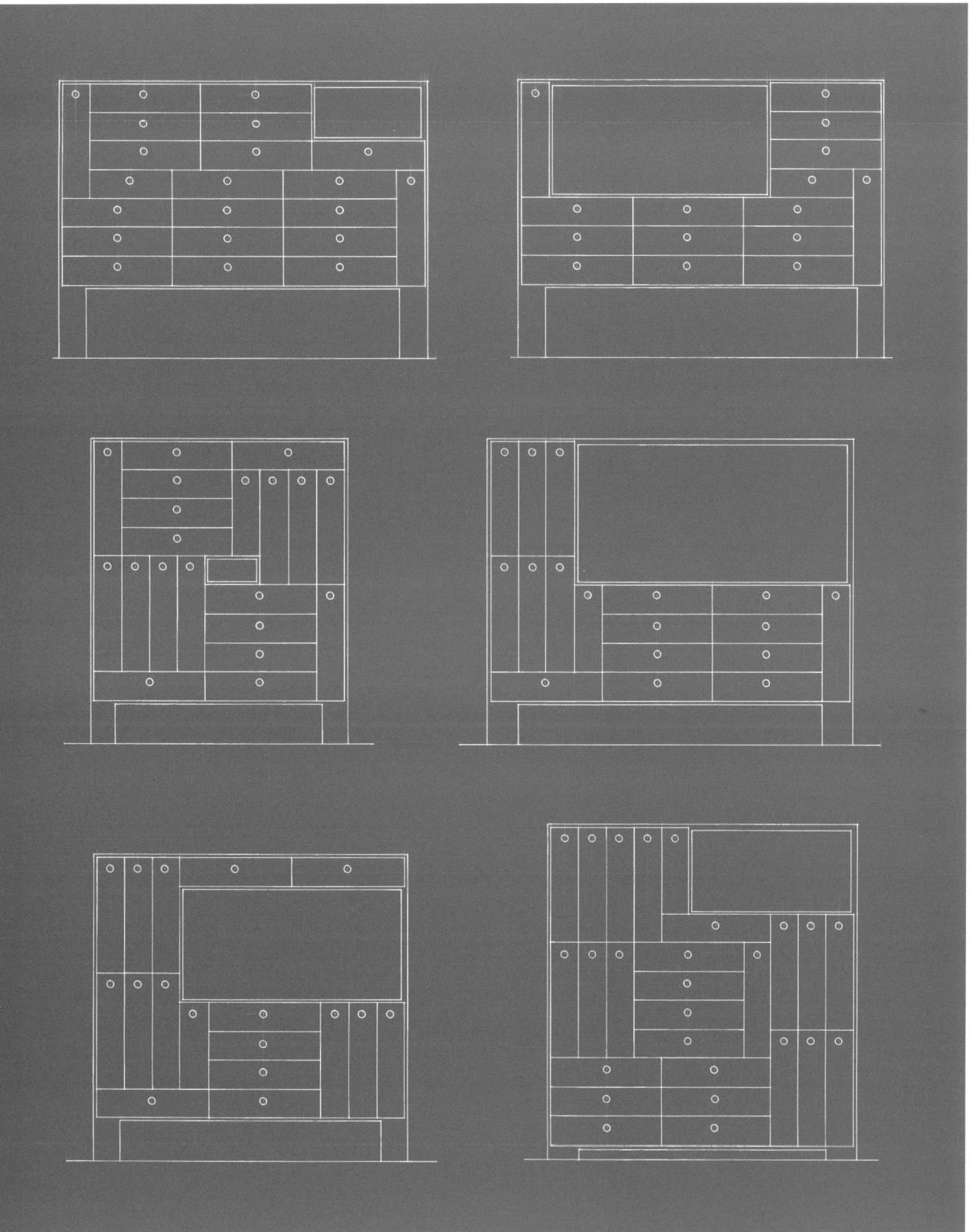

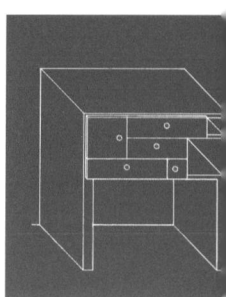

P48. Odd number, three primes

It is thought that every odd number greater than 5 is the sum of three primes.

Every odd prime is either a 4n+1 prime or a 4n-1 prime.

Let those odd numbers which consist of both 4n+1 and 4n-1 primes be picked out.

A 4n+1 prime being the sum of two squares can be represented by two squares.

And a 4n-1 prime can be represented by a certain number of 1x4 strips and one 1x3 strip.

Then an odd number being the sum of one 4n+1 prime and two 4n-1 primes will be represented by two squares made as shelves, by the strips expressing the smaller 4n-1 prime made as shelves and the strips expressing the larger 4n-1 prime made as drawers.

And an odd number being the sum of one 4n-1 prime and two 4n+1 primes will be represented by strips made as drawers, by the two squares expressing the smaller 4n+1 prime made as shelves and the two squares expressing the larger 4n+1 prime made as storage compartments.

Each object in this project consists of squares and strips, shelves and drawers/storage compartments, which are fitted within a rectangle the area of which in units is the number represented.

194 objects are generated until a supplementary rule stops the process.

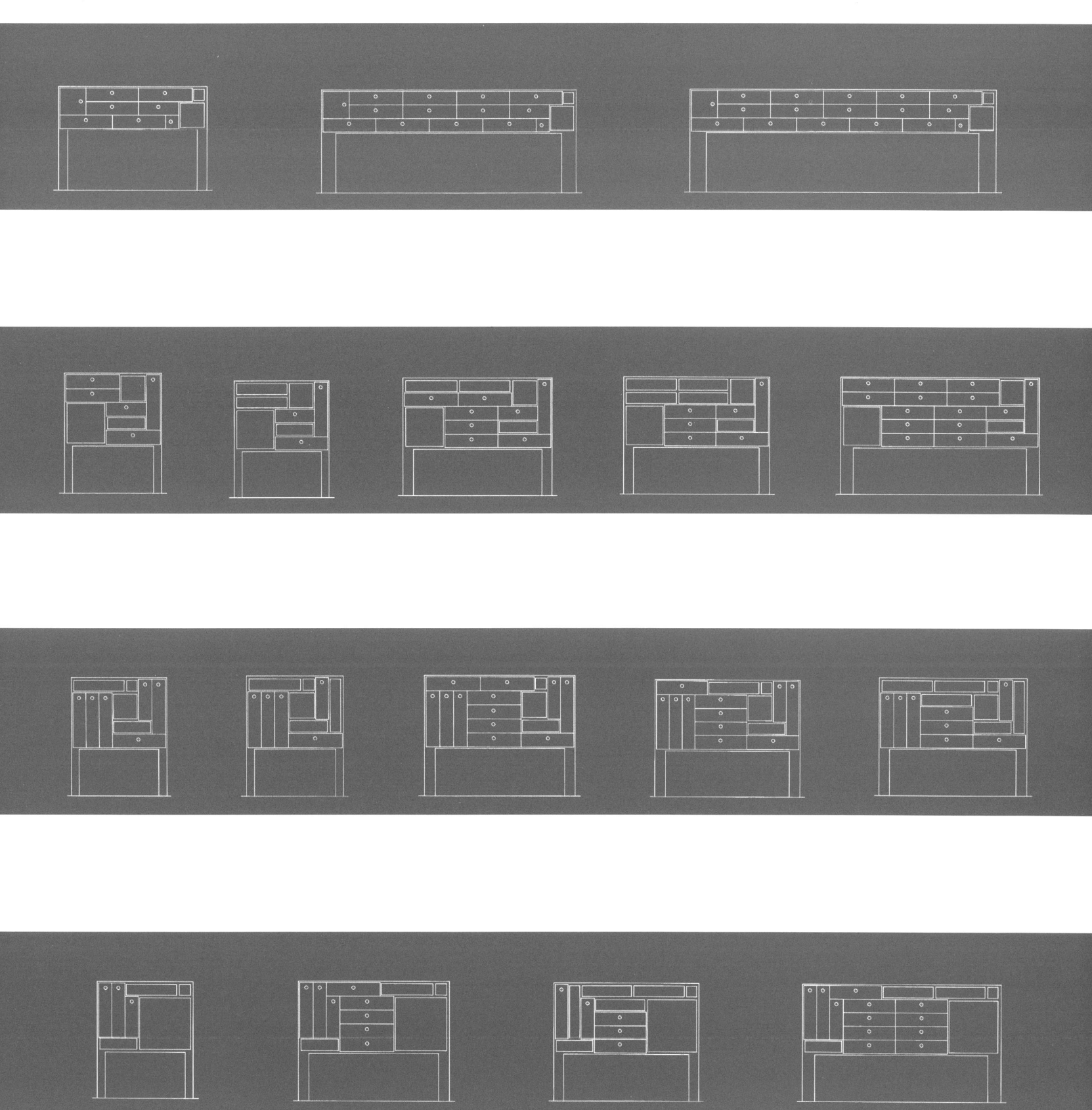

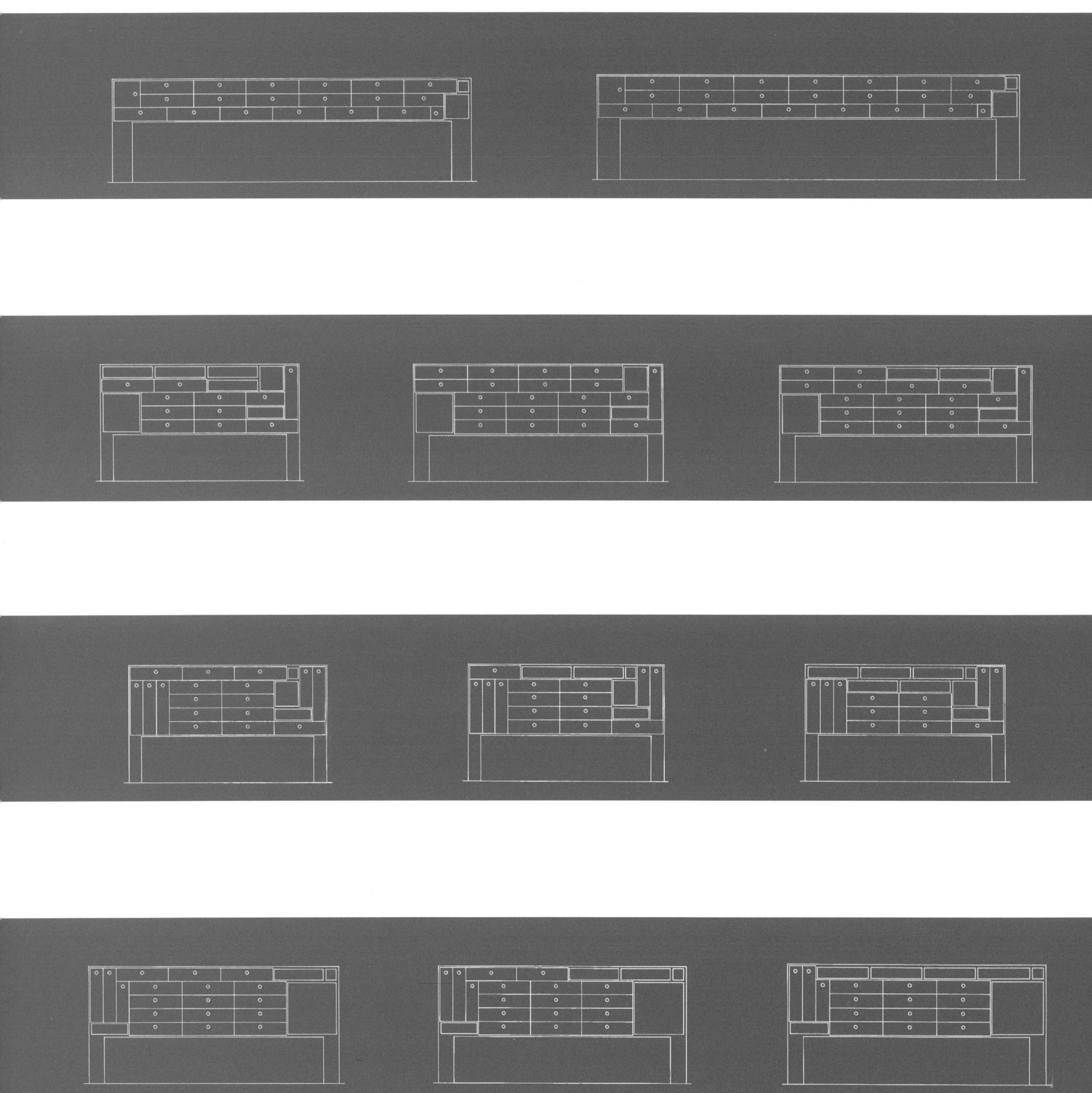

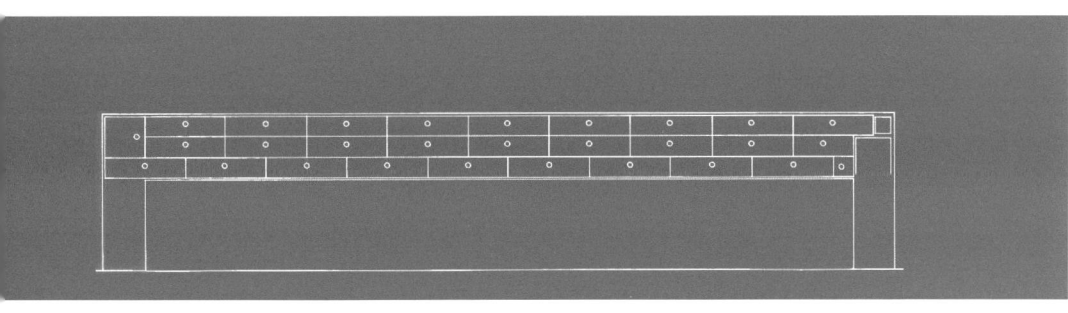

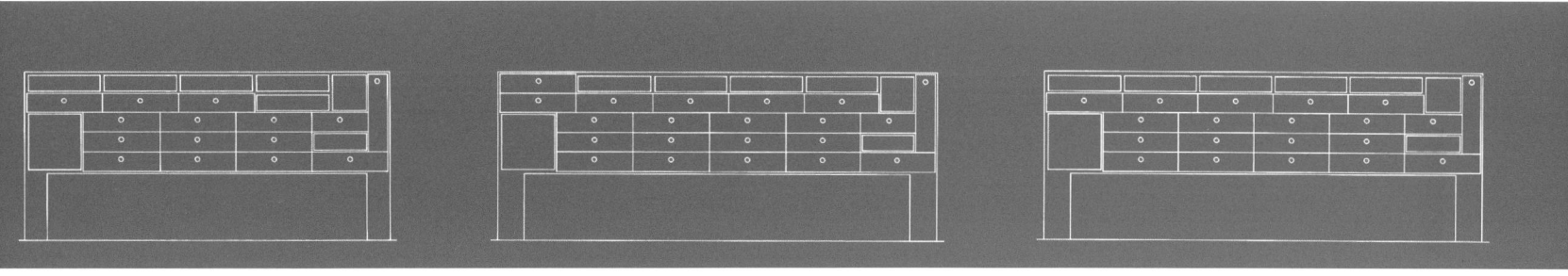

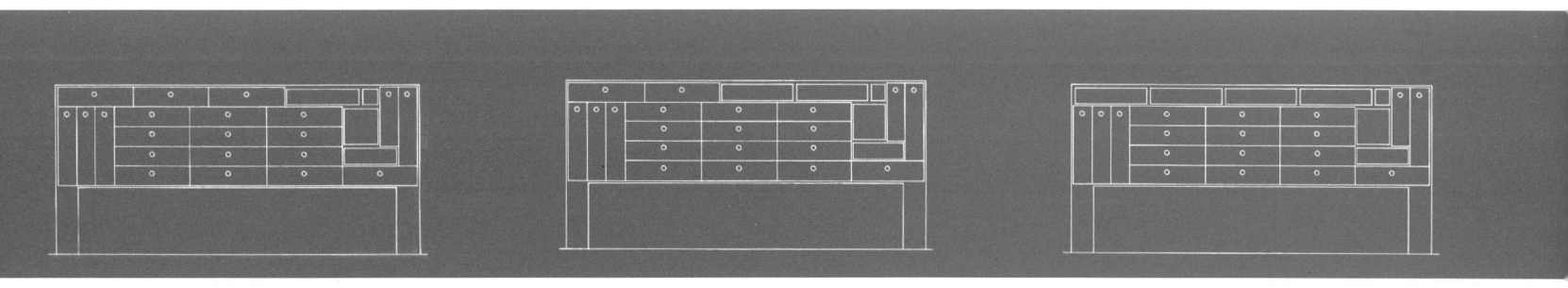

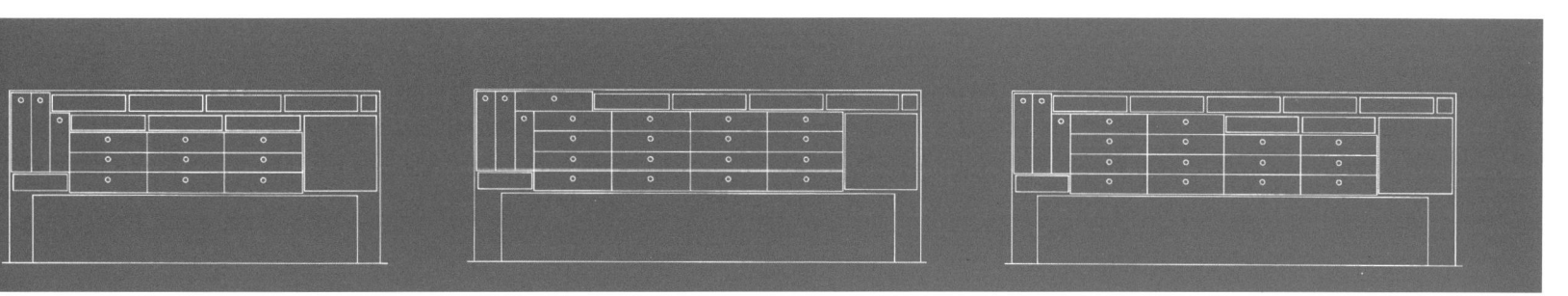

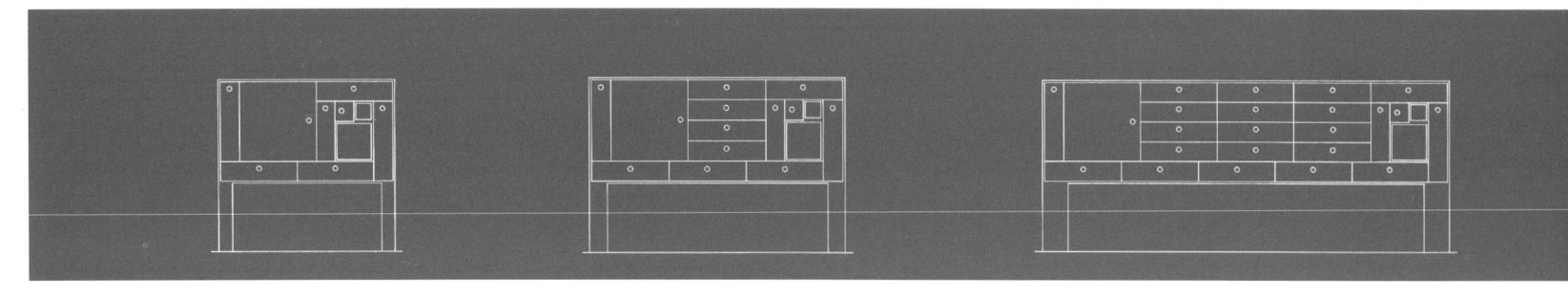

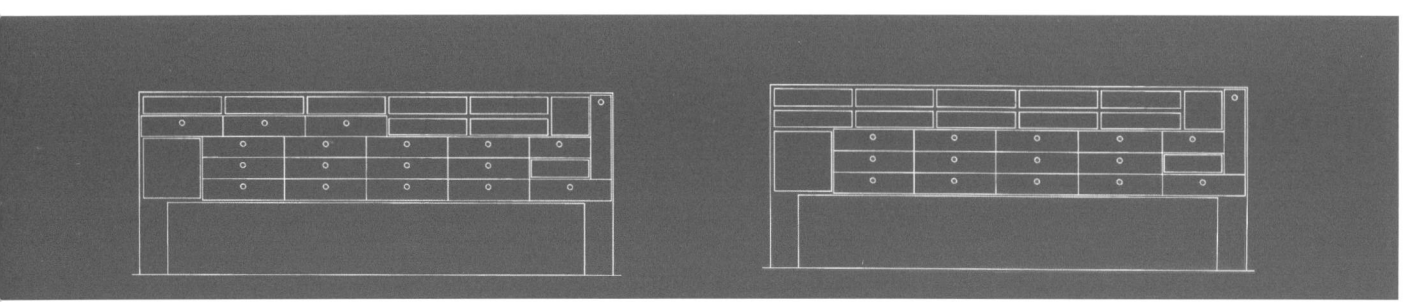

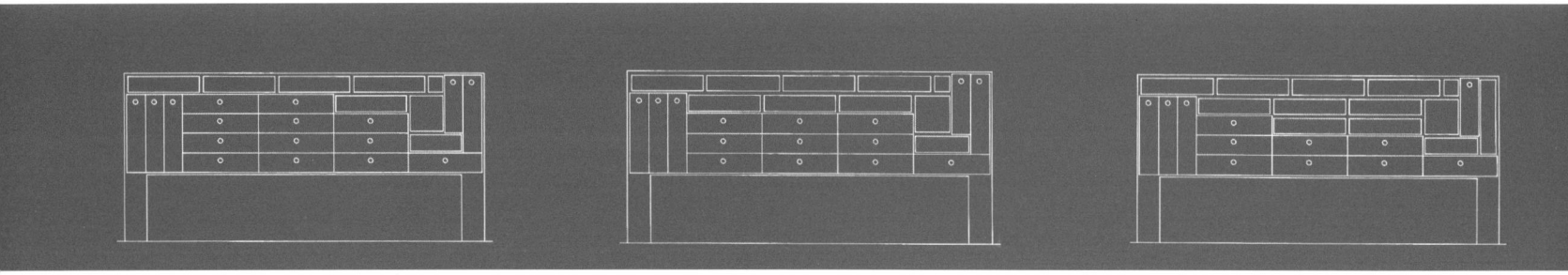

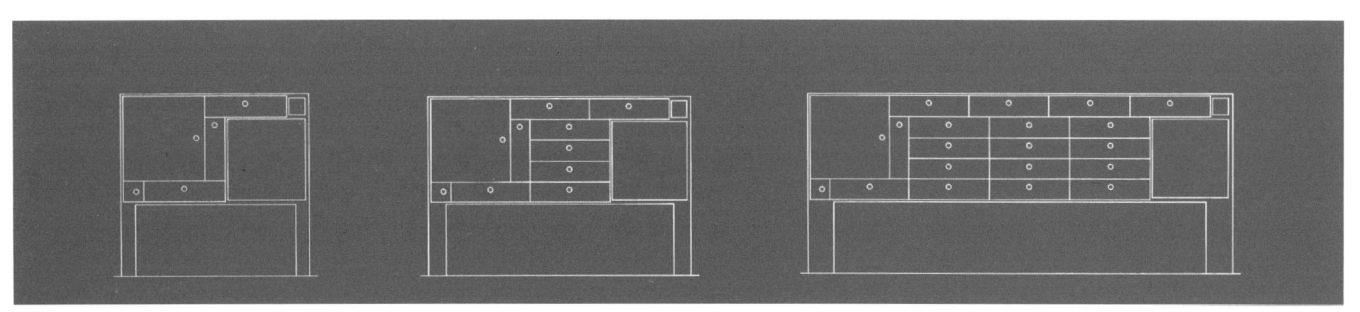

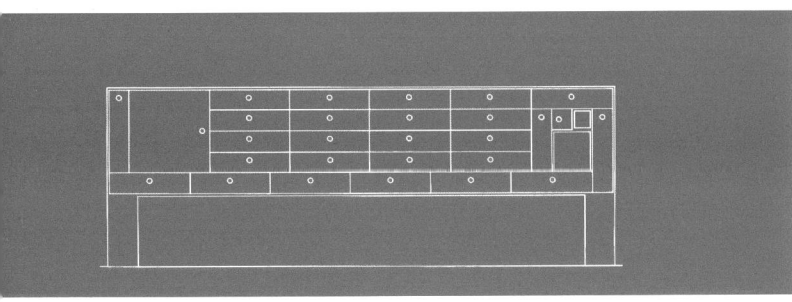

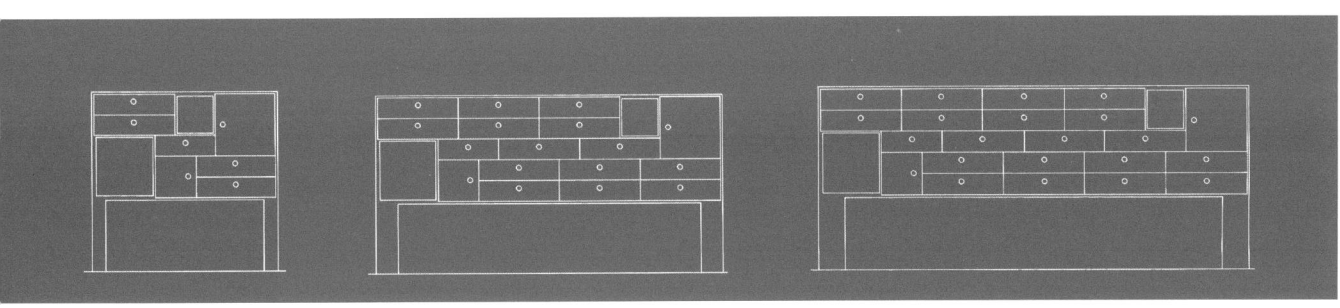

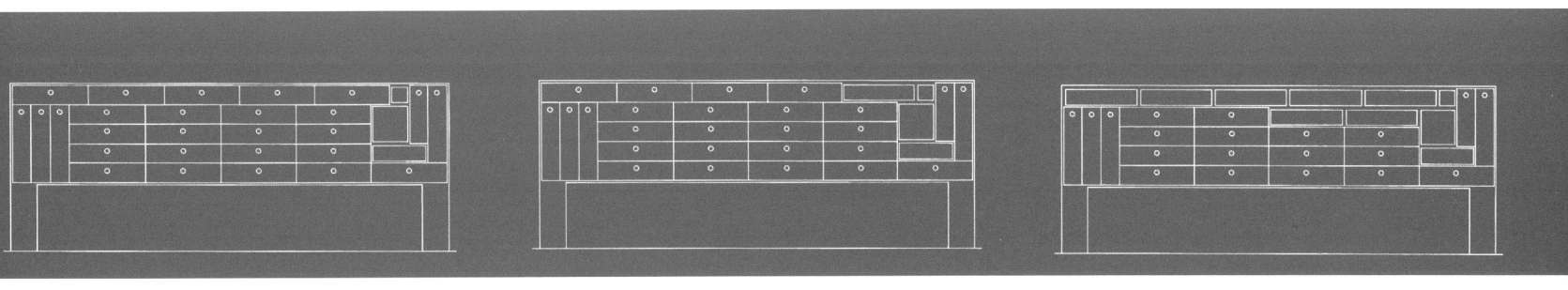

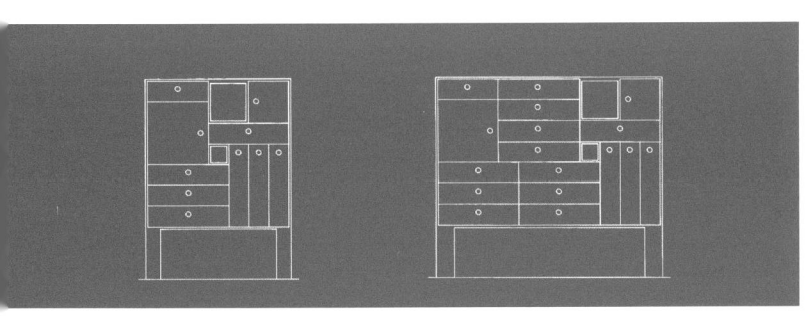

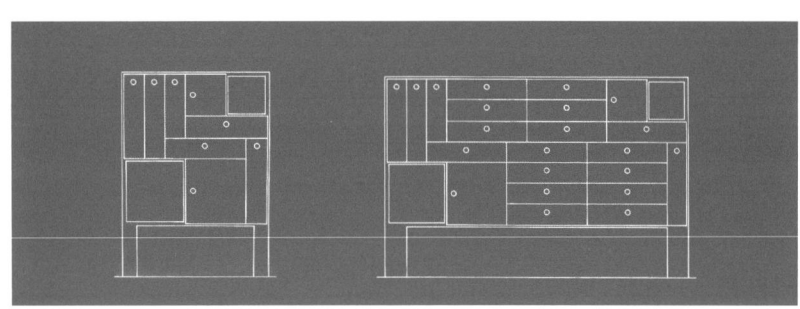

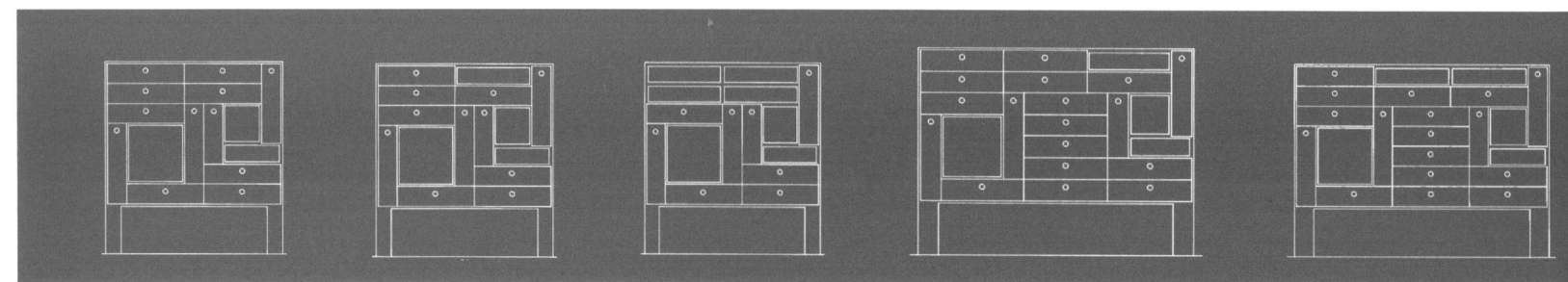

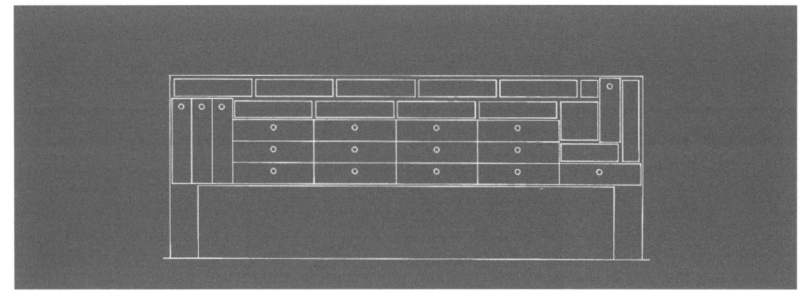

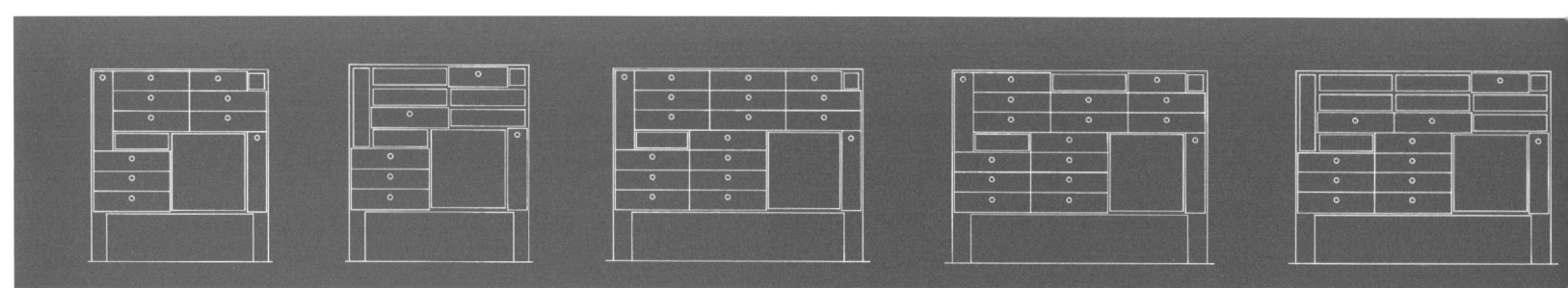

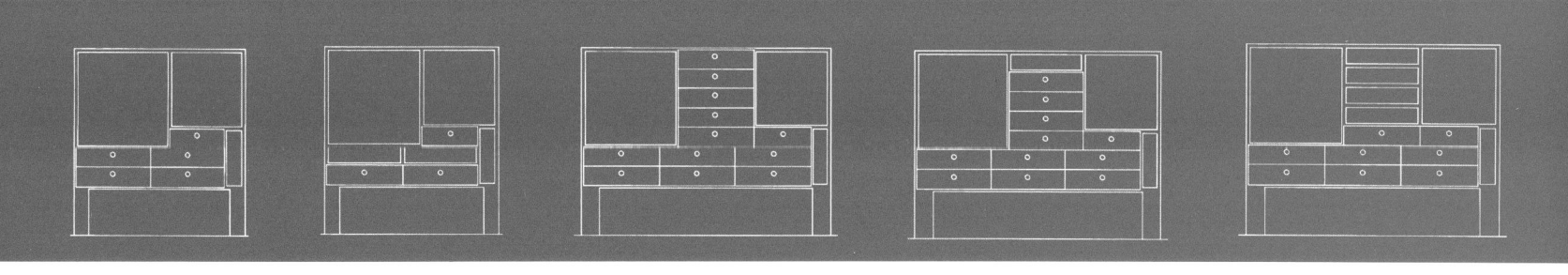

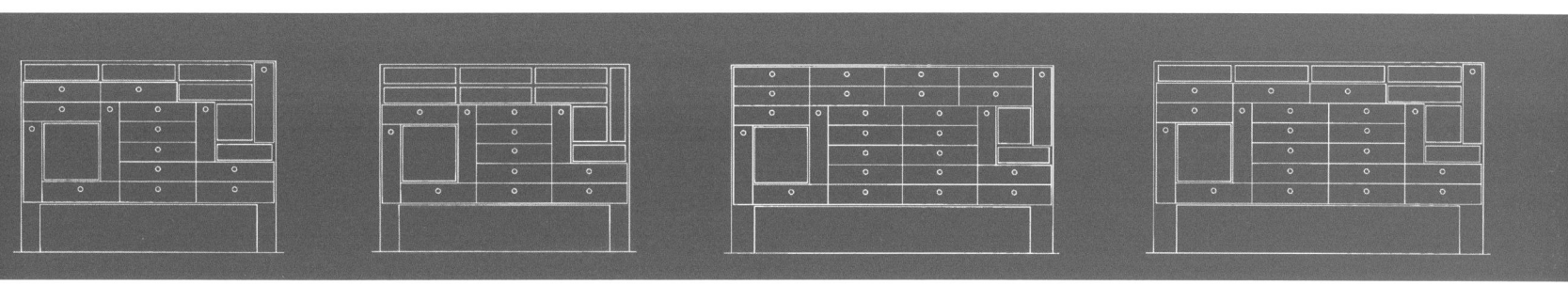

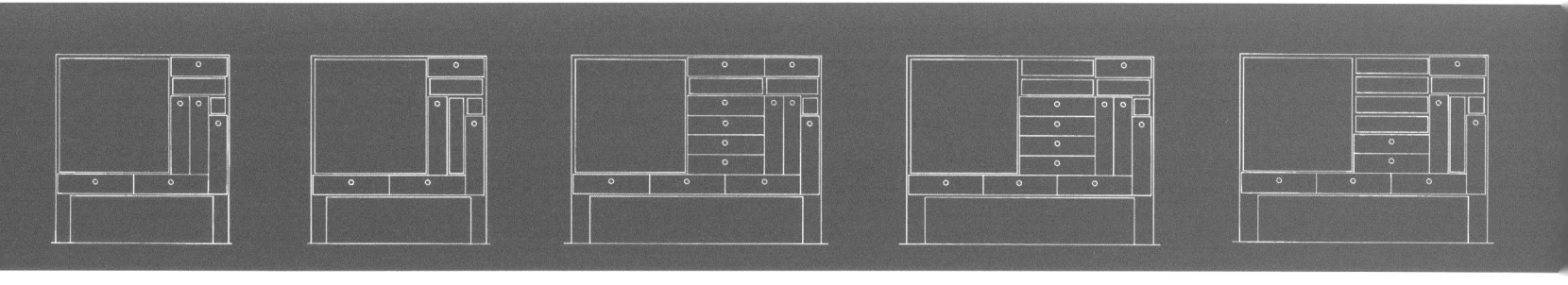

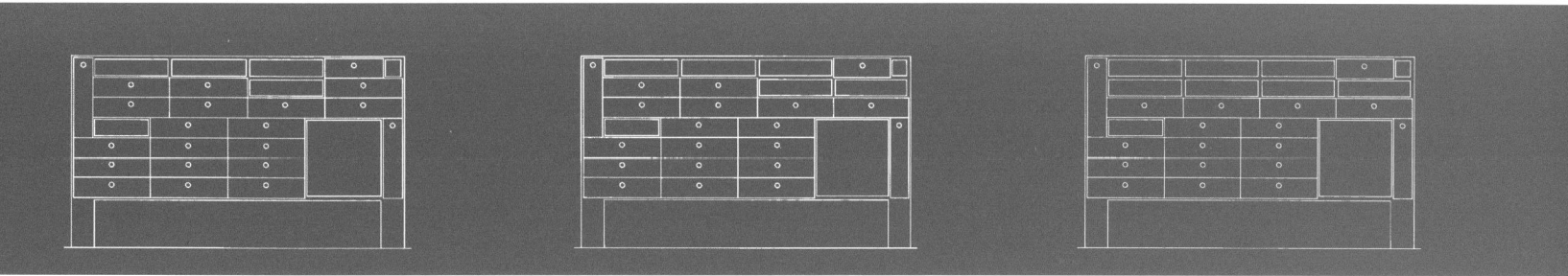

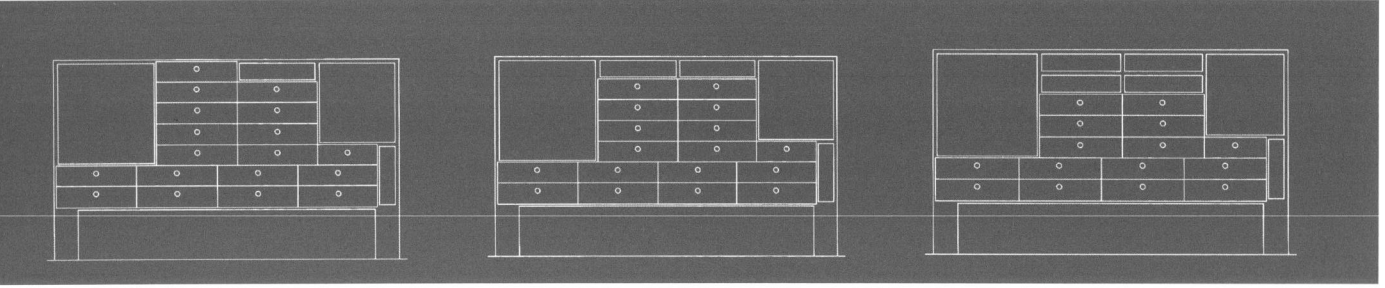

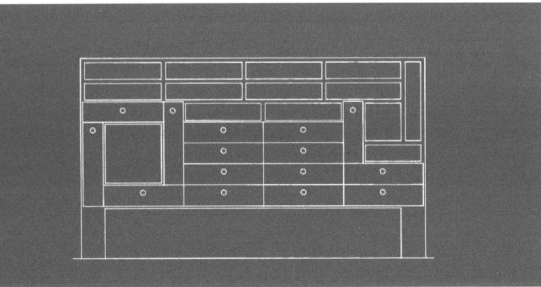

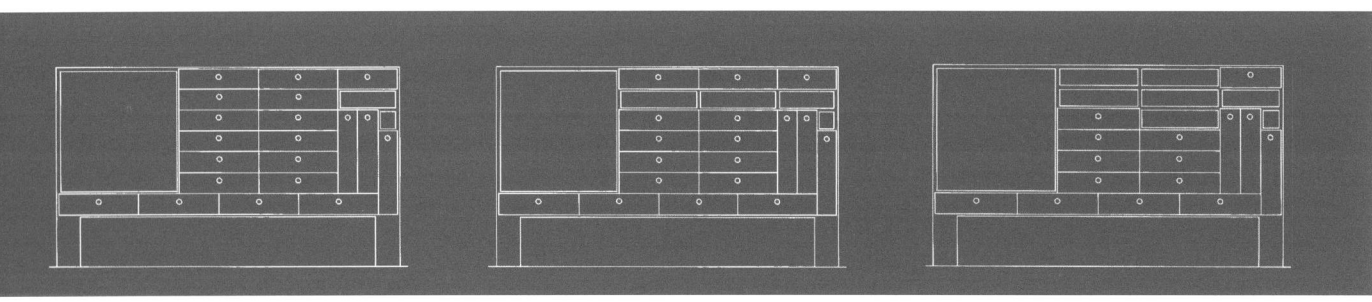

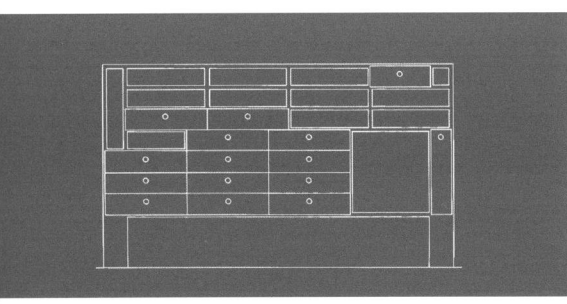

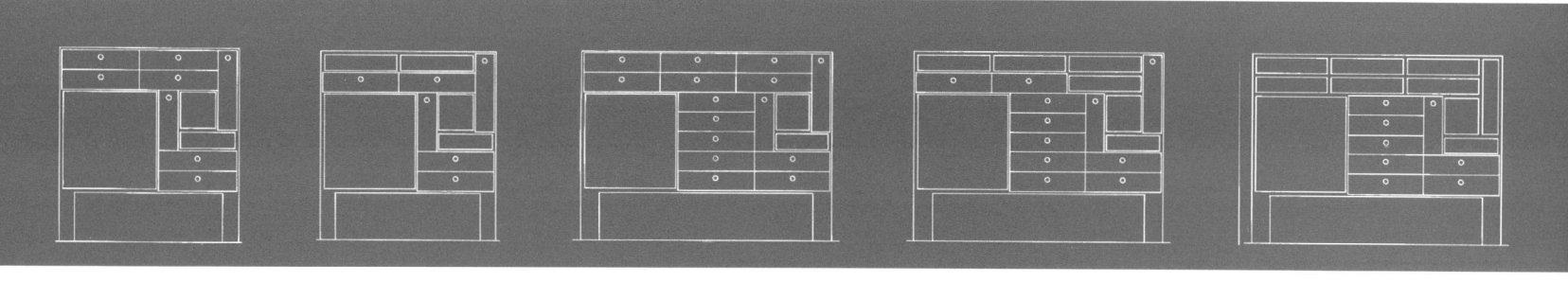

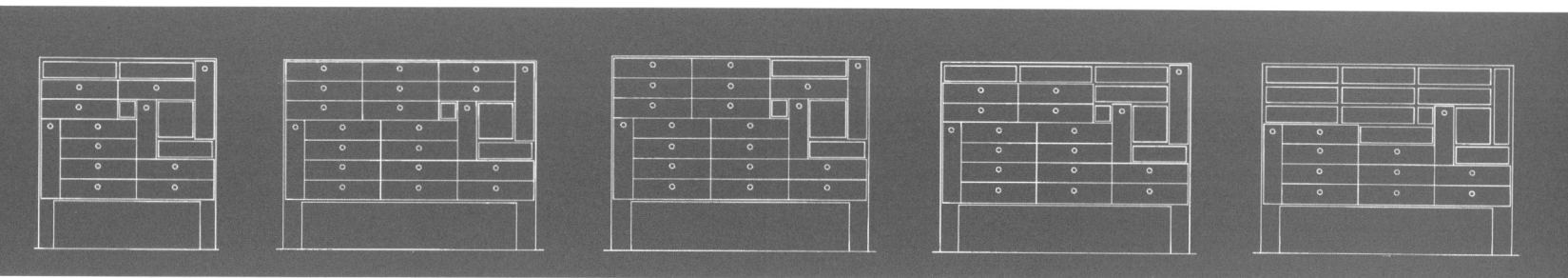

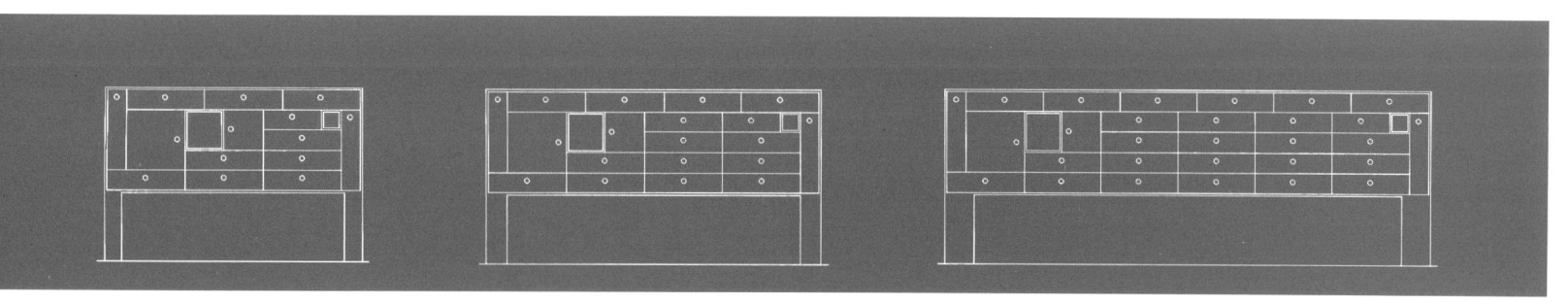

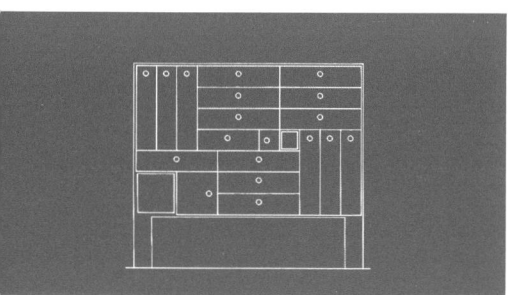

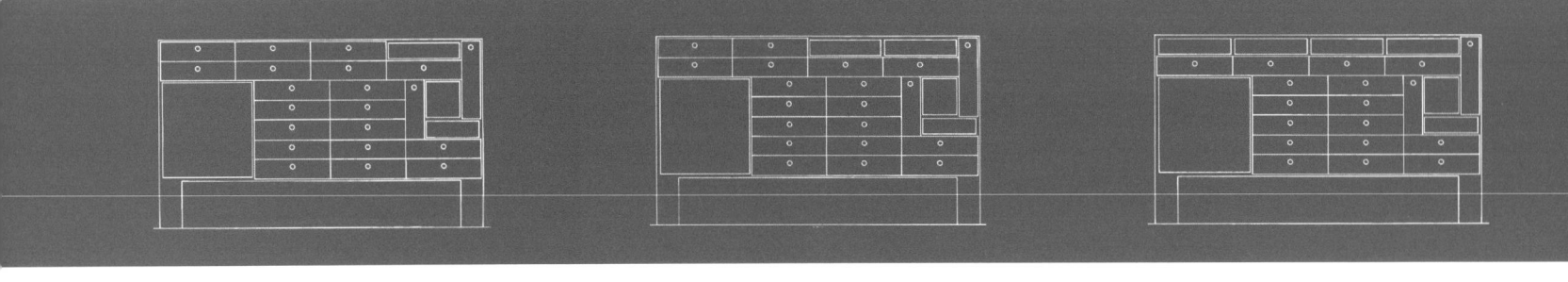

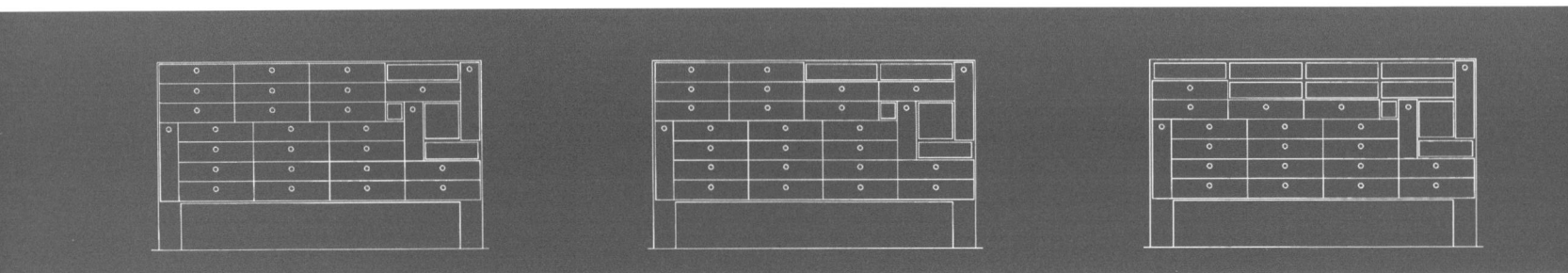

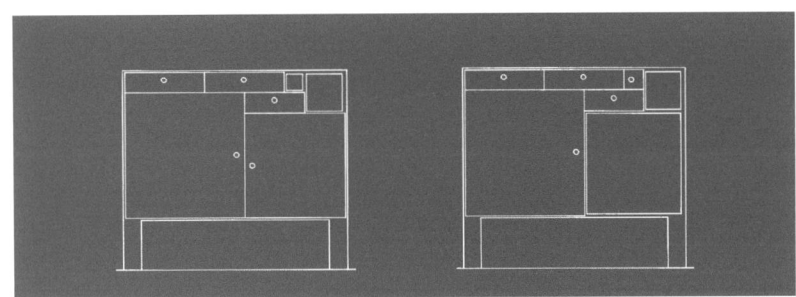

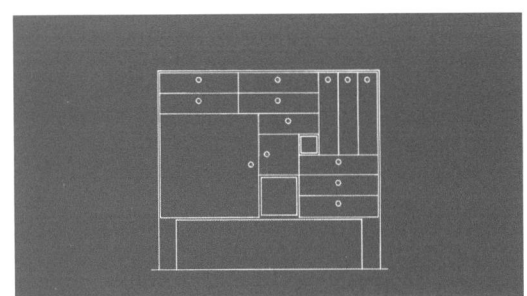

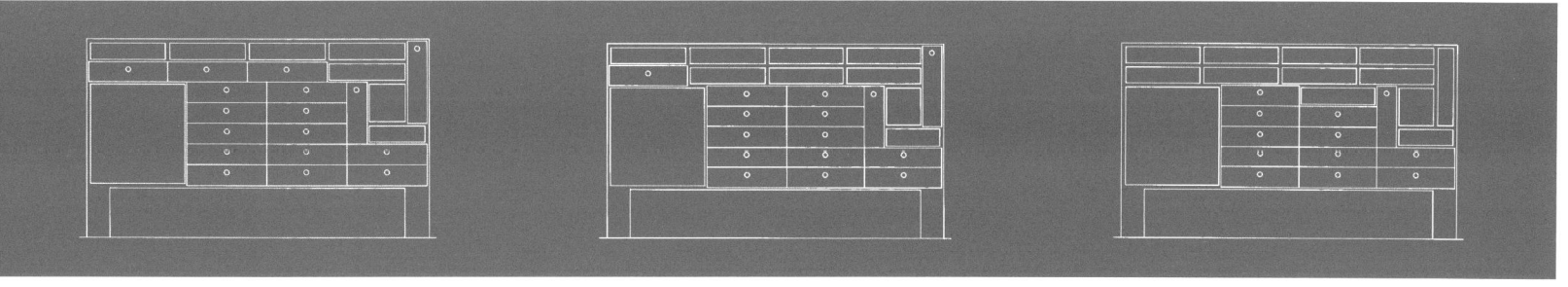

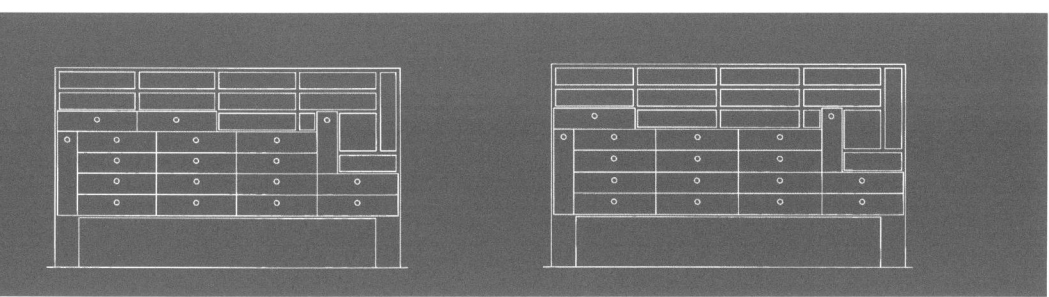

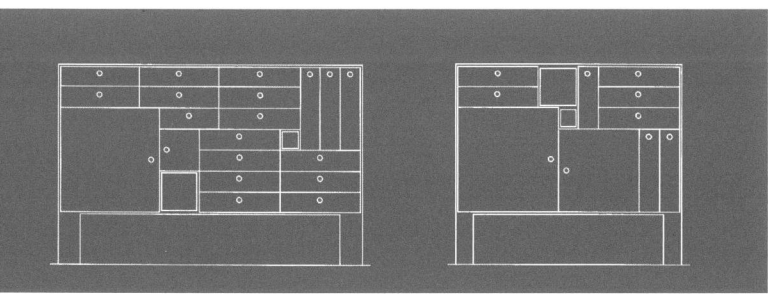

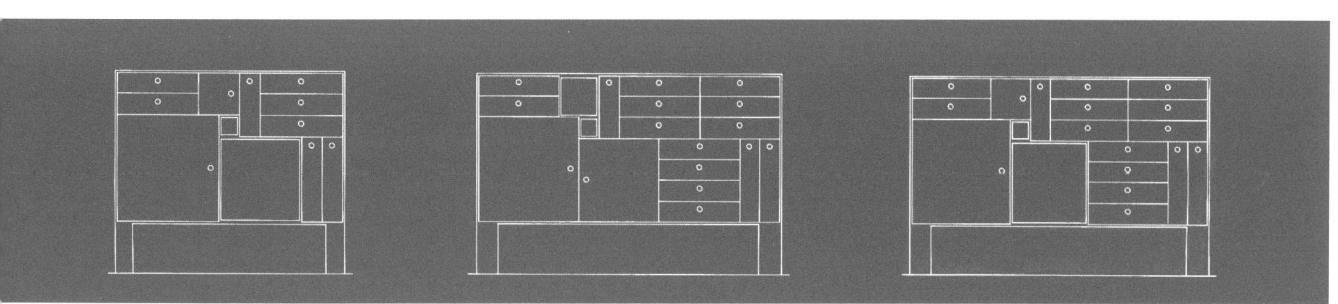

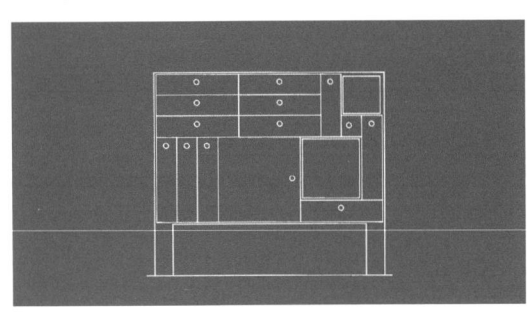

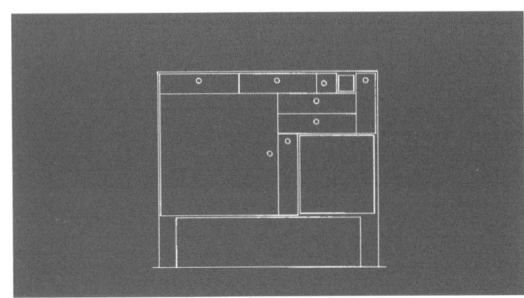

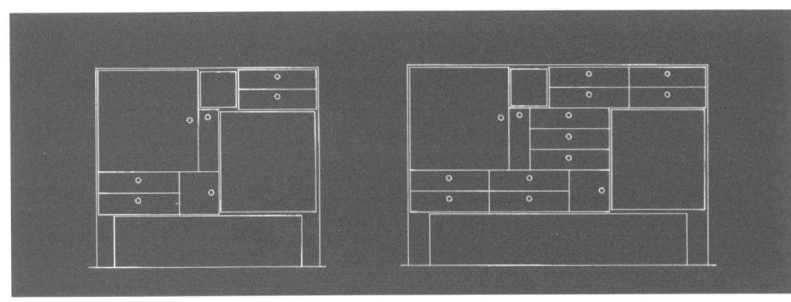

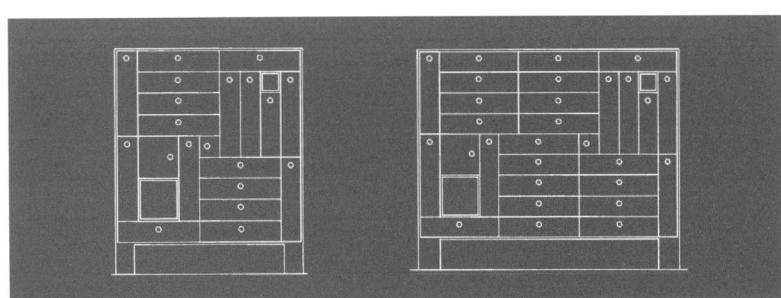

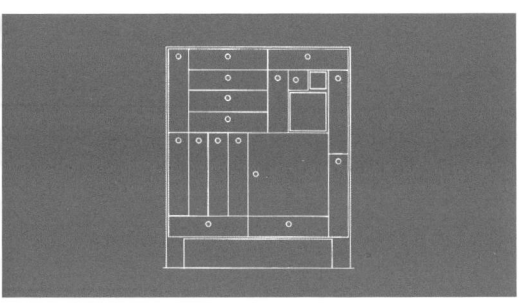

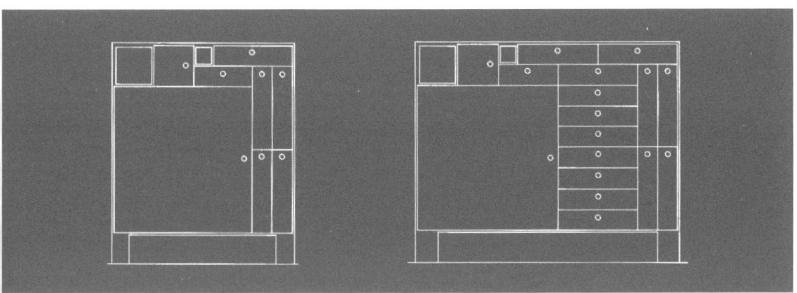

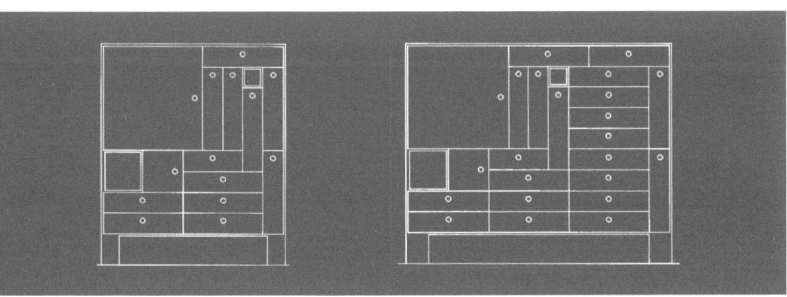

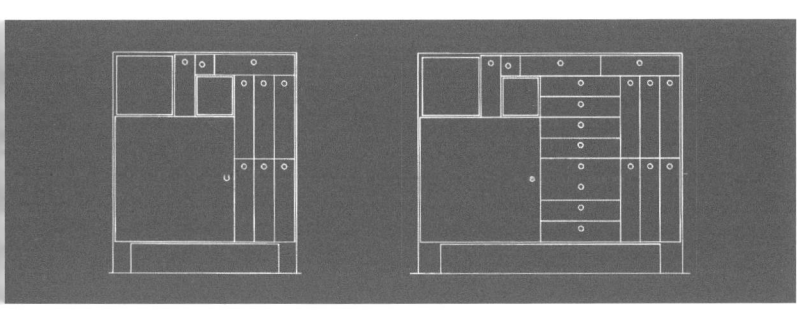

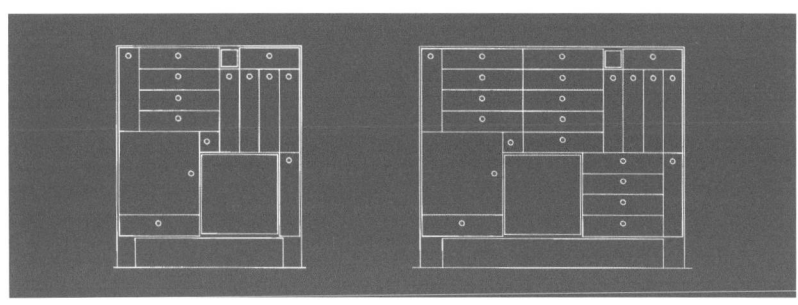

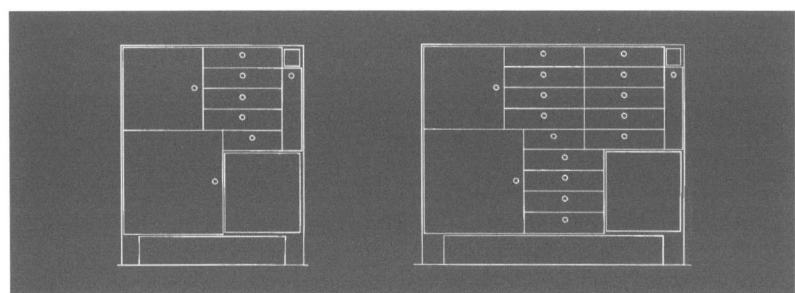

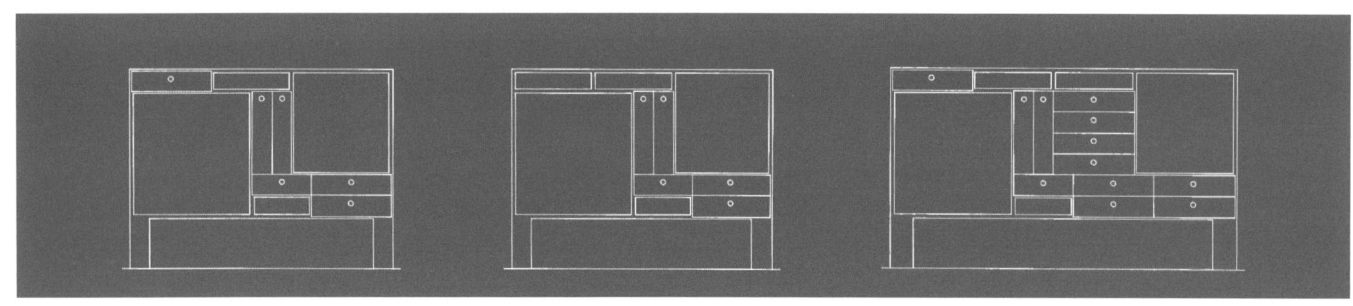

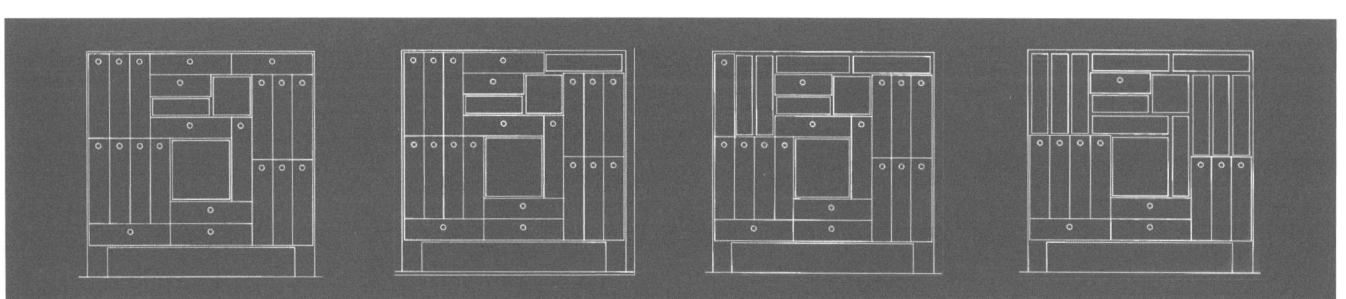

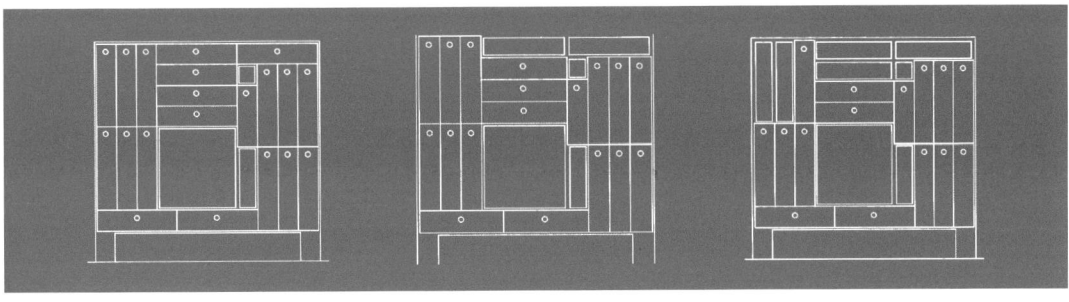

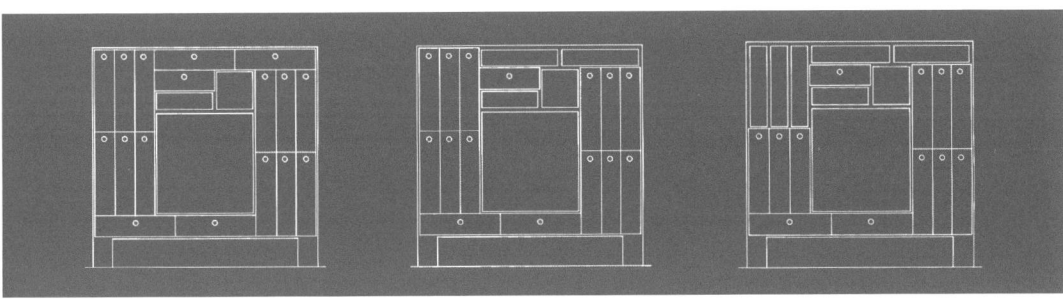

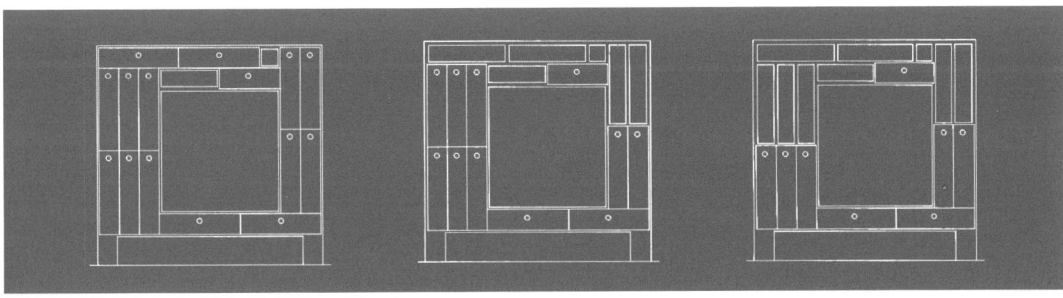

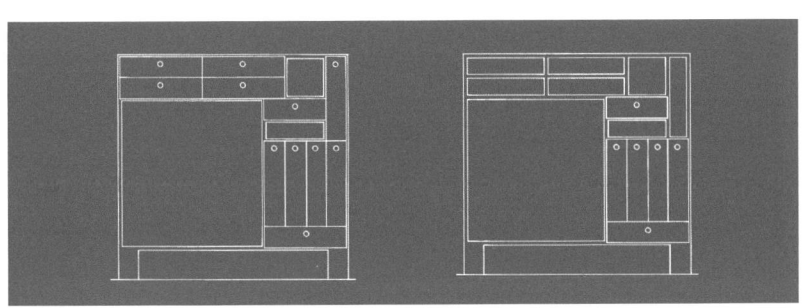

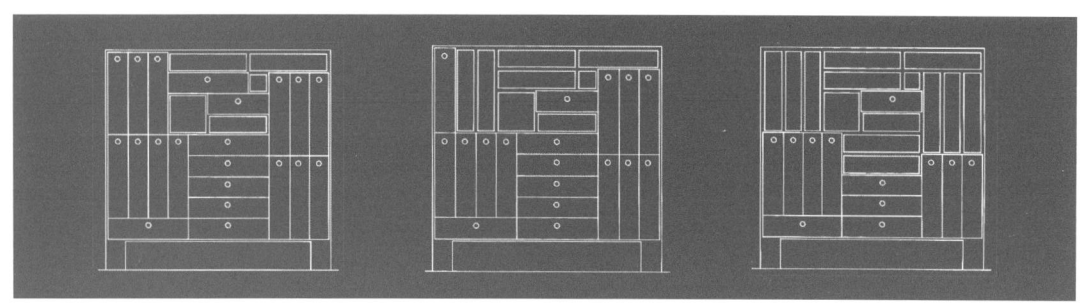

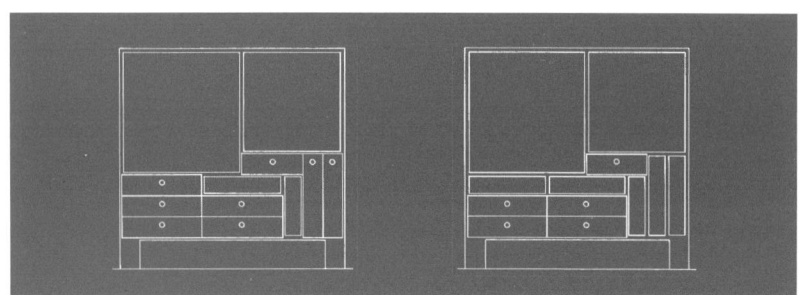

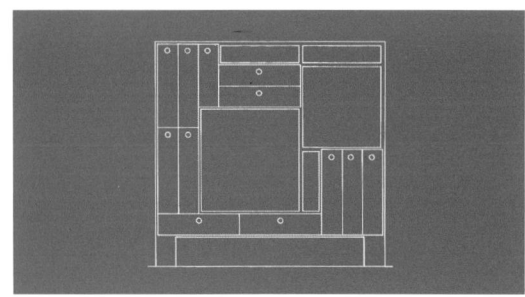

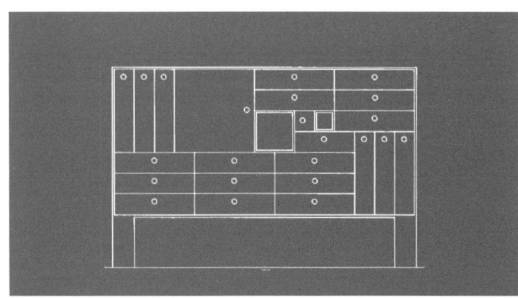

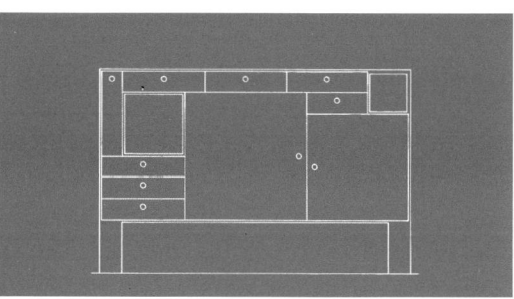

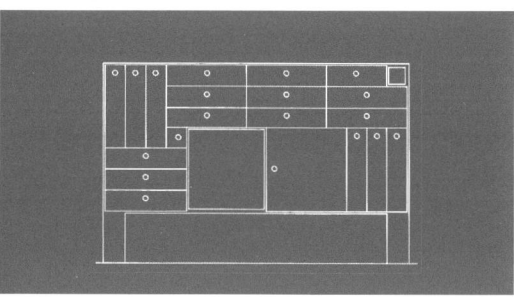

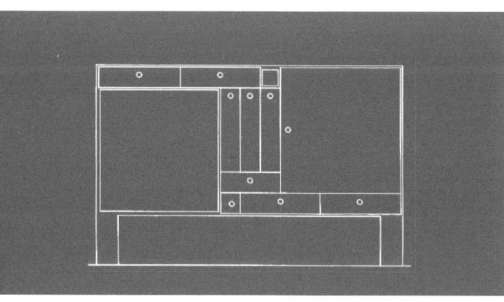

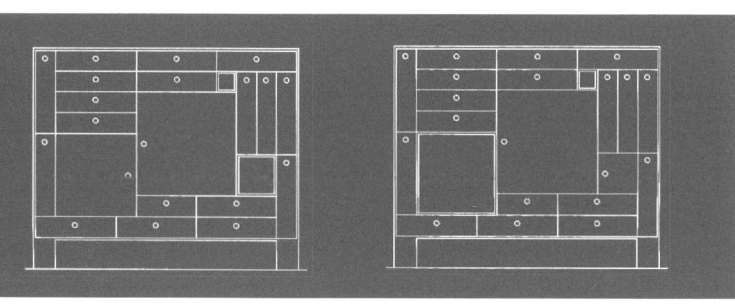

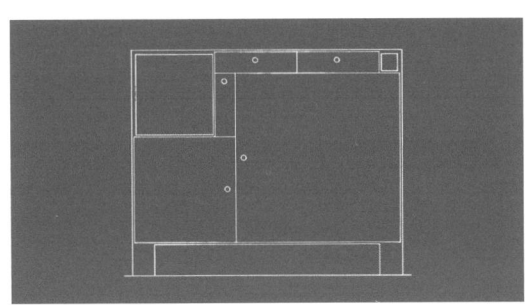

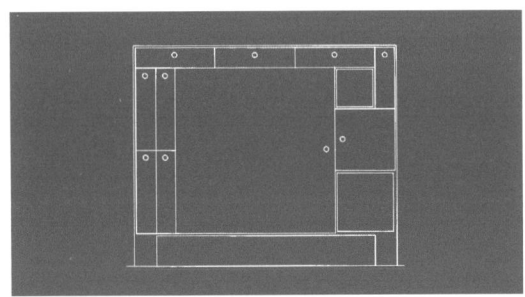

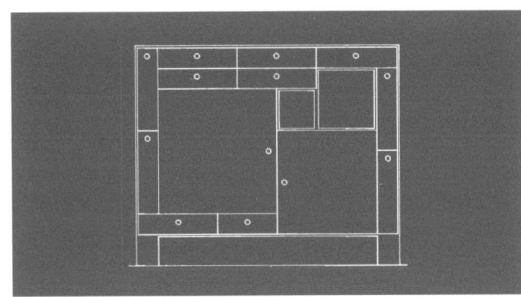

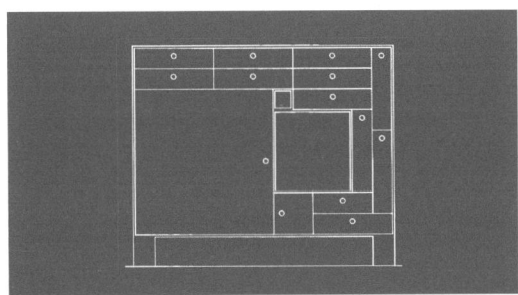

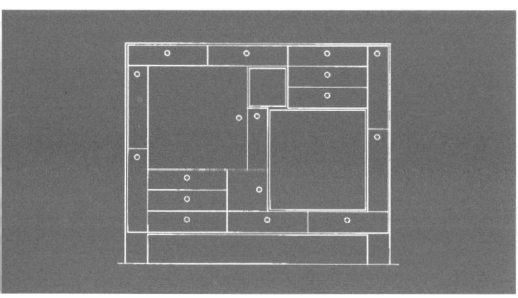

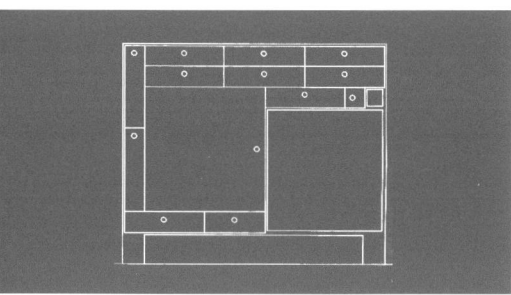

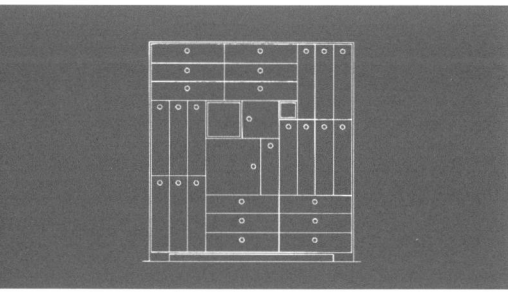

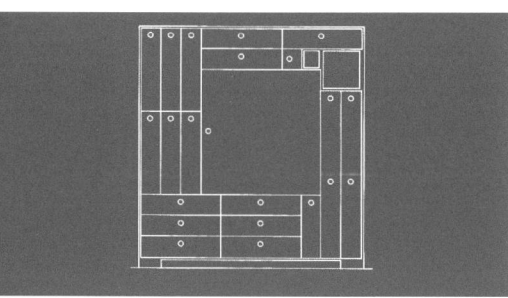

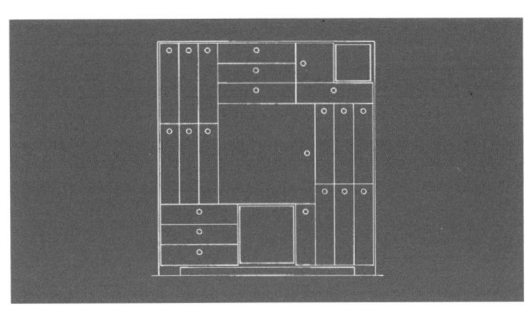

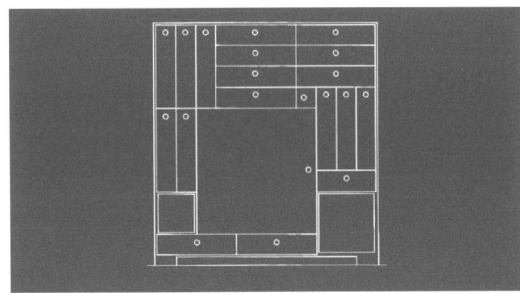

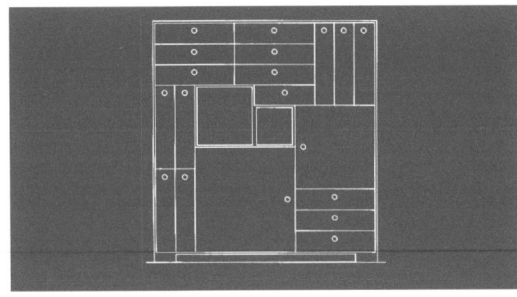

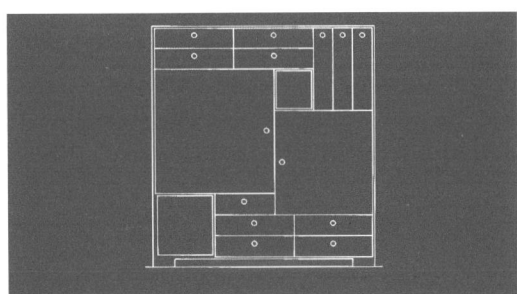

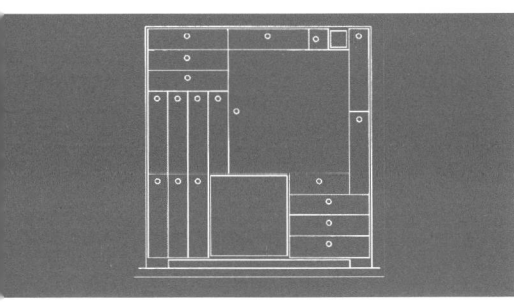

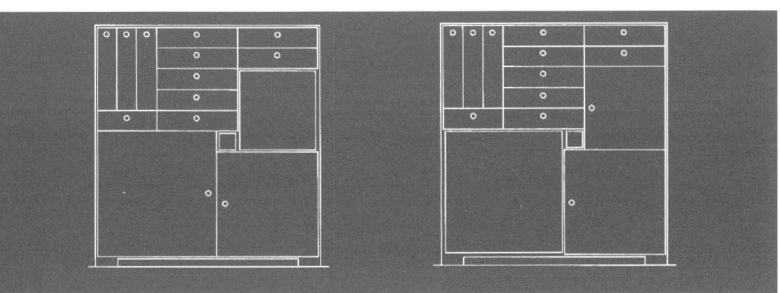

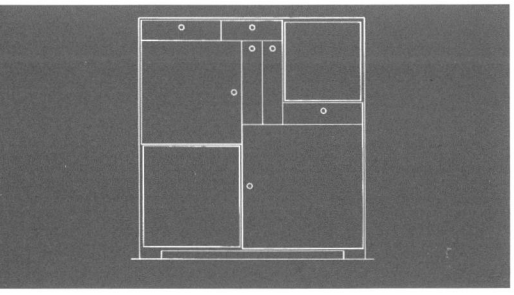

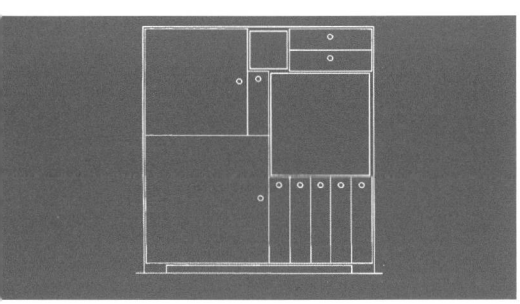

© 2008 BLACK DOG PUBLISHING limited
and the author
All rights reserved

Designed by David Hillman

Black Dog Publishing Limited
10A Acton Street
London
WC1X 9NG
UK

t. +44 (0)207 713 5097
f. +44 (0)207 713 8682
e. info@blackdogonline.com

British Library Cataloguing-in-Publication Data.
A CIP record for this book is available from the
British Library.

ISBN   978 1 906155 35 3

BLACK DOG PUBLISHING is an environmentally
responsible company. *Tables Boxes Screens Cabinets...*
is printed on Fedrigoni Symbol Freelife Satin, an
environmentally-friendly ECF (Elemental Chlorine Free)
woodfree paper with a high content of selected
preconsumer recycled material.

architecture art design
fashion history photography
theory and things

black dog
publishing

www.blackdogonline.com   london uk